OXFORD EARLY CHRISTIAN STUDIES

General Editors

Gillian Clark   Andrew Louth

THE OXFORD EARLY CHRISTIAN STUDIES series includes scholarly volumes on the thought and history of the early Christian centuries. Covering a wide range of Greek, Latin, and Oriental sources, the books are of interest to theologians, ancient historians, and specialists in the classical and Jewish worlds.

Making Amulets Christian

Artefacts, Scribes, and Contexts

THEODORE DE BRUYN

OXFORD
UNIVERSITY PRESS

OXFORD

UNIVERSITY PRESS

Great Clarendon Street, Oxford, OX2 6DP,
United Kingdom

Oxford University Press is a department of the University of Oxford.
It furthers the University's objective of excellence in research, scholarship,
and education by publishing worldwide. Oxford is a registered trade mark of
Oxford University Press in the UK and in certain other countries

First Edition published in 2017
Impression: 1

Published in the United States of America by Oxford University Press
198 Madison Avenue, New York, NY 10016, United States of America

British Library Cataloguing in Publication Data
Data available

Library of Congress Control Number: 2016962751

ISBN 978-0-19-968788-6

Printed and bound by
CPI Group (UK) Ltd, Croydon, CR0 4YY

For Calum

Acknowledgements

This book would not have come about had Geoff Jenkins not alerted me, many years ago, to the wealth of materials unearthed in Egypt. The work of identifying and analysing the amulets discussed in this book was supported by a research grant from the Social Sciences and Humanities Research Council of Canada. I am grateful for the assistance of Hazel Atkins, Steven Scott, Stephen Quinlan, and Michael Caligiuri at that time. My colleague Jitse Dijkstra has patiently tutored me in the ways of papyrologists, and has been unfailingly ready with advice on difficult readings and all matters Egyptian. The University of Ottawa and the Faculty of Arts have been generous in granting release from teaching at various times, a year-long sabbatical leave in 2013–14, and a short leave of absence in 2015, without which I would not have been able to complete this manuscript. I owe a great debt to the staff of the interlibrary loan office of the University of Ottawa Library for their prompt service over more than a decade. The work of research and writing was enriched by visits to a number of research centres: the Centre for Early Christian Studies in the Australian Catholic University; the Ancient History Documentary Research Centre in Macquarie University; the Department of History and the Department of Near Eastern Languages and Cultures in the University of California at Los Angeles; and the Center for the Study of Christianity and the Israel Institute for Advanced Studies in the Hebrew University of Jerusalem. I am especially appreciative of the warm hospitality shown me by curators of several papyrological collections during my visits to examine papyri: Traianos Gagos (†) at the University of Michigan Library, Robert Daniel at the Institut für Altertumskunde in the University of Cologne, Cornelia Römer at the Austrian National Library in Vienna, Fabian Reiter at the Egyptian Museum in Berlin, and Rosario Pintaudi at the Biblioteca Medicea Laurenziana in Florence. At various points the manuscript has benefited from comments from Juan Chapa, Jitse Dijkstra, Sophie Lunn-Rockliffe, Ágnes Mihálykó, and Joseph Sanzo; I of course remain responsible for what came of their suggestions. Finally, it gives me much pleasure to be able to publish with Oxford University Press again. I am obliged to Tom Perridge for commissioning the manuscript; to the editors of this series, Gillian Clark and Andrew Louth, for accepting it; and to Karen Raith, Dan Harding, Joy Mellor, and Kavya Ramu for shepherding it through the process of editing and production.

Contents

List of Figures

List of Abbreviations

For abbreviations of titles of Greek Christian works, see G. H. E. Lampe (ed.), *A Greek Patristic Lexicon* (Oxford: Clarendon Press, 1961). For abbreviations of titles of Latin Christian works, see A. Blaise (ed.), *Dictionnaire latin-français des auteurs chrétiens* (Turnhout: Brepols, 1954). Items published in papyrological series are cited according to the abbreviations found in J. F. Oates, W. H. Willis, J. D. Sosin, R. Ast, R. S. Bagnall, J. M. S. Cowey, M. Depauw, A. Delattre, R. Maxwell, P. Heilporn, *Checklist of Greek, Latin, Demotic and Coptic Papyri, Ostraca and Tablets*, <http://www.papyri.info/docs/checklist>, which replaces the previous site, <http://library.duke.edu/rubenstein/scriptorium/papyrus/texts/clist.html>.

ABD	D. N. Freedman (ed.), *The Anchor Bible Dictionary*, 6 vols (New York: Doubleday, 1992)
ACM	M. Meyer and R. Smith (eds), *Ancient Christian Magic: Coptic Texts of Ritual Power* (San Francisco: HarperCollins, 1994)
ACO	Acta Conciliorum Oecumenicorum
AcOr	*Acta Orientalia*
ACW	Ancient Christian Writers
AJSL	*American Journal of Semitic Languages and Literatures*
AKZ	A. Kropp, *Ausgewählte Koptische Zaubertexte*, 3 vols (Brussels: Édition de la Fondation égyptologique Reine Élisabeth, 1930–1)
AnalPap	*Analecta Papyrologica*
ANRW	H. Temporini and W. Haase (eds), *Aufstieg und Niedergang der römischen Welt: Geschichte und Kultur Roms im Spiegel der neueren Forschung*, Part 2: *Principat* (Berlin: de Gruyter, 1972–)
APF	Archiv *für Papyrusforschung*
ARG	*Archiv für Religionsgeschichte*
ArOr	*Archiv Orientální*
ASE	*Annali di storia dell'esegesi*
AW	*Antike Welt*
BASP	*Bulletin of the American Society of Papyrologists*
BBGG	*Bollettino della Badia Greca di Grottaferrata*
BCH	*Bulletin de correspondance hellénique*
BCNH	Bibliothèque Copte de Nag Hammadi
BIFAO	*Bulletin de l'Institut français d'archéologie orientale*
BJ	*Bonner Jahrbücher*

BL	F. Preisigke et al. (eds), *Berichtigungsliste der griechischen Papyrusurkunden aus Ägypten* ([Multiple publishers], 1922–)
BN	*Biblische Notizen*
BNP	H. Cancik and H. Schneider (eds), *Brill's New Pauly: Encyclopaedia of the Ancient World: Antiquity*, 16 vols (Leiden: Brill, 2002–10)
CCSL	Corpus Christianorum, series Latina
CdE	*Chronique d'Égypte*
CE	A. S. Atiya (ed.), *The Coptic Encyclopedia*, 8 vols (New York: Macmillan, 1991)
ClAnt	*Classical Antiquity*
CMAnc	*Cahiers 'Mondes anciens'*
CSCO	Corpus Scriptorum Christianorum Orientalium
CSEL	Corpus Scriptorum Ecclesiasticorum Latinorum
DACL	F. Cabrol and H. Leclercq (eds), *Dictionnaire d'archéologie chrétienne et de liturgie*, 15 vols (Paris: Letouzey et Ané, 1907–53)
DAWWPh	*Denkschriften der kaiserlichen Akademie der Wissenschaften in Wien, Philosophisch-historisch Classe*
DOP	*Dumbarton Oaks Papers*
EBR	H.-J. Klauck et al. (eds), *Encyclopedia of the Bible and its Reception*, 12 vols (Berlin: Walter de Gruyter, 2009–16)
EkklPh	*Ekklesiastikos Pharos*
EME	*Early Medieval Europe*
ET	English translation
ETL	*Ephemerides Theologicae Lovanienses*
EVO	*Egitto e Vicino Oriente*
FVC	*Forhandlinger i Videnskabsselskabet i Christiania*
GCS	Die griechischen christlichen Schriftsteller der ersten Jahrhunderte
GCS N.F.	Die griechischen christlichen Schriftsteller der ersten Jahrhunderte, Neue Folge
GMA	R. Kotansky (ed.), *Greek Magical Amulets: The Inscribed Gold, Silver, Copper, and Bronze Lamellae, Part I: Published Texts of Known Provenance* (Opladen: Westdeutscher Verlag, 1994)
GMPT	H. D. Betz (ed.), *The Greek Magical Papyri in Translation, Including the Demotic Spells*, 2nd edn (Chicago and London: University of Chicago Press, 1992)
GRBS	*Greek, Roman, and Byzantine Studies*
HeidJahr	*Heidelberger Jahrbücher*
HSCP	*Harvard Studies in Classical Philology*
HTR	*Harvard Theological Review*

IEJ	Israel Exploration Journal
JAC	Jahrbuch für Antike und Christentum
JANER	Journal of Ancient Near Eastern Religions
JBL	Journal of Biblical Literature
JCSCS	Journal of the Canadian Society of Coptic Studies
JEA	Journal of Egyptian Archaeology
JECS	Journal of Early Christian Studies
JJP	Journal of Juristic Papyrology
JLH	Jahrbuch für Liturgik und Hymnologie
JOB	Jahrbuch der Österreichischen Byzantinistik
JRS	Journal of Roman Studies
JSQ	Jewish Studies Quarterly
JTS	Journal of Theological Studies
JWAG	Journal of the Walters Art Gallery
JWI	Journal of the Warburg and Courtauld Institute
LCL	Loeb Classical Library
MHNH	MHNH: Revista internacional de investigación sobre magia y astrología antiguas
MPER	Mittheilungen aus der Sammlung der Papyrus Erzherzog Rainer
MPER N.S.	Mitteilungen aus der Papyrussammlung der österreichischen Nationalbibliothek in Wien, Neue Serie
NA^{28}	Novum Testamentum Graece, ed. E. Nestle and E. Nestle, 28th edn, ed. B. Aland and K. Aland et al. (Stuttgart: Deutsche Bibelgesellschaft, 2012)
NAWG	Nachrichten der Königlichen Gesellschaft der Wissenschaften zu Göttingen
NHMS	Nag Hammadi and Manichaean Studies (formerly Nag Hammadi Studies)
NPNF[1]	Nicene and Post-Nicene Fathers, Series 1
OCP	Orientalia Christiana Periodica
OEAE	D. B. Redford (ed.), The Oxford Encyclopedia of Ancient Egypt, 3 vols (New York: Oxford University Press, 2001)
OMRM	Oudheidkundige Mededeelingen uit het Rijksmuseum van Oudheden te Leiden
PAM	Polish Archaeology in the Mediterranean
PDM	Papyri Demoticae Magicae (as cited in GMPT only)
PG	J.-P. Migne (ed.), Patrologiae cursus completes, series graeca, 161 vols (Paris, 1857–66)
PGM	K. Preisendanz and A. Henrichs (eds), Papyri Graecae Magicae: Die griechischen Zauberpapyri, 2 vols, 2nd edn (Stuttgart: Teubner, 1973–4; repr. Munich and Leipzig: K. G. Saur, 2001)

PL	J.-P. Migne (ed.), *Patrologiae cursus completes, series latina*, 221 vols (Paris, 1844–55)
PLS	A. Hamman (ed.), *Patrologiae cursus completes, series latina: supplementum*, 5 vols in 6 (Paris: Garnier, 1958–74)
PO	Patrologia orientalis
PP	*La Parola del Passato*
PTA	Papyrologische Texte und Abhandlungen
PTS	Patristische Texte und Studien
PW	G. Wissowa et al. (eds), *Paulys Realencyclopädie der classischen Altertumswissenschaft: neue Bearbeitung*, 34 vols (Stuttgart: J. B. Metzler and A. Druckenmüller, 1893–1972)
PWSup	G. Wissowa et al. (eds), *Paulys Realencyclopädie der classischen Altertumswissenschaft: Supplementum Band*, 15 vols (Stuttgart: J. B. Metzler and A. Druckenmüller, 1903–78)
RAC	T. Klauser et al. (eds), *Reallexikon für Antike und Christentum*, 26 vols (Stuttgart: A. Hiersemann, 1950–2015)
RBK	K. Wessel and M. Restle (eds), *Reallexikon zur byzantinischen Kunst*, 6 vols (Stuttgart: A. Hiersemann, 1966–2005)
REAC	*Ricerche di egittologia e di antichità copte*
REAug	*Revue d'Études Augustiniennes et Patristiques*
REByz	*Revue des Études Byzantines*
REG	*Revue des études grecques*
ROC	*Revue de l'orient chrétien*
RRE	*Religion in the Roman Empire*
RSBN	*Rivista degli studi bizantini e neoellenici*
RTPE	*Recueil de travaux relatifs à la philologie et à l'archéologie égyptiennes et assyriennes*
SB	F. Preisigke et al. (eds), *Sammelbuch griechischer Urkunden aus Aegypten* ([Multiple publishers], 1915–)
SC	Sources Chrétiennes
SCO	*Studi classici e orientali*
SIFC	*Studi italiani di filologia classica*
SM	R. W. Daniel and F. Maltomini (eds), *Supplementum Magicum*, 2 vols (Opladen: Westdeutscher Verlag, 1991–2)
SMSR	*Studi e materiali di storia delle religioni*
SO	*Symbolae Osloenses*
SOC	*Studi sull'Oriente Cristiano*
SPAW	*Sitzungsberichte der Preussischen Akademie der Wissenschaften*

SPP	C. Wessely (ed.), *Studien zur Palaeographie und Papyruskunde* (Leipzig, 1901–24)
StudLit	*Studia Liturgica*
StudPap	*Studia Papryologica*
StudPatr	*Studia Patristica*
ThesCRA	*Thesaurus Cultus et Rituum Antiquorum (ThesCRA)*, 9 vols (Los Angeles: J. Paul Getty Museum, 2004–12)
TM	Trismegistos Texts Database, <http://www.trismegistos.org/index.html>
TNDT	G. Kittel and G. Friedrich (eds), *Theological Dictionary of the New Testament*, tr. G. W. Bromiley, 10 vols (Grand Rapids: Eerdmans, 1964–76)
TTZ	*Trierer Theologische Zeitschrift*
TU	Texte und Untersuchungen zur Geschichte der altchristlichen Literatur
VetChr	*Vetera Christianorum*
VigChr	*Vigiliae Christianae*
ZAC	*Zeitschrift für antikes Christentum*
ZAS	*Zeitschrift für ägyptische Sprache und Altertumskunde*
ZNW	*Zeitschrift für die neutestamentliche Wissenschaft und die Kunde der älteren Kirche*
ZPE	*Zeitschrift für Papyrologie und Epigraphik*
ZWT	*Zeitschrift für wissenschaftliche Theologie*

A Note on References

To eliminate the need for lengthy references when referring to editions of papyri, parchments, ostraca, and other materials discussed in this book, I have adopted a simplified version of the system used by papyrologists.

The main identifier of an item is, in order of precedence: (1) its reference in the corpora *Papyri Graecae Magicae* or *Supplementum Magicum*; (2) its reference in a papyrological series; or (3) its inventory number in an institutional collection (for items published outside of both of the above in a journal or a book). Items published in a papyrological series are cited according to the abbreviations found in the *Checklist of Greek, Latin, Demotic and Coptic Papyri, Ostraca and Tablets* (<http://www.papyri.info/docs/checklist>, see List of Abbreviations), which may be consulted for full bibliographical details. The volume of a series is given in Roman numerals; the number of the item in the volume is given in Arabic numerals, e.g., *P.Köln* IV 171. Items held in an institutional collection are identified by location and inventory number in an unitalicized form, e.g., P.Vindob. inv. G 29418.

When an item published in a corpus (e.g., *PGM* or *SM*) is previously published in a papyrological series, the reference to the series is given in parentheses after the reference to the corpus at the first instance in each chapter, e.g., *PGM* P2 (*P.Oxy.* VII 1060), *SM* I 22 (*P.Amst.* I 26). For prior editions published outside of a papyrological series, or other prior bibliography, the reader is referred to the introduction to the item in the corpus. When discussion warrants citing prior literature, I give the reference. When an item published in a corpus is subsequently republished in a papyrological series, the reference to the series is given after the reference to the corpus, e.g., *SM* I 31 (*P.Turner* 49) = *BKT* IX 134.

Reference to lines in a text takes the form, e.g., *PGM* P19.6; *P.Köln* IV 171.5; *SM* I 27.6. Normally I refer to lines of an item as published in a corpus (*PGM* or *SM*), but at times it is preferable to refer to the edition in a papyrological series. Reference to the introduction of an item takes the form, e.g., *P.Prag.* I 6 intro. If the introduction is long, a specific page number may be given. Reference to a comment on one or more lines in a text takes the form, e.g., *P.Prag.* I 6.1–5 comm.

In *Papyri Graecae Magicae* non-Christian papyri and parchments are identified with a Roman numeral in capitals preceded by 'P'; Christian papyri and parchments are identified with an Arabic numeral preceded by 'P'; ostraca and tablets are identified with an Arabic numeral preceded by 'O' and 'T' respectively. It has become customary to refer to the non-Christian papyri and parchments simply by their Roman numeral, e.g., *PGM* LVII.

For English translations of *Papyri Graecae Magicae* I–LXXXI, the reader is referred to *The Greek Magical Papyri in Translation*; I do not give the reference. (*The Greek Magical Papyri in Translation* follows the numbering of *Papyri Graecae Magicae* for non-Christian Greek papyri and parchments [I–LXXXI] and continues this form of numeration for Greek materials published subsequently [LXXXII–CXXX]; translations of Demotic materials are identified with lower-case Roman numerals, e.g., PDM xiv.) For English translations of texts published in *Supplementum Magicum*, the reader is referred to *Supplementum Magicum*. When an item is translated in *Ancient Christian Magic*, I give the reference for convenience, e.g., *ACM*, no. 20.

Papyrological transcriptions employ the so-called Leiden system of critical signs (cf. B. A. van Groningen, 'Projet d'unification des systems de signes critiques, *CdE*, 7 (1932), 262–9):

[ ] lacuna
< > omission in the original
⟦ ⟧ deletion in the original
` ´ interlinear addition
( ) resolution of symbol or abbreviation
{ } cancelled by the editor of the text
... uncertain or illegible letters

Introduction

I fell into this project by accident. I had spent a number of years reading the sermons of Augustine, exploring how Augustine in his discourse had to take account of the attitudes and actions of the people whose outlook and conduct he was seeking to shape. By giving voice to his audience, recording not only their acclamations and interruptions but also their supposed concerns and complaints, Augustine's sermons offered some access to 'everyday' people in North Africa in the first decades of the fifth century. Their voices were evidently managed, but not entirely within the control of the bishop. This is what made the sermons interesting. What emerged was a sense of the perspectives and preoccupations of 'everyday' Christians within a context that 'official' Christians did not necessarily dominate.

In a number of sermons Augustine evokes the scenario of a Christian wracked with pain on his sickbed but resolutely refusing to tie on an amulet despite the urging of those around him.[1] When I became aware that many textual amulets have survived from Late Antiquity, I was enticed to peruse them in the hope of getting a little closer to routine, mundane, personal expressions of religious devotion than is possible in the discourses of elites. I eventually came across an amulet whose text was derived from a pre-immersion formula of anointing introduced into Eastern baptismal liturgies in the latter half of the fourth century.[2] This connection, overlooked by the papyrus's editor, alerted me to the intersection between the writing of amulets and the rituals of the church that is a feature of the transformation of amulet production in late antique Egypt. I was persuaded that a study of amulets would yield further insights into the ways in which the production and use of amulets transected what had in the past been referred to as 'official' and 'popular' religion.[3] In many ways the lineaments of this book were born then,

---

[1] See Chapter 1 n. 69.

[2] T. S. de Bruyn, 'P. Ryl. III.471: A Baptismal Anointing Formula Used as an Amulet', *JTS*, n.s. 57 (2006), 94–109, doi: 10.1093/jts/flj089.

[3] On this distinction, see, e.g., P. Brown, *The Cult of the Saints: Its Rise and Function in Latin Christianity* (Chicago: University of Chicago Press, 1981), 12–22; N. Z. Davis, 'From "Popular Religion" to Religious Cultures', in S. Ozment (ed.), *Reformation Europe: A Guide to Research*

though in the intervening decade it has been enriched and complicated by various fields of scholarship.

This book investigates how a customary practice changed in an increasingly Christian environment by studying textual incantations and amulets preserved in Egypt that incorporate Christian elements. I focus on Egypt since it is the source of most of the textual amulets that have survived from Late Antiquity. I ask three questions. First, how did the formulation of incantations and amulets change as the Christian church became the prevailing religious institution in Egypt in the last centuries of the Roman Empire? (As I explain in the section on terms, by 'incantations' I mean texts that appeal to or adjure supernatural powers to heal, protect, constrain, or avenge, and by 'amulets' I mean objects that are worn, affixed, or deposited for healing, protective, or propitious purposes. Since amulets may be written with texts that are not incantations, I use both terms in what follows.) Second, what can we learn from incantations and amulets containing Christian elements about the cultural and social location of the people who wrote them? Finally, how were incantations and amulets indebted to the rituals or ritualizing behaviour of Christians?

I.1. FORMULATIONS

When answering the first question—how did the formulation of incantations and amulets change as the Christian church became the prevailing religious institution in Egypt in the last centuries of the Roman Empire?—we must consider not only innovation but also continuity, for, as in other aspects of the transformation of the religious culture of late antique Egypt, the two are always in play.[4] Certainly, there was a long tradition in Egypt of dealing with difficult circumstances by means of incantations, amulets, figurines, and other devices, extending back to Pharaonic times.[5] In the Ptolemaic and early Roman periods the field of practice expands, absorbing media, idioms,

---

(St Louis: Center for Reformation Research, 1982), 321–43; L. N. Primiano, 'Vernacular Religion and the Search for Method in Religious Folklife', *Western Folklore*, 54 (1995), 37–56, esp. 45–7, doi: 10.2307/1499910.

[4] Important studies of the religious transformation of Egypt in Late Antiquity are R. S. Bagnall, *Egypt in Late Antiquity* (Princeton: Princeton University Press, 1993), chapter 8; D. Frankfurter, *Religion in Roman Egypt: Assimilation and Resistance* (Princeton: Princeton University Press, 1998); J. H. F. Dijkstra, *Philae and the End of Ancient Egyptian Religion: A Regional Study of Religious Transformation (298–642 CE)* (Leuven: Peeters, 2008). On differences in their methods and conclusions, see Dijkstra, *Philae*, 11–23.

[5] There is a sizeable literature; for a recent survey with ample bibliography, see G. Pinch, *Magic in Ancient Egypt*, 2nd edn (London: British Museum Press, 2006). On the Egyptian concept of 'magic' or *heka*, see R. K. Ritner, 'Magic: An Overview', *OEAE*, 2.321–6;

and objectives from the wider Hellenistic world.[6] Egyptian traditions of symbolizing and invoking divine power are juxtaposed, intermingled, or fused with Greek, Jewish, and Near Eastern traditions. The needs addressed go beyond the customary Pharaonic ones of healing and protection to include pan-Mediterranean preoccupations with competition in love, sport, and business. The purveyors become more diverse, less tied to the Egyptian temples, and Greek becomes the language of incantation, at least in written materials.

By the fourth century CE, when incantations and amulets with Christian elements begin to appear in the material record,[7] a large, eclectic, and syncretistic body of Graeco-Egyptian recipes for various procedures and purposes was in circulation, as well as incantations and objects that were actually prepared for or used by individuals (applied materials).[8] These materials form the backdrop to what follows from the fourth to the eighth centuries, the period with which this book is concerned. It allows us to observe how amulets with Christian elements preserve customary Graeco-Egyptian forms of invocation and adjuration, juxtapose these forms with Christian ones, modulate them into Christian ones, or replace them entirely with Christian texts that are nevertheless similar in function.

This study will deal primarily with materials written in Greek.[9] Many of these materials have been gathered together in several major corpora: Richard Wünsch's 'Defixionum tabellae Atticae' and Augustus Audollent's *Defixionum tabellae*, collections of binding incantations (*defixiones*);[10] Karl Preisendanz's

---

R. K. Ritner, 'The Religious, Social, and Legal Parameters of Traditional Egyptian Magic', in M. Meyer and P. Mirecki (eds), *Ancient Magic and Ritual Power* (Leiden: Brill, 1995), 43–60.

[6] For what follows, see J. Dieleman, 'Coping with a Difficult Life: Magic, Healing, and Sacred Knowledge', in C. Riggs (ed.), *The Oxford Handbook of Roman Egypt* (Oxford: Oxford University Press, 2012), 337–61 at 338–42. On the relative scarcity of, e.g., erotic or amatory incantations from Egypt prior to the Graeco-Roman period, see S. Nagel and F. Wespi, 'Ägypter, Griechen und Römer im Liebesbann—Antiker "Liebeszauber" im Wandel der Zeiten', in A. Jördens (ed.), *Ägyptische Magie und ihre Umwelt* (Wiesbaden: Harrassowitz, 2015), 218–80 at 221–5.

[7] For a description of Christian elements in these materials and problems associated with their interpretation, see T. S. de Bruyn and J. H. F. Dijkstra, 'Greek Amulets and Formularies from Egypt Containing Christian Elements: A Checklist of Papyri, Parchments, Ostraka, and Tablets', *BASP*, 48 (2011), 163–216 at 168–71, <http://hdl.handle.net/2027/spo.0599796.0048.001:14>.

[8] Although the position taken by R. K. Ritner, 'Egyptian Magical Practice under the Roman Empire: The Demotic Spells and their Religious Context', *ANRW*, 18/5.3333–79 at 3358–71, on the Egyptian character of these materials has been contested—see J. Dieleman, *Priests, Tongues, and Rites: The London-Leiden Magical Manuscripts and Translation in Egyptian Ritual (100–300 CE)* (Leiden: Brill, 2005), 19–20—his argument in favour of the term 'Graeco-Egyptian' remains valid.

[9] For an introduction to the papyri and a comprehensive survey of editions and scholarship of the last century, see W. M. Brashear, 'The Greek Magical Papyri: An Introduction and Survey; Annotated Bibliography (1928–1994)', *ANRW*, 18/5.3380–684.

[10] R. Wünsch, 'Defixionum tabellae Atticae', in W. Dittenberger and R. Wünsch (eds), *Inscriptiones Atticae aetatis romanae*, Inscriptiones Graecae 3.3 (Berlin: Georgium Reimerum, 1897), Appendix; A. Audollent, *Defixionum tabellae* (Paris: A. Fontemoing, 1904).

seminal compilation of Graeco-Egyptian manuals, recipes, and applied materials, *Papyri Graecae Magicae* (abbreviated as *PGM*),[11] subsequently revised and expanded by Albert Henrichs;[12] Robert Daniel and Franco Maltomini's supplementary compilation, *Supplementum Magicum* (abbreviated as *SM*),[13] presenting Greek materials published after the second edition of *Papyri Graecae Magicae*;[14] and Roy Kotansky's volume of protective texts written on *lamellae* (metal foil) of known provenance around the Roman world (not only Egypt), *Greek Magical Amulets* (abbreviated as *GMA*).[15] These corpora are not, of course, exhaustive, since editions of materials held by institutions, purchased from dealers, or found by archaeologists continue to be published.[16] For instance, in the case of binding incantations, the surveys of David Jordan are an essential supplement to Wünsch's and Audollent's corpora.[17]

Although Greek was the principal language used when writing manuals and incantations during our period of study, materials were also written in Demotic and Coptic, two Egyptian writing systems. Demotic was a cursive script used to write the Egyptian language from the mid-seventh century BCE to Roman times. Under the Ptolemies and the Romans, Demotic gave way to Greek, initially as the language of higher administration, and eventually for most administrative, legal, and commercial matters.[18] Several bilingual Demotic and Greek manuals of procedures and incantations have survived from the Roman period.[19] By the time they were compiled—around the third century CE[20]—Demotic was relegated to the scriptoria of Egyptian temples. Greek would remain the dominant language of public life and, indeed, the Christian church until the Arab conquest. One shortcoming of *Papyri Graecae Magicae* was the omission of the Demotic portions of the Graeco-Egyptian manuals.[21] This was

---

[11] K. Preisendanz (ed.), *Papyri Graecae Magicae: Die griechischen Zauberpapyri*, 2 vols (Stuttgart: Teubner, 1928–31).

[12] K. Preisendanz and A. Henrichs (eds), *Papyri Graecae Magicae: Die griechischen Zauberpapyri*, 2 vols, 2nd edn (Stuttgart: Teubner, 1973–4; repr. Munich and Leipzig: K. G. Saur, 2001).

[13] R. W. Daniel and F. Maltomini (eds), *Supplementum Magicum*, 2 vols (Opladen: Westdeutscher Verlag, 1991–2).

[14] Daniel and Maltomini were stricter in their inclusion criteria than Preisendanz and Henrichs. Whereas *Papyri Graecae Magicae* included, for instance, procedures for divination and oracles, *Supplementum Magicum* limited itself to what it termed 'charms' and 'spells' and formularies (collections of recipes) for 'charms' and 'spells'.

[15] R. Kotansky (ed.), *Greek Magical Amulets: The Inscribed Gold, Silver, Copper, and Bronze Lamellae, Part I: Published Texts of Known Provenance* (Opladen: Westdeutscher Verlag, 1994).

[16] For materials published after the above corpora appeared, consult TM-Magic, <http://www.trismegistos.org/magic/index.php>, a thematic metadata database hosted by Trismegistos.

[17] D. R. Jordan, 'A Survey of Greek Defixiones Not Included in the Special Corpora', *GRBS*, 26 (1985), 151–97, <http://grbs.library.duke.edu/article/view/5281>; D. R. Jordan, 'New Greek Curse Tablets (1985–2000)', *GRBS*, 41 (2000), 5–46, <http://grbs.library.duke.edu/article/view/1371>.

[18] Bagnall, *Egypt in Late Antiquity*, 235–8.   [19] See Section 3.1.

[20] Dieleman, *Priests, Tongues, and Rites*, 41–4; K. Dosoo, 'A History of the Theban Magical Library', *BASP*, 53 (2016), 251–74 at 255 n. 15.

[21] Ritner, 'Egyptian Magical Practice', 3333–42, 3358–60.

remedied, in part, by their inclusion, translated by Janet H. Johnson, in the anthology of Graeco-Egyptian materials in English translation edited by Hans Dieter Betz, *The Greek Magical Papyri in Translation* (abbreviated as *GMPT*; the Demotic materials in this volume are referred to by the abbreviation PDM).[22]

In the third century CE, bilingual Greek-Egyptian speakers developed a new writing system for the Egyptian language that used the Greek alphabet with six additional characters taken from Demotic script.[23] Coptic—the name for this writing system as well as the hellenized Egyptian language it expressed—flourished from the fourth century onward in the production of both 'translation literature' (translations of the Bible, apocryphal works, and 'gnostic' and Manichaean texts) and 'original literature' (hagiographical literature, sermons, liturgical texts, some treatises).[24] It was also used for private letters (particularly among monks) and occasional legal documents.[25] After the Arab conquest, the use of Coptic for all types of writing increased dramatically until Arabization drove Coptic into disuse.[26] Coptic was used for incantations of various kinds. The first major collection and study of these materials was published by Angelicus Kropp in *Ausgewählte Koptische Zaubertexte* (abbreviated as *AKZ*).[27] Other important publications followed.[28] The anthology edited by Marvin Meyer and Richard Smith, *Ancient Christian Magic* (abbreviated as *ACM*), provided English translations of many of these materials.[29] An exhaustive catalogue of Coptic incantations, long a *desideratum*, is about to be published.[30]

The procedures and incantations recorded in these materials were meant to deal with an array of personal problems, needs, and desires. We find

---

[22] H. D. Betz (ed.), *The Greek Magical Papyri in Translation, Including the Demotic Spells*, 2nd edn (Chicago and London: University of Chicago Press, 1992).

[23] For a description of the development of Coptic, see T. S. Richter, 'Greek, Coptic, and the "Language of the Hijra": Rise and Decline of the Coptic Language in Late Antique and Medieval Egypt', in H. M. Cotton et al. (eds), *From Hellenism to Islam: Cultural and Linguistic Change in the Roman Near East* (Cambridge: Cambridge University Press, 2012), 401–46 at 406–17.

[24] T. Orlandi, 'Coptic Literature', in B. A. Pearson and J. E. Goehring (eds), *The Roots of Egyptian Christianity* (Philadelphia: Fortress Press, 1986), 51–81; T. Orlandi, 'Literature, Coptic', *CE*, 5.1450–60; S. Emmel, 'Coptic Literature in the Byzantine and Early Islamic World', in R. S. Bagnall (ed.), *Egypt in the Byzantine World, 300–700* (Cambridge: Cambridge University Press, 2007), 83–102.

[25] J.-L. Fournet, 'The Multilingual Environment of Late Antique Egypt: Greek, Latin, Coptic, and Persian Documentation', in R. S. Bagnall (ed.), *The Oxford Handbook of Papyrology* (Oxford: Oxford University Press, 2009), 418–51 at 430–41.

[26] Fournet, 'The Multilingual Environment', 441.

[27] A. Kropp, *Ausgewählte koptische Zaubertexte*, 3 vols (Brussels: Édition de la Fondation égyptologique Reine Élisabeth, 1930–1).

[28] See W. Kammerer, *A Coptic Bibliography* (Ann Arbor: University of Michigan Press, 1950), 97–100; S. Pernigotti, 'La magia copta: i testi', *ANRW*, 18/5.3685–730 at 3690–8.

[29] M. Meyer and R. Smith (eds), *Ancient Christian Magic: Coptic Texts of Ritual Power* (San Francisco: HarperCollins, 1994).

[30] One is currently being prepared by Roxanne Bélanger Sarrazin under the supervision of my colleague, Jitse Dijkstra.

procedures and incantations to constrain or curse an adversary; to enhance sexual desire or prowess, attract a lover, or separate the person one desires from his or her mate; to bring about favour, good fortune, success at the races or in business; to protect oneself or one's household from evil and harm; to heal various illnesses or ailments; to obtain a vision or induce a revelatory dream.[31] While individual instances of each type of procedure or incantation may differ considerably in its particular instructions and phrasing, they typically follow or incorporate recognizable, customary forms. This allows us to observe how Christian elements are introduced into customary forms, or how customary forms come to be expressed in a Christian idiom.

The transformation of the practice was not, however, limited to the alteration of customary forms of incantation. Amulets written with passages from scripture, litanies, prayers, liturgical excerpts, names of martyrs, or Christian symbols came to be used as well. Classifying such materials can be problematic. In the absence of characteristics typical of customary incantations, how can one determine whether a papyrus written with a passage of scripture, a prayer, a list of names, and the like was in fact used, or meant to be used, as an amulet?[32] There are other possible reasons for writing such texts. Folding may provide a clue, but is not decisive, because documents were folded for other reasons than to be worn or buried as an amulet. In some cases the type of text—the opening words of LXX Ps. 90 or a gospel,[33] for example—increases the likelihood that the artefact was meant to serve as an amulet. In other cases the classification must remain tentative. Nevertheless, these types of amulets will be included in this study along with customary incantations.[34]

I.2 SCRIBES

In addressing the second question—what can we learn from incantations and amulets containing Christian elements about the cultural and social location of the people who wrote them?—this book aims to bring the producers of incantations and amulets with Christian elements into greater relief. There has

---

[31] Brashear, 'Greek Magical Papyri', 3499–505; F. Naether, 'Griechisch-Ägyptische Magie nach den *Papyri Graecae et Demoticae Magicae*', in Jördens, *Ägyptische Magie*, 191–217 at 204–5. See also Meyer and Smith, *Ancient Christian Magic*, chapters 4–8.

[32] On this problem, see T. S. de Bruyn, 'Papyri, Parchments, Ostraca, and Tablets Written with Biblical Texts in Greek and Used as Amulets: A Preliminary List', in T. J. Kraus and T. Nicklas (eds), *Early Christian Manuscripts: Examples of Applied Method and Approach* (Leiden: Brill, 2010), 145–89; de Bruyn and Dijkstra, 'Greek Amulets', 172–3.

[33] References to the Psalms in this book follow the numbering of the Septuagint (LXX).

[34] For Greek materials, the items listed in de Bruyn and Dijkstra, 'Greek Amulets', tables 1–3, comprise the initial basis for this study.

been an effort in recent years to appreciate more fully the individuality of people's religious activity in antiquity.[35] While individuals were necessarily conditioned by the expectations, habits, customs, rituals, and institutions of the collective,[36] they still expressed varying degrees of individuality in the roles they assumed, the ways they participated in collective activities, the symbolic world they appropriated, and the authorities and institutions they tacitly or explicitly recognized. There was necessarily variability in what individuals did, and also a potential for individualized expression, as one can see in the texts of incantations and amulets. While these texts are usually instances of a typical formula or model, they are not without variation or even innovation in their construction or expression.

There are a number of reasons to expect, and thus look for, individuality in these materials. First, from the configuration and articulation of customary and Christian elements in these materials we can reasonably surmise that they were written by scribes with different sorts of training, expertise, occupations, and roles. David Frankfurter has advanced a multifaceted model for understanding the types of individuals to whom people in a community in late antique Egypt might have turned for a remedy, incantation, or amulet, and why people would have turned to these individuals. The status accorded these individuals could be a function of a number of qualities, all of which are socially constructed: their accessibility and cost; their perceived expertise in dealing with personal problems; the prestige and indeed utility they enjoy because they were able to write; their affiliation with religious institutions such as a temple, church, shrine, or monastery; their ability to enact rituals and configure incantations derivative of the activities of those institutions; their physical and social location on the periphery of the community and its institutions, combined with the value attributed to something obtained by travelling to a holy site.[37] Indeed, the materials discussed in this book suggest a variety of purveyors. Some materials display technical expertise that had traditionally been the preserve of priests of the Egyptian temples. As the political and economic fortunes of the great temples declined, this social class, and their children, turned to other types of occupations, taking whatever

[35] J. Rüpke and W. Spickermann (eds), *Reflections on Religious Individuality: Greco-Roman and Judaeo-Christian Texts and Practices* (Berlin: De Gruyter, 2012); J. Rüpke (ed.), *The Individual in the Religions of the Ancient Mediterranean* (Oxford: Oxford University Press, 2013); see also J. Rüpke et al., 'Editorial', *RRE*, 1 (2015), 1–7 at 1–4, doi: 10.1628/219944615X14234960199597.

[36] F. Graf, 'Individual and Common Cult: Epigraphic Reflections', in Rüpke, *Individual*, 115–35 at 131–13; G. Woolf, 'Ritual and the Individual in Roman Religion', in Rüpke, *Individual*, 136–60 at 153–5; J. Leemans, 'Individualization and the Cult of the Martyrs: Examples from Asia Minor in the Fourth Century', in Rüpke, *Individual*, 187–212 at 206–7.

[37] D. Frankfurter, 'Dynamics of Ritual Expertise in Antiquity and Beyond: Towards a New Taxonomy of "Magicians"', in P. Mirecki and M. Meyer (eds), *Magic and Ritual in the Ancient World* (Leiden: Brill, 2002), 159–78.

expertise they retained with them.[38] Other materials display liturgical knowledge or ritual habits that one would expect to find in a priest or monk of the Christian church. Moreover, these putative candidates do not exhaust all the possibilities. From an exchange of letters between two Manichaean scribes, we know that scribes whose principal occupation was writing and copying documents had copies of incantations in their possession.[39] Similarly, *literati* might collect these materials, as an incantation preserved among the papers of Dioscorus of Aphrodite shows.[40]

Second, while all the individuals who produced the materials discussed in this book were able, evidently, to write, the nature of that ability and the purposes to which it was put varied. In other words, we are dealing with different types of writers who benefited from varying degrees of training and were accustomed (or not) to certain kinds of writing. At a fundamental level, we can distinguish levels of skill and experience in writing.[41] Some writers could only form letters laboriously one by one ('slow writers'), but most writers were more practiced. They often write in an informal semi-cursive or cursive hand.[42] Sometimes the execution is fairly regular; other times it is erratic or even clumsy. Occasionally the hand approximates the formal sloping or upright majuscule styles used to copy books (as well as write documents).[43] (Biblical majuscule or Alexandrian majuscule hands appear less frequently.) Various characteristics of the hand, apart from the skill and speed with which it is written, may disclose the experience and skill of the scribe: letters that are regular in formation, size, and incline;[44] letters contained (apart from some usual exceptions) between two notional lines (bilinearity);[45] even spacing of

---

[38]　Frankfurter, *Religion in Roman Egypt*, 210–17.

[39]　P. A. Mirecki, I. Gardner, and A. Alcock, 'Magical Spell, Manichaean Letter', in P. Mirecki and J. D. BeDuhn (eds), *Emerging from Darkness: Studies in the Recovery of Manichean Sources* (Leiden: Brill, 1997), 1–32; *P.Kellis* V 35.

[40]　D. Jordan, 'A Prayer Copied by Dioskoros of Kômê Aphroditês (PGM 13a)', *Tyche*, 16 (2001), 87–90, <http://tyche-journal.at/tyche/index.php/tyche/article/view/477/595>.

[41]　For what follows, see Section 2.2.2.

[42]　On the distinction between semi-cursive and cursive writing, see G. Cavallo, *La scrittura greca e latina dei papiri: una introduzione* (Pisa: Fabrizio Serra, 2008), 39, 51. In a semi-cursive hand, individual letters are written in single stroke and neighbouring letters may occasionally be joined, but ligatures (a common stroke shared by two letters) are rare. In a cursive hand, letters are written continuously in a fluid sequence with more frequent ligatures, and the speed of writing can result in simplified or reduced letter-forms. This use of the terms differs from E. G. Turner, *Greek Manuscripts of the Ancient World*, 2nd edn, ed. P. J. Parsons (London: Institute of Classical Studies, 1987), 1–2. For examples of semi-cursive and cursive hands used in documents, see H. Harrauer, *Handbuch der griechischen Paläographie*, 2 vols (Stuttgart: Anton Hiersemann, 2010).

[43]　On the emergence of these styles, see Cavallo, *La scrittura*, 111–16. See also G. Cavallo and H. Maehler, *Greek Bookhands of the Early Byzantine Period: A.D. 300–800* (London: Institute of Classical Studies, 1987), 3–4.

[44]　Cribiore, *Writing, Teachers, and Students*, 103.

[45]　Turner, *Greek Manuscripts*, 3.

lines; facility in writing adjoining letters or ligatured letters (letters that share a common stroke);[46] use of abbreviations; use of lectional signs.[47]

In addition to characteristics that distinguished writers in general, the materials under consideration display other features that offer clues to the cultural location of the scribe. Customary Graeco-Egyptian incantations often incorporated oral and visual devices:[48] vowels; esoteric names, words, or sounds (*nomina barbara* and *voces mysticae*); esoteric signs (*charaktêres*); word-shapes; figures. The use of such devices and the nature of their execution give us a sense of where an individual scribe fits in the larger field of Graeco-Egyptian ritual expertise. Similarly, in the incantations and amulets under consideration we encounter scribal features more widely employed in Christian manuscripts and documents:[49] *nomina sacra* (abbreviated forms of the Greek words for 'God', 'Lord', 'father', 'son', 'spirit', 'Jesus', 'Christ', and certain other names), crosses, staurograms (·⳨· or *tau-rho*), christograms (⳩ or *chi-rho*, used less frequently), and other symbols, such as the sequence *XMΓ*. What a scribe's use of such conventions in an incantation or amulet implies must be handled case by case. In correspondence, for instance, it had become an almost universal convention by the sixth century to precede the first line with a cross,[50] whereas *nomina sacra* were employed erratically and appear less frequently over time.[51] Nevertheless, when considered together with other aspects of an amulet, these features contribute to a more fine-grained analysis of the culture of the scribe.

I.3 RITUALS

What scribes might write by way of an incantation or an amulet, and how they might write it, would not only have been conditioned by their individual training, expertise, occupations, and roles, both as writers and as purveyors of amulets. It would also have been shaped by aspects of their cultural and social context, such as the habits and expectations of people who went to them for help. One dimension of that context—the ritual dimension—needs to be considered in detail since it supplied resources that scribes consciously or unconsciously drew upon when formulating incantations or selecting protective texts. Hence the third question addressed in this book: how were

---

[46] On this distinction, see Harrauer, *Handbuch*, 1.8.

[47] Turner, *Greek Manuscripts*, 8–13; Cribiore, *Writing, Teachers, and Students*, 81–8. See also Chapter 2.

[48] For what follows, see Chapter 2.   [49] For what follows, see Chapter 2.

[50] L. H. Blumell, *Lettered Christians: Christians, Letters, and Late Antique Oxyrhynchus* (Leiden: Brill, 2012), 44.

[51] Blumell, *Lettered Christians*, 50–1.

incantations and amulets indebted to the rituals or ritualizing behaviour of Christians?

Purveyors of incantations and amulets did not work in a cultural vacuum. The materials they devised or copied drew on specialized traditions of invoking or adjuring supernatural power and on more general institutional and personal religious practices. In other words, as proposed in a recent working definition of 'tradition', purveyors of incantations and amulets were constrained by 'resources that individuals, communities, and institutions understand as authentic and regard as authoritative'.[52] Even a cursory reading of Graeco-Egyptian manuals and incantations reveals that their purveyors valued the sense that their procedures and incantations were 'traditional'.[53] Sometimes the scribes explicitly declare their procedure to be authentic or authoritative.[54] They attribute the procedure to a god or say that it is god-given. They explain that they copied the procedure from a stele or from an inscription or 'holy book' in a temple. They attribute the procedure to a legendary Egyptian, Greek, Semitic, or Persian figure renowned for his skill or power, such as Apollobex, Pythagoras, Moses, or Ostanes. More often, however, the appropriation of tradition is implicit in the procedure. The structure of the incantation corresponds to the structure of prayer in the ancient world.[55] The language of the incantation echoes phrases, motifs, and themes associated with rituals of the Egyptian temple and court.[56] The deities or powers that are named may be associated with a particular cult or cultic setting, or may evoke well-known and deeply ingrained mythic narratives of deities and heroes.[57] Even the formulaic phrasing of a specific sort of incantation—for fever, favour, or vengeance—conveys the sense that the incantation is authentic and authoritative because it is like others before it.[58]

So too, if we turn to Christian elements found in incantations and amulets, we find that they echo or replicate rituals or ritualizing behaviour of Christians

---

[52] M. L. Satlow, 'Tradition: The Power of Constraint', in R. A. Orsi (ed.), *The Cambridge Companion to Religious Studies* (Cambridge: Cambridge University Press, 2012), 130–50 at 133.

[53] For an overview of what follows, see R. Gordon, 'Memory and Authority in the Magical Papyri', in B. Dignas and R. R. R. Smith (eds), *Historical and Religious Memory in the Ancient World* (Oxford: Oxford University Press, 2012), 145–80.

[54] Dieleman, *Priests, Tongues, and Rites*, 261–76.

[55] F. Graf, 'Prayer in Magical and Religious Ritual', in C. A. Faraone and D. Obbink (eds), *Magika Hiera: Ancient Greek Magic and Religion* (Oxford: Oxford University Press, 1991), 188–213 at 189–91.

[56] Ritner, 'Egyptian Magical Practice', 3362; Dieleman, *Priests, Tongues, and Rites*, 149–70; J. F. Quack, 'From Ritual to Magic: Ancient Egyptian Precursors of the Charitesion and their Social Setting', in G. Bohak, Y. Harari, and S. Shaked (eds), *Continuity and Innovation in the Magical Tradition* (Leiden: Brill, 2011), 43–84.

[57] S. I. Johnston, 'The Authority of Greek Mythic Narratives in the Magical Papyri', *ARG*, 16 (2015), 51–65, doi: 10.1515/arege-2014-0006.

[58] E.g., T. S. de Bruyn, 'An Anatomy of Tradition: The Case of the *Charitêsion*', *ARG*, 16 (2015), 31–50, doi: 10.1515/arege-2014-0005.

in various communal settings. The incantations incorporate acclamations from the liturgy of the church. They call upon God, Christ, Mary, and the saints by means of formal invocations. They recite prayers or psalms routinely chanted in services of morning and evening prayer. They draw on rituals of healing and exorcism.

Thus, to understand how practices of invoking power for protection, healing, or assistance became more or less 'Christian', we must appreciate the role of Christian rituals and ritualizing behaviour in supplying resources for the scribes of incantations and amulets. It was rituals or ritualizing behaviour that made the elements the scribe employed, however commonplace, authentic means for securing supernatural assistance. But at the same time it was the individual scribe who combined these resources, customary as well as Christian, into a specific incantation or amulet. It was the individual scribe, conditioned by the habits of the collective but also exercising some individuality, who mediated the particular expression of 'lived religion' that is preserved for us today on a piece of papyrus or some other material. When exploring the relationship between the practices of the wider institutional church and the incantations and amulets written by these scribes, we shall want to focus on specific instances of this interactive cultural phenomenon.[59]

I.4 OVERVIEW OF THE BOOK

To summarize, in this book I seek to draw out how scribes working within personal and collective constraints produced incantations and amulets that were 'Christianized' in a variety of recognizable but nevertheless idiosyncratic ways. In Chapter 1, I begin by setting out normative stances of Christian authorities as conveyed in treatises, sermons, saint's lives, canons, and the like. Although what scribes and their clients did in an increasingly Christian environment did not correspond to this normative discourse, neither was it unaffected by it. Some of the practices we shall observe later in the book correspond to the admonitions or counsels of Christian authorities, revealing how 'lived religion' encompasses officially sanctioned practices. The next chapter, Chapter 2, provides an introduction to the materials, formats, hands, and oral and visual devices that scribes used when preparing amulets. These are all aspects of an artefact that come into play when examining textual amulets and interpreting their features. Then, as a backdrop to the individual artefacts that are the focus of this book, Chapter 3 surveys manuals of

---

[59] See R. Raja and J. Rüpke, 'Appropriating Religion: Methodological Issues in Testing the "Lived Ancient Religion" Approach', *RRE*, 1 (2015), 11–19 at 17, doi: 10.1628/219944615X14234960199632, on 'culture in interaction'.

procedures and collections of recipes—writings that preserved, at various moments, the techniques and incantations available to a given group of practitioners. We shall observe when and how Christian elements emerge in these manuals and collections, and glean what we can about the scribes who collected and recorded the recipes, evidently practitioners who had acquired some degree of expertise in the practice.

The next two chapters are devoted to applied materials, that is, artefacts that were prepared for or used by an individual client (also called 'finished products').[60] The aim here will be to bring the individuality of the artefacts and their writers to the fore. In Chapter 4, I examine the scribal features of amulets whose formulation still bears the imprint of customary practices. In Chapter 5, I examine the scribal features of amulets that consist only or mainly of one or more biblical passages or similar Christian texts that substituted for customary incantations. Although these two types of amulets are not mutually exclusive (some amulets combine customary incantations with scriptural passages), I have chosen to divide the material into two chapters in order to be able to compare groups of amulets that are similar in their formulation. Such comparisons bring the individuality of specific amulets and their scribes into greater relief, while at the same time highlighting the common resources on which groups of amulets drew.

In the last chapter, Chapter 6, I turn to the Christian ritual context in which scribes of incantations and amulets with Christian elements lived and worked. I describe how Christian acclamations, invocations, doxologies, and the like made their way from rituals of the Christian church into incantations and amulets, and argue that this was due in part to the significance vested in such formulations through collective ritual action. I discuss how incantations and amulets were extensions of rituals, both customary and Christian, used to dispel evil spirits or protect against harm. I also explore the diversity of Christian communities reflected in these formulations.

Finally, in the Conclusion I draw out the implications of the preceding chapters for our understanding of how the practice of creating incantations and amulets changed in the increasingly Christian environment of late antique Egypt. In the past few decades the term 'ritual expert' has replaced the term 'magician' to refer to these purveyors in order to relieve them of the mostly negative connotations of the latter term. But the new term is still abstract and anonymous. The evidence and analysis of this study will allow us to populate the category with distinct and diverse individuals. It will enable us to see how different scribes, working with resources that were, inevitably, circumscribed, left the imprint of their individual abilities and cultural formation on the products of their work.

---

[60] 'Finished product' is the preferred expression of G. Bohak, *Ancient Jewish Magic: A History* (Cambridge: Cambridge University Press, 2008), 144 and throughout.

This book was written within some constraints of its own. It focuses on textual amulets from Egypt written mainly on papyrus or parchment. I leave aside amulets from workshops around the late antique world in the form of gems,[61] cameos, pendants, medallions, armbands,[62] and coins.[63] Though such amulets combined text with image,[64] the techniques used to produce them (engraving, casting) were different than for amulets written on papyrus and parchment, and thus entail different forms of analysis. Moreover, while textual amulets and engraved amulets serve similar purposes (love, health, and general success),[65] they draw on different iconographic traditions; they are complementary forms of practice.[66] I thus take engraved amulets into account only tangentially as *comparanda* to the textual amulets that are the focus of this study.

Furthermore, I deal mainly with materials written in Greek. While I occasionally deal with materials written in Coptic, they do not receive the systematic treatment that the Greek materials receive. There are a number of

[61] The major collections are C. Bonner, *Studies in Magical Amulets, Chiefly Graeco-Egyptian* (Ann Arbor: University of Michigan, 1950); A. Delatte and P. Derchain, *Les intailles magiques gréco-égyptiennes* (Paris: Bibliothèque nationale, Cabinet des médailles et antiques, 1964); S. Michel, *Magischen Gemmen im Britischen Museum*, 2 vols (London: British Museum Press, 2001); J. Spier, *Late Antique and Early Christian Gems* (Wiesbaden: Reichert, 2007), esp. chapters seven and eleven, supplemented by J. Spier, 'Late Antique Gems: Some Unpublished Examples', in C. Entwistle and N. Adams (eds), *'Gems of Heaven': Recent Research on Engraved Gemstones in Late Antiquity c. AD 200–600* (London: The British Museum, 2011), 193–213; and the Campbell Bonner Magical Gems Database, <http://www2.szepmuveszeti.hu/talismans/visitatori_salutem>. On gems, see also A. M. Nagy, 'Engineering Ancient Amulets: Magical Gems of the Roman Imperial Period', in D. Boschung and J. M. Bremmer (eds), *The Materiality of Magic* (Munich: Wilhelm Fink, 2015), 205–40; Entwistle and Adams, *'Gems of Heaven'*; S. Michel, *Die magischen Gemmen: Zu Bildern und Zauberformeln auf geschnittenen Steinen der Antike und Neuzeit* (Berlin: Akademie Verlag, 2004).

[62] On pendants, medallions, and armbands, see G. Vikan, 'Art, Medicine, and Magic in Early Byzantium', *DOP*, 38 (1984), 65–86; G. Vikan, 'Two Byzantine Amuletic Armbands and the Group to Which They Belong', *JWAG*, 49/50 (1991–2), 35–51; J. Spier, 'Medieval Byzantine Magical Amulets and their Tradition', *JWI*, 56 (1993), 25–62, doi: 10.2307/751363 (esp. appendix II for early Byzantine amulets); J. Spier, 'An Antique Magical Book Used for Making Sixth-Century Byzantine Amulets?', in V. Dasen and J.-M. Spieser (eds), *Les savoirs magiques et leur transmission de l'Antiquité à la Renaissance* (Florence: SISMEL—Edizioni del Galluzzo, 2014), 43–66.

[63] On coins or pseudo-coins, see H. Maguire, 'Money and Magic in the Early Middle Ages', *Speculum*, 72 (1997), 1037–54, doi: 10.2307/2865957; M. M. Fulghum, 'Coins Used as Amulets in Late Antiquity', in S. R. Asirvatham, C. O. Pache, and J. Watrous (eds), *Between Magic and Religion: Interdisciplinary Studies in Ancient Mediterranean Religion and Society* (Lanham: Rowman and Littlefield, 2001), 139–47; C. Morrisson, 'Monnaies et amulettes byzantines à motifs chrétiens: croyance ou magie?', in Dasen and Spieser, *Les savoirs magiques*, 409–29, esp. 409–14.

[64] See, e.g., Spier, 'An Antique Magical Book'. On the evolution of practice—beginning with the stone, then adding an image, and finally adding text—see C. A. Faraone, 'Text, Image and Medium: The Evolution of Graeco-Roman Magical Gemstones', in Entwistle and Adams, *'Gems of Heaven'*, 50–61.

[65] Nagy, 'Engineering Ancient Amulets', 215–18.

[66] Nagy, 'Engineering Ancient Amulets', 218–20.

reasons for this. The dating of Coptic materials is more difficult than the dating of Greek materials because the study of Coptic palaeography is not as advanced as the study of Greek palaeography.[67] To identify those that should be assigned to Egypt up to the eighth century would require palaeographical and philological skills that I do not have. As well, given their *longue durée*, extending into the ninth, tenth, and eleventh centuries, Coptic materials deserve to be treated in light of circumstances in the centuries after as well as before the Arab conquest. This is beyond the scope of this book, despite the desirability of longer time-frames in studies of the transformation of the culture and society of the Mediterranean and Near Eastern world of Late Antiquity.[68] I regret this limitation. Ideally, studies of the late antique world should integrate evidence from all the relevant linguistic cultures, as others have rightly argued.[69] Coptic manuals, incantations, and amulets deserve much more systematic and expert treatment than I can give them.

I.5 TERMS

Any study dealing with the practices this book treats must, it seems, explain its terminology. I shall be brief, since the problems of terminology have been the subject of exhaustive, and to some extent inconclusive, scholarly discussion.[70] The focus of debate has been the validity and utility of the term 'magic' as an analytical category. On the one hand, there are those who argue that it is almost impossible to avoid the term, or one like it, since it continues to be used in modern parlance in most societies to refer to esoteric and arcane activities.[71] On the other hand, there are those who point out that in each society the salience of language used to refer to 'magic' is constructed through discourse.[72]

---

[67] B. Layton, 'Towards a New Coptic Paleography', in T. Orlandi and F. Wisse (eds), *Acts of the Second International Congress of Coptic Study* [sic], *Roma, 22–26 September 1980* (Rome: C.I.M., 1985), 149–58; R. Kasser, 'Paleography', *CE*, 8.175–84.

[68] G. Fowden, *Before and After Muḥammad: The First Millennium Refocused* (Princeton: Princeton University Press, 2014).

[69] Ritner, 'Egyptian Magical Practice', 3358–71; Bagnall, *Reading Papyri*, 19–22.

[70] For the history of the discussion, see R. L. Fowler, 'The Concept of Magic', *ThesCRA*, 3.283–6 (with ample bibliography); Y. Harari, 'What is a Magical Text? Methodological Reflections Aimed at Redefining Early Jewish Magic', in S. Shaked (ed.), *Officina Magica: Essays on the Practice of Magic in Antiquity* (Leiden: Brill, 2005), 91–124; K. B. Stratton, *Naming the Witch: Magic, Ideology, and Stereotype in the Ancient World* (New York: Columbia University Press, 2007), 4–15.

[71] E.g., H. S. Versnel, 'Some Reflections on the Relationship Magic–Religion', *Numen*, 38 (1991), 177–97, doi: 10.1163/156852791X00114; Harari, 'What is a Magical Text?', 111–15.

[72] E.g., A. F. Segal, 'Hellenistic Magic: Some Questions of Definition', in R. van den Broek and M. J. Vermaseren (eds), *Studies in Gnosticism and Hellenistic Religion* (Leiden: Brill, 1981), 349–75; Stratton, *Naming the Witch*, 15–18.

Since terms like 'magic' and 'magician' cannot be used without importing socially constructed connotations, these scholars argue, it is preferable to be more specific about the phenomena or activities being discussed. Thus, rather than trying to subsume a wide array of phenomena or activities under 'magic', one should speak of curses, adjurations, amulets, divination, oracles, and so on—so-called 'mid-range' taxa.[73] Such terms also have socially constructed connotations, but they have the advantage of referring to narrower fields of practice.

In the course of my own research I have found the second approach to be more viable than the first, though I have benefited from the writings of scholars who have attempted to develop definitions of 'magic', particularly those who have argued for a provisional polythetic definition of the term.[74] I agree that provisional polythetic definitions are a practical and defensible means of distinguishing phenomena that in reality never correspond to ideal types but are nevertheless readily identifiable as instances of such types. But I find that this approach works only to generate a notion of what was considered 'magic' in a particular culture or society, not as a universal, cross-cultural term.[75] Thus, in this book I use the term 'magic' only as it or its equivalents are used in the normative discourses of Roman and Christian authorities to denote practices they derided or condemned on a variety of grounds. Typically, these practices were deemed dangerous or undesirable because they coerced rather than supplicated the divine, invoked the restless dead or evil spirits, were performed in private rather than in public, sought personal gain rather than collective benefit, and served immoral or anti-social ends.[76] Otherwise, when describing the practices discussed in this book, I use the more specific, but nevertheless polythetic, mid-range terms 'incantation' and 'amulet'.

By 'incantation' I mean a text that appeals to or adjures supernatural powers to heal, protect, constrain, or avenge a particular individual (or a number of individuals), sometimes hastening the desired outcome by accelerating, commanding, or threatening phrases.[77] By 'amulet' I mean an object that is

---

[73] J. Z. Smith, 'Trading Places', in Meyer and Mirecki, *Ancient Magic and Ritual Power*, 13–27 at 16–17; Stratton, *Naming the Witch*, 8–9.

[74] Versnel, 'Some Reflections', 185–6; Harari, 'What is a Magical Text?', 109–15.

[75] J. N. Bremmer, 'The Birth of the Term "Magic"', *ZPE*, 126 (1999), 1–12 at 11, <http://www.uni-koeln.de/phil-fak/ifa/zpe/downloads/1999/126pdf/126.html>; J. N. Bremmer, 'Appendix: Magic and Religion', in J. N. Bremmer and J. R. Veenstra (eds), *The Metamorphosis of Magic from Late Antiquity to the Early Modern Period* (Leuven: Peeters, 2002), 265–71 at 269–70.

[76] Versnel, 'Some Reflections', 178–9; J. Braarvig, 'Magic: Reconsidering the Grand Dichotomy', in D. R. Jordan, H. Montgomery, and E. Thomassen (eds), *The World of Ancient Magic: Papers from the First International Samson Eitrem Seminar at the Norwegian Institute at Athens, 4–8 May 1997* (Bergen: Norwegian Institute at Athens, 1999), 21–54 at 52–3; Fowler, 'The Concept of Magic', 285; Stratton, *Naming the Witch*, 12.

[77] See Harari, 'What is a Magical Text?', 119–20, on the features of a Jewish adjuration text.

worn, affixed, or deposited by an individual for healing, protective, or propitious purposes. I prefer 'incantation' to the more specific names given to various types of adjurations in antiquity (though I shall on occasion use these terms as well) because it can be applied throughout to more than one type of invocation or adjuration. For example, 'incantation' subsumes both 'curses' and 'prayers for justice', which are similar in that they both seek retribution but different in how they go about it. The term groups together texts that function in similar ways but would have registered on different points of the 'approved'–'suspect' continuum in ancient normative discourses.[78]

As we have already observed, amulets with Christian elements may be written with an incantation or with other types of texts, such as passages from scripture. Thus 'incantations' and 'amulets' each comprise phenomena that the other does not, while at the same time comprising phenomena included by the other. They are intersecting but not entirely overlapping sets. For instance, lead tablets written with 'binding spells'—customarily referred to as *defixiones*—are incantations but not amulets, while papyri written with verses from the Psalms are amulets but not incantations (in the narrowest sense of that term). Since, however, there are structural and functional similarities between phenomena within each of these two sets, I use a collective term to refer to all the phenomena in the set (e.g., 'incantation') and modify the collective term to refer to specific types of procedures within the set (e.g., 'healing incantation', 'binding incantation').

I.6 A FINAL NOTE

In writing this book, I have tried to make the material accessible to those who are not specialists in ancient Christian literature, magic, and papyrology. I have sought to balance evidentiary detail with expository narrative. Since I draw upon the materials under consideration for different reasons throughout the book, items discussed in one chapter may reappear in another. Some repetition in the narrative is inevitable, but to keep it to a minimum items are discussed in detail where they are most pertinent.

---

[78] See n. 76.

1

Normative Christian Discourse

The educated classes of the Roman Empire were largely hostile toward or contemptuous of magical techniques and their purveyors, even though some of these critics might at the same time have recourse to such interventions or investigate how they worked.[1] Their attitudes are exemplified in different ways by, for instance, Pliny's catalogue of magical remedies in Book Thirty of his *Natural History*, the charge of magical wrongdoing brought against Apuleius and his defence against that charge in his *Apologia*, or Lucian's *exposés* of charlatans who pass themselves off as 'philosophers' and 'wonder-workers' in *Alexander, or the False Prophet* and *Philopseudes* ('Lover of Lies'). A generally negative assessment of magical techniques is characteristic of Christian writers as well, which is hardly surprising, given that the cultural and educational formation of Christian writers was like that of their pagan peers. But just as pagan critics of magic singled out certain aspects of the practice for critique or derision and assumed a particular set of interests and prejudices on the part of their intended audiences, so too Christian critics discussed what they considered to be magical activities with a view to advancing their own objectives with their intended audiences.

The ways in which Christian writers and leaders framed magical activities—and specifically the production and use of incantations and amulets—in their discourses are of particular interest to us. It gives us some idea of the normative stances that purveyors and users of incantations and amulets may have encountered in an increasingly Christian environment. Although 'lived

---

[1] For more detailed discussions, see F. Graf, *Magic in the Ancient World*, tr. F. Philip (Cambridge, M.A.: Harvard University Press, 1997), chapter 3; R. Gordon, 'Imaging Greek and Roman Magic', in B. Ankarloo and S. Clark (eds), *Witchcraft and Magic in Europe: Ancient Greece and Rome* (Philadelphia: University of Pennsylvania Press, 1999), 159–275 at 191–243; M. W. Dickie, *Magic and Magicians in the Greco-Roman World* (London: Routledge, 2001), chapters 7 and 8; B.-C. Otto, *Magie: Rezeptions- und diskursgeschichtliche Analysen von der Antike bis zur Neuzeit* (Berlin: De Gruyter, 2011), chapter 7. For an overview of ancient perspectives, see the relevant chapters in D. J. Collins (ed.), *The Cambridge History of Magic and Witchcraft in the West: From Antiquity to the Present* (Cambridge: Cambridge University Press, 2015), which came to my attention after this manuscript was complete.

religion' may not correspond to officially sanctioned norms, it is not unaffected by those norms and the institutions that promote them. This will be evident in subsequent chapters, where we explore how and why Christian elements enter into incantations and amulets.

From the fourth century onward, admonitions against using incantations and amulets appear with some frequency in the sermons and canons of Christian bishops, revealing a slippage between what Christians did and what, according to the bishops, they were supposed to do. In many ways, the stance of the bishops was anticipated by earlier Christian writers. Therefore, before we turn to the pronouncements of Christian bishops and the slippage between admonition and conduct, it will be useful to sketch the lineaments of the discourse of Christian writers in the second and third centuries on magic in general and incantations in particular.

1.1 EARLY CHRISTIAN DISCOURSE

In Christian writings from the second and third centuries, the use of incantations and amulets is subsumed under the larger discursive fields of magic and sorcery.[2] These terms are associated with danger, evil, illusion, and fraud. When early Christian writers refer to incantations within this discourse, they frequently call attention to their harmful and reprehensible objectives: to exact vengeance, handicap a competitor, attract a lover, or arouse sexual desire. When the desired end is not objectionable, as in the case of healing incantations, Christian writers locate the wrong in a misplaced attribution of agency. A passage from Tatian's *Oration to the Greeks*, written in the second half of the second century,[3] illustrates this two-pronged rhetoric. After mentioning people who avail themselves of an incantation because they are sick or in love or angry or vengeful, Tatian asks, 'How could it be good to help acts of adultery? How is it virtuous to come forward to aid other people's feuds? Or how can it be right to ascribe help given to the insane to matter and not to God?'[4] Arnobius of Sicca, writing under persecution in the early years of the fourth century,[5] is even more expansive:

---

[2] For a survey of the evidence, see F. C. R. Thee, *Julius Africanus and the Early Christian View of Magic* (Tubingen: J. C. B. Mohr, 1984), 316–448.

[3] M. Marcovich, 'Introduction', in M. Marcovich (ed.), *Tatiani Oratio ad Graecos*, PTS 43 (Berlin: Walter de Gruyter, 1995), 1–3; M. Wallraff, 'The Beginnings of Christian Universal History from Tatian to Julius Africanus', *ZAC*, 14 (2011), 540–55 at 543 n. 12, doi: 10.1515/ZAC.2010.29.

[4] Tatian, *Orat.* 17 (Marcovich, 36); ET: Tatian, *Oratio ad Graecos and Fragments*, ed. and tr. M. Whittaker (Oxford: Clarendon Press, 1982), 35 (modified).

[5] M. B. Simmons, *Arnobius of Sicca: Religious Conflict and Competition in the Age of Diocletian* (Oxford: Clarendon Press, 1995), 47–93.

Who is not aware that these men (i.e., *magi*) are eager to know in advance what is about to happen, things which will come to pass in any case, whether they wish it or not, as a natural result of their inherent character; or to inflict a deadly, wasting disease upon whomever they please; or to break up the affections of families; or to open without keys places that are locked; or to bind the mouth in silence; or to weaken, speed on, or slow down horses in chariot races; or inspire in the wives and children of others, both males and females, the flames and frenzied passions of illicit love; or if they seem to attempt anything useful, to be able to do it not by their own force but by the power of those they pray to?[6]

Not only are the ends of such activity objectionable; the means are as well. Early Christian writers usually attribute the effects of incantations and similar techniques, whether real or illusory, to the agency of demons, who deceive and ensnare people by these practices.[7] Alternatively, the explanation is found in the techniques and tricks of the sorcerer, which also deceive. The description of magical tricks in the *Refutations of All Heresies* attributed to Hippolytus is a noteworthy instance of this type of explanation.[8]

Early Christian writers often have two larger objectives when they mention the contemporary use of incantations and related techniques. They aim, first, to differentiate Christian practices from practices commonly found in the wider environment (which I shall refer to as 'customary practices'), and, second, to critique the people or groups who are said to employ customary practices. Christian discourse about incantations is thus an instance of the more general polemical function of discourse about magic and magicians in the ancient world, where to characterize a person as a magician or a practice as magic was to marginalize, discredit, or threaten the person or the practice.[9]

The writings of Justin, composed in the mid-second century, illustrate this aspect of Christian discourse nicely. When Justin addresses a Hellenistic audience and describes how Christians changed after they escaped the deceiving influence of the demons,[10] he says that they abandoned 'magical techniques' ($\mu\alpha\gamma\iota\kappa\alpha\hat{\iota}\varsigma\ \tau\acute{\epsilon}\chi\nu\alpha\iota\varsigma$) to devote themselves to the 'good and ungenerated God'.[11] Exorcisms performed by Christians, an expression of Christ's victory

---

[6] Arnobius of Sicca, *Adv. nat.* 1.43 (CSEL 4.29); ET: Arnobius of Sicca, *The Case against the Pagans*, tr. G. E. McCracken, 2 vols, ACW 7–8 (Westminster, M.D.: The Newman Press, 1949), 1.91 (modified).

[7] Thee, *Julius Africanus*, 330, 336–8, 349–50, 356, 373–4, 378–81, 404–6, 418, 425–6, 431–2; Otto, *Magie*, 299–304.

[8] Hippolytus, *Haer.* 4.28–42, in *Hippolytus, Refutatio omnium haeresium*, ed. M. Marcovich, PTS 25 (Berlin: Walter de Gruyter, 1986), 115–27. See Thee, *Julius Africanus*, 394–5; J. A. Kelhoffer, '"Hippolytus" and Magic: An Examination of *Elenchos* IV 28–42 and Related Passages in Light of the Papyri Graecae Magicae', *ZAC*, 11 (2008), 517–48, doi: 10.1515/ZAC.2007.028.

[9] M. Choi, 'Christianity, Magic, and Difference: Name-Calling and Resistance between the Lines in *Contra Celsum*', *Semeia*, 79 (1997), 75–92.

[10] On the deceptions worked by demons, see Justin, *1 Apol.* 24.1–26.8 (SC 507.194–202).

[11] Justin, *1 Apol.* 14.1–3 (SC 507.162–4).

over the demons, reveal the impotence of such magical techniques:[12] whereas the demon-possessed are not healed by 'all the other exorcists and enchanters and sorcerers', 'many of our people have healed them and still heal them today, exorcizing them by the name of Jesus Christ'.[13] When Justin's objective is to demonstrate the superiority of Christian faith to Jewish tradition, the same is true, *mutatis mutandis*. Christian exorcists are superior to Jewish exorcists. The latter may perhaps succeed if they exorcise 'by the God of Abraham, of Isaac, and of Jacob', but typically they use the same techniques as the gentiles, employing 'fumigations and binding adjurations'.[14] Jewish exorcists are aligned with pagan exorcists by their techniques—techniques that Christians, according to Justin, have abandoned. Even if Justin may have an accurate knowledge of details of others' practice,[15] his main objective is to differentiate Christians from pagans or Jews.

Such recourse to the negative connotations of magical techniques to differentiate one's own practice from the practice of others was not, of course, unique to Christian writers. Jewish and pagan polemics against Christians likewise attempted to discredit the new movement by alleging that its founder and his followers resorted to magic to work wonders,[16] as Justin himself attests.[17] Celsus' *The True Doctrine*, written only a few decades after Justin's floruit, is a primary witness to this strategy.[18] As quotations preserved in Origen's *Against Celsus* reveal, Celsus alleges that Jesus accomplished his marvels through sorcery,[19] having acquired the power to perform such feats during his youth in Egypt.[20] He asks whether sorcerers who perform their wonders in the marketplace—driving out demons, blowing away diseases, calling up the souls of dead heroes, causing sumptuous banquets to appear, making things move as if they are alive—should be considered sons of God or, rather, wicked persons possessed by an evil daimon.[21] Jesus himself

---

[12] On the relationship between Christ's victory over the demons and exorcism of demons in his name, see T. Korteweg, 'Justin Martyr and his Demon-ridden Universe', in N. Vos and W. Otten (eds), *Demons and the Devil in Ancient and Medieval Christianity* (Leiden: Brill, 2011), 145–58 at 151–3.

[13] Justin, *2 Apol.* 5(6).6 (SC 507.334).

[14] Justin, *Dial.* 85.3, in *Justin Martyr, Dialogue avec Tryphon*, ed. P. Bobichon, 2 vols (Fribourg: Academic Press and Éditions Saint-Paul, 2003), 1.416.

[15] See A. Nicolotti, *Esorcismo cristiano e possessione diabolica tra II e III secolo* (Turnhout: Brepols, 2011), 146–55.

[16] M. Hengel, *The Charismatic Leader and his Followers*, tr. J. C. G. Greig (Edinburgh: T. & T. Clark, 1981), 41 n. 14 (originally published in German in 1968); M. Smith, *Jesus the Magician* (San Francisco: Harper and Row, 1978), 45–67; P. Schäfer, *Jesus in the Talmud* (Princeton: Princeton University Press, 2007), 102–6.

[17] Justin, *Dial.* 69.7 (Bobichon, 376); *1 Apol.* 30 (SC 507.208).

[18] See Nicolotti, *Esorcismo cristiano*, 374–89.   [19] Origen, *Cels.* 1.6 (SC 132.92).

[20] Origen, *Cels.* 1.28, 38 (SC 132.152, 181).

[21] Origen, *Cels.* 1.68 (SC 132.266). On the typical feats of these travelling wonder-workers, see Dickie, *Magic*, 236–43. The connotations of the term *daimon* were different in ancient and Hellenistic Greek thought than in later Christian thought. To reflect that difference, I use the

acknowledges, he says, that wonders can be the work of wicked frauds when he warns his disciples against imitators.[22] As Celsus points out, 'Is it not a miserable argument that on the basis of the same works he is deemed a god but they are deemed sorcerers?'[23]

Celsus explicitly assimilates Christians to sorcerers. He says that Christians 'seem to exercise power by invoking the names of certain daimones',[24] and he reports that he 'has seen books with the barbarous names of daimones and charlatanry in the possession of some presbyters'.[25] The allegations are something of a flashpoint for Origen.[26] He replies that Christians 'exercise power not by invocations, but by the name of Jesus, together with a recital of narratives about him'.[27] He brushes off the report about presbyters owning occult books, equating it with the manifestly false accusations that Christians eat the flesh of infants or have unrestrained sex with women, accusations which even non-Christians know to be false.[28] What differentiates Christian healings and exorcisms, according to Origen, from sorcery is precisely the absence of the incantations that others use to control and command demons.[29] Origen does not dispute that demons can be manipulated by incantations and by the divine names employed in incantations.[30] But for that reason he maintains that Christians appeal only to the power of God and the name of Jesus. In short, both Celsus and Origen trade on the negative connotations of seeming to command spirits by means of esoteric incantations. The former evokes the practice to discredit Christians; the latter, to differentiate them from pagans.

The accusation of magic also proved to be a useful tool to differentiate 'false' Christians from 'true' Christians. We cannot be certain of the extent to which Justin associated 'false' teachers with magical techniques—as he does when discussing Simon and his disciple Menander in the *First Apology*[31]—since his *Treatise against All the Heresies* is lost.[32] But the association is a recurring motif in the heresiological writings of Irenaeus, Hippolytus, and Tertullian.[33]

---

word 'daimon' when the term is used in a Hellenistic context or by a pagan writer and 'demon' when the term is used in a Christian context or by a Christian writer.

[22] Origen, *Cels.* 2.49 (SC 132.396). [23] Origen, *Cels.* 2.49 (SC 132.396).

[24] Origen, *Cels.* 1.6 (SC 132.90).

[25] Origen, *Cels.* 6.40 (SC 147.274); see also *Cels.* 6.39 (SC 147.272). On the meaning of πρεσβύτεροι, see Nicolotti, *Esorcismo*, 384–5, who rightly takes it to refer to Christian clergy and dismisses the notion that here Celsus is referring only to heterodox or 'gnostic' Christians.

[26] See G. S. Gasparro, 'Origene e la magia: teoria e prassi', in L. Peronne with P. Bernardino and D. Marchini (eds), *Origeniana Octava: Origen and the Alexandrian Tradition*, 2 vols (Leuven: Leuven University Press and Peeters, 2003), 1.733–56; Nicolotti, *Esorcismo cristiano*, 417–34, 442–59.

[27] Origen, *Cels.* 1.6 (SC 132.90). [28] Origen, *Cels.* 6.40 (SC 147.274).

[29] Origen, *Cels.* 7.4 (SC 150.22); see also *Cels.* 2.51 (SC 132.404).

[30] Thee, *Julius Africanus*, 373–4, 377–84. [31] Justin, *1 Apol.* 26.2, 4 (SC 507.198, 200).

[32] Justin, *1 Apol.* 26.8 (SC 507.202).

[33] Thee, *Julius Africanus*, 346–8, 396, 413; Kelhoffer, '"Hippolytus" and Magic', 539–42.

Irenaeus' *Against Heresies*, the earliest extant heresiological writing to make extensive use of the tool, is illustrative.[34] It would be an overstatement to say that Irenaeus always associates heretics with magic, since he does not level this charge against every heretic. But whenever Irenaeus uses the terms 'magic' or 'magician' of a heretic, they are pejorative and discrediting. Marcus, Simon and his followers, the followers of Basilides, and Carpocrates and his followers are all said to have practiced magic.[35] Occasionally Irenaeus specifies what magic entails: adjurations and incantations;[36] love charms or potions, and attraction spells;[37] daimones-assistants and dream-senders.[38] While one cannot rule out that these techniques were used by some of the teachers or groups Irenaeus attacks—'gnostics' may have used incantations to ascend through the layers of the *pleroma* to their heavenly home[39]—several aspects of Irenaeus' discourse suggest that he is availing himself of a stereotype. First, in all but one of these passages he describes whole groups. It is unlikely that he in fact knew much about what individual members of these purported groups did. Second, Irenaeus mentions only what he considers to be deceiving or coercive techniques, not what others might consider to be beneficial techniques, such as healing and protective incantations. Finally, Irenaeus, like Justin before him and Origen after him, sharply differentiates the church's practices from customary practices. When he later summarizes his arguments against 'false knowledge', he contrasts what 'true' Christians do with what 'false' Christians do.[40] The former drive out demons, see visions and utter prophecies, heal the sick by laying hands upon them, and even raise the dead[41]—a description that echoes Paul's list of spiritual gifts (1 Cor. 12: 4–11). These gifts are exercised, Irenaeus says, not 'by angelic invocations . . . or by incantations or by any other wicked inquisitiveness', but by 'praying in an innocent, pure, and open manner to the Lord who made everything, invoking the name of Jesus

[34] See G. S. Gasparro, 'Eretici e maghi in Ireneo: l'accusa di maghia comme strumento della polemico anti-gnostica', in R. Barcellona and T. Sardella (eds), *Munera amicitiae: studi di storia e cultura sulla tarda antichità offerti a Salvatore Pricoco* (Soveria Mannelli: Rubbettino, 2003), 471–501; Nicolotti, *Esorcismo cristiano*, 229–35, 253–8.

[35] Irenaeus, *Haer.* 1.13.1, 1.23.1, 1.23.4, 1.23.5, 1.24.5, 1.25.3 (SC 264.188–90, 312, 318, 320, 330, 336).

[36] Irenaeus, *Haer.* 1.23.4 (SC 264.318): *exorcismis et incantationibus utuntur*; see also *Haer.* 1.24.5 (SC 264.330). On the meaning of *exorcismis*, see Nicolotti, *Esorcismo cristiano*, 232.

[37] Irenaeus, *Haer.* 1.13.5, 1.23.4, 1.25.3 (SC 264.200, 318, 336).

[38] Irenaeus, *Haer.* 1.13.3, 1.23.4, 1.25.3 (SC 264.192–4, 318, 336). On daimones as assistants, see L. J. Ciraolo, 'Supernatural Assistants in the Greek Magical Papyri', in M. Meyer and P. Mirecki (eds), *Ancient Magic and Ritual Power* (Leiden: Brill, 1995), 279–95; A. Scibilia, 'Supernatural Assistance in the Greek Magical Papyri: The Figure of the *Parhedros*', in J. N. Bremmer and J. R. Veenstra (eds), *The Metamorphosis of Magic from Late Antiquity to the Early Modern Period* (Leuven: Peeters, 2002), 71–86.

[39] See Irenaeus, *Haer.* 1.24.5–7 (SC 264.328–32); G. S. Gasparro, 'Tra gnosi e magia: spazio e ruolo della prassi magica nell'universo religioso dello gnosticismo', in G. Lanata (ed.), *Il tardoantico alle soglie del Duemila: diritto, religione, società* (Pisa: ETS, 2000), 1–35.

[40] See Nicolotti, *Esorcismo cristiano*, 238–45.   [41] Irenaeus, *Haer.* 2.32.4 (SC 294.340).

Christ'.[42] This dichotomy cannot admit of any ambiguity, any combination of Christian and customary practice.

There are exceptions to this negative portrayal of the use of incantations, substances, and objects, and the corresponding dichotomy between Christian and customary practice. Julius Africanus' *Cesti* is a case in point. This technical and scientific compendium, completed around 231 CE,[43] includes an array of procedures involving organic substances (from plants, animals, and humans), incantations, inscriptions, and amulets.[44] Most of these procedures are remedies or cures for illnesses, wounds, or other physical problems in animals and humans. Some are designed for use against the enemy in military campaigns. A few erotic remedies are included. But Africanus does not present this knowledge as magic; the terms 'magic' (μαγεία) and 'sorcery' (γοητεία) do not appear in the compendium.[45] Rather, he aligns himself with a tradition of esoteric knowledge of the secret properties of nature.[46] Words typically used in incantations (ὁρκίζω, ἐξορκίζω, ἐπικαλοῦμαι, ἐπακούω) are rare or absent.[47] Uncanny effects are obtained by the hidden natural properties of things, not by adjuring spirits or daimones,[48] though the absence of adjurations could be a result of censorship by Byzantine excerptors, to whom we owe the transmission of much of the work.[49] In short, Africanus' lack of concern about the suitability of the procedures he compiled (or even the fact that he compiled them) is not really compatible with the discursive antithesis found in Christian apologetical and polemical writings. This no doubt led Jerome to omit the *Cesti* in his list of Africanus' writings, and Rufinus of Aquileia to remove a reference to the work when he translated Eusebius of Caesarea's *Ecclesiastical History*.[50] Were it not for Eusebius' mention of the work and the subscription 'Kestos 18 of Julius Africanus' below an excerpt of the work in a mid-third-century

---

[42] Irenaeus, *Haer.* 2.32.5 (SC 294.342). On invocations of angels, see Irenaeus, *Haer.* 1.24.5 (SC 264.330). The vice of inquisitiveness also figures in Augustine's critique of theurgy two centuries later; see F. Graf, 'Augustine and Magic', in Bremmer and Veenstra, *The Metamorphosis of Magic*, 87–103 at 100–1.

[43] M. Wallraff, 'Dating and Structure', in M. Wallraff et al. (eds), *Iulius Africanus. Cesti: The Extant Fragments*, GCS N.F. 18 (Berlin: Walter de Gruyter, 2012), xix–xxii at xix.

[44] Thee, *Julius Africanus*, 193–309; C. Guignard, 'Technical and/or Magical Character', in Wallraff et al., *Iulius Africanus. Cesti*, xxvii–xxxii.

[45] Guignard, 'Technical', xxviii–xxix.

[46] Guignard, 'Technical', xxviii–xxx; Thee, *Julius Africanus*, 309–11.

[47] M. Wallraff, 'Magie und Religion in den Kestoi des Julius Africanus', in M. Wallraff and L. Mecella (eds), *Die Kestoi des Julius Africanus und ihre Überlieferung* (Berlin: Walter de Gruyter, 2009), 39–52 at 49.

[48] Thee, *Julius Africanus*, 308–9; Guignard, 'Technical', xxx.

[49] In his critical reading of the contents of the *Cesti*, Michael Psellus notes Africanus' recourse to incantations and amulets at a few points; see Julius Africanus, *Cesti*, T7, lines 23–5, 46–7 (Wallraff et al., 12–14).

[50] M. Wallraff, 'Iulius Africanus and the Background of the *Cesti*', in Wallraff et al., *Iulius Africanus. Cesti*, xi–xvii at xvi, with Julius Africanus, *Cesti*, T1a (Wallraff et al., 2).

papyrus (*P.Oxy.* III 412),[51] the *Cesti* might still be considered incompatible with Africanus' Christian identity and *œuvre*.[52] The *Cesti* is the exception that proves the rule with regard to the prevailing view of incantations and amulets in normative Christian discourse.

1.2 LATER CHRISTIAN DISCOURSE

In light of the prevailingly negative depiction of magical techniques (including incantations and amulets) in Christian literature from the second and third centuries, it is hardly surprising that the pronouncements of Christian bishops in later centuries would be equally censorious.[53] By then the normative stance of Christian orthodoxy regarding such practices was well established. What is more interesting, for the purposes of this study, is a shift in focus as the church acquires legal status, privileges, and adherents after the change in imperial policy initiated by Constantine. The discourse is no longer intent mainly on refuting anti-Christian polemics and exposing 'fraudulent' Christian teachers. While these concerns do not entirely disappear, they give way to efforts to persuade Christians—people who participate in Christian services or identify themselves as members of the church—to abandon practices deemed to be 'pagan' or 'Jewish'.[54] In all likelihood this 'failure to differentiate' was already an aspect of Christian affiliation in the second and third centuries. What had changed in the fourth and fifth centuries, from the point of view of Christian authorities, was the magnitude of the problem as more and more people identified as Christian.

The admonitions of bishops from all regions of the Roman Empire—Athanasius in Alexandria, Cyril (or John) in Jerusalem, John Chrysostom in Antioch, Basil of Caesarea and Gregory of Nazianzus in Cappadocia, Augustine in North Africa, and (in the first half of the sixth century) Caesarius

---

[51] Re-edited in J. Hammerstaedt, 'Magie und Religion in den Kestoi des Julius Africanus', in Wallraff and Mecella, *Die Kestoi des Julius Africanus*, 53–69, plate at p. 69.

[52] Wallraff, 'Magie und Religion', 49–50.

[53] There is now an accumulation of studies. For an overview, both of the evidence and of changing approaches to it, see N. Brox, 'Magie und Aberglaube an den Anfängen des Christentums', *TTZ*, 83 (1974), 157–80; H. F. Stander, 'Amulets and the Church Fathers', *EkklPhar*, 75 (1993), 55–66; M. W. Dickie, 'The Fathers of the Church and the Evil Eye', in H. Maguire (ed.), *Byzantine Magic* (Washington, D.C.: Dumbarton Oaks Research Library and Collection, 1995), 9–34; Dickie, *Magic*, chapters 9 and 10; S. Trzcionka, *Magic and the Supernatural in Fourth-Century Syria* (London and New York: Routledge, 2007).

[54] On the concern in discourse on amulets to create boundaries between Christians and others, see J. E. Sanzo, 'Magic and Communal Boundaries: The Problems with Amulets in Chrysostom, *Adv. Iud.* 8, and Augustine, *In Io. tra.* 7', *Henoch* (forthcoming).

in Arles and Severus in Antioch—have much in common.[55] The uttering of incantations and the making of amulets are grouped together with various forms of sorcery, all of which are condemned, along with the many methods of divination. These practices are denounced as superstitious frauds or, more seriously, demonic snares: whatever effects incantations and amulets (and the like) achieve are the work of demons, who work through human agents or material properties. Christians who resort to these remedies in effect renounce their baptism (if they have been baptized) and place themselves once more under the dominion of the Devil. Instead of turning to incantations and amulets to protect themselves or their children, they should pray, give alms, make the sign of the cross (by which the Devil was vanquished), recite passages from scripture, and, if they still need some physical token of power, use a gospel (or some portion of it).[56]

This outlook is often expressed in scenarios evoked by the writer or speaker to make a particular point. For all their apparent vividness, these scenarios are shaped by the genre of the work and the occasion for the remarks. For instance, in sermons to those about to be baptized, the act of renouncing the Devil prior to baptism becomes an occasion to classify customary practices among the Devil's works.[57] In sermons on the feast of a martyr, the preacher, looking for contemporary parallels to martyrdom, likens it to the refusal to resort to incantations and amulets when one is deathly ill.[58] For the writer of a commentary on scripture, a passage that suggests that the apostle Paul may have believed in the 'evil eye' (Gal. 3: 1) requires explanation.[59] For the writer of a saint's life, a story about the malignant effects of a binding incantation or the urgent need for healing is an opportunity to demonstrate the saint's power to rebuke demons or to supplant customary remedies. So we must be wary of accepting everything in these scenarios at face value.[60] At the same time they offer valuable insight into customary practices and, more to the point, into the space allowed for the scribes who produced amulets and the people who commissioned or used them.

---

[55] See Stander, 'Amulets'.

[56] On portions of a gospel, see T. S. de Bruyn, 'Papyri, Parchments, Ostraca, and Tablets Written with Biblical Texts in Greek and Used as Amulets: A Preliminary List', in T. J. Kraus and T. Nicklas (eds), *Early Christian Manuscripts: Examples of Applied Method and Approach* (Leiden: Brill, 2010), 145–89 at 159–60.

[57] E.g., Cyril or John of Jerusalem, *Catech. myst.* 1.8 (SC 126 *bis*.94–6).   [58] See n. 69.

[59] See Dickie, 'The Fathers of the Church and the Evil Eye', 21–6.

[60] See, e.g., the debate between D. Frankfurter, 'Hagiography and the Reconstruction of Local Religion in Late Antique Egypt: Memories, Inventions, and Landscapes', in J. H. F. Dijkstra and M. van Dijk (eds), *The Encroaching Desert: Egyptian Hagiography and the Medieval West* (Leiden: Brill, 2006), 13–37, and P. van Minnen, 'Saving History? Egyptian Hagiography in Space and Time', in Dijkstra and van Dijk, *The Encroaching Desert*, 57–91. For an intermediate position, see J. van der Vliet, 'Bringing Home the Homeless: Landscape and History in Egyptian Hagiography', in Dijkstra and van Dijk, *The Encroaching Desert*, 39–55.

1.2.1 Sermons

We already know from the material record that people routinely used incantations and amulets to protect themselves from harm and to heal themselves from sickness. The observations of Augustine and John Chrysostom, among others, reveal how ubiquitous and customary such remedies were. When Augustine in *On Christian Doctrine* describes the category of 'human superstitions' to which incantations and amulets belong,[61] he mentions wearing earrings on the tip of an ear or rings made of ostrich bones on one's fingers; holding the left thumb with the right hand when hiccupping; what to do if a stone or a dog or a slave-boy comes between friends walking together (cuff the boy or the dog); what to do when you pass in front of your own house (tread on the threshold); what to do if you sneeze while putting on your shoes (go back to bed); what to do if you trip when leaving your house (go back inside).[62] The impression conveyed by this grouping of practices is of routine behaviour meant to avert misfortune or misadventure—behaviour, however, that according to Augustine relies on a system of meaning created and operated by demons.[63] A similar impression is gained from accounts of behaviour associated with common life-cycle occurrences such as birth or sickness. In one sermon, after a critique of customs and festivities associated with marriage, John Chrysostom turns to customs associated with what comes next, childbirth. He deplores the practice of hanging thread and bells from the hands of infants and of daubing their foreheads with mud against the evil eye or envy.[64] Chrysostom compares such actions with the rituals of midwives during childbirth and the wailing of mourners at funerals, all of which are diabolical.[65] According to Chrysostom, such practices cannot be defended on the grounds that they are 'customary', as his imaginary interlocutor protests in defence of public processions of a bride prior to her marriage.[66] But this is precisely the point: the practices the bishops decry were durable because they were customary.

There were many reasons people were reluctant to abandon customary practices.[67] The scenarios evoked by Christian preachers intimate some of them. One of the more frequent commonplaces in the sermons of bishops is

---

[61] Augustine, *Doct. chr.* 2.19.29–30, in *Augustine: De Doctrina Christiana*, ed. R. P. H. Green (Oxford: Clarendon Press, 1995), 90–2.

[62] Augustine, *Doct. chr.* 2.20.30–1 (Green, 92).

[63] Graf, 'Augustine and Magic', 95–102.

[64] John Chrysostom, *Hom. 12 in 1 Cor.* 7 (PG 61.105–6).

[65] John Chrysostom, *Hom. 12 in 1 Cor.* 7 (PG 61.106).

[66] John Chrysostom, *Hom. 12 in 1 Cor.* 7 (PG 61.104).

[67] See W. E. Klingshirn, *Caesarius of Arles: The Making of a Christian Community in Late Antique Gaul* (Cambridge: Cambridge University Press, 1994), 209–26, for a fine-grained analysis of customary practices in sixth-century Gaul.

how people would resort to incantations and amulets—or would be tempted to resort to them—in the event of sickness, either their child's or their own.[68] The sickness often presents itself as some sort of fever or pain whose cause would have been unknown, but whose pattern and outcome would have been all too familiar. Just how agonizing and terrifying such sicknesses could be is suggested by a scenario used to recommend 'martyrdom' to Christians, now that persecution was a thing of the past (at least for 'orthodox' Christians). Augustine draws the scene often in sermons on the feasts of martyrs.[69] One example will suffice:

> I on occasion am reminded of the leaflets on the miracles of the martyrs, which are read in your presence. A few days ago a leaflet was read, in which a sick woman, wracked with the severest pains said, 'I can't bear it.' The martyr, to whom she had come to be healed, said, 'What if you were enduring martyrdom?' So it is that many people endure martyrdom on their sickbeds, very many indeed. Satan has a certain method of persecution, more hidden and cunning than the ones he employed in those times. A believer is lying in bed, wracked with pain; he prays, he isn't listened to; or rather, he is listened to, but he is being tested, being put through his paces, being chastised in order to be received as a son. So while he's being wracked with pain, along comes trial and temptation by tongue; either some female, or a man, if man he can be called, approaches the sickbed, and says to the sick man, 'Tie on that amulet (*ligaturam*), and you will get better; let them apply that incantation (*praecantatio*), and you will get better. So-and-so, and So-and-so and So-and-so; ask, they all got better by using it.' He doesn't yield, he doesn't agree, he doesn't give his consent; he has to struggle, all the same. He has no strength, and he conquers the devil. He becomes a martyr on his sickbed, and he is crowned by the one who hung for him on the tree.[70]

The depiction of someone in the throes of sickness is probably not exaggerated. The sermonic illustration undoubtedly owed its effectiveness (as well as its frequency in Augustine's repertoire) to the fact that inexplicable and deadly illness was a common occurrence, experienced by 'very many indeed' (Augustine's phrase).[71] As John Chrysostom remarks in another context, 'There are evils which by reason of their severity cannot be mitigated by being common . . . Tell me, I ask you, if we have ever been attacked by a violent

---

[68] Athanasius of Alexandria, *De amuletis* (PG 26.1320); Basil of Caesarea, *Hom. in Ps.* 45.2 (PG 29.417); John Chrysostom, *Hom. 8 in Col.* 5 (PG 62.358); Augustine, *Psal.* 70, *sermo* 1.17 (CCSL 39.955).

[69] Augustine, *Serm.* 318.3 (PL 38.1439–40); *Serm.* 328.8 (PLS 2.801); *Serm.* 335D.3, 5 (PLS 2.778–80); *Serm.* 360F.7, in *Augustin d'Hippone. Vingt-six sermons au peuple d'Afrique*, ed. F. Dolbeau (Paris: Institut d'Études Augustiniennes, 1996), 215; see also John Chrysostom, *Hom. 8 in Col.* 5 (PG 62.357–8).

[70] Augustine, *Serm.* 286.7 (PL 38.1300–1); ET: *The Works of Saint Augustine: A Translation for the 21st Century*, Part III: *Sermons*, vol. 8: *Sermons 273–305A*, tr. E. Hill (Hyde Park: New City Press, 1994), 105 (slightly modified).

[71] Augustine, *Serm.* 286.7 (PL 38.1300).

fever, have we not found that all consolation has failed us? And rightly so; for when terror strikes, the soul is in no mood to be consoled.'[72]

But the durability of the practice was not simply a result of the urgency of the need to which it responded. It was also—if not even more so—a result of the social matrix in which people lived.[73] When Augustine and Chrysostom describe the social pressure to use incantations and amulets at crucial moments in the life cycle, they populate their scenes with spouses, servants, friends, and neighbours. It is 'the women in the bath, nurses and waiting-maids' who, according to Chrysostom, daub the child's forehead with mud.[74] It is a friend, a neighbour, a neighbour's maid, or the woman she brings along (a *dematricula*), expert in such remedies,[75] who, according to Augustine, urges the sick man to submit to customary procedures.[76] Or it may be a wife or a husband who presses the remedy upon the invalid[77]—remedies that are 'approved' or 'tested',[78] a further indication of social approbation. William Klingshirn's observation about divinatory and healing practices in sixth-century Gaul is no doubt relevant for prior centuries and other locales: 'It was the variety and reliability of these old remedies, their widespread availability, and their wide social acceptance that promoted their use among country people'[79]—and, one might add, not only 'country people'. Klingshirn points out that for many people it would have been cheaper and easier to obtain traditional remedies in the event of a sudden illness or mishap than to consult a physician or even find their way to a church or a monk.[80] This is confirmed by a remark by Basil of Caesarea (that, however, is silent about the practical, social, and economic reasons for such behaviour): when a child is ill, people first seek out the singer of incantations or get amulets to hang around their child's neck, and only later turn to a doctor and his medicines.[81]

In addition, people who attended church had a different notion of what it meant to be Christian than their bishops did. When Augustine draws scenes of sickbed 'martyrdom', he has those at the bedside defend customary practices by saying that people who use or offer such remedies are Christians, no less:

> But the one who says, 'I won't do it'... well, he gets this answer from the one who is suggesting it: 'Do it, and you'll get well. So-and-so and Such-and-such did it. What? Aren't they Christians? Aren't they believers? Don't they hurry off to

---

[72] John Chrysostom, *Hom. 10 in 1 Tim.* 3 (PG 62.552); ET: J. Tweed, NPNF¹ 13.441 (modified).
[73] See the Introduction, nn. 35–6.
[74] John Chrysostom, *Hom. 12 in 1 Cor.* 7 (PG 61.105–6); see also Caesarius of Arles, *Serm.* 52.6 (CCSL 103.232).
[75] On the meaning of *dematricula*, see Dickie, *Magic*, 309–10.
[76] Augustine, *Serm.* 335D.3, 5 (PLS 2.778, 880).
[77] Augustine, *Psal.* 93.20 (CCSL 39.1322).   [78] Augustine, *Serm.* 335D.3 (PLS 2.778).
[79] Klingshirn, *Caesarius*, 223.   [80] Klingshirn, *Caesarius*, 222.
[81] Basil of Caesarea, *Hom. in Ps.* 45.2 (PG 29.417).

church? And yet they did it and got well. So-and-so did it and was cured immediately. Don't you know Such-and-such, that he's a Christian, a believer? Look, he did it, and he got well.'[82]

Augustine, of course, introduces this dialogue in order to differentiate 'good' Christians from 'bad' ones, the 'wheat' from the 'chaff'.[83] But at the same time he reveals that what identified a person as a Christian in the minds of the faithful was not their view of customary remedies but their attendance at church services.[84] John Chrysostom acknowledges as much in an imaginary dialogue with a Christian mother who applies an incantation to her sick child:

> Tell me, then, if someone says, 'Take him to an idol's temple, and he will live,' would you allow it? 'No', she says. 'Why not?' 'Because he is urging me to commit idolatry. In this case, there is no idolatry, but only incantation,' she says.[85]

In other words, what counted as appropriate behaviour for bishops trying to inculcate a distinctive Christian identity was not altogether what counted for the people in their congregations.[86] This has many implications for the 'market' for incantations and amulets in the fourth and fifth centuries, and probably later. For some Christians, one should suppose, neither the supplier nor the product had to be identifiably 'Christian'. Or, if they were identifiably 'Christian' in some way, the Christian element may have been, from a bishop's point of view, superficial or formal.

It is significant that this sort of ambiguity surfaces in homiletic discourse only in relation to protective and healing procedures. Only with regard to such purposes—protection and healing—did bishops find it necessary to make their case by giving voice to what likely were common views among Christians. (No imaginary Christian speaks up in defence of erotic and aggressive procedures, which are unequivocally evil and demonic.) To manage the demand for protective or healing amulets, bishops were obliged to accept or even commend Christian substitutes, such as making the sign of the cross or wearing a gospel. The way these substitutes are framed rhetorically suggests that there was no settled opinion—and often considerable ambivalence—among Christian authorities regarding their use. In some contexts John Chrysostom refers to Christian women who wear the gospel around their neck without any

---

[82] Augustine, *Serm.* 335D.3 (PLS 2.778); ET: *The Works of Saint Augustine: A Translation for the 21st Century*, Part III: *Sermons*, vol. 9: *Sermons 306–340A*, tr. E. Hill (Hyde Park: New City Press, 1994), 230. See also Augustine, *Serm.* 260D.2 (PLS 2.586); Augustine, *Psal.* 93.20 (CCSL 39.1321–2); John Chrysostom, *Hom. 8 in Col.* 5 (PG 62.358).

[83] Augustine, *Psal.* 93.20 (CCSL 39.1321).

[84] See Klingshirn, *Caesarius*, 211–12, on Caesarius of Arles' criticisms of 'pagan' behaviour among those who attended mass. See also E. Rebillard, *Christians and their Many Identities in Late Antiquity, North Africa, 200–450 CE* (Ithaca: Cornell University Press, 2012), 68–9.

[85] John Chrysostom, *Hom. 8 in Col.* 5 (PG 62.358).

[86] Rebillard, *Christians and their Many Identities*, 74–9.

criticism, indeed with approbation.[87] But Jerome calls such women 'superstitious', adding that 'indeed they have zeal for God, but without understanding'.[88] Augustine commends the Christian who puts a gospel by his head
when he has a fever only because to do so is preferable to using an amulet,
not because it is what a Christian should do.[89] By 'amulet' Augustine
means customary devices, including those, he says, that incorporate the
name 'Christ' in order to seduce Christians.[90] Caesarius of Arles is, by
comparison, categorical—a difference worth noting, given Caesarius' debt as
a preacher to Augustine.[91] He condemns amulets even if they are made by
monks or priests and contain Christian inscriptions: they are still means
whereby the Devil kills the soul; Christians who use them turn themselves
into pagans; the Eucharist and anointing of the sick suffice to protect and heal
both body and soul.[92] Elsewhere Caesarius proclaims that those who persist in
customary practices (which include incantations, potions, amulets of herbs or
amber, and written amulets) commit sacrilege and lose the sacrament of
baptism.[93] Such remarks reveal an overriding concern to distinguish sharply
between things 'pagan' and 'Christian'. As Severus of Antioch argues in one of
his sermons, since it is impossible to tell the difference outwardly between a
Christian amulet and a pagan one, Christians should avoid wearing even
amulets obtained from saints, so as not to harm other believers who might
then resort out of custom to diabolical incantations.[94]

1.2.2 Saints' Lives

Real and perceived tensions between customary practices and Christian norms
also figure in the literary products of early Christian monasticism—saints'
lives, sayings, 'beneficial tales', and the like.[95] What saints do to help Christians

---

[87] John Chrysostom, *Hom. 72 in Matt.* 2 (PG 58.669); *Stat.* 19.14 (PG 49.196).

[88] Jerome, *Matt.* 4 on Matt. 23: 6 (SC 259.164).

[89] Augustine, *Tract. Io.* 7.12 (CCSL 36.73).   [90] Augustine, *Tract. Io.* 7.6 (CCSL 36.70).

[91] See Dickie, *Magic*, 307; T. O'Loughlin, 'Caesarius of Arles', in A. D. Fitzgerald (ed.),
Augustine through the Ages: An Encyclopedia (Grand Rapids: Eerdmans, 1999), 115–16 at 115;
Klingshirn, *Caesarius*, 147–51, with 142–3, for another instance of a loss of nuance in the transfer
from Augustine to Caesarius.

[92] Caesarius of Arles, *Serm.* 50.1 (CCSL 103.225). See also the sermon preserved in the *Life* of
Eligius of Noyon, *Vit. Elig.* 2.16 (PL 87.524–50 at 527–9), now believed to be the work of an
eighth-century redactor; see J. McCune, 'Rethinking the Pseudo-Eligius Sermon Collection',
EME, 16 (2008), 445–76 at 446 n. 4, doi: 10.1111/j.1468-0254.2008.00238.x.

[93] Caesarius of Arles, *Serm.* 13.5 (lose the sacrament of baptism), *Serm.* 14.4 (commit
sacrilege), *Serm.* 52.6 (commit sacrilege if they permit others to do what they themselves
would not do) (CCSL 103.68, 71–2, 232–3).

[94] Severus of Antioch, *Hom.* 79 (PO 20/2.321).

[95] H. J. Magoulias, 'The Lives of Byzantine Saints as Sources of Data for the History of Magic
in the Sixth and Seventh Centuries A.D.: Sorcery, Relics and Icons', *Byzantion*, 37 (1967),

in this literature plays out, implicitly if not explicitly, against what other purveyors offer. Some episodes, in fact, stereotypically pit the Christian saint against the pagan sorcerer, cause of an array of harms: demonic possession, sickness, pain, paralysis, amorous infatuation, failure to compete at the races or in athletic contests, and even inability to launch a new ship down its slipway. (When the sorcerer is a Christian, he is presented as a lapsed one, usually a dissolute cleric.) What is interesting for our purposes, apart from what the saint does to defeat the sorcerer, is the extent to which the saint's remedies are distinguishable from customary alternatives.

We begin with Athanasius of Alexandria's *Life of Antony*, so influential in subsequent Christian hagiography.[96] The saint's method of healing and exorcism, as portrayed by Athanasius, corresponds to the norms of Christian apologetic literature. The saint repels demons by praying, making the sign of the cross, reciting scripture, speaking the name of Christ, and breathing on the demons.[97] The sick and the possessed who come to him are healed either by their own prayers or his, sometimes accompanied by the sign of the cross.[98] Athanasius has Antony contrast these Christian methods (calling upon Christ and making the sign of the cross) with traditional ones (philosophical reasoning, magical techniques, invocation of idols) in his discourse with some philosophers who come to him to argue the irrationality of Christ's crucifixion.[99] 'Where one makes the sign of the cross,' he says, 'magic ($\mu\alpha\gamma\epsilon\acute{\iota}\alpha$) is enervated and sorcery ($\varphi\alpha\rho\mu\alpha\kappa\epsilon\acute{\iota}\alpha$) has no effect'[100]—the rudiments, so to speak, of the stereotypical opposition between a saint and a sorcerer.

With Jerome's *Life of Hilarion*, whose debt to the *Life of Antony* is apparent,[101] the repertoire of personae and action in this opposition expands. The saint's actions when healing the sick and the possessed incorporates gestures and

---

228–69; J. Wortley, 'Some Light on Magic and Magicians in Late Antiquity', *GRBS*, 42 (2001), 289–307, <http://grbs.library.duke.edu/article/view/1891>; Trzcionka, *Magic, passim*.

[96] G. J. M. Bartelink, 'Introduction', in G. J. M. Bartelink (ed.), *Athanase d'Alexandrie, Vie d'Antoine*, SC 400 (Paris: Les Éditions du Cerf, 1994), 25–108 at 68–70; W. Harmless, *Desert Christians: An Introduction to the Literature of Early Monasticism* (New York: Oxford University Press, 2004), 97–100; E. Poirot, *Saint Antoine le Grand dans l'Orient chrétien: dossier littéraire, hagiographique, liturgique, iconographique en langue française*, 2 vols (Frankfurt am Main: Peter Lang, 2014), 1.27–30. In early Egyptian-speaking monastic circles, however, it appears that Antony's letters were more influential than Athanasius' *Life*; see M. Choat, 'The *Life of Antony* in Egypt', in B. Leyerle and R. Darling Young (eds), *Ascetic Culture: Essays in Honor of Philip Rousseau* (Notre Dame: University of Notre Dame Press, 2013), 50–74.

[97] Athanasius of Alexandria, *V. Anton.* 35.2, 39.1–40.6 (SC 400.230, 240–4).

[98] Athanasius of Alexandria, *V. Anton.* 48.2–3, 58.4–5, 61.1–3, 64.1–2, 71.1–2 (SC 400.264, 290–2, 298–300, 302, 318–20).

[99] Athanasius of Alexandria, *V. Anton.* 80.1–4 (SC 400.338).

[100] Athanasius of Alexandria, *V. Anton.* 78.5 (SC 400.334).

[101] P. Leclerc, 'Jérôme et le genre littéraire de la biographie monastique', in E. M. Morales and P. Leclerc (eds), *Jérôme, Trois vies de moines (Paul, Malchus, Hilarion)*, SC 508 (Paris: Les Éditions du Cerf, 2007), 33–72 at 48–51.

utterances in addition to prayer and making the sign of the cross.[102] Some of the gestures are modelled on Jesus in the gospels: raising eyes to heaven, applying spit.[103] Hilarion, like Jesus, addresses and commands a legion of demons directly, using the second-person imperative.[104] Oil blessed by the saint is a medium of healing power;[105] people of all ranks flock to Hilarion to obtain oil he has blessed.[106] On several occasions people seeking Hilarion's help are victims of binding incantations: a leading citizen of Gaza, a Christian, whose racehorses are handicapped by incantations commissioned by his rival;[107] a young woman who is madly infatuated with a young man who, having acquired the necessary skills in Memphis, had deposited incantations and figurines beneath the threshold of her house;[108] a Frankish officer of the emperor Constantius II's personal body-guard (*candidatus*) who is possessed by a demon that, ensconced by incantations, has the officer answer in perfect Syriac and Greek though he normally speaks only Frankish and Latin.[109] In each instance Jerome takes pains to explain how the saint, in responding, sought to avoid appearing like a magician. Hilarion has his own drinking cup filled with water to protect the Gazan's horses after the Gazan explains that a Christian should seek help from a servant of Christ rather than use magic arts;[110] he purges the woman of her demon before exposing the young man and his devices, so as not to seem to have himself succeeded by means of incantations;[111] he is not interested in the magical constraints that prevent the demon from leaving the Frankish officer, and simply commands him to leave in the name of Jesus Christ.[112] Although the Gazan crowd accuses Hilarion of being 'the sorcerer of the Christians' (*maleficium christianorum*), Jerome's narrative frames him as the antithesis of a sorcerer.

In the portraits of Egyptian ascetics compiled by visitors to the region in the late fourth century—the so-called *History of the Monks of Egypt*, an inquiry into the emerging monastic movement, occasioned by a pilgrimage of seven Palestinian monks to monasteries and hermitages along the Nile and in the Delta in 394–5 and published by 397,[113] and the *Lausiac History*, a memoir composed by Palladius in the early 420s of his decade among the monks in the

---

[102] Jerome, *V. Hil.* 3.8, 8.8 (SC 508.222–4, 234).

[103] Jerome, *V. Hil.* 7.4, 9.3 (SC 508.232, 236).

[104] Jerome, *V. Hil.* 10.5, 8 (SC 508.240); see Mark 5: 8.

[105] Jerome, *V. Hil.* 32.2 (SC 508.294).   [106] Jerome, *V. Hil.* 20.2, 22.6 (SC 508.266, 274).

[107] Jerome, *V. Hil.* 11.3–13 (SC 508.242–6); see Trzcionka, *Magic*, 43–5.

[108] Jerome, *V. Hil.* 12.1–9 (SC 508.246–8); see Trzcionka, *Magic*, 88–91.

[109] Jerome, *V. Hil.* 13.1–10 (SC 508.248–52); see Trzcionka, *Magic*, 150–1. On *candidati*, see A. H. M. Jones, *The Later Roman Empire 284–602: A Social, Economic, and Administrative Survey*, 2 vols (Oxford: Basil Blackwell, 1964), 1.613, 2.1253 n. 11.

[110] Jerome, *V. Hil.* 11.7 (SC 508.244).   [111] Jerome, *Vit. Hil.* 12.10 (SC 508.248).

[112] Jerome, *Vit. Hil.* 13.9 (SC 508.250–2).

[113] On this work, see now A. Cain, *The Greek Historia monachorum in Aegypto: Monastic Hagiography in the Late Fourth Century* (Oxford: Oxford University Press, 2016).

Delta (chiefly Kellia) in the 390s[114]—monks are regularly sought out by the sick and the possessed. The healings and exorcisms they perform are among the 'signs' and 'wonders' and 'powerful deeds' that, recalling the age of the apostles in the New Testament, attest to the presence and power of God.[115] The reports of these healings and exorcisms are mostly general and generic.[116] Those that are more detailed usually refer to prayer, laying on of hands, and anointing with oil or sprinkling with water as the means of healing.[117] One story relates the ability of a monk to undo an erotic incantation: Macarius restores a woman who had been turned into a mare by the magical arts of a certain evildoer.[118] Despite the imaginary qualities and edifying objectives of the portrayals, they suggest that Christian ascetics were perceived and presented as substitutes for their pagan competitors. The monks inhabit a world where people come to them for healing (as they would have gone to traditional healers); where the monks send people on their way with empowered substances, chiefly water or oil (as did those who uttered incantations over herbs and potions);[119] where the monks are adept in managing the dangers of the desert and the Nile—the scorpion, the snake, and the crocodile (as were the purveyors of protective amulets);[120] where the monks, gifted with clairvoyance and discernment, are able to see into the future or from afar (as had the oracles of the Egyptian temples).[121]

The reality was undoubtedly more complex than these hagiographical tales would lead one to believe, as an excerpt from a work by Shenoute shows.[122] The abbot complains about the amulets and oils that Christians obtain from various purveyors, including monks:

> at the time of suffering, those fallen into poverty or in sickness or indeed some other trial abandon God and run after enchanters or diviners or indeed seek other acts of deception, just as I myself have seen: the snake's head tied on someone's hand, another one with the crocodile's tooth tied to his arm, and another with fox

---

[114] Harmless, *Desert Christians*, 275–9.   [115] Harmless, *Desert Christians*, 290–9.

[116] *Hist. mon.* 2.6, 6.1, 7.2, 8.7, 10.1, 15.1, 24.10, in *Historia monachorum in Aegypto*, ed. A.-J. Festugière (Brussels: Société des Bollandistes, 1961), 37, 43–4, 46, 49, 75, 111, 133; Palladius, *H. Laus.* 12.1, in *The Lausiac History of Palladius*, ed. C. Butler, Texts and Studies 6/2 (Cambridge: Cambridge University Press, 1904), 35.

[117] *Hist. mon.* 1.12, 1.16 (Festugière, 12–13, 14–15); Palladius, *H. Laus.* 12.1, 18.11, 18.22 (Butler, 35, 51, 54–5).

[118] *Hist. mon.* 21.17 (Festugière, 128). For a different version, see Palladius, *H. Laus.* 17.6–9 (Butler, 44–6).

[119] Palladius, *H. Laus.* 12.1 (Butler, 35). For other examples, see B. Kranemann, 'Krankenöl, *RAC*, 21.915–65 at 931–3.

[120] *Hist. mon.* 20.12 (Festugière, 122).

[121] *Hist. mon.* 1.1–2, 1.10–11, 11.4, 12.11, 22.5–6, 22.8 (Festugière, 9–10, 12, 90, 96, 129–30).

[122] On the work in question (Acephalous work A14), transmitted without *incipit* and *explicit* and erroneously included in Shenoute's *Contra Origenistas* by Tito Orlandi, see S. Emmel, *Shenoute's Literary Corpus*, 2 vols (Leuven: Peeters, 2004), 2.692–3; H.-J. Cristea, *Schenute von Atripe: Contra Origenistas* (Tübingen: Mohr Siebeck, 2011), 12.

claws tied to his legs—especially since it was an official who told him that it was wise to do so! Indeed, when I demanded whether the fox claws would heal him, he answered, 'It was a great monk who gave them to me, saying "Tie them on you [and] you will find relief."' Listen to this impiety! Fox claws! Snakes' heads! Crocodiles' teeth! And many other vanities that people put on themselves for their own relief, while others deceive them. Moreover, this is the manner that they anoint themselves with oil or that they pour over themselves water while receiving [ministrations] from enchanters or drug-makers, with every deceptive kind of relief. . . . Still again, they pour water over themselves or anoint themselves with oil from elders of the church, or even from monks![123]

Clearly, in the mind of Shenoute, the ministrations of monks resembled customary 'pagan' remedies far too closely. But then, not all abbots were as rigorous as Shenoute in the boundaries they set for their monks.[124]

1.3 STANDARDS FOR THE FAITHFUL AND THE CLERGY

The negative stance of Christian authorities toward practices subsumed under the terms 'magic' and 'sorcery', including the making and wearing of amulets, is also reflected in documents setting out expectations of members of the church or candidates for admission to the church. One of the earliest articulations of such expectations is the teaching on the 'Two Ways', 'the way of life' and 'the way of death'. This teaching, which is Jewish in origin and can be found in various Jewish contexts,[125] made its way into a number of Christian documents from the second, third, and fourth centuries: the *Didache*, the *Doctrina apostolorum*, the *Letter of Barnabas*, the *Apostolic Church Order* (also known as *Ecclesiastical Canons of the Apostles*), and the *Epitome of the Canons of the Holy Apostles*.[126] The relationship among these works, and the putative sources on which they drew, is now clearer, thanks to several recent

---

[123] Shenoute, Acephalous work A14, §§255–9, in *Shenute: Contra Origenistas*, ed. T. Orlandi (Rome: C.I.M., 1985), 18; ET: D. Frankfurter, 'Syncretism and the Holy Man in Late Antique Egypt', *JECS*, 11 (2003), 339–85 at 375 (modified), doi: 10.1353/earl.2003.0043; cf. T. Orlandi, 'A Catechesis against Apocryphal Texts by Shenute and the Gnostic Texts of Nag Hammadi', *HTR*, 75 (1982), 85–95 at 90, <http://www.jstor.org/stable/1509665>.

[124] J. E. Goehring, *Ascetics, Society, and the Desert: Studies in Early Egyptian Monasticism* (Harrisburg: Trinity Press International, 1999), 218–19.

[125] J. A. Draper, 'The *Didache* in Modern Research: An Overview', in J. A. Draper (ed.), *The Didache in Modern Research* (Leiden: Brill, 1996), 1–42 at 7–10, 13–16; H. van de Sandt and D. Flusser, *The Didache: Its Jewish Sources and its Place in Early Judaism and Christianity* (Assen: Van Gorcum, 2002), 140–90; A. Stewart(-Sykes) (ed.), *On the Two Ways: Life or Death, Light or Darkness: Foundational Texts in the Tradition* (Yonkers: St Vladimir's Seminary Press, 2011), 13–26.

[126] Stewart(-Sykes), *On the Two Ways*, gives a convenient overview, with translations of all the texts.

studies. The injunctions that concern us can be found in the *Didache* and the *Doctrina apostolorum* (each drawing independently on a common source),[127] and again in the *Apostolic Church Order* and the *Epitome of the Canons of the Holy Apostles* (likewise drawing on a common source).[128] In these documents those who follow 'the way of life' are exhorted, among many other prohibitions, not to 'practice magic' or 'use potions' (i.e., practice sorcery).[129] They are not to be an enchanter (i.e., one who utters incantations) or a purifier (i.e., one who performs purificatory rituals), or even to witness such things, since such things lead to idolatry (i.e., to the honouring of demons).[130]

The teaching of the 'Two Ways' had a long life as a form of instruction for Christians.[131] Of particular relevance for our study are the direct and indirect witnesses to its presence and influence in Egypt. Egypt is the source of the two oldest witnesses to the *Didache*:[132] leaves from a fourth-century Greek codex of the work,[133] and leaves, probably from the fifth century, preserving an excerpt of the work in Coptic.[134] The church in Egypt appears to have used the *Didache* or the teaching of the 'Two Ways' in catechetical instruction.[135] (In the *Didache* itself, the teaching is presented as instruction to be given prior to baptism.[136]) Athanasius of Alexandria included the *Didache* (or an independent manual of the 'Two Ways') among the books that are not in the canon of scripture but have been approved as reading for those who are currently

---

[127] Van de Sandt and Flusser, *The Didache*, 61–3, 112–39. See also W. Rordorf and A. Tullier, 'Introduction', in W. Rordorf and A. Tullier (eds), *La doctrine des douze apôtres (Didachè)*, SC 248 *bis* (Paris: Les Éditions du Cerf, 1998), 11–128, supplemented by 221–46.

[128] A. Stewart-Sykes, *The Apostolic Church Order: The Greek Text with Introduction, Translation and Annotation* (Strathfield: St Pauls Publications, 2006), 2–30; van de Sandt and Flusser, *The Didache*, 64–5.

[129] *Did.* 2.2 (SC 248 *bis*.148): οὐ μαγεύσεις, οὐ φαρμακεύσεις; *Doct. apost.* 2.2 (SC 248 *bis*.207): *non magica facies, non medicamenta mala facies*; so too *Apostolic Church Order* 6 (Stewart-Sykes, *Apostolic Church Order*, 92); *Epitome* (Stewart-Sykes, *Apostolic Church Order*, 117, reproducing the Greek text from *Eine Elfapostelmoral oder die X-Rezension der 'beiden Wege'*, ed. T. Schermann [Munich: Lentner'sche Buchhandlung, 1903], 16–18). See also *Did.* 5.1 (SC 248 *bis*.166); *Doct. apost.* 5.1 (SC 248 *bis*.209).

[130] *Did.* 3.4 (SC 248 *bis*.152–4): μηδὲ ἐπαοιδὸς μηδὲ μαθηματικὸς μηδὲ περικαθαίρων, μηδὲ θέλε αὐτὰ βλέπειν < μηδὲ ἀκούειν>· ἐκ γὰρ τούτων ἁπάντων εἰδωλολατρία γεννᾶται; *Doct. apost.* 3.4 (SC 248 *bis*.208): *noli esse mathematicus neque delustrator, quae res ducunt ad vanam superstitionem; nec velis ea videre nec audire*; *Apostolic Church Order* 10 (Stewart-Sykes, *Apostolic Church Order*, 94); *Epitome* (Stewart-Sykes, *Apostolic Church Order*, 117). On purificatory rituals, see Dickie, *Magic*, 91–2, 189–90, 245–6.

[131] Van de Sandt and Flusser, *The Didache*, 81–111; W. Rordorf, 'An Aspect of the Judeo-Christian Ethic: The Two Ways', in Draper, *The Didache in Modern Research*, 148–64 at 159–64.

[132] Van de Sandt and Flusser, *The Didache*, 24–5.

[133] *P.Oxy.* XV 1782.

[134] See now F. S. Jones and P. A. Mirecki, 'Considerations on the Coptic Papyrus of the *Didache* (British Library Oriental Manuscript 9271)', in C. N. Jefford (ed.), *The Didache in Context: Essays on its Text, History, and Transmission* (Leiden: Brill, 1995), 47–87.

[135] Van de Sandt and Flusser, *The Didache*, 86–8.

[136] *Did.* 7.1 (SC 248 *bis*.170); see Rordorf, 'An Aspect', 153–9.

entering the church and desire instruction in godliness,[137] and Didymus the Blind, whom Athanasius appointed as head of the catechetical school in Alexandria, refers to it as a book 'of instruction' (τῆς κατηχήσεως).[138] Although the *Didache* seems to have waned in influence after the fifth century,[139] the teaching of the 'Two Ways' continued to be transmitted in documents incorporating it in some form or other (including those already mentioned). Of particular note is its role in the formation of monks.[140] Two Egyptian monastic manuals of instruction from the late fourth century, the *Syntagma doctrinae* and the Pseudo-Athanasian *Fides CCCXVIII patrum*, draw on it,[141] and a seventh-century Arabic *Life of Shenoute* includes a version of the teaching, confirming that the monks of the White Monastery had access to the teaching.[142] The *Life* expands on the relatively concise counsels of the teaching in its earlier forms: 'O my son, do not frequent the enchanters and magicians, flee them, these people and their words; for the one who frequents them draws himself away from God'.[143] Such use of the teaching would naturally have lent continuing authority to injunctions against magical practices.

A normative stance against magic and magicians is also reflected in conditions placed on admission to baptism in the so-called 'church orders'.[144] The earliest of these is the much discussed *Apostolic Tradition*.[145] Although the oldest extant witness to this composite work dates from the last quarter of the fourth century, it preserves what is thought to be more ancient traditions.[146] It describes the inquiries that are to be made into the positions and

---

[137] Athanasius of Alexandria, *Ep. fest.* 39.11, in P.-P. Joannou, *Discipline générale antique (IVᵉ-IXᵉ s.)*, vol. 2: *Les canons des pères grecs* (Vatican: Tipografia Italo-Orientale 'S. Nilo', 1963), 75.

[138] Didymus, *Ps.* 34: 20, in *Didymos der Blinde: Psalmenkommentar (Tura-Papyrus)*, vol. 3: *Kommentar zu Psalm 29–34*, ed. M. Gronewald, with A. Geschéb (Bonn: Rudolf Habelt, 1969), 389 (codex p. 227, lines 26–7); Didymus, *Eccl.* 3: 7, in *Didymos der Blinde: Kommentar zum Ecclesiastes (Tura-Papyrus)*, vol. 2: *Kommentar zu Eccl. Kap. 3–4, 12*, ed. M. Gronewald (Bonn: Rudolf Habelt, 1977), 70 (codex p. 78, line 22).

[139] Van de Sandt and Flusser, *The Didache*, 3–5.

[140] C. Davis, 'The *Didache* and Early Monasticism in the East and West', in Jefford, *The Didache in Context*, 352–67.

[141] Van de Sandt and Flusser, *The Didache*, 68–71.

[142] Van de Sandt and Flusser, *The Didache*, 66–70; Davis, 'The *Didache*', 355–8, with an English translation of the version of the teaching of the 'Two Ways' in the Arabic *Life* at 365–7.

[143] É. Amélineau, *Monuments pour servir à l'histoire de l'Égypte chrétienne aux IVᵉ-VIIᵉ siècles*, 2 vols (Paris: E. Leroux, 1888), 1.279–478 at 291–2; ET: Davis, 'The *Didache*', 366.

[144] For an overview of these documents, see P. F. Bradshaw, *The Search for the Origins of Christian Worship: Sources and Methods for the Study of Early Liturgy*, 2nd edn (Oxford: Oxford University Press, 2002), chapter 4.

[145] P. F. Bradshaw, M. E. Johnson, and L. E. Phillips, *The Apostolic Tradition: A Commentary* (Minneapolis: Fortress, 2002).

[146] Bradshaw, Johnson, and Phillips, *Apostolic Tradition*, 7–8, 13–15; C. Markschies, 'Wer schrieb die sogenannte *Traditio Apostolica*? Neue Beobachtungen und Hypothesen zu einer kaum lösbaren Frage aus der altkirchlichen Literaturgeschichte', in *Tauffragen und Bekenntnis: Studien zur sogenannten 'Traditio Apostolica', zu den 'Interrogationes de fide' und zum 'Römischen Glaubensbekenntnis'* (Berlin: Walter de Gruyter, 1999), 1–74 at 4–6, 49–50.

occupations of people wishing to become catechumens. Among other stipu-
lations, it states: 'The enchanter or the astrologer, or the wizard, or the one
who interprets dreams or the one who stirs up crowds, or the one who ruins
the hems of garments... or the one who makes phylacteries, either let them
cease or be cast out.'[147] A magician is not even to be admitted to instruction.[148]
An expanded version of this injunction—which does not, however, exclude
magicians—can be found in Book Eight of the *Apostolic Constitutions*, a Syrian
work dated to around 380,[149] which draws on the *Apostolic Tradition*:[150] 'a
magician, a charlatan, an enchanter, an astrologer, a diviner, a charmer of wild
animals, a pimp, a maker of amulets, a purifier, an augur, an interpreter of
portents or tremors, one who in encounters observes defects in the eyes or feet,
birds or cats, noises or significant sounds: let these be tested for some time, for
this sort of wickedness is hard to wash out; if they cease, let them be received;
but if they do not obey, let them be rejected'.[151] The *Canons of Hippolytus*, an
Egyptian collection whose author also drew on the *Apostolic Tradition* and
whose extant Arabic text is based on a Coptic version from the late fourth or
early fifth century,[152] likewise specifies the terms under which all such practitioners may be admitted to instruction: 'a magician, or an astrologer, or a
diviner, or an interpreter of dreams, or a snake charmer, or an agitator who
agitates the people, or one who makes phylacteries... all these and the like, do
not catechize them and baptize them until they have renounced all occupations of this sort, and three witnesses have testified that they really have
renounced all these vices'.[153]

These injunctions are similar to the terms set for admission to communion
by the so-called *Canons of Athanasius*, a treatise on the recruitment and duties
of the clergy written by a high cleric in Alexandria in the first half of the fifth
century.[154] It is preserved in fragmentary Sahidic manuscripts, the earliest of
which has been assigned to around 600, and in medieval Arabic canonical
collections of the Coptic Church.[155] (The organization of the work into 107

---

[147] The earliest extant witness to this section is the Sahidic version assigned to around 500 CE:
Trad. ap. 16.14, in *Der koptische Text der Kirchenordnung Hippolyts*, ed. W. Till and J. Leipoldt,
TU 58 (Berlin: Akademie Verlag, 1954), 12; ET: Bradshaw, Johnson and Phillips, *Apostolic
Tradition*, 90, with later versions in parallel columns.

[148] *Trad. ap.* 16.13 (Till and Leipoldt, 12).

[149] M. Metzger, 'Introduction', in M. Metzger (ed.), *Les Constitutions Apostoliques. Tome I:
Livres I et II*, SC 320 (Paris: Les Éditions du Cerf, 1985), 54–60.

[150] Metzger, 'Introduction', 14–19.   [151] *Const. apost.* 8.32.11 (SC 336.238).

[152] See Markschies, 'Wer schrieb die sogenannte *Traditio Apostolica*?', 8–11, 63–9; Bradshaw,
Search, 83–4; E. Wipszycka, *The Alexandrian Church: People and Institutions* (Warsaw: Journal
of Juristic Papyrology, 2015), 28–9.

[153] *Can. Hipp.* 15 (PO 31/2.368–70); ET: Bradshaw, Johnson, and Phillips, *Apostolic
Tradition*, 19.

[154] W. E. Crum and W. Riedel, *The Canons of Athanasius of Alexandria* (London: Williams
and Norgate, 1904), x–xxvi; Wipszycka, *The Alexandrian Church*, 29–31.

[155] Crum and Riedel, *Canons*, x, xxvi, 81–5.

canons and its attribution to Athanasius is found only in the Arabic witnesses.) At several points in the treatise, the author attempts to regulate contact with horoscope readers, enchanters, diviners, and magicians.[156] They are not to be admitted to the liturgy of the faithful or to receive communion without undergoing a period of penance to prove that they have abandoned their profession.[157] A magician must burn his books and fast daily for three years;[158] the Arabic version of the *Canons* adds that a horoscope reader, enchanter, or diviner must fast daily for one year.[159] Any Christian who goes to such persons must undergo a penance of three years before being readmitted to communion.[160]

Similarly, if we look beyond Egypt, the advice given by Basil of Caesarea and Gregory of Nyssa in response to questions from fellow bishops about the discipline that should be applied in a myriad of specific circumstances—advice that eventually was taken up into the canons of the Byzantine church, the fundamental source of ecclesiastical law—underscores the seriousness with which bishops viewed the activities of diviners and sorcerers.[161] Basil stipulates that the discipline for a Christian who confesses to practicing sorcery or devotes himself to divination should be the same as for one who commits murder.[162] His stance was no doubt influenced by the fact that in Roman law private forms of divination and sorcery were deemed to be socially harmful and potentially treasonous acts, punishable by execution. His advice also takes into account situations where a potion results in the death of the person who drinks it, particularly potions meant to induce amorous desires or an abortion.[163] The discipline imposed on a Christian who merely seeks out such services, while less severe, is still exacting. Those who consult soothsayers or who bring purifiers into their homes to discover and eliminate incantations may be readmitted to communion only after six years, having spent a year beseeching the prayers of the faithful as they enter the church for the Eucharist, a year as hearers (dismissed from the Eucharist after the liturgy of the word with no special recognition), three years as kneelers (dismissed after the liturgy

---

[156] For the terms in Sahidic, see Crum and Riedel, *Canons*, §41, 88.

[157] Crum and Riedel, *Canons*, §25, f. 105a–105b (Arabic), 30 (English); the fragmentary Sahidic version is missing most of the canons prior to Canon 40.

[158] Crum and Riedel, *Canons*, §72, f. 112b (Arabic), 47 (English), 108–9 (Coptic), 135–6 (English).

[159] Crum and Riedel, *Canons*, §73, f. 112b (Arabic), 47 (English).

[160] Crum and Riedel, *Canons*, §41, f. 107a (Arabic), 34 (English), 88 (Coptic), 118 (English). Whereas the Coptic version speaks of 'any of the church', the Arabic version refers specifically to priests as well as, in one manuscript, believers.

[161] See Dickie, *Magic*, 258–9.

[162] Basil of Caesarea, *Ep.* 217, canons 65 (sorcery) and 72 (divination), in *Saint Basile, Lettres*, ed. Yves Courtonne, 3 vols (Paris: Belles Lettres, 1957–66), 2.212, 213; Joannou, *Discipline générale antique*, 2.148, 150.

[163] Basil of Caesarea, *Ep.* 188, canon 8 (Courtonne, 2.127–8); Joannou, *Disciplina generale antica*, 2.107.

of the word with a laying on of hands), and one year among the faithful for the entire Eucharist but without communicating.[164] For Gregory of Nyssa, Christians who turn to sorcerers or diviners or seek out demonic purifying or protective remedies are to be treated as apostates; they are barred from communion until their dying days, like Christians who voluntarily join up with polytheists, Jews, or Manicheans. Only if they acted under some severe affliction is their penance to be mitigated.[165]

Disciplinary measures were also directed at clerics.[166] An oft-cited prohibition among the canons of the synod of Laodicea—a collection of Phrygian canons assembled in the late fourth or early fifth century and not, in fact, the canons of a specific synod[167]—states that 'consecrated and lower clergy must not be magicians or enchanters or mathematicians or astrologers, nor make what are called phylacteries, which are chains for their souls'.[168] Presumably the canon was the result of instances where clerics were reputed to have acted in one or more of these capacities. Certainly, accounts of charges levelled against bishops—usually in the heat of some ecclesiastical dispute—reveal that they might possess magical books and enact magical procedures.[169] The books in question are said to have been collections of incantations (as in the case of Paulinus of Dacia, whose *libri maleficorum* were burned by Macedonius of Mopsuestia),[170] astrological treaties (as in the case of Sophronius of Constantia),[171] or possibly philosophical works (particularly works of theurgy).[172] But for the most part we are not told exactly what procedures or remedies these clerics enacted. (The divination ritual allegedly performed by Sophronius is a rare exception.[173]) The Phrygian canon, like its subsequent iterations,[174] assumes that it is understood what an enchanter or amulet-maker is. Still, whoever wrote the canon felt it necessary to explain that amulets are not what they are said to be—protective devices—but rather 'chains for the soul'.

---

[164] Basil of Caesarea, *Ep.* 217, canon 83 (Courtonne, 2.216); Joannou, *Disciplina generale antica*, 2.156–7. For a description of the six-year penance, see canon 75 in the same letter (Courtonne, 2.213–14).

[165] Gregory of Nyssa, *Ep. can.* (PG 45.225, 228); Joannou, *Disciplina generale antica*, 2.211–12.

[166] See Dickie, *Magic*, 260–2.

[167] P.-P. Joannou, *Discipline générale antique (IVᵉ-IXᵉ s.)*, vol. 1/2: *Les canons des synodes particuliers* (Vatican: Tipografia Italo-Orientale 'S. Nilo', 1962), 127–8.

[168] Council of Laodicea, canon 36, in Joannou, *Disciplina generale antica*, 1/2.145: Ὅτι οὐ δεῖ ἱερατικοὺς ἢ κληρικοὺς ἢ μάγους ἢ ἐπαοιδοὺς εἶναι ἢ μαθηματικοὺς ἢ ἀστρολόγους, ἢ ποιεῖν τὰ λεγόμενα φυλακτήρια, ἅτινά εἰσι δεσμωτήρια τῶν ψυχῶν αὐτῶν.

[169] See Dickie, *Magic*, 274–9.

[170] Hilary of Poitiers, *Collectanea antiariana Parisina* A IV 1.27.6 (CSEL 65.66).

[171] *Akten der ephesinischen Synode vom Jahre 449*, ed. J. Flemming (Berlin: Weidmann, 1917), 82–3.

[172] Dickie, *Magic*, 279.

[173] Flemming, *Akten der ephesinischen Synode*, 80–3, summarized in Dickie, *Magic*, 277–8.

[174] E.g., Fulgentius Ferrandus of Carthage, *Breu. can.* 110 (CCSL 149.296): *ut diaconus aut clericus magus et incantator non sit neque phylateria faciat*. On the author and the work, compiled in the second quarter of the sixth century, see CCSL 149.284–6.

This brings us, finally, to an important difference between the stance of church authorities and that of imperial authorities on magic. As Matthew Dickie has observed,[175] Roman civil authorities were in most circumstances unconcerned about protective or healing rituals, incantations, or devices. The strictures of Roman law were directed primarily at private forms of divination or sorcery that threatened the regime or harmed its subjects.[176] But, as we have seen, protective and healing remedies are not exempt from the strictures of church authorities. Such seemingly benign remedies are especially insidious because they allow the Devil or demons to ensnare believers in times of crisis.

The attitude of Roman authorities is evident in the edicts of the emperor Constantine I and his successors, collected in the *Theodosian Code* under the heading 'Concerning sorcerers, astrologers, and others of this sort' (*de maleficis et mathematicis et ceteris similibus*).[177] Like his predecessors in the early empire, Constantine was concerned chiefly with non-traditional private divination for personal advantage or political advancement, which was seen to be socially harmful and potentially treasonous.[178] But in an edict probably issued in 318,[179] condemning 'the science of those who are equipped with magic arts (*magicis artibus*) and who are revealed to have worked against the welfare of people or to have turned virtuous minds to lust' (a reference to aggressive or binding incantations and devices), Constantine explicitly exempts from criminal indictment those whose remedies or rituals are meant to heal a person or protect a harvest:

> But remedies sought for human bodies (*remedia humanis quaesita corporibus*) shall not be involved in criminal accusation, nor the assistance that is innocently employed in rural districts in order that rains may not be feared for the ripe grape harvests or that the harvests may not be shattered by the stones of ruinous hail, since by such devices no person's safety or reputation is injured, but by their action they bring it about that divine gifts and the labors of men are not destroyed.[180]

---

[175] Dickie, *Magic*, 257.

[176] On the conceptualization of magic in Roman law, see H. G. Kippenberg, 'Magic in Roman Civil Discourse: Why Rituals Could Be Illegal', in P. Schäfer and H. G. Kippenberg, *Envisioning Magic: A Princeton Seminar and Symposium* (Brill: Leiden, 1997), 137–63; Gordon, 'Imaging Greek and Roman Magic', 253–65; J. B. Rives, 'Magic in Roman Law: The Reconstruction of a Crime', *CA*, 22 (2003), 313–39, doi: 10.1525/ca.2003.22.2.313. On the edicts and prosecutions of the fourth century, see A. Lotz, *Der Magiekonflikt in der Spätantike* (Bonn: Rudolf Habelt, 2005); Dickie, *Magic*, 251–7.

[177] *C.Th.* 9.16.0, in *Theodosiani libri XVI cum Constitutionibus Sirmondianis et Leges novellae ad Theodosianum pertinentes*, ed. T. Mommsen and P. M. Meyer, 2 vols in 3 (1905; repr. Berlin: Weidmann, 1962), 1/2.459.

[178] *C.Th.* 9.16.1–2 (Mommsen and Meyer, 1/2.459–60); see Gordon, 'Imaging Greek and Roman Magic', 260–1; Dickie, *Magic*, 251–2.

[179] On the date of the edict (*C.Th.* 9.16.3), see Lotz, *Der Magiekonflikt*, 138 n. 439.

[180] *C.Th.* 9.16.3 (Mommsen and Meyer, 1/2.460); ET: *The Theodosian Code and Novels, and the Sirmondian Constitutions*, tr. C. Pharr (Princeton: Princeton University Press, 1952), 237.

It is important to note that this edict was not only republished in the *Theodosian Code* of 438 but also in the Justinianic Code of 539,[181] even though the latter is on the whole more restrictive in such matters than the former, eliminating, for instance, protections that Valentinian I maintained for public forms of divination.[182] Thus, tolerance for popular remedies against harm and sickness was ensconced in Roman law during the reigns of successive Christian emperors from Constantine I to Justinian I.

1.4 CONCLUSION

In the first several centuries of the Christian church, the overwhelming preoccupation of its writers and leaders was to differentiate 'true' Christians from those who might resemble or mislead them—from Jews, pagans, 'erroneous' Christians, 'lax' Christians. The tendency of their arguments and examples was to sharpen the difference between the things that Christians should do and others did, between the company that Christians should keep and others kept. In this discourse the ubiquitous peddlers of knowledge, advice, and help in the ancient world—astrologers, horoscope-casters, dream-interpreters, amulet-makers, spell-casters, and the like—are inevitably grouped together as professions to be abandoned and figures to be avoided. The impetus for the discourse was not merely to create social distance between Christians and others, though this was evidently its objective. The discourse was motivated at a more profound level by the belief that demonic forces were at work in all these practices, deceiving and ensnaring those who had recourse to them even if they did so naively and unthinkingly. For the fourth-century Roman historian Ammianus Marcellinus, incantations and amulets of the sort that 'old women' provide against pain and fever are harmless, possibly foolish, but nevertheless permissible remedies;[183] they enter his narrative to illustrate the level of paranoia and danger that obtained in a context of political intrigue, when otherwise common remedies could become a pretext for suspicion, accusation, and prosecution.[184] For the fourth-century Christian bishop Augustine, however, the spouse, friends, servants, or 'old women' who press a gravely ill Christian to tie on an amulet are the agents of Satan, tempting the believer to deny Christ just as much as when, in the past, friends and family urged the believer to offer a libation to the gods.

---

[181] *C.Iust.* 9.18.4, in *Corpus juris civilis*, vol. 2: *Codex Iustinianus*, ed. P. Krueger (Berlin: Weidmann, 1892), 380.

[182] *C.Th.* 9.16.9 (Mommsen and Meyer, 1/2.462).

[183] Ammianus Marcellinus, *Res gest.* 16.8.2, LCL, 3 vols (Cambridge, M.A.: Harvard University Press, 1939–1950), 1.232.

[184] Ammianus Marcellinus, *Res gest.* 16.8.2, 19.12.13, 29.2.26 (LCL 1.232, 540; 3.230–2).

The problem this discourse poses for the historian, in the face of the material record attesting to widespread and continued use of incantations and amulets in Late Antiquity, is not just that it is categorical. It is also that it is parsimonious with details about the purveyors of these remedies and the sorts of remedies they provided. The standards set out for catechumens and clergy, for instance, simply prohibit them from making amulets. Nothing is said about the nature of the amulets being made or the culture of the person making them. The prohibitions assume that the activity is 'not Christian'. The scenarios evoked by Augustine and Chrysostom are something of an exception. Despite their prejudices, they offer precious insight into the social matrix that sustained customary practices and rare details about, for instance, what nurse maids and others did to protect an infant or relieve a fever. But they still do not reveal much about the culture of these purveyors, except to suggest that it is 'not Christian' or 'insufficiently Christian'.

Such an approach, admitting of no or few gradations in dealing with a customary practice, was bound to fall short of its objectives. The very nature of the practice—the fact that it was ubiquitous, routine, and accepted in the social circles of many in the population—ensured that it would continue. Ironically, widespread social acceptance of amulets and their makers rendered them suspect in the eyes of Christian authorities, on the one hand, and undermined the effect of ecclesiastical prohibitions, on the other. It is not surprising, therefore, that the material record reveals a more adaptive and sustainable approach, whereby Christian idioms enter the repertoire of protective and healing incantations and Christian biblical and liturgical materials take on apotropaic functions. In later chapters we shall investigate how this happened.[185] Nevertheless, the normative stance of Christian authorities played a part in this adaptive process, since it created both a context and an impetus for the production of suitable Christian alternatives to customary remedies.

---

[185] Chapters 4–6.

2

Materials, Format, and Writing

In the next several chapters we shall be examining manuals, incantations, and amulets with Christian elements to learn more about the scribes who wrote these materials and, by inference, how these scribes worked with the re-sources available to them. However, before we launch into this investigation, it will be useful to give an overview of aspects of the production of these materials, since I refer to these aspects of production in later chapters. In this chapter, therefore, I describe materials used to make textual amulets, how texts might be written on these materials, and a number of oral and visual devices that could be employed in the texts. While the focus is on incantations and amulets with Christian elements, I take account of incan-tations and amulets that do not have Christian elements, since in fact the materials and techniques were common to the practice as a whole. I have done so selectively, identifying relevant *comparanda* with the help of several databases of Egyptian materials (Trismegistos, TM Magic, and the Leuven Database of Ancient Books).[1]

2.1 MATERIALS

Scribes had a variety of materials at their disposal on which they might write an amulet: papyrus, parchment, potsherds (the most common form of ostraca), strips of metal (*lamellae*), wooden tablets, and stone. The choice depended in part on the purpose of the artefact, in part on the availability and cost of the material, and in part on the use of these materials for other purposes (receipts, accounts, letters, school exercises, books, and so on).

---

[1] For a description of these databases, see <http://www.trismegistos.org/about.php> (Trismegistos), <http://www.trismegistos.org/magic/index.php> (TM Magic), and <http://www.trismegistos.org/ldab/about.php> (Leuven Database of Ancient Books).

2.1.1 Papyrus

Papyrus was by far the material that most scribes used for an incantation or amulet, with the exception of binding incantations, for which metal or other durable materials were customarily used (see Sections 2.1.4). There are several reasons for this. First, papyrus was widely and easily available in Egypt. It was used for the great majority of Greek and Latin documentary and literary texts throughout the Roman period,[2] and it continued to be made and used well after the Roman period until it was eventually superseded by paper in the eleventh century.[3] Second, papyrus could be cut to a size suited to the text or its application, and could be folded or rolled into a format that could be worn—important qualities for an amulet. Parchment also had these qualities, but it was more expensive than papyrus; on one estimate, it cost about 2.5 times as much as papyrus.[4] Parchment was therefore used almost exclusively for literary texts, and even then the majority of literary texts—70 per cent, by one calculation—were still copied on papyrus.[5]

2.1.2 Parchment

Although papyrus predominates among the materials used for amulets in Egypt throughout Late Antiquity, a small but significant change is noticeable from, roughly, the fifth century onward. We see more amulets written on parchment. Most of these amulets consist only of verses of scripture;[6] a few include an appeal for help or protection.[7] This increase in the use of parchment for amulets coincides with a considerable increase in the use of parchment for codices—the format that Christians preferred for their books—between the fourth and seventh centuries.[8] Scribes who used parchment for amulets, particularly

---

[2] A. Bülow-Jacobsen, 'Writing Materials in the Ancient World', in R. S. Bagnall (ed.), *The Oxford Handbook of Papyrology* (Oxford: Oxford University Press, 2009), 3–29 at 3–4.

[3] P. M. Sijpesteijn, 'Arabic Papyri and Islamic Egypt', in Bagnall, *Oxford Handbook of Papyrology*, 452–72 at 452–3.

[4] R. S. Bagnall, *Early Christian Books in Egypt* (Princeton: Princeton University Press, 2009), 52–7.

[5] Bülow-Jacobsen, 'Writing Materials', 4.

[6] T. S. de Bruyn and J. H. F. Dijkstra, 'Greek Amulets and Formularies from Egypt Containing Christian Elements: A Checklist of Papyri, Parchments, Ostraka, and Tablets', *BASP*, 48 (2011), 163–216 at 175–6, <http://hdl.handle.net/2027/spo.0599796.0048.001>.

[7] *BKT* VI 7.1; MPER N.S. XVII 10; see also *PGM* P4 (*P.Oxy.* VIII 1077), which has a heading.

[8] W. A. Johnson, 'The Ancient Book', in Bagnall, *Oxford Handbook of Papyrology*, 256–81 at 266. A search of the Leuven Database of Ancient Books <http://www.trismegistos.org/ldab/index.php, accessed 30/10/2015> for the material of literary texts by century (strictly defined) yielded the following data (total number, number and percent papyrus, number and percent parchment): IV: 398, 284 (71 per cent), 111 (27 per cent); V: 507, 172 (33 per cent), 331 (65 per cent); VI: 682, 225 (32 per cent), 450 (65 per cent); VII: 377, 83 (22 per cent), 269 (71 per cent).

amulets consisting of scriptural verses, may at times have been working in or close to centres, such as monasteries, where Christian books were copied.[9] They would have had readier access to scraps of parchment and might also have been in the habit of writing scripture on parchment.

2.1.3 Ostraca

Ostraca in the form of potsherds were, of course, even cheaper than papyrus, since they could be gathered freely from the ground. They were favoured in areas where pottery was plentiful but papyrus had to be brought in, as in the Egyptian desert.[10] Numerous texts written on ostraca have been found, for instance, among the remains of the monasteries in the region of Thebes. Many of the texts are letters or short documents,[11] but the finds also include biblical and liturgical texts.[12] Ostraca were not as malleable or easy to carry as papyrus, which limited their usefulness for amulets. They were more suited to binding incantations, antagonistic devices that were deposited in earth or water (a grave, the baths, the target's house or workplace) in order to take effect.[13] Often, evidence that scribes may have used ostraca for amulets is ambiguous: ostraca with Christian texts that could be protective—verses from the Psalms, the names of the Forty Martyrs of Sebaste, the correspondence between Abgar and Jesus—may have been written for other reasons.[14] Nevertheless, ostraca could be used to write amulets. Among the numerous ostraca written by Frange, a monk living in Djeme (western Thebes) in the first half of the eighth century,[15] are two letters that refer to amulets to be used to protect animals by being placed in their vicinity or tied around their neck.[16] He has also left us an example of such an amulet, a prayer addressed to Jesus Christ, asking him to protect the inhabitants and animals of a monastery.[17]

---

[9] On the role of monks in the production of books, see C. Rapp, 'Christians and their Manuscripts in the Greek East in the Fourth Century', in G. Cavallo, G. de Gregori, and M. Maniaci (eds), *Scritture, libri e testi nelle aree provinciali di Bisanzio*, 2 vols (Spoleto: Centro italiano di studi sull'alto Medioevo, 1991), 1.127–48; C. Kotsifou, 'Books and Book Production in the Monastic Communities of Byzantine Egypt', in W. E. Klingshirn and L. Safran (eds), *The Early Christian Book* (Washington, D.C.: Catholic University of America Press, 2007), 48–66.

[10] Bülow-Jacobsen, 'Writing Materials', 15.

[11] Bülow-Jacobsen, 'Writing Materials', 3, 16.

[12] A. T. Mihálykó, 'Writing the Christian Liturgy in Egypt (3rd to 9th cent.)', PhD thesis, University of Oslo, Oslo, 2016, 109 and *passim*.

[13] R. Martín-Hernández and S. Tovar Torallas, 'The Use of the *Ostracon* in Magical Practice in Late Antique Egypt: Magical Handbooks vs. Material Evidence', *SMSR*, 80/2 (2014), 780–800.

[14] Martín-Hernández and Torallas, 'The Use of the *Ostracon*', 789–94.

[15] *O.Frangé*, pp. 10–11.

[16] *O.Frangé* 190 and 191. I am indebted to Ágnes Mihálykó for bringing these letters to my attention.

[17] *O.CrumST* 18; French translation at *O.Frangé* 190 intro.

2.1.4 Metal

Among the types of metal used for incantations or amulets in Egypt, lead was reserved for binding incantations, as was customary elsewhere in the Graeco-Roman world. A search of lead tablets from Egypt in the database Trismegistos yielded twenty-five items.[18] The majority of these have been assigned to the third or fourth century CE, and most of the remainder belong to the first or second century CE.[19] None of the tablets incorporate Christian elements.

In Egypt, as elsewhere,[20] bronze, silver, and gold strips of metal were used for incantations for healing, deliverance, or favour. But examples of such amulets are relatively rare when compared with the many amulets on papyrus that have survived from Egypt.[21] This is no doubt because papyrus was more available and less costly. Most of the silver and gold amulets have been assigned to the third or fourth century.[22] One silver amulet from the fifth century has specifically Christian elements; only the invocation remains: 'Lord Jesus, Lord Christ, Michael, Gabriel, my Lord'.[23] (The spellings of 'Jesus' and 'Christ' are irregular.[24])

2.1.5 Wood

Wood was also used for amulets. A recent survey of inscribed wooden tablets from antiquity includes approximately twenty items from Egypt that were or may have been used as amulets.[25] About half of these consist of small wooden

---

[18] Trismegistos, <http://www.trismegistos.org/tm/search.php>, accessed 18 April 2015 (search parameters: Egypt only; material: metal *and* lead; type: magic).

[19] I–II (2 items); II (2 items); II–III (4 items); II–IV (1 item); III (6 items); III–IV (4 items); IV (4 items); V–VI (1 item); VI–VII (1 item).

[20] See *GMA* I.

[21] A search of Trismegistos, <http://www.trismegistos.org/tm/search.php>, accessed 14 April 2015 (search parameters: Egypt only; material: metal *but not* lead; type: magic), yielded eleven items (TM no. given in parentheses): J. Naveh and S. Shaked, *Amulets and Magic Bowls: Aramaic Incantations of Late Antiquity* (Jerusalem: Magnes Press, 1985), 82–4 (TM 113528); *P.Köln* VIII 338 (TM 109622); *P.Köln* VIII 339 (TM 109623); *SB* XVIII 13603 (TM 30981); *SB* XVIII 13605 (TM 30982); *SB* XX 14986 (TM 34182); *SB* XXIV 15916 (TM 79240); *SB* XXVI 16677 (TM 97920); *SEG* XLII 1582 (TM 105444); *SM* I 2 (TM 92846); *SM* II 64 (TM 92333).

[22] II–III (2 items); III (3 items); III–IV (2 items); IV (1 item); V (2 items); VII (1 item).

[23] H. Harrauer, 'Von Silber beschützt', in H. Lang and H. Harrauer (eds), *Mirabilia artium librorum recreant te tuosque ebriant: dona natalicia Ioanni Marte oblata* (Vienna: Phoibos, 2001), 90–3 = *SB* XXVI 16677; image at <http://data.onb.ac.at/rec/RZ00001890> (Österreichischen Nationalbibliothek Katalog der Papyrussammlung; P.Vindob. inv. G 60398).

[24] Lines 1–5: κυριο- | s Iησ- | os K̄χ̄- | ειστ- | os, with Harrauer, 'Von Silber beschützt', 92–3 (lines 2–3 comm.).

[25] K. A. Worp, *A New Survey of Greek, Coptic, Demotic and Latin Tabulae Preserved from Classical Antiquity* (Leuven: Trismegistos Online Publications, 2012), <http://www.trismegistos.org/top.php>.

pendants inscribed with variants of the word βους, sometimes accompanied by Βαινχωωχ (the Greek transliteration of the Egyptian name 'spirit of darkness'[26]), the opening words of LXX Ps. 90, or a cross.[27] (Bone was also used for such amulets.[28]) To these we can add a few other small wooden tablets or pendants that were certainly used as amulets.[29] But, as with the ostraca discussed in Section 2.1.3, the uses of the remaining wooden tablets are less clear. They consist of larger boards written with Christian texts that could have a protective purpose—LXX Ps. 90, verses from other Psalms, the Lord's Prayer, the correspondence between Abgar and Jesus, prayers, and litanies.[30] The position of the text in relation to the holes along the edges of these boards shows that the holes were not made to affix the text to a door or wall, but rather to allow the board to be gathered with others into a codex.[31] If the board was used as an amulet, it could only have been by being positioned in an appropriate spot, such as a niche or a tomb.[32]

2.1.6 Other Materials

A few other materials were also used for amulets: bone, limestone, and semiprecious stones. The first two were used only occasionally.[33] The third falls largely outside our purview, since we are focusing on the scribal features of written materials, not chiselled ones. But it is important to be aware that many semiprecious rings, pendants, and medallions engraved with figures, names, symbols, *voces mysticae*, invocations, and adjurations survive from the

---

[26] W. M. Brashear, 'The Greek Magical Papyri: An Introduction and Survey; Annotated Bibliography (1928–1994)', *ANRW* 18/5.3380–684 at 3581.

[27] For surveys of the items, see G. Nachtergael, 'Une amulette chrétienne du Musée des Beaux-Arts de Dijon', *REAC*, 4 (2002), 93–101; G. Menci, 'Un amuleto "Bous" da Antinoe', *ZPE*, 159 (2007), 249–52; , <http://www.jstor.org/stable/20191210>; T. J. Kraus, 'Βους, Βαινχωωχ und Septuaginta-Psalm 90? Überlegungen zu den sogenannten "Bous"-Amuletten und dem beliebtesten Bibeltext für apotropäische Zwecke', *ZAC*, 11 (2008), 479–91, doi: 10.1515/ZAC.2007.025. Two additional items were subsequently published in A. Delattre and K. A. Worp, 'Trois tablettes de bois du Musée de Leyde', *CdE*, 87 (2012), 361–82 at 363–8, 377–8, doi: 10.1484/J. CDE.1.103137.

[28] Kraus, 'Βους', nos. 1, 2, 3, and 6.

[29] E.g., D. Wortmann, 'Neue magische Texte', *BJ*, 168 (1968), 56–111 at 107 (no. 10; Cologne, Private collection); P. J. Sijpesteijn, 'Objects with Script in the Collection Moen', *ZPE*, 42 (1981), 111–12 at 112 (no. 2; Moen inv. 595), <http://www.jstor.org/stable/20186069>; P. J. Sijpesteijn, 'A Wooden Disk', *ZPE*, 49 (1982), 72, <http://www.jstor.org/stable/20183689> = *SB* XVI 12992.

[30] Delattre and Worp, 'Trois tablettes', 379–82.

[31] Delattre and Worp, 'Trois tablettes', 382.

[32] For wooden tablets found in a tomb, see *P.Bad* IV, pp. 47–9, regarding *P.Bad*. IV 60 and *P. Bad*. IV 65 + *P.Bad*. V 127.

[33] For amulets written on bone, see n. 27 (four 'βους' amulets). For a possible amulet written on limestone, see MPER N.S. XVIII 196.

Roman period.[34] The fashion for such amulets, whose production began in the Hellenistic period, peaked in the second and third centuries CE, followed by a slow decline.[35] As with other materials, some of these amulets incorporate Christian figures, words, or symbols.[36]

2.2 FORMAT AND WRITING

As we have already seen, there was a practical relationship between the purpose of an object, its material, and its format. Amulets that were meant to be worn had to be portable: hence rings, pendants, and malleable materials (papyrus, parchment, or metal) that could be folded or rolled and carried in a tube or pouch. Incantations that were meant to be deposited had to be durable: hence metal (chiefly lead, for a variety of practical and customary reasons[37]), potsherds, and stone. I shall describe some typical formats, giving as examples incantations without Christian elements as well as incantations with Christian elements. Sometimes the format is meant to set off features of the incantation. At other times it is simply the format used to write other types of texts, such as letters.

2.2.1 Formats

Since most of the incantations with Christian elements that have survived from Egypt were written on papyrus, we focus on papyri. Although the manuals often give lengthy and elaborate procedures for preparing and applying an incantation, the text that was to be written down could be relatively short. It might consist simply of an invocation or series of *voces mysticae* followed by an adjuration or command. For such texts scribes typically used a rectangular piece of papyrus that would have to be folded

---

[34] For representative samples, see C. Bonner, *Studies in Magical Amulets, Chiefly Graeco-Egyptian* (Ann Arbor: University of Michigan, 1950); S. Michel, *Magischen Gemmen im Britischen Museum*, 2 vols (London: British Museum Press, 2001); and now the Campbell Bonner Magical Gems Database, <http://www2.szepmuveszeti.hu/talismans/visitatori_salutem>. Further bibliography at the Introduction, nn. 61–2.

[35] A. M. Nagy, 'Engineering Ancient Amulets: Magical Gems of the Roman Imperial Period', in D. Boschung and J. M. Bremmer (eds), *The Materiality of Magic* (Munich: Wilhelm Fink, 2015), 205–40 at 209–10; J. Spier, *Late Antique and Early Christian Gems* (Wiesbaden: Reichert, 2007), 14, 81.

[36] Spier, *Late Antique and Early Christian Gems*, 81–6; see also Michel, *Magischen Gemmen im Britischen Museum*, 268–92.

[37] J. G. Gager (ed.), *Curse Tablets and Binding Spells from the Ancient World* (New York: Oxford University Press, 1992), 3–4.

only a few times horizontally and vertically in order to be carried.[38] For longer texts scribes could use either a large rectangle of papyrus that would have to be folded more often or into larger segments,[39] or a long oblong piece of papyrus that might be rolled or folded mostly or only in one direction.[40] The latter might be written in long lines across the papyrus or in short lines down the papyrus.[41] It is noteworthy that papyrus codex sheets (sheets of papyrus folded in half to form two leaves) were not normally used for customary incantations.[42] Amulets in this format consist almost exclusively of scriptural passages or incantations incorporating a scriptural passage.[43]

The manuals routinely instruct practitioners to write their incantations on a new piece of papyrus,[44] not on the back of previously written papyrus. While this is usually the practice of scribes, occasionally they write their incantation on previously written material.[45] Scriptural passages or liturgical prayers that may have functioned as amulets are also found on the back of previously written material.[46] Thus, use of previously written material does not rule out the possibility that a given text was meant to serve as an amulet.[47] (Some amulets are written on the back of a *protokollon*, a sheet attached to the beginning of a papyrus roll in order to protect the roll against damage, which could bear an official mark in a distinctive form of writing [*Stempelschrift*];[48] it is arguable that, once detached from the roll, the papyrus was deemed to be 'new'.[49])

---

[38] E.g., *PGM* LXXIX = *P.Prag.* I 4; *SM* I 4 (*PUG* I 6); *SM* I 7; *SM* I 9 (*P.Michael.* 27); *SM* I 12. With Christian elements: *PGM* P2 (*P.Oxy.* VII 1060); *PGM* P5a (*P.Oxy.* VI 924); *PGM* P6a (*P.Oxy.* VIII 1152); *SM* I 21 (*P.Köln* VI 257); *SM* I 22 (*P.Amst.* I 26); *SM* I 23 (*P.Haun.* III 51); *SM* I 25 (*P.Prag.* I 6); *SM* I 26 = *BKT* IX 206; *SM* I 27; *SM* I 28; *SM* I 33; *SM* I 34; *SM* I 35 (*P.Batav.* 20). For the dimensions of the incantations with Christian elements, see de Bruyn and Dijkstra, 'Greek Amulets and Formularies', table 1.

[39] E.g., *PGM* XIXa, *PGM* XXIIb. With Christian elements: *PGM* P13 (*P.Cair.Cat.* 10263); *PGM* P17 (*P.Iand.* I 6) = *P.Giss.Lit.* 5.4; *PGM* P21.

[40] E.g., *SM* I 10 = *BKT* IX 68. With Christian elements: *PGM* P5b (*P.Oxy.* VIII 1151); *PGM* P15a (*P.Ross.Georg.* I 24); *P.Köln* VIII 340; *SM* I 31 (*P.Turner* 49) = *BKT* IX 134; *SM* I 32.

[41] Across: *SM* I 31 (*P.Turner* 49) = *BKT* IX 134; *SM* I 32. Down: *PGM* P5b (*P.Oxy.* VIII 1151); *PGM* P15a (*P.Ross.Georg.* I 24); *P.Köln* VIII 340.

[42] On the construction of codex sheets and quires, see Bülow-Jacobsen, 'Writing Materials', 23–4.

[43] De Bruyn and Dijkstra, 'Greek Amulets and Formularies', 176 n. 62. *PGM* P21, a *charitêsion* or good-luck charm written on two leaves of a sheet of papyrus once folded in half, is a rare exception.

[44] E.g., *PGM* III.17–18; *PGM* IV.78; *PGM* VII.193–4, 219, 703, 940–1; *PGM* XXXVI.71-2 (*P.Oslo* I 1); *PGM* XXXVIII.2 (*P.Oslo* I 3).

[45] E.g., Wortmann, 'Neue magische Texte', 106 (*P.Köln* inv. 521a); *SM* I 34; *SM* II 62.

[46] E.g., the probable amulets listed at Bruyn and Dijkstra, 'Greek Amulets and Formularies', 177 n. 65.

[47] *Pace* H. Förster, 'Heilige Namen in Heiligen Texten', *AW*, 33 (2002), 321–4 at 321–2; *MPER* N.S. XV 184 intro.

[48] H. I. Bell, 'The Greek Papyrus Protocol', *JHS*, 37 (1917), 56–8 at 56.

[49] For amulets written on the back of a *protokollon*, see *PGM* P6d, with de Bruyn and Dijkstra, 'Greek Amulets and Formularies', 188 n. 132; *PGM* P19 (*PSI* VI 719), with R. Pintaudi, 'Per la datazione di PSI VI 719', *AnalPap*, 2 (1990), 27–8; *SM* I 22 intro. (*P.Amst.* I 26).

When writing an incantation, the scribe could write the text in continuous lines across the papyrus or could visually set off parts of the incantation. I shall discuss visual schemes in Section 2.4.1. In the case of incantations written in continuous lines, the regularity of the hand and the spacing of the lines varies, as one might expect. In some amulets the lines are more or less evenly spaced in a regular informal hand (see Section 2.2.2);[50] in other amulets the writing is irregular or even crude and the lines are compressed.[51] When writing more or less continuous script, scribes sometimes left a space between *voces mysticae*, since otherwise it would not be evident when one name ends and another begins.[52] But this is not always the case.[53] Usually the incantation fits within the space of the papyrus without the need to write lines perpendicular to the main body of the text,[54] as sometimes happens in the writing of letters. There may even be room to spare. Scribes either anticipated the space needed for the incantation, adapted the incantation to the size of the papyrus, or cut the papyrus to size after writing the text. Sometimes the width of the text is determined by the length of the heading, invocation, or sequence of *voces mysticae* with which the incantation begins.[55] But in other instances the width of the text bears no relation to the contents of the first line; the lines are simply of a length that would permit the incantation to be written on the rectangle of papyrus. This is nicely illustrated by two identical incantations to restrain anger, *PGM* LXXIX = *P.Prag.* I 4 and *PGM* LXXX = *P.Prag.* I 5.[56] The width of lines in the former corresponds to the length of the heading; the width of lines in the latter, to the extent of the papyrus.

2.2.2 Hands

When describing the writing styles of scribes, it is common to speak of 'book hands' and 'documentary hands'. The former refers to the hands found in

---

[50] E.g., *SM* I 12, image at <http://www2.szepmuveszeti.hu/talismans/cbd/9?orderby=cbd_id&orderdir=asc> (Campbell Bonner Magical Gems Database). With Christian elements: *PGM* P3 (*P.Oslo* I 5), image at <http://ub-prod01-imgs.uio.no/OPES/jpg/303r.jpg> (Oslo Papyri Electronic System) and fig. 4.2 below; *SM* I 22 (*P.Amst.* I 26), image at *P.Amst.* I, plate XIII.

[51] E.g., *SM* I 43, image at <https://papyri.uni-koeln.de/stueck/tm30843> (Kölner Papyrussammlung). With Christian elements: *PGM* P5a (*P.Oxy.* VI 924), image at M. de Haro Sanchez, 'Le vocabulaire de la pathologie et de la thérapeutique dans les papyrus iatromagiques grecs: fièvres, traumatismes et "épilepsie"', *BASP*, 47 (2010), 131–53 at 136, <http://hdl.handle.net/2027/spo.0599796.0047.001>.

[52] E.g., *SM* I 12.1, 3–5; *SM* I 43.1–3; see also *P.Mich.* XVIII 768.1–4.

[53] E.g., *PGM* P3.1, 6–7 (*P.Oslo* I 5).

[54] As occurs, e.g., in *PGM* XLIII, where, after writing a series of angel-names in a column in the middle of the papyrus, the scribe then turned the papyrus ninety degrees (clockwise) and continued to write angel names in the space below the wing-shape to the left of the column and between the wing-shape and the column. Image at <http://data.onb.ac.at/rec/RZ00002489> (Österreichischen Nationalbibliothek Katalog der Papyrussammlung; P.Vindob. inv. G 335).

[55] E.g., *SM* I 12.1 (possibly also line 2); *SM* I 22.1 (*P.Amst.* I 26).

[56] Images at *P.Prag.* I, plates XIII and XIV.

copies of literary texts; the latter, to hands found in letters, receipts, accounts, and the like. In reality, however, the distinction was not so tidy. In Late Antiquity one finds documents written in literary hands, and literary texts copied in hands used for documents.[57] This can be observed in earlier periods of Greek writing as well.[58] Thus, while it is convenient at times to employ the phrases 'book hand' or 'documentary hand', it is more precise to use descriptors derived from letter-forms and writing styles than from types of texts.[59]

Hands may be identified with a given 'style' of writing on the basis of the form (size, shape, and inclination) and structure (number, sequence, and direction of strokes) of individual letters, as well as the overall manner of writing in which the letter-forms appear.[60] A style may in turn be classified in a 'stylistic class', writings that share a general framework, form, and structure of some letters, but may contain graphic variants of the same letter. In Late Antiquity certain styles of writing achieve the status of a 'formal' or 'canonical' or 'normative' script, where the style follows precise rules and is repeated over time with minimal variation in technique or execution.[61] The main types of formal scripts that are occasionally found in amulets are sloping majuscule, upright majuscule, Biblical majuscule, and Alexandrian majuscule.[62]

Few of the incantations and amulets with which we are concerned are written in a formal script.[63] Many are written in informal hands that manifest characteristics belonging to a stylistic class. They may be more or less regular in their execution. A more regular hand is able to write individual letters with a consistent shape, structure, and inclination (upright, sloping to the left, or sloping to the right); to write within the notional parallel lines that define the upper and lower bounds of the letters (bilinearity), excepting the long ascenders or descenders of certain letters (e.g., *rho, upsilon, phi, psi*); and to maintain even distances between lines.

The letter-forms of a hand may be majuscule, semi-cursive, or cursive. In majuscule hands, particularly formal majuscule scripts, the scribe writes the constituent strokes of the letter with a separate movement of the calamus

---

[57] G. Cavallo and H. Maehler, *Greek Bookhands of the Early Byzantine Period: A.D. 300–800* (London: Institute of Classical Studies, 1987), 1–2.

[58] G. Cavallo, *La scrittura greca e latina dei papiri: una introduzione* (Pisa: Fabrizio Serra, 2008), 57–61, 89–91.

[59] For what follows, see P. Orsini and W. Clarysse, 'Early New Testament Manuscripts and their Dates: A Critique of Theological Palaeography', *ETL*, 88 (2012), 443–74 at 448–9, doi: 10.2143/ETL.88.4.2957937.

[60] See also E. G. Turner, *Greek Manuscripts of the Ancient World*, 2nd edn, ed. P. J. Parsons (London: Institute of Classical Studies, 1987), 19–20.

[61] See also Cavallo and Maehler, *Greek Bookhands*, 3–5; G. Cavallo, 'Greek and Latin Writing in the Papyri', in Bagnall, *Oxford Handbook of Papyrology*, 101–48 at 127–34. For a chart of the principal formal scripts, see Orsini and Clarysse, 'Early New Testament Manuscripts', fig. 3.

[62] Cavallo and Maehler, *Greek Bookhands*, 4–5.

[63] E.g., MPER N.S. XVII 10; *P.Mich.* III 132; *PGM* P4 (*P.Oxy.* VIII 1077)—all discussed in Chapter 5.

(a reed pen).[64] In semi-cursive hands, some or all of the movements required to form the letter may be joined, so that the letter is written in a more continuous movement. Individual letters may occasionally be joined to a neighbouring letter (adjoining letters). In cursive hands, letters are written continuously in a fluid sequence, adjoining letters may share a common stroke (ligatures), and the speed of writing may result in simplified or reduced letter-forms.[65] In the material with which we are concerned we see mainly semi-cursive and cursive hands. The regularity with which they are executed varies widely.

Writers may be classified as 'slow', practiced, or professional on the basis of the skill and speed of their writing. In Egypt children learned to write by first forming the individual letters of the alphabet and then copying out series of meaningless syllables. If a child did not have the opportunity or aptitude to advance from copying letters, syllables, and words to creating sentences, their development might be arrested when they were able only to write individual letters or copy text as a sequence of individual majuscule letters.[66] Hence the phenomenon of 'slow writers'—adult writers who can laboriously form letters in order to be able to write their name or a short text, but cannot write much more.[67] (Skilled writers who chose to form letters slowly obviously do not belong in this category.[68]) A few amulets among our materials were written by 'slow writers'. However, most of the scribes with which we are concerned were more or less practiced writers. That is to say, they were accustomed to writing, even if their writing could be irregular.

Men had much greater opportunity than women not only to learn how to write but also to become proficient at writing. Only the most privileged girls learned to read and write, and their schooling consisted of primary and perhaps secondary education, but not advanced rhetorical training.[69] However, if a woman became proficient at writing, as could happen in wealthy and propertied families, their writing could match those of similarly proficient

---

[64] Turner, *Greek Manuscripts*, 1–2; see also R. Cribiore, *Writing, Teachers, and Students in Graeco-Roman Egypt* (Atlanta: Scholars Press, 1996), 106–11.

[65] Cavallo, *La scrittura greca*, 38–9, 51.

[66] On learning how to write and read, see Cribiore, *Writing, Teachers, and Students*, 148–52; R. Cribiore, *Gymnastics of the Mind: Greek Education in Hellenistic and Roman Egypt* (Princeton: Princeton University Press, 2001), 164–78.

[67] Herbert C. Youtie, '*Βραδέως γράφων*: Between Literacy and Illiteracy', *GRBS*, 12 (1971), 239–61, <http://grbs.library.duke.edu/issue/view/1701>, repr. in H. C. Youtie, *Scriptiunculae*, 2 vols (Amsterdam: A. M. Hakkert, 1973), 2.629–51; T. J. Kraus, '"Slow Writers"—*ΒΡΑΔΕΩΣ ΓΡΑΦΟΝΤΕΣ*: What, How Much, and How Did They Write?', in Thomas J. Kraus (ed.), *Ad fontes: Original Manuscripts and their Significance for Studying Early Christianity—Selected Essays* (Leiden: Brill, 2007), 130–47.

[68] Turner, *Greek Manuscripts*, 2–3.

[69] Cribiore, *Gymnastics of the Mind*, 86–91; R. S. Bagnall and R. Cribiore, *Women's Letters from Ancient Egypt, 300 BC–AD 800* (Ann Arbor: The University of Michigan Press, 2006), 6–9.

men. From the writing itself there is no way of telling whether the text was written by a man or a woman.[70] The same is true of less proficient, more personal hands. While it is possible by various means to identify such hands as written for or by women,[71] less proficient or clumsy hands were, obviously, also produced by men.

How likely is it that among our materials we have an amulet written by a woman? We know that learned privileged women could be esteemed as philosophers and mentors in both pagan and Christian contexts.[72] It is not outside the realm of the possible that such women might have had some knowledge of amulets and that people in their immediate social circle—family, neighbours, clients—might have turned to them for help. Moreover, the requirements and activities of Christian monastic communities would have extended basic literacy to more women than might otherwise have been the case,[73] just as it did for men. Still, the odds that an amulet examined in this study was written by a woman are small, given the lower rate of schooling among women in general, the less advanced level of education available to women, and the social circumstances and preoccupations of women who did receive an education. Therefore, when discussing scribes, I shall typically use the masculine pronoun rather than repeatedly referring to 'him or her'. Nevertheless, at times I shall add the female pronoun, simply as a reminder that women may have been among the writers of our material.

2.2.3 Reading Aids and Lectional Signs

Since it was common practice to write letters in continuous lines without separating words (*scriptio continua*), scribes introduced aids to assist the reader. Some of these are found in the materials with which we are concerned. Scribes could separate recipes in a collection by a horizontal line, a device used, for instance, by teachers to separate different sections of declensions and conjugations.[74] They could also use several other aids to distinguish parts of a text:[75] *ekthesis*, projecting the first line of a section out into the left margin (a 'hanging indent'); *eisthesis*, indenting the first line of a section; a *paragraphos*,

---

[70] Bagnall and Cribiore, *Women's Letters*, 48–9.

[71] Bagnall and Cribiore, *Women's Letters*, 46–8, 49–53.

[72] See, e.g., N. Denzey Lewis, 'Living Images of the Divine: Female Theurgists in Late Antiquity', in K. B. Stratton and D. S. Kalleres (eds), *Daughters of Hecate: Women and Magic in the Ancient World* (New York: Oxford University Press, 2014), 274–97.

[73] M. J. Albarrán Martínez, 'Women Reading Books in Egyptian Monastic Circles', in J. P. Monferrer-Sala, H. Teule, and S. Torallas Tovar (eds), *Eastern Christians and their Written Heritage: Manuscripts, Scribes and Context* (Leuven: Peeters, 2012), 199–212 at 207–10.

[74] Cribiore, *Writing, Teachers, and Students*, 76.

[75] Turner, *Greek Manuscripts*, 8, 12; Cribiore, *Writing, Teachers, and Students*, 81–2.

a short horizontal line written at the left margin below the line that marks the beginning of a break or section; or a *diple obelismene*, a short forked horizontal line used to mark a section of verse or prose, that in school exercises functioned much like a *paragraphos*.

Scribes of incantations and amulets might also use lectional signs to distinguish words or letters within a group of words. The most common of these is the *trema* or *diairesis*: a pair of dots (sometimes a single dot or a horizontal line) placed over a vowel (usually *iota* or *upsilon*) to indicate that it should be pronounced separately within a cluster of vowels ('organic' *diairesis*) or to mark the initial (or, less often, final) vowel of a word ('inorganic' *diairesis*).[76] Sometimes a scribe will place dots or other markers between words or groups of words. Occasionally a scribe will use some form of punctuation.[77]

2.2.4 Orthography and Syntax

Greek papyri have yielded a wealth of data on the development of Greek as a language during the Ptolemaic and Roman periods. The language as it was spoken, not surprisingly, influenced the language as it was written.[78] We see this as well in the texts with which we are concerned. Often the Greek is spelled phonetically and follows the syntax of the spoken language.[79] The texts display, for instance, common phonetic interchanges between the signs for long vowels and diphthongs and the signs for short vowels, such as the interchange between $\epsilon\iota$, ι, and η, one of the more frequent instances of itacism, where previously distinct sounds are reduced to /i/.[80] The texts may reflect the general confusion between single and double consonants (e.g., λ for $\lambda\lambda$ and vice versa) and the weakened pronunciation of final *nu*. They may betray the influence of Egyptian in a bilingual speaker and writer.[81] Since phonetic spellings, misspellings, and irregular syntax are common occurrences in our material, what stands out are scribes at either ends of the continuum of orthography and syntax: those whose writing is relatively 'classical' and 'correct' and those whose writing is almost unintelligible. We shall note these as we come across them.

---

[76] Turner, *Greek Manuscripts*, 10–11; Cribiore, *Writing, Teachers, and Students*, 83–4.

[77] Turner, *Greek Manuscripts*, 9.

[78] For an overview, see E. Dickey, 'The Greek and Latin Languages in the Papyri', in Bagnall, *Oxford Handbook of Papyrology*, 149–69 at 150–7.

[79] The standard reference is F. T. Gignac, *A Grammar of the Greek Papyri of the Roman and Byzantine Periods*, 2 vols (Milan: Istituto Editoriale Cisalpino-La Goliardica, 1976–81).

[80] Gignac, *Grammar*, 1.234, 330.

[81] For consonants, see Gignac, *Grammar*, 1.179.

2.3 ACOUSTIC ELEMENTS

Graeco-Egyptian incantations often reinforce their adjurations with unintelligible sounds (*voces mysticae*, also called *voces magicae*), foreign names (*nomina barbara*),[82] and voiced letters (usually the seven Greek vowels, which were used to express the incomprehensible names of God and channel the power of the seven planetary spheres governing all aspects of earthly life).[83] The boundary between *voces mysticae* and *nomina barbara* is, in fact, indistinct, since over time names of higher powers from other cultures and languages would be misread by the purveyors of incantations to the point that they became unintelligible. (Efforts to recover their provenance can be misleading.[84]) These unintelligible or semi-intelligible sequences are presented as the secret names of the powers being petitioned or adjured. The practitioner is instructed to utter (as well as write) the sequences to gain the attention of the powers being invoked, to identify the petitioner with such powers, or to ensure that they do the petitioner's bidding. Since the sequences might be written as well as spoken, they are not only acoustic but also visual in their presentation, as we shall see shortly. In some amulets with Christian elements, such esoteric modes of speech continue to function as the means of addressing higher powers, usually alongside Christian forms of address.[85] But otherwise they are replaced by Christian acclamations or invocations.

---

[82] On *voces mysticae* and *nomina barbara*, see Bonner, *Studies in Magical Amulets*, 186–92; Brashear, 'Greek Magical Papyri', 3429–38, 3576–603; D. Ogden, 'Binding Spells: Curse Tablets and Voodoo Dolls in the Greek and Roman Worlds', in B. Ankarloo and Stuart Clark (eds), *Witchcraft and Magic in Europe: Ancient Greece and Rome* (Philadelphia: University of Pennsylvania Press, 1999), 1–90 at 46–9; K. Dzwiza, *Schriftverwendung in antiker Ritualpraxis anhand der griechischen, demotischen und koptischen Praxisanleitungen des 1.—7. Jahrhunderts*, 4 vols in 2 (Erfurt and Heidelberg, 2013), 1.81–114, 2.298–303, 644–51, 882–5, 911–44, <http://www.db-thueringen.de/servlets/DocumentServlet?id=23500>; M. Tardieu, A. Van Den Kerchove, and M. Zago (eds), *Noms barbares I: formes et contextes d'une pratique magique* (Turnhout: Brepols, 2013).

[83] See *PGM* I.25–6; *PGM* IV.1002–7; *PGM* V.79–81; cf. *SM* I 3.2 and *SM* I 20.1. On the power of sounds represented by vowels, see P. C. Miller, 'In Praise of Nonsense', in A. H. Armstrong (ed.), *Classical Mediterranean Spirituality: Egyptian, Greek, Roman* (London: Routledge and Kegan Paul), 481–505; D. Frankfurter, 'The Magic of Writing and the Writing of Magic: The Power of the Word in Egyptian and Greek Traditions', *Helios*, 21 (1994), 179–221 at 199–202; N. Janowitz, *Icons of Power: Ritual Practices in Late Antiquity* (University Park, Pennsylvania State University Press, 2002), 45–61. On the planetary spheres (Saturn, Jupiter, Mars, Sun, Venus, Mercury, Moon) that circulated between the fixed stars and the fixed earth, see W. Hübner, 'Planets. II. Astrology and Mythology', *BNP*, 11.328–34.

[84] Bonner, *Studies in Magical Amulets*, 187–8; G. Bohak, 'Hebrew, Hebrew Everywhere? Notes on the Interpretation of *Voces Magicae*', in S. Noegel, J. Walker, and B. Wheeler (eds), *Prayer, Magic, and the Stars in the Ancient and Late Antique World* (Philadelphia: Pennsylvania State University Press, 2003), 69–82.

[85] E.g., *PGM* P3 (*P.Oslo* I 5); *PGM* P11; *SB* XXII 15234; *SM* I 20; *SM* I 28; *SM* I 29 (*P.Princ.* II 107).

2.4 VISUAL ELEMENTS

As I have already intimated, the devices scribes incorporated into incantations were not only acoustic but also visual: word-shapes, *charaktêres* (letters or signs written in a non-standard script), and, less frequently, figures. Although these visual elements are not as ubiquitous in Graeco-Egyptian manuals and applied materials as acoustic ones, they are conspicuous precisely because they are visible. They constitute a repertoire of techniques designed to be used specifically when *writing* incantations or amulets. When they appear in incantations or amulets with Christian elements, the manner in which they are incorporated is among the features that differentiate the writers of these materials. In what follows I shall briefly describe these customary visual techniques as they appear in Graeco-Egyptian manuals and incantations. I shall then describe visual elements associated with Christian scribal culture in late antique books, documents, and letters from Egypt (*nomina sacra*, crosses, staurograms, and christograms), and consider what their use in incantations and amulets may or may not imply.

2.4.1 Word-shapes

In Graeco-Egyptian incantations certain words and or groups of letters are often written in a diminishing shape formed by dropping a letter from the beginning and/or end of the sequence in each successive line.[86] The shape may be centred (the grape-cluster or heart-shape) or aligned to one side (the wing-shape).[87] The significance of the shape appears to have been its power to diminish or incapacitate the target: the ailment or afflicting demon in the case of healing incantations; the rival or competitor in the case of binding incantations.[88] Other shapes are also used, such as an inverted grape-cluster or pyramid-shape (an increasing sequence), an egg-shape (an increasing and a diminishing sequence),[89] or a rectangle (a set number of letters per line).

---

[86] On this practice, see F. Dornseiff, *Das Alphabet in Mystik und Magie*, 2nd edn (Leipzig: Teubner, 1925), 63–5; Brashear, 'Greek Magical Papyri', 3433–4; R. Gordon, 'Shaping the Text: Innovation and Authority in Graeco-Egyptian Malign Magic', in H. F. J. Horstmanshoff et al. (eds), *Kykeon: Studies in Honour of H. S. Versnel* (Leiden: Brill, 2002), 69–111 at 85–97; A. Mastrocinque, 'Le pouvoir de l'écriture dans la magie', *CMAnc*, 1 (2010) [online], doi: 10.4000/mondesanciens.168; R. Martín-Hernández, 'Reading Magical Drawings in the Greek Magical Papyri', in P. Schubert (ed.), *Actes du 26ᵉ Congrès internationale de papyrologie, Genève, 16–21 août 2010* (Geneva: Librarie Droz, 2012), 491–8 at 495–6.

[87] On the Greek terms used in the manuals for these shapes, see *GMA* I, pp. 202–3.

[88] Martín-Hernández, 'Reading Magical Drawings', 495–6; C. A. Faraone, 'Magic and Medicine in the Roman Imperial Period: Two Case Studies', in G. Bohak, Y. Harari, and S. Shaked (eds), *Continuity and Innovation in the Magical Tradition* (Leiden: Brill, 2011), 135–57 at 144–6.

[89] E.g., *PGM* XVIIa.

Usually the letters form an esoteric name, a common one being the palindrome 'Ablanathanalba', another, the name 'Akrammachamari'.[90] Occasionally the name of a mythical hero that is threatening to the present ailment is used.[91] Sometimes the letters comprise the seven vowels of the Greek alphabet. (Vowels appear in several shapes: grape-clusters; pyramids; rectangles.[92]) The text of the incantation is usually written below or beside the word-shape,[93] occasionally above the word-shape or even around it.[94] Sometimes the schema is extremely elaborate.[95] It may also include figures.[96]

2.4.2 *Charaktêres*

Charaktêres are esoteric signs,[97] an invented script that defies reading. Like *voces mysticae*, which they often accompany, they purport to be signifiers but remain unintelligible.[98] Richard Gordon has published several studies of these signs as they appear in papyri, *lamellae*, and gems. He has identified over a thousand individual signs to date. Gordon argues that most of these signs were generated by modifying the letters of the Greek alphabet, some Latin letters, and five simple graphic shapes (the bar, the cross, the rectangle, the star, and the lozenge) with a number of 'estranging devices'.[99] The diversity of signs that could be created by such techniques is virtually unlimited, indicating that the signs were never meant to function as an intelligible system, as a 'secret alphabet'. However, although the number of distinct signs is very large, the repertoire of recurring signs is quite small. Gordon counted twelve that occur in precisely the same form more than fifteen times in his sample.[100] More recently, Kirsten Dzwiza has categorized, counted, and displayed all the *charaktêres* occurring in a set of thirty-seven Demotic, Greek, and Coptic

---

[90] On these names and their use in word-shapes, see *P.Mich.* XVI, 108–10.

[91] *SM* I, pp. 4–6; Mastrocinque, 'Le pouvoir de l'écriture'.

[92] Dornseiff, *Das Alphabet*, 57–60; Frankfurter, 'The Writing of Magic', 199–200. To the examples noted by Frankfurter one may add *SM* I 3 (grape-cluster).

[93] Below: *PGM* XXXIII (*P.Tebt.* II 275); *PGM* XXXIX (*P.Oslo* I 4); *SM* I 9 (*P.Michael.* 27); *SM* I 11 (*P.Princ.* III 159); *SM* I 40 (*P.Princ.* II 76). Beside: *PGM* XXXVI.115–33 (*P.Oslo* I 1); *PGM* XLIII; *SM* I 7; *SM* I 21 (*P.Köln* VI 257); *SM* I 34.

[94] Above: *SM* I 3. Around: *PGM* XVIIIb (*BGU* III 956).

[95] *PGM* XIXa; *PGM* LXII.76–106; *SM* I 48 = *P.Mich.* XVI.

[96] *PGM* XXXVI.115–24 (*P.Oslo* I 1); *PGM* XXXIX (*P.Oslo* I 4).

[97] On *charaktêres*, see Frankfurter, 'The Magic of Writing', 205–11; R. Gordon, '*Signa nova et inaudita*: The Theory and Practice of Invented Signs (*charaktêres*) in Graeco-Egyptian Magical Texts', *MHNH*, 11 (2011), 15–44; R. Gordon, '*Charaktêres* between Antiquity and Renaissance: Transmission and Re-Invention', in V. Dasen and J.-M. Spieser (eds), *Les savoirs magiques et leur transmission de l'Antiquité à la Renaissance* (Florence: SISMEL—Edizioni del Galluzzo, 2014), 253–300; Dzwiza, *Schriftverwendung*, 1.113–27.

[98] Gordon, '*Signa nova et inaudita*', 26–7; Gordon, '*Charaktêres*', 263–4.

[99] Gordon, '*Signa nova et inaudita*', 28–9; Gordon, '*Charaktêres*', 266–7.

[100] Gordon, '*Signa nova et inaudita*', 28; Gordon, '*Charaktêres*', 264.

manuals and individual recipes with procedures that clearly entail the writing of a text.[101] Her typology of signs proceeds on a different basis than Gordon's.[102] Nevertheless, in her data, too, the number of signs that recur in more than one procedure is relatively small.[103] Thus, while the technique of writing *charaktêres* gave a scribe considerable scope to improvise and impress, it also could be reduced to something of a convention, with a scribe simply adding a few of the more common signs to an incantation.

One of the 'estranging devices' used to create signs was adding little circles (or squares and triangles when working in hard surfaces) at the ends of strokes. This technique has given rise to the term 'ring-letters' or, as Gordon prefers, *signes pommetés*.[104] In manuals and applied materials one can observe an increasing prevalence of 'ring-letters' in Late Antiquity.[105] A distinctive feature of Coptic incantations is, in fact, the profusion of 'ring-letters', used to call the reader's attention to the power and majesty of a spiritual entity rather than to call the spiritual entity's attention to the petitioner's request.[106] We find figures of Jesus, angels, or demonic entities drawn in the style of 'ring-letters', emblazoned with them, and accompanied by them.[107] The number and placement of these 'ring-letters' corresponds to the power and status of the spiritual entity: Jesus and archangels, for instance, will have many such letters on their torso or around them, whereas demonic entities will have only a few or none.

Charaktêres are not as ubiquitous in incantations as *voces mysticae*. Thus, the absence of *charaktêres* in an incantation or amulet with Christian elements is probably less significant than the absence of *voces mysticae*. What the presence of *charaktêres* tells us about the culture of the scribe depends on the overall composition of the incantation. The culture of the scribe who wrote, for example, *SM* I 23 (*P.Haun.* III 51), which combines an acclamatory christological creed with an appeal to deliberately written *charaktêres*, or *SPP* XX 294, which frames several biblical verses with two lines of *charaktêres*, is different than the culture of the scribe who wrote *SM* I 20 or *PGM* P11, where Christian references are simply inserted into a traditional repertoire of powerful names, sounds, and signs. We shall have occasion to discuss these instances in their contexts in Chapters 4, 5, and 6.[108]

---

[101] Dzwiza, *Schriftverwendung*, 1.29–35.   [102] Dzwiza, *Schriftverwendung*, 1.115–16.

[103] Dzwiza, *Schriftverwendung*, 2.296–7 (the most complete and intelligible set of procedures); see also 2.642–3, 881.

[104] Gordon, 'Charaktêres', 257 n. 13.   [105] Gordon, 'Charaktêres', 270.

[106] Frankfurter, 'The Magic of Writing', 208; Gordon, 'Charaktêres', 274–6.

[107] In addition to Gordon, 'Charaktêres', figs 3–5, see *AKZ* 3, plates I–III, V–VIII, and the list of illustrations in *ACM*, 393–4. On the use of 'ring-letters' in London, British Library, Or. Ms. 6796 (*AKZ* 3, plate I; *ACM*, 292), see J. E. Sanzo, 'The Innovative Use of Biblical Traditions for Ritual Power: The Crucifixion of Jesus on a Coptic Exorcistic Spell (Brit. Lib. Or. 6796[4], 6796) as a Test Case', *ARG*, 16 (2015), 67–98 at 79–82, doi: 10.1515/arege-2014-0007.

[108] In addition to the items already named, *charaktêres* appear in *P.Köln* VIII 340; *P.Köln* X 425; *P.Oxy.* LXV 4469; *SM* I 21 (*P.Köln* VI 257); *SM* I 27; *SM* I 32; *SM* I 34; *SM* I 36.

2.4.3 Figures

Figures of certain deities and astral powers dominate pendants and rings, as a perusal of the major collections readily shows.[109] Figures are less prominent in textual materials, where the dominant means of channelling divine power is oral rather than figurative. Nevertheless, Graeco-Egyptian manuals occasionally instruct the practitioner to draw the figure of the god or spirit being invoked to do the work of the incantation.[110] Drawings of these entities or the person targeted by the incantation can be found in applied materials as well.[111] One can observe continuities with earlier Graeco-Egyptian iconographic motifs and arrangements in later Coptic manuals and recipes.[112]

In the Greek materials with which we are primarily concerned, however, figures occur infrequently. They depict mainly the persons who are the petitioners or beneficiaries of the text:[113] the bust of a certain Paulus Julianus between the busts of the powers that are expected to bring him good fortune (*PGM* XXXV [*PSI* I 29]);[114] two *orantes* representing the intended beneficiary of a healing incantation (*P.Köln* VIII 340);[115] the bust of a person to be protected by a frequently cited verse from the Gospel of Matthew, Matt. 4: 23 (*PGM* P4 [*P.Oxy.* VIII 1077]).[116] Since we are dealing with found materials, the relative infrequency of figures in Greek amulets with Christian elements may simply be the result of chance. Other fragmentary papyri and parchments with drawings believed to have had a 'magical' purpose show figures of *orantes*,

---

[109] See also C. A. Faraone, 'Text, Image and Medium: The Evolution of Graeco-Roman Magical Gemstones', in C. Entwistle and N. Adams (eds), *'Gems of Heaven': Recent Research on Engraved Gemstones in Late Antiquity c. AD 200–600* (London: The British Museum, 2011), 50–68; Nagy, 'Engineering Ancient Amulets', 206–20.

[110] E.g., *PGM* II.11–12, 59–60, 169–73, with plate I, fig. 2 (the 'headless one'); *PGM* IV.2111–25 (a lion-faced man, Hekate, Osiris); *PGM* VII.586–90, with plate I, fig. 4 (an ouroboros); *PGM* VII.939–40, with plate I, fig. 3; *PGM* VIII.109–10, with plate I, fig.6 (Bes); *PGM* XII.376–7, with plate II, fig. 10; *PGM* XXXVI.2, 38, 71–3, 102–3, 179–85, 231–3, with plate III, fig. 13–18 (multiple figures; see also *P.Oslo* I, plates I–IV, VII, X); *PGM* LXXVIII.3–4, with plate IV, fig. 2; *SM* II 96 A.13–22. The images are traced within the English translations in *GMPT*; for *SM* II 96 A.13–22, see *GMPT*, no. CXXIIIa. For bibliography on selected figures in manuals and applied materials, see Brashear, 'Greek Magical Papyri', 3442–3; additional discussion at R. Gordon, 'Shaping the Text', 97–107.

[111] Agents: *PGM* XXXIX; *PGM* LXIV; *SM* I 38. Targets: *PGM* LXVI, with plate IV, fig. 1.

[112] I. Grumach, 'On the History of a Coptic Figura Magica', in D. H. Samuel (ed.), *Proceedings of the Twelfth International Congress of Papyrology* (Toronto: A. M. Hakkert, 1970), 169–81.

[113] See J. H. F. Dijkstra, 'The Interplay between Image and Text on Greek Amulets Containing Christian Elements from Late Antique Egypt', in Boschung and Bremmer, *The Materiality of Magic*, 271–92 at 280–6.

[114] See T. S. de Bruyn, 'An Anatomy of Tradition: The Case of the *Charitêsion*', *ARG*, 16 (2015), 31–50 at 39–40, doi: 10.1515/arege-2014-0005.

[115] The amulet is discussed in Section 4.2.2.

[116] The amulet is discussed in Section 5.3.

angels, and demons.[117] Nevertheless, it is noteworthy that in Greek materials we see neither the simple nor the elaborate figures emblazoned or surrounded by 'ring-letters' that we observe in Coptic materials.

2.4.4 Nomina sacra

Nomina sacra, a term introduced by Ludwig Traube in his seminal study,[118] refers to abbreviated forms of certain words in early Greek manuscripts of Christian texts. The words so abbreviated include the Greek words for 'God', 'Lord', 'Jesus', and 'Christ'—these four being the most frequently and regularly abbreviated—as well as 'spirit', 'father', 'heaven', 'David', 'Israel', 'Jerusalem', 'son', 'saviour', 'cross', and 'mother'.[119] The most common method of abbreviation is contraction: the first and last letters of the word-form, and sometimes one or more medial letters, are retained. This method had the advantage of indicating the case of the word. An alternative and early method of abbreviation, used mostly for 'Jesus' and 'Christ', is suspension: the first two letters of the word are retained. Typically, a horizontal stroke is written above the contracted or suspended form. Whatever the reason for the supralinear stroke may originally have been,[120] it had the effect of distinguishing the abbreviation visually. While it could serve as an aid to reading, it also became part of the visual appearance of the text, which is why we treat it as a visual element in incantations and amulets.

These abbreviated forms have been the subject of much discussion among scholars of the early Christian movement, where debate has turned on when the technique was introduced, whether it originated in Jewish or Christian contexts, and how it came to be standardized.[121] These questions do not concern us, since by the fourth century the abbreviations were routinely used by scribes working in a Christian milieu. The abbreviations appear not

---

[117] U. Horak (ed.), *Illuminierte Papyri, Pergamente und Papiere I* (Vienna: A. Holzhausens, 1992), nos. 48–52, 54–60.

[118] L. Traube, *Nomina Sacra: Versuch einer Geschichte der christliche Kürzung* (Munich: Beck, 1907), 17–18.

[119] A. H. R. E. Paap, *Nomina Sacra in the Greek Papyri of the First Five Centuries A.D.: The Sources and Some Deductions* (Leiden: Brill, 1959), 76–99.

[120] L. W. Hurtado, 'The Origin of the Nomina Sacra: A Proposal', *JBL*, 117 (1998), 655–73 at 668–9, doi: 10.2307/3266633; C. M. Tuckett, '"Nomina Sacra": Yes and No', in J.-M. Auwers and H. J. de Jonge (eds), *The Biblical Canons* (Leuven: Leuven University Press, 2003), 431–58 at 444–5; L. W. Hurtado, *The Earliest Christian Artifacts: Manuscripts and Christian Origins* (Grand Rapids: Eerdmans, 2006), 112–16.

[121] For a recent position on the origins of the practice that summarizes prior research, see Hurtado, *Earliest Christian Artifacts*, 99–120. On the development of a systematic approach to writing *nomina sacra* in biblical manuscripts, see S. D. Charlesworth, 'Consensus Standardization in the Systematic Approach to *nomina sacra* in Second- and Third-Century Gospel Manuscripts', *Aegyptus*, 86 (2006), 37–68, <http://www.jstor.org/stable/41217448>.

only in manuscripts of the Septuagint and canonical and apocryphal Christian scriptures, but also in homilies, documents, letters, school exercises, and, of course, amulets.[122]

The questions that interest us when we encounter *nomina sacra* in incantations and amulets are ones that interrogate a scribe's familiarity with the conventions of the practice. What names or words are abbreviated? Are all instances of the name or word abbreviated? Are the abbreviated forms relatively common or are they idiosyncratic? Are the abbreviations accompanied by a supralinear stroke? What the answers to such questions may reveal about the scribe's culture, however, is complicated by the vagaries of scribal practice more generally.

In general, scribes of biblical manuscripts are consistent and regular in abbreviating the words for 'God', 'Lord', 'Jesus', and 'Christ', but they may also inadvertently abbreviate 'god' and 'lord' when these words occur in the singular in a 'mundane' sense.[123] Other *nomina sacra* are not always abbreviated in biblical manuscripts; if they are, they may not be abbreviated consistently, and both 'sacred' and 'mundane' senses of the word may be abbreviated.[124]

Writers of letters are much less consistent and regular, as scholars have observed.[125] Lincoln Blumell's study of letters from Oxyrhynchus that were certainly or almost certainly written by Christians is illustrative.[126] *Nomina sacra* appear in thirty-five of 191 letters.[127] In almost every instance the abbreviations appear in the opening or closing formula of address, which inevitably reduces the number of candidates for abbreviation, since these formulae typically refer to 'the Lord' or 'God' or 'the Lord God'. There are a few anomalies in the abbreviations employed,[128] but in most instances the forms are standard ones.[129] In some letters the writer writes a word in both an

---

[122] Paap, *Nomina Sacra*, 22–49, lists evidence assigned to the third-fourth or fourth century. Additional data for *nomina sacra* in copies of the Septuagint and the New Testament are given in S. Jankowski, 'I "nomina sacra" nei papyri dei LXX (secoli II e III d.C.)', *StudPap*, 16 (1977), 81–116; J. O'Callaghan, *'Nomina Sacra' in Papyris Graecis Saeculi III Neotestamentariis* (Rome: Biblical Institute Press, 1970); and J. O'Callaghan, '"Nominum sacrorum" elenchus in Graecis Novi Testamenti papyris a saeculo IV usque ad VIII', *StudPap*, 10 (1971), 99–122.

[123] Data from second- and third-century gospel manuscripts are conveniently presented in Charlesworth, 'Consensus Standardization', 41–62. See also Paap, *Nomina Sacra*, 100–1, 107–10.

[124] In addition to the data presented by Charlesworth, see, e.g., Paap's summary of data from the Freer Gospels at p. 117.

[125] See, e.g., Paap, *Nomina Sacra*, 101; M. Choat, *Belief and Cult in Fourth-Century Papyri* (Turnhout: Brepols, 2006), 119–22.

[126] On the criteria used to determine Christian authorship, see L. H. Blumell, *Lettered Christians: Christians, Letters, and Late Antique Oxyrhynchus* (Leiden: Brill, 2012), chapter 2. For the list of letters of certain or near certain authorship, see the appendix, table 1.

[127] Blumell, *Lettered Christians*, appendix, table 6, lists thirty-five letters, though at p. 50 Blumell gives the number as 'thirty-six'.

[128] Blumell, *Lettered Christians*, 51 n. 114.

[129] Blumell, *Lettered Christians*, appendix, table 6.

abbreviated form and in full.[130] The names 'Jesus' and 'Christ' never appear in
an abbreviated form; these names are always written out in full.[131] In some
formulae of address, 'Lord' and 'God' are written in full.[132] Most interesting of
all, over time *nomina sacra* decrease in frequency whereas other Christian
symbols increase in frequency. The abbreviations are most prominent in
letters from the late third or fourth century, appear occasionally in letters
from the fifth century, and are rare in letters from the sixth or seventh century,
where they almost never appear with a supralinear stroke.[133]

What does this imply for our interpretation of *nomina sacra* (or their
absence) in Greek incantations and amulets with Christian elements?[134] On
the one hand, we cannot infer from the absence of *nomina sacra*—that is,
writing the words or names out in full rather than in an abbreviated form—
that the writer did not work in a Christian milieu or lacked a Christian
formation. On the other hand, we may infer from consistent and regular use
of *nomina sacra* that the writer was trained in the conventions of the system
and probably worked in a Christian milieu. Inconsistent and irregular use of
nomina sacra presents the greatest interpretative challenges, since it could be
the result of any number of circumstances: unfamiliarity with the conventions;
speed or sloppiness in writing; vague awareness of *nomina sacra* as a feature of
Christian biblical and liturgical books. In addition, one must take account of
the fact that the writer of an incantation or amulet may have been copying
from an exemplar. Moreover, one must differentiate between what might be
expected of the writer of an incantation and what might be expected of the
writer of an amulet comprising scriptural passages. All these considerations
should be weighed in light of the other textual and scribal features of the item.

2.4.5 Crosses, Staurograms, and Christograms

In incantations and amulets with Christian texts—in other words, with texts
whose Christian character is unambiguous—one often finds signs that, for
convenience, we shall call the cross (·┼·, an equilateral cross, also called the
Greek cross),[135] the staurogram (·ϼ·, a monogram comprising the Greek letters

---

[130] Blumell, *Lettered Christians*, 51 nn. 114, 116.

[131] Blumell, *Lettered Christians*, 51 n. 116.

[132] Blumell, *Lettered Christians*, appendix, table 7. The letters range from the third to the fifth
or sixth century.

[133] Blumell, *Lettered Christians*, 51, and appendix, table 7.

[134] For occurrences of *nomina sacra*, see de Bruyn and Dijkstra, 'Greek Amulets and
Formularies', tables 1–3.

[135] For forms of the cross, see P. C. Finney, 'Cross', in E. Ferguson (ed.), *Encyclopedia of Early
Christianity*, 2nd edn, 2 vols (New York: Garland, 1998), 1.303–5 at 304. For examples and
discussion, see H. Leclercq, 'Croix, crucifix', *DACL*, 3/2.3045–131.

tau and *rho*), and the christogram (☧, a monogram comprising the Greek letters *chi* and *rho*).[136] These signs were not uniquely and specifically Christian in antiquity.[137] In particular, both the *tau-rho* ligature and the *chi-rho* ligature appear in non-Christian manuscripts as abbreviations by suspension for certain Greek words.[138] By the third century, however, both ligatures had taken on Christian meanings. In manuscripts of the gospels from around the beginning of that century the *tau-rho* ligature is used in abbreviations for the Greek words for 'cross' (σταυρός) and 'crucify' (σταυρόω),[139] where, it has been argued, it functions as 'a visual reference to the crucified Jesus'.[140] In the fourth century the ligature appears in manuscripts as a self-standing symbol, an evolution from its function within a *nomen sacrum*. By that time as well, but independently of the scribal system of *nomina sacra*, the *chi-rho* ligature was being used as a monogram for the Greek word for 'Christ' (Χριστός). The monogram appears on a number of third-century gems believed to have come from Syria or Asia Minor and to have been produced a generation or two before the reign of the emperor Constantine, with whom the symbol is famously associated.[141]

From the fourth century onward, one of the means of determining whether the writer of a document or a letter may have been a Christian is the presence of a cross or a staurogram (or, to a much lesser extent, a christogram). In the fourth century, writers had taken to preceding the first line of a document or the greeting or address of a letter with a cross or a staurogram.[142] By the sixth century the practice was common and widespread.[143] The cross was used much more frequently than the staurogram. In the letters from Oxyrhynchus studied by Blumell, the cross appears on almost every letter from the fifth and sixth centuries, whereas the staurogram appears on only thirty-two of the

---

[136] For occurrences of these signs (including texts whose Christian character is *not* unambiguous), see de Bruyn and Dijkstra, 'Greek Amulets and Formularies', tables 1–3.

[137] The literature on the emergence of these signs as Christian signs is considerable. For an overview, see S. Heid, 'Kreuz', *RAC*, 21.1099–148, discussing non-Christian use at 1100–1.

[138] E. Dinkler-Von Schubert, 'ΣΤΑΥΡΟΣ: Vom "Wort vom Kreuz" (1 Kor. 1,18) zum Kreuz-Symbol', in C. Moss and K. Kiefer (eds), *Byzantine East, Latin West: Art-Historical Studies in Honor of Kurt Weitzmann* (Princeton: Department of Art and Archaeology, Princeton University, 1995), 29–39 at 33–4; E. Dinkler and E. Dinkler-Von Schubert, 'Kreuz I', *RBK*, 5.1–219 at 36–7; Hurtado, *Earliest Christian Artifacts*, 137–8.

[139] Paap, *Nomina Sacra*, 112–13; K. Aland, 'Bemerkungen zum Alter und zur Entstehung des Christogrammes anhand von Beobachtungen bei 𝔓66 und 𝔓75', in K. Aland (ed.), *Studien zur Überlieferung des Neuen Testaments und seines Textes* (Berlin: Walter de Gruyter, 1967), 173–9 at 173–5; Dinkler-Von Schubert, 'ΣΤΑΥΡΟΣ', 31–2; Hurtado, *Earliest Christian Artifacts*, 140–2, with plates 4–5.

[140] Hurtado, *Earliest Christian Artifacts*, 146–52, quotation at 151.

[141] J. Spier, *Late Antique and Early Christian Gems*, 30–4; additional examples at J. Spier, 'Late Antique Gems: Some Unpublished Examples', in Entwistle and Adams, *'Gems of Heaven'*, 193–213 at 196–7.

[142] Choat, *Belief and Cult*, 117 nn. 529 (documents) and 530 (letters).

[143] Blumell, *Lettered Christians*, 43–5.

letters.[144] (The one possible instance of a christogram is too indistinct to bear much weight.[145])

It is interesting to compare these data with the frequency of crosses, staurograms, and christograms in the materials that form the basis for our study.[146] Crosses appear more frequently than staurograms, and staurograms appear more frequently than christograms.[147] If we limit ourselves to materials whose purpose is unambiguous (i.e., materials that were certainly used as an incantation or amulet),[148] we may note, as well, that both crosses and staurograms frequently appear in the same text, or that more than one cross or staurogram appear in the same text. Precisely where crosses or staurograms appear in a text varies: singly at the beginning of a text; singly at the beginning of a section or sections within a text; in a series at the head of the text; in a series at the end of a text; together with other symbols, letters, or words, such as the letters *alpha* and *omega*. When crosses and staurograms appear in a series, they are often in groups of three or seven.[149]

In Christian ritual and thought, the sign of the cross was believed to repel demons and protect against their stratagems.[150] The power vested in the sign—an extension of the power displayed by Christ when he vanquished the Devil through his death—undoubtedly accounts for its use in incantations and amulets. However, the widespread use of the cross in all manner of writing dilutes its value as an indicator of an individual scribe's culture. As with *charaktêres* and *nomina sacra*, the significance of a particular scribe's use of crosses, staurograms, and associated signs will depend upon other features of the text and artefact.

2.4.6 Other Christian Markers

Other Christian markers that are at once visual and symbolic also make their way into incantations and amulets. One is the letters *alpha* and *omega*, which,

---

[144] Blumell, *Lettered Christians*, appendix, table 4.

[145] *P.Oxy.* XXXI 2069.3, discussed at Blumell, *Lettered Christians*, 45–6, with plate 3.

[146] De Bruyn and Dijkstra, 'Greek Amulets and Formularies', tables 1–3.

[147] In table 1 crosses appear in 41 items and staurograms in 19 items (including two questionable instances). The monogram at *PGM* XII.138 cannot plausibly be read as an abbreviation for Χριστόν; see table 1 n. 127.

[148] De Bruyn and Dijkstra, 'Greek Amulets and Formularies', table 1.

[149] Three: *PGM* P16.25 (*P.Ross.-Georg.* I 23); *PGM* P19.6 (*PSI* VI 719); *P.Oxy.* LXXXII 5311.9; *SM* I 27.6; *SM* I 34 head of text; *SM* II 59v.1 (*P.Ups.8*), two groups of three; C. A. La'da and A. Papathomas, 'A Greek Papyrus Amulet from the Duke Collection with Biblical Excerpts', *BASP*, 41 (2004), 93–113 at 97–8, <http://hdl.handle.net/2027/spo.0599796.0041.001:06> (P.Duke inv. 778r.1, v.26); Wortmann, 'Neue magische Texte', 106 (P.Köln inv. 521a.1). Seven: *P.Köln* VIII 340a, fr. A.1; *SM* I 35.15 (*P.Batav.* 20); W. M. Brashear, *Magica Varia* (Brussels: Fondation Égyptologique Reine Élisabeth 1991), 63–70 at 64, l. 19 (*SB* XVIII 13602).

[150] Heid, 'Kreuz', 1126–9.

as we have just noted, often appear alongside a cross or staurogram on stelae and gems. Their frequent use in engravings or inscriptions in Late Antiquity is no doubt an expression of the tradition, originating in Revelations, that Christ is 'the Alpha and the Omega, the first and the last, the beginning and the end' (Rev. 22: 13; cf. Rev. 1: 8, 17–18; 21: 6).[151] Another is the letters *koppa* and *theta* which, read as numbers, equal the sum of the letters that comprise the Greek word 'amen'. In Greek, numbers were denoted by letters accompanied by a horizontal stroke or a tick written to the side to indicate that the symbol was to be read as a number rather than a letter. Consequently, the sequence of letters in a word or phrase could also be read as a sequence of numbers, giving rise to the art of isopsephism—a modern term derived from the Greek word *ἰσόψηφον*, meaning 'equal in numerical value'—whereby one could arrive at a numerical sum for the series of letters.[152] One common technique was simply to add up the values of the letters, which in the case of 'amen' yields 99 ($a = 1 + \mu = 40 + \eta = 8 + \nu = 50$), a number indicated by the letters *koppa theta* ($\varphi = 90 + \theta = 9$). In letters from Oxyrhynchus this is the earliest identifiable Christian isopsephism, appearing in letters assigned to the fourth century.[153] In the fifth and sixth centuries, the isopsephism appears often in documents together with other Christian symbols, such as the letters *χμγ* and a cross or staurogram.[154]

The meaning of the letters *χμγ* has itself been the subject of considerable debate. It can be read as an isopsephism for the phrase 'God [is] helper' (*θεὸς βοηθός*), which yields the sum 643 (*χμγ* read as a number).[155] It can also be read as an acrostic, but as such its resolution remains an open question. Among the proposals that have been put forward for its meaning as a Christian marker,[156] *χριστὸν μαρία γεννᾷ* ('Mary gives birth to Christ'),[157] *χριστὸς μαρίας γέννα* ('Christ, offspring of Mary'),[158] and *χριστὸς μάρτυς*

---

[151] For examples in gems, see Spier, *Late Antique and Early Christian Gems*, nos. 573, 578, 677, 678; for inscriptions, see F. Cabrol, '*A Ω*', *DACL*, 1/1.1–25 at 6–14. See also H. Froschauer, '*A* = Ligatur von Alpha und Omega?' *AnalPap*, 14–15 (2002–2003), 91–9 at 93–4.

[152] For an overview of the technique, see Dornseiff, *Das Alphabet*, 91–118; R. Ast and J. Lougovaya, 'The Art of the Isopsephism in the Greco-Roman World', in A. Jördens (ed.), *Ägyptische Magie und ihre Umwelt* (Wiesbaden: Harrassowitz, 2015), 82–98.

[153] Blumell, *Lettered Christians*, 47.

[154] *CPR* XXIII 34.1 comm. gives numerous instances.

[155] S. R. Llewelyn, 'The Christian Symbol *XMΓ*, an Acrostic or an Isopsephism?' in S. R. Llewelyn (ed.), *New Documents Illustrating Early Christianity*, vol. 8: *A Review of the Greek Inscriptions and Papyri Published 1984–85* (Sydney and Grand Rapids: Ancient History Documentary Research Centre, Macquarie University, and Eerdmans, 1998), 156–68.

[156] The literature is noted at Llewelyn, 'The Christian Symbol *XMΓ*', 157 n. 5; *CPR* XXIII 34.1 comm.; Choat, *Belief and Cult*, 114–15; B. Nongbri, 'The Lord's Prayer and *XMΓ*: Two Christian Papyrus Amulets', *HTR*, 104 (2011), 59–64 at 67, doi: 10.2307/41234070.

[157] J.-O. Tjäder, 'Christ, Our Lord, Born of the Virgin Mary (*XMΓ* and VDN)', *Eranos*, 68 (1970), 148–90; A. Blanchard, 'Sur quelques interpretations de *XMΓ*', in *Proceedings of the XIV International Congress of Papyrologists, Oxford, 24–31 July 1974* (London: British Academy, 1975), 19–24.

[158] *P.Naqlun* I, 'Appendix: The Christian Symbol *XMΓ*', pp. 179–87 at 179–84.

γένοιτο ('Christ is my witness'), each have some support.[159] But none of the proposals has been decisive, leading one to conclude that the sequence probably had several meanings in antiquity.[160] Whatever its origins and meanings, however, the sequence was used as a Christian marker in Egypt already in the fourth century,[161] and appears often at the head of the text together with other Christian symbols in Egyptian documents from the fifth, sixth, and seventh centuries.[162] Likewise, the sequence appears in letters from Oxyrhynchus from the late fourth to the early seventh century, usually at the head of the text.[163]

The protective power attributed to these symbols is well illustrated by two amulets. One assigned to the sixth century,[164] P.Köln inv. 521a,[165] has a line of three crosses at the head of the text, followed by seven lines with alternating *A Ω* and *Ω A*, concluding with ⳨ Ἰ(ησοῦ)ς Χρ(ιστό)ς[166] ⳨ | ⳨ βοήθεια ⳨ ('Jesus Christ, help') at the bottom of the text. The letter *alpha* is written in a majuscule form frequently found in inscriptions (Λ), with the horizontal linking the two diagonal strokes in the form of an 'x' or *chi*, suggesting that the writer may have been influenced by the frequent occurrence of *A Ω* on grave stelae.[167] The papyrus was folded three times vertically and three times horizontally,[168] a strong indication that it was in fact carried as an amulet. The other amulet, P.CtYBR inv. 4710,[169] written in a large, at times ungainly cursive assigned to the fifth or sixth century, consists simply of the sequence χμγ̄ written four times in a single line across a long, narrow strip of papyrus. It, too, was folded, from left to right in half three times, likewise indicating that it was carried as an amulet. It is possible that the writer intended the sequence χμγ̄ to be read as numbers, since they are combined with a supralinear stroke. Nevertheless, their meaning is cryptic, as is the meaning of *A Ω* and *Ω A* in the previous amulet. So, like *charaktêres*, these Christian symbols were seen as powerful signs that could protect simply by virtue of having been written, even if the referent was obscure or understood only by the initiated.

---

[159] A. Gostoli, 'Una nuova ipotesi interpretativa della sigla *XMΓ*', StudPap, 22 (1983), 9–14; see also G. Robinson, '*KMΓ* and *ΘMΓ* for *XMΓ*', Tyche, 1 (1986), 175–7.

[160] *P.Naqlun* I, pp. 185–7; Nongbri, 'The Lord's Prayer', 68.

[161] Choat, *Belief and Cult*, 115–16.   [162] *CPR* XXIII 34.1 comm.

[163] Blumell, *Lettered Christians*, 48, and appendix, table 5.

[164] The crude capitals of the amulet cannot be easily dated. Wortmann's assigned date of the sixth century was no doubt based on the two lines written in a Byzantine hand on the other side (P.Köln inv. 521av in the Kölner Papyrussammlung). The amulet would have been written later (P.Köln inv. 521ar in the Kölner Papyrussammlung).

[165] Wortmann, 'Neue magische Texte', 106.

[166] The *nomen sacrum* is χρ̄ς, not χ̄ς as read by Wortmann.

[167] Froschauer, 'Λ = Ligatur von Alpha und Omega?', 92–3. For numerous occurrences in Coptic stelae, see M. Cramer, *Das altägyptische Lebenszeichen [ankh] im christlichen (koptischen) Ägypten: Eine kultur- und religionsgeschichtliche Studie*, 3rd edn (Wiesbaden: Harrassowitz, 1955).

[168] Autopsy 29 April 2008.   [169] Nongbri, 'The Lord's Prayer', 64–8.

2.5 CONCLUSION

In this chapter we have surveyed the materials, skills, and techniques that were available to producers of textual amulets in late antique Egypt. Some of what we have reviewed was not unique to incantations or amulets. It can be observed in various types of writing—in the materials, format, and hands used to write, for instance, a private letter, a personal copy of a literary work, or even a school exercise. This is to be expected. Writers of incantations and amulets were trained—to whatever extent they were trained—first of all as writers. They would inevitably and unconsciously have been shaped by the conventions of their training, just as they would have been constrained or enabled by their individual capabilities and habits as writers. For that very reason, the way in which an incantation or amulet is written, or the manner in which it incorporates commonplace scribal conventions, tells us something about the formation of the writer and his or her social location.

These more general qualities are the substratum, if you will, for aspects of incantations and amulets that *are* unique or peculiar to the genre, such as the structure of the incantation, the use of customary expressions to invoke a higher power or expedite a request, and the presence or absence of acoustic or visual devices. Here again, producers of incantations and amulets were working with resources available to them—with what they and their clients perceived to be an authoritative and effective way of devising an incantation or amulet. What exactly those resources might have been, and how individual scribes left traces of their particular cultural formation in working with those resources, are the subject of the remaining chapters in this book. In the process we shall observe varying degrees of 'christianization' in the making of amulets, and I shall offer some suggestions as to how and where such 'christianization' came about.

3

Manuals of Procedures and Incantations

The amulets with which this book is concerned emerged out of a long-standing practice that evolved as the broader cultural context changed. The practice perpetuated itself not only through knowledge and techniques passed on from one generation of purveyors to the next, but also in manuals of procedures and incantations (collections of recipes, also called 'formularies'). We know from various sources that such manuals—'magical' books—circulated fairly widely in the Roman Empire. Few of them have survived. This is not simply a result of the environmental hazards to which all manuscripts were subject. Manuals of procedures and incantations were suspect in the eyes of Roman and Christian authorities. Legal and literary sources tell us that if 'magical' books came to light, they were confiscated and burned.[1] Moreover, these types of books did not benefit from social or institutional systems that ensured that manuscripts were in demand, copied, and collected. The manuals were not, for example, among the works of poetry, satire, tragedy, history, rhetoric, philosophy, and other genres used in education or read by *literati*,[2] nor among the biblical, liturgical, theological, and

---

[1] On book burning in the Roman empire, see W. Speyer, *Büchervernichtung und Zensur des Geistes bei Heiden, Juden und Christen* (Stuttgart: Hiersemann, 1981); M. W. Dickie, *Magic and Magicians in the Greco-Roman World* (London: Routledge, 2001), 259–60, 263–7, 277, 314; D. Sarefield, 'Bookburning in the Christian Roman Empire: Transforming a Pagan Rite of Purification', in H. A. Drake (ed.), *Violence in Late Antiquity: Perceptions and Practices* (Farnham: Ashgate, 2006), 287–96; D. Sarefield, 'The Symbolics of Book Burning: The Establishment of a Christian Ritual of Persecution', in W. E. Klingshirn and L. Safran (eds), *The Early Christian Book* (Washington, D.C.: Catholic University of America Press, 2007), 159–73; J. Herrin, 'Book Burning as Purification', in P. Rousseau and E. Papoutsakis (eds), *Transformations of Late Antiquity: Essays for Peter Brown* (Farnham: Ashgate, 2009), 205–22.

[2] On books used in education, see R. Cribiore, *Gymnastics of the Mind: Greek Education in Hellenistic and Roman Egypt* (Princeton: Princeton University Press, 2001), 137–47. On books collected by readers and scholars, see, e.g., E. G. Turner, 'Scribes and Scholars', in A. K. Bowman et al. (eds) *Oxyrhynchus: A City and its Texts* (London: Egypt Exploration Society, 2007), 256–61; D. Obbink, 'Readers and Intellectuals', in Bowman, *Oxyrhynchus*, 271–82. For lists of books held in collections or sought by readers, see H. Harrauer, 'Bücher in Papyri', in H. W. Lang (ed.), *Flores litterarum Ioanni Marte sexagenario oblati: Wissenschaft in der Bibliothek* (Vienna: Böhlau Verlag, 1995), 59–77; R. Otranto, *Antiche liste di libri su papiro* (Rome: Edizioni di storia e letteratura, 2000). For local or regional studies, see, e.g., J. Krüger, *Oxyrhynchos in der*

hagiographical books that dominated the libraries of Christian churches and monasteries.[3]

There is one remarkable exception to this pattern: an archive of manuscripts from Thebes (the 'Theban Magical Library'), the largest extant collection of Graeco-Egyptian manuals of procedures and incantations, a product of the interests and activity of priests associated with the Egyptian temples. As well, we have fragments of formularies written in Greek and Coptic, and a variety of Coptic manuals, some of which were copied by groups of scribes working together. These allow us to see not only what circulated in such manuals, but also where and how Christian elements begin to appear in customary recipes. In this chapter we shall examine instances where Christian elements enter into the repertoire of the scribes who copied or collected such recipes—into the cultural horizon, as it were, of people who had a particular interest, as compilers or purveyors, in techniques of incantation and adjuration.

3.1 THE THEBAN ARCHIVE

The manuscripts of the Theban archive were acquired in the early nineteenth century by Giovanni Anastasi, a merchant and diplomat in Alexandria, and sold during his lifetime and after his death to various European museums and institutions.[4] A recent investigation of the provenance of the manuscripts, the documents associated with their sales, and the contents of the manuscripts has concluded that the archive almost certainly included the following rolls and codices: *PGM* I, *PGM* II, *PGM* IV, *PGM* V, *P.Holm.* + *PGM* Va (an alchemical codex), *PGM* XII/PDM xii, *PGM* XIII, *PGM* XIV/PDM xiv, PDM Supp, and *P.Leid.* II no. X (an alchemical codex).[5] Other manuscripts have at one time or

Kaiserzeit: Studien zur Topographie und Literaturrezeption (Frankfurt am Main: Lang, 1990), 144–260; P. van Minnen and K. A. Worp, 'The Greek and Latin Literary Texts from Hermopolis', *GRBS*, 34 (1993), 151–86, <http://grbs.library.duke.edu/article/view/3441>.

[3] For an overview, see C. Kotsifou, 'Books and Book Production in the Monastic Communities of Byzantine Egypt', in Klingshirn and Safran, *The Early Christian Book*, 48–66 at 51–3. For Christian books named in lists, see Harrauer, 'Bücher'; R. Otranto, '*Alia tempora, alii libri*: Notizie ed elenchi di libri cristiani su papiro', *Aegyptus*, 77 (1997), 101–24, <http://www.jstor.org/stable/41217691>, repr. in Otranto, *Antiche liste*, 123–44. See also n. 113.

[4] On the acquisition and sale of these manuscripts and associated documents, see now K. Dosoo, 'A History of the Theban Magical Library', *BASP*, 53 (2016), 251–74, which surveys prior literature. Still useful, despite inaccuracies corrected by later scholars, is W. M. Brashear, 'The Greek Magical Papyri: An Introduction and Survey; Annotated Bibliography (1928–1994)', *ANRW*, 18/5.3380–684 at 3402–11.

[5] For the institutional inventory numbers of these and the following manuscripts, see Dosoo, 'A History', 255–8.

another been associated with the archive, but are no longer considered to belong to it: *PGM* III, *PGM* VI, *PGM* VII, *PGM* VIII, *PGM* XIa, *PGM* XXXVI, *PGM* LXI/PDM lxi, *P.Leid.* II no. U, and *P.Leid.* II no. Y.[6]

The Theban manuals, which were compiled in the third and fourth centuries CE,[7] consist mainly of recipes giving instructions for rituals, incantations, material preparations, and objects (figurines, bones, amulets, tablets, rings, etc.), to be used toward various ends. The recipes appear to have been compiled for archival purposes rather than to guide practitioners. Four of the manuals have text written in Demotic and Greek, as well as, to varying extents, passages in Old Coptic, hieratic, and cipher script.[8] This, as well as their contents, indicates that they were compiled by scribes trained in Egyptian temple scriptoria, since only temple scribes would have had the requisite knowledge of these scripts as well as of details of Egyptian myth and ritual.[9]

This has been demonstrated conclusively by Jacco Dieleman with regard to the Demotic-Greek manuals *PGM* XII/PDM xii and *PGM* XIV/PDM xiv.[10] The Demotic sections of these two manuals are linguistically more complex but culturally more homogeneous than the Greek sections, which incorporate elements from Egypt, Greece, the Near East, and Persia. Nevertheless, both sections derive from an Egyptian milieu. Their juxtaposition and, at points, intersection in a single manuscript show that at the time of writing—the turn of the third century, according to Dieleman[11]—the scribe was knowledgeable and receptive of Hellenistic as well as Egyptian traditions of incantation and adjuration. Indeed, these bilingual manuscripts suggest that Egyptian temple priests were adapting to the confluence of Egyptian and Hellenistic culture in Egypt by combining Greek material composed for a Hellenistic clientele with Demotic material presented according to a Hellenistic model.

The Theban manuals therefore allow us to glimpse the extent to which the Christian cult figured in the materials available to and compiled by temple scribes. We begin with sporadic references to 'Jesus'. In a few formularies the name appears within a series of divine names; it is one of several ways to identify with or invoke the god. At *PGM* XII.190–2, a request for an oracle, the name appears at the beginning of the prescribed invocation, the rest of which is lost. In the same manual, at *PGM* XII.385–95, the name may appear in an incantation to induce insomnia, depending on how one reads the continuous

---

[6] Dosoo, 'A History', 251–63. [7] See Dosoo, 'A History', 255 n. 15.

[8] J. H. Johnson, 'Introduction to the Demotic Magical Papyri', in *GMPT*, lv–lviii; J. Dieleman, *Priests, Tongues, and Rites: The London-Leiden Magical Manuscripts and Translation in Egyptian Ritual (100–300 CE)* (Leiden: Brill, 2005), 34–5 (on the *absence* of Old Coptic in *PGM* XII/PDM xii), 47–101.

[9] R. K. Ritner, 'Egyptian Magical Practice under the Roman Empire: The Demotic Spells and their Religious Context', *ANRW*, 18/5.3333–79 at 3361–2.

[10] For a summary of his findings, see Dieleman, *Priests, Tongues, and Rites*, 285–94.

[11] Dieleman, *Priests, Tongues, and Rites*, 41–4.

script.[12] And at *PGM* III.418–20, a manual whose use of Old Coptic alongside Greek suggests that it comes from a milieu similar to that of the Demotic-Greek manuals, the name appears at the end of an incantation written in Coptic. It is unlikely that the individuals who composed such texts or later copied them into a manual knew much, if anything, about the deity or the name being invoked. Indeed, it is clear from the Demotic section of *PGM* XIV/ PDM xiv that the scribe did not always understand the *voces mysticae* being transcribed or glossed.[13] Moreover, customary ways of addressing a deity in Graeco-Egyptian incantations, such as a litany of epithets or attributes, are absent. 'Jesus' is just within the cultural horizon of these texts; little is said about him. Still, it is noteworthy that 'Jesus' has entered the repertoire of powerful names in a Graeco-Egyptian milieu.

In *PGM* IV, the so-called 'Great Magical Papyrus of Paris', we encounter more specific Christian references in two recipes. This manual is the longest of the Anastasi manuscripts and indeed of all the extant manuals from Egypt. It belongs to the same find as *PGM* XII/PDM xii and *PGM* XIV/PDM xiv. In fact, the collection begins with an Old Coptic incantation in which there is an invocation to Osiris that parallels an invocation in a Demotic incantation in PDM xiv.[14] The manuscript has been assigned to the late third or fourth century.[15] One of its rituals for driving out a demon, *PGM* IV.3007–86, begins its adjuration with the words, 'I adjure you by the god of the Hebrews, Jesus'. Another, *PGM* IV.1227–64, contains an invocation addressed to 'Jesus Christ'. Not surprisingly, both passages have received much attention over the years.

3.1.1 PGM IV.3007–86

In the ritual in *PGM* IV.3007–86, the exorcist is instructed to prepare a mixture while reciting *voces mysticae*, write *voces mysticae* on a tin amulet and hang it on the possessed, and recite a long adjuration while facing the possessed. The adjuration—in fact a series of adjurations—is replete with allusions to important events in Jewish biblical and parabiblical narratives (*PGM* IV.3019–78).[16] The knowledge of Jewish lore in this litany is impressive

---

[12] R. W. Daniel (ed.), *Two Greek Magical Papyri in the National Museum of Antiquities in Leiden: A Photographic Edition of J 384 and J 395 (= PGM XII and XIII)* (Opladen: West-deutscher Verlag, 1991), 25; *PGM* XII.391 apparatus.

[13] Dieleman, *Priests, Tongues, and Rites*, 56–62.

[14] *PGM* IV.11–14 and PDM xiv.627–9; see F. Ll. Griffith and H. Thompson (eds), *The Demotic Magical Papyrus of London and Leiden* (London: H. Grevel, 1904), 134, for the relevant literature.

[15] F. Ll. Griffith, 'The Date of the Old Coptic Texts and their Relation to Christian Coptic', *ZAS*, 39 (1901), 78–82, <https://archive.org/stream/zeitschriftfr3639deutuoft#page/n529/mode/2up>.

[16] This exorcism has attracted considerable scholarly attention over the years. See, e.g., A. Deissmann, *Light from the Ancient East: The New Testament Illustrated by Recently*

within the overall repertoire of the extant manuals.[17] Most scholars agree, therefore, that the exorcism originated in a Jewish milieu, but that the text as we have it has been reworked by an 'outsider' impressed by the reputed power of Jewish rituals.[18] There are several indications of this, as others have noted. The exorcism is attributed to Pibechis, an Egyptian name that occurs frequently in lists of alchemists and which Preisendanz identified with the Egyptian magician Apollobex.[19] There are anomalous spellings or references that are difficult to attribute to a Jewish scribe even after allowing for the idiosyncratic character of long-standing Jewish communities in Egypt:[20] 'Israel' is spelled 'Osraêl' (*PGM* IV.3034), 'Hierosolyma' is spelled 'Hierosolymos' (*PGM* IV.3069), and the spirits associated with enemies of the Israelites in the land of Canaan are named 'Ebousaios or Chersaios or Pharaisios' (*PGM* IV.3044), appearing to confuse the 'Pherezaioi' of the Septuagint (LXX Gen. 15: 20–21; Exod. 3: 8, 17) with the 'Pharisaioi' of the gospels.[21] The recipient of the exorcism is enjoined not to eat pork (*PGM* IV.3079–80), one of the more commonly known, and thus stereotypical, Jewish prohibitions.[22] And the text concludes by asserting that 'the spell is Hebraic' (*PGM* IV.3084–5), the sort of additional explanation one expects of an 'outsider'.

Discovered Texts of the Graeco-Roman World, tr. L. R. M. Strachan from the 4th German edn (New York, 1927; repr. Peabody: Hendrickson, 1995), 260–3; W. L. Knox, 'Jewish Liturgical Exorcism', *HTR*, 31 (1938), 191–203, <http://www.jstor.org/stable/1508308>; S. Eitrem, *Some Notes on the Demonology in the New Testament*, 2nd edn (Oslo: Universitetsforlaget, 1966), 15–30; R. Kotansky, 'Greek Exorcistic Amulets', in M. Meyer and P. Mirecki (eds), *Ancient Magic and Ritual Power* (Leiden: Brill, 1995), 243–77 at 262–6; B. Kollmann, *Jesus und die Christen als Wundertäter: Studien zu Magie, Medizin und Schamanismus in Antike und Christentum* (Göttingen: Vandenhoeck and Ruprecht, 1996), 156–60; R. Merkelbach (ed.), *Abrasax: Ausgewählte Papyri religiösen und magischen Inhalts*, vol. 4: *Exorzismen und jüdisch/christlich beeinflusste Texte* (Cologne: Westdeutscher Verlag, 1996), 36–43. Observations from other studies are adduced in notes 17–18 and 20–2.

[17] M. Smith, 'Jewish Elements in the Magical Papyri', in S. J. D. Cohen (ed.), *Studies in the Cult of Yahweh: New Testament, Early Christianity, and Magic* (Leiden: Brill, 1996), 241–56 at 246–7, 249–52.

[18] E.g., Smith, 'Jewish Elements', 250; P. S. Alexander, 'Jewish Elements in Gnosticism and Magic *c.* CE 70–*c.* CE 270', in W. Horbury, W. D. Davies, and J. Sturdy (eds), *The Cambridge History of Judaism: The Early Roman Period* (Cambridge: Cambridge University Press, 1999), 1052–78 at 1073–4; P. W. van der Horst, 'The Great Magical Papyrus of Paris (PGM IV) and the Bible', in P. W. van der Horst (ed.), *Jews and Christians in their Graeco-Roman Context: Selected Essays on Early Judaism, Samaritanism, Hellenism, and Christianity* (Tübingen: Mohr Siebeck, 2006), 269–79 at 278–9; G. Bohak, *Ancient Jewish Magic: A History* (Cambridge: Cambridge University Press, 2008), 206–7.

[19] K. Preisendanz, 'Pibechis', *PW*, 20.1310–12.

[20] Smith, 'Jewish Elements', 242; van der Horst, 'The Great Magical Papyrus', 278.

[21] Deissmann, *Light from the Ancient East*, 261 n. 11; van der Horst, 'The Great Magical Papyrus', 275–6.

[22] L. LiDonnici, '"According to the Jews:" Identified (and Identifying) "Jewish" Elements in the *Greek Magical Papyri*', in L. LiDonnici and A. Lieber (eds), *Heavenly Tablets: Interpretation, Identity and Tradition in Ancient Judaism* (Leiden: Brill, 2007), 87–108 at 97–8.

The reference to 'the god of the Hebrews, Jesus' (*PGM* IV.3019–20) should be read in light of these permutations. Origen reports that the expression 'the god of the Hebrews', which figures in the biblical account of the Exodus,[23] was often used against demons.[24] Others would have known this as well. So while a Jewish 'insider' might use this phrase when writing for an 'outsider', it is also possible that an 'outsider' might use it to invoke the Jewish God, perhaps in an effort to serve a Jewish (or Christian) client.[25] If the phrase 'the god of the Hebrews, Jesus' was part of the original incantation, it would appear that its author was an 'outsider' to the traditional phraseology of not only Jews but also Christians. It is possible, of course, that 'Jesus' was inserted into the incantation at some later date, as some have suggested.[26] But this simply reveals that the redactor, rather than the author, judged the expression to be suitable and effective.[27] In the version preserved in the manual, we find a *nomen sacrum* for 'god' ($\overline{\theta v}$), as one sees elsewhere in the manuscript,[28] but not for 'Jesus'.[29] This suggests that the exemplar from which this recipe was copied was not written by someone familiar with Christian scribal conventions, though we must always allow for inconsistent application of those conventions.

3.1.2 PGM IV.1227–64

The second ritual for driving out demons, *PGM* IV.1227–64, gives an incantation that is to be recited over the head of the client, along with instructions on preparing a bundle of olive branches to be used when reciting the incantation and an amulet that is to be worn by the client after the demon has been cast out.[30] The incantation begins with an invocation and adjuration expressed in Coptic but written in Greek script (*PGM* IV.1231–9).[31] These Coptic lines were in all likelihood not part of the original Greek exorcism. (The Greek text reads fluently if these lines are removed.) The Coptic reads as follows:[32]

---

[23] Exod. 3: 18; 5: 3; 7: 16; 9: 1, 13; 10: 3.   [24] Origen, *Cels.* 4.34 (SC 136.270).

[25] As suggested by LiDonnici, '"According to the Jews"', 96–7, 107.

[26] E.g., Deissmann, *Light from the Ancient East*, 260 n. 4; Knox, 'Jewish Liturgical Exorcism', 193; Eitrem, *Some Notes*, 16.

[27] Van der Horst, 'The Great Magical Papyrus', 274.

[28] L. Traube, *Nomina Sacra: Versuch einer Geschichte der christliche Kürzung* (Munich: Beck, 1907), 38–40.

[29] By way of contrast, *nomina sacra* are used for the words 'God Jesus Christ' copied as *voces mysticae* in the Jewish formulary discussed by G. Bohak, 'Greek, Coptic, and Jewish Magic in the Cairo Genizah', *BASP*, 36 (1999), 27–44 at 35–6, <http://hdl.handle.net/2027/spo.0599796.0036. 001:03>.

[30] ET: *GMPT*, 62; *ACM*, no. 19.

[31] I follow the normalized reading of G. Möller at *PGM*, 1.115 n. 3; see the introductory note at *PGM*, 1.65–6.

[32] I am indebted to Jitse Dijkstra for advice on the translation and interpretation of this passage.

> Greetings, God of Abraham; greetings, God of Isaac; greetings, God of Jacob. Jesus Christ,[33] the Holy Spirit, the Son of the Father, who is above the seven,[34] who is in the seven. Bring Iaô Sabaôth; let your (pl.) power go away (out?) from NN until you (pl.) drive away this unclean demon, Satan, who is upon him.

This passage presents a number of interpretative difficulties that are hard to resolve for lack of context. What should we make of the juxtaposition of 'the God of Abraham, the God of Isaac, and the God of Jacob', often invoked in incantations,[35] with 'Jesus Christ, the Holy Spirit, the Son of the Father'? What, in turn, should we make of the juxtaposition of these latter three names? They could issue from an early christological tradition that does not distinguish sharply between the Son and the Holy Spirit. One sees such fluidity in, for instance, writings of Hermas,[36] which were read in Egypt already in the second century.[37] Then, if the expression 'above the seven' refers to Jesus' position above the seven planetary spheres that regulate earthly phenomena,[38] which seems warranted by traditions that describe Jesus ascending to the seventh heaven,[39] what is meant by saying that he is also 'in the seven'? Finally, how exactly should one construe the Coptic of the concluding command? It has been translated in various ways so as to make sense.[40]

[33] On 'Christ' spelt with an *eta*, see W. M. Shandruk, 'The Interchange of ι and η in Spelling χριστ- in Documentary Papyri', *BASP*, 47 (2010), 205–19 at 211, <http://hdl.handle.net/2027/spo.0599796.0047.001:16>. The variant spelling is attested, for instance, in Valentinian writings preserved in the Nag Hammadi codices; see *Le Traité Tripartite (NH I, 5)*, ed. E. Thomassen, BCNH, section Textes 19 (Québec: Les Presses de l'Université Laval, 1989), 435. In view of what follows immediately—'the Holy Spirit, the Son of the Father'—I think it unlikely that ⲡⲓⲭⲣⲏⲥⲧⲟⲥ should be read as 'the excellent one', as suggested at *GMPT* 62 n. 168; M. J. Edwards, 'Χρηστος in a Magical Papyrus', *ZPE*, 85 (1991), 232–6 at 234, <http://www.uni-koeln.de/phil-fak/ifa/zpe/downloads/1991/085pdf/085.html>; Merkelbach, *Abrasax*, 4.62.

[34] I read 'above the seven' (with *GMPT*, 62, and Merkelbach, *Abrasax*, 4.62), not 'below the seven' (as in *PGM*, 1.115, and *ACM*, no. 19); see W. E. Crum, *A Coptic Dictionary* (Oxford: At the Clarendon Press, 1939), *s.v.* ϩⲣⲁⲓ (at p. 698b under ⲥⲁϩⲣⲁⲓ).

[35] Origen, *Cels.* 4.33 (SC 136.266–8), remarks on the widespread invocation of 'the God of Abraham, the God of Isaac, and the God of Jacob' in incantations and magical books. For other references, see M. Rist, 'The God of Abraham, Isaac, and Jacob: A Liturgical and Magical Formula', *JBL*, 57 (1938), 289–303.

[36] See, e.g., Hermas, *Sim.* 5.6.1–7 (GCS 49.56–7), with C. Osiek, *Shepherd of Hermas: A Commentary* (Minneapolis: Fortress, 1999), 179–81.

[37] On the early circulation in Egypt of writings by Hermas, see now R. S. Bagnall, *Early Christian Books in Egypt* (Princeton: Princeton University Press, 2009), 40–8. For a list of extant witnesses, see the Leuven Database of Ancient Books, <http://www.trismegistos.org/ldab/index.php>, 'Hermas' as author, accessed 17 May 2016.

[38] On the planetary spheres, see W. Hübner, 'Planets. II. Astrology and Mythology', *BNP*, 11.328–34 at 331–3.

[39] See, e.g., *PGM* P13.8–9: 'who has gone up to the seventh heaven' (ὁ ἀνελθὼν εἰς τὸν ἕβδομον οὐρανόν), with A. T. Mihálykó, 'Christ and Charon: PGM P13 Reconsidered', *SO*, 89 (2016), 183–209 at 196, doi: 10.1080/00397679.2015.1108051.

[40] *PGM* 1.115: 'möge eure Kraft fort sein von NN, bis ihr vertreibt diesen unreinen Dämon'; *GMPT*, 62: 'may your power issue forth from him, NN, until you drive away this unclean daimon' (similarly, *ACM*, no. 19); Merkelbach, *Abrasax*, 4.59: 'Möge eure Kraft sich ereignen weg von N.N., möget ihr vertreiben diesen unreinen Dämon'.

Alongside such questions of interpretation are questions about the origin and transmission of the passage. From what sort of Christian milieu did the Coptic passage issue? How did it come to be inserted into the exorcism? Was it inserted because of some affiliation or knowledge of the scribe or to serve the need of a particular client? What accounts for the irregular spellings of Coptic words in Greek script? Was this the work of a Greek writer who was not a native speaker of Coptic, or of a Greek writer who was attempting to render in Greek a formula known to him orally in Coptic? Did the passage undergo further changes in the course of the exorcism's transmission? Was it present in the other example to which the compiler of the manual refers (*PGM* IV.1261–3), the one with an amulet bearing the sign of Chnoubis rather than a series of *voces mysticae*?[41] How did these particular examples of the exorcism come into the possession of this compiler? Those well versed in early Coptic will be in a better position to answer these questions than I am. But we would like to know more, since this is a rare early example of not only the intersection between customary and Christian forms of incantation, but also the intersection between Greek scribes and Coptic speech—one that pre-dated the fourth century, if we assume that the recipes collected in the manual were in existence prior to being gathered and copied.

3.2 FRAGMENTARY GREEK COLLECTIONS

The large manuals we have just discussed are extraordinary for having been preserved intact. We also have a number of fragments from rolls or codices, as well as individual sheets, with recipes for procedures or incantations.[42] Usually these materials are the remains of a manual. Sometimes someone appears to have recorded just a few recipes for their own use or reference.[43] For the most part, these materials lack any Christian elements, a point that is noteworthy in itself. But there are a few exceptions.

3.2.1 A Transposed Litany

P.Berol. inv. 17202,[44] a fragmentary sheet of papyrus that has been assigned to the fourth century, preserves six recipes separated from each other by horizontal

---

[41] See *GMPT*, 62 n. 170.

[42] E.g., from the fourth century and later, *SM* II 86, 88, 90, 93, 94, 95, 96, 97, 98, 99.

[43] E.g., *PGM* LXV, *SM* II 89 (*O.Ashm.Shelt.* 194).

[44] W. M. Brashear and R. Kotansky, 'A New Magical Formulary', in P. Mirecki and M. Meyer (eds), *Magic and Ritual in the Ancient World* (Leiden: Brill, 2002), 3–24.

lines, a common device used to demarcate entries in a manual or collection.[45] The editors concluded that all the recipes were written by a single scribe, but over a period of time, since the writing varies in style and size: the first four recipes are written in a semi-cursive hand which slopes slightly to the right, whereas the fifth and sixth recipes are written with lighter ink in a smaller cursive hand.[46] (The fourth recipe also is separated from the fifth by two horizontal lines rather than one.) The collection is eclectic. It includes the litany, an incantation to silence opponents, a hymnic invocation, an adjuration against a thief, a procedure to get an erection (or dispel fleas?), and a procedure involving a stele.

The litany is evidently Christian in substance and phraseology, echoing language found in patristic literature and later Byzantine manuals.[47] The transcript employs *nomina sacra* for 'Jesus Christ' as well as 'Lord',[48] unlike *PGM* IV.3019–20, suggesting that the text originated at some point with a scribe familiar with Christian conventions. In the course of transmission, errors were introduced by a copyist who misread cursive characters,[49] such that certain phrases no longer make sense.[50] Although traces of the structure of the original litany can be seen in the interlinear lines of the present text, that structure is no longer clearly preserved. As reconstructed by the editors of the papyrus, the original litany may have read as follows (the line numbers of the text as written on the papyrus are given in parentheses):[51]

VERSICLE: 'The one having lo[osed] the one punished [. . .]' (line 2)

RESPONSORY: *'Lord by your command to men . . .'* (line 1a, written between lines 1 and 2)

VERSICLE: 'And the one having sent for his only begot- | ten child . . .' (lines 3–4)

RESPONSORY: *'As you have willed it . . .'* (line 4a, written between lines 4 and 5)

VERSICLE: 'And having indwelled the womb of the Vir- | gin . . .' (lines 4–5)

RESPONSORY: *'The race of humans has not been able to discover the nature of your birth, Lord Jesus Christ . . .'* (lines 5–7)

---

[45] See Chapter 2 n. 75.

[46] Brashear and Kotansky, 'A New Magical Formulary', 6. Image at <http://smb.museum/berlpap/index.php/04194> (Berliner Papyrusdatenbank).

[47] The expressions 'only-begotten child' (ὁ μονογενὴς παῖς) and 'from the Virgin's womb' (ἐκ λαγόνων παρθενικῶν) are, for instance, attested in patristic literature; see G. H. E. Lampe (ed.), *A Greek Patristic Lexicon* (Oxford: At the Clarendon Press, 1961), *s.v.* παῖς 2; λαγών 3. See also the Byzantine parallels to phrases in the litany adduced by the editors in their comments.

[48] Line 1a: κε (without a supralinear stroke, contrary to the reading of the first edition); line 7: κε Ῑϲ Χ̄ϲ; line 11: κε.

[49] Brashear and Kotansky, 'New Magical Formulary', 7.

[50] See, e.g., Brashear and Kotansky, 'New Magical Formulary', 13–14 (line 1 comm.), 21 (lines 23–4 comm.).

[51] Brashear and Kotansky, 'New Magical Formulary', 10–12.

VERSICLE: 'The one having walked upon the waters, not having sullied his feet.' (lines 7–8)

'The one having from five loaves filled five-thousand men...' (lines 9–10)

RESPONSORY: *'For all have obeyed your command, O Lord...'* (lines 10–11)

'Come, by your mercy, to me, a sinner...' (line 12)

It is evident from other recipes in the collection that the scribe transcribed words without understanding their meaning.[52] Thus, we have here an instance of a scribe collecting incantations deemed to be powerful without entirely understanding the import of those incantations. What is more, the collection shows that Christian liturgical materials had begun to circulate among such scribes already in the fourth century, if the date assigned to the papyrus is correct.

3.2.2 A Multilingual Collection

A group of papyri in the collection of the University of Milan, of unknown provenance but found together, is especially interesting for a number of reasons. The group comprises a short codex written in Coptic,[53] a section of a roll and a large number of fragments written mainly in Greek (*SM* II 96–8),[54] and several fragments written in Aramaic.[55] The codex contains three incantations written by a single scribe. The roll preserves fourteen sections of a manual (*SM* II 96 A), separated from one another by a horizontal line. The first four sections of this manual contain *voces mysticae*, *charaktêres*, names, and figures. The remaining sections consist of short prescriptions. Several of the Greek fragments repeat text found on the roll (*SM* II 96 B–F). Some of these fragments are written by the scribe who wrote the roll, others not. On the back of two Greek fragments (*SM* II 98, nos. 2, 6) there is writing in Aramaic. Thus, the entire group of papyri, which have been assigned to the fifth or sixth century,[56] is the work of a multilingual group of scribes. What is more, the scribes not only copied materials in multiple languages, but occasionally also drew on a common fund of techniques: in the Coptic codex and in another fragmentary Greek manual that was part of the find (*SM* II 97), the scribes drew an identical figure with its hands raised behind its head (not an

---

[52] Brashear and Kotansky, 'New Magical Formulary', 7, 21–3.

[53] S. Pernigotti, 'Il codice copto', *SCO*, 29 (1979), 19–53; re-edited in S. Pernigotti, 'Una rilettura del P.Mil. Vogl. Copto 16', *Aegyptus*, 73 (1993), 93–125, <http://www.jstor.org/stable/41217102> (TM 102252).

[54] F. Maltomini, 'I papiri greci', *SCO*, 29 (1979), 55–124, republished in *SM* II 96–8.

[55] P. Marrassini, 'I frammenti aramaici', *SCO*, 29 (1979), 125–30.

[56] Pernigotti, 'Una rilettura', 96; Maltomini, 'I papiri greci', 55.

orans), surmounted by the same seven *charaktêres*.[57] In the Greek manual it is clear that the drawing refers to the figurine described in the surrounding text.

Among the mix of idioms in these materials, by now common in Graeco-Egyptian manuals, there are a few Christian elements. The most obvious one occurs in the short prescriptions in the Greek manual. It is a recipe to ease the birth of a child: 'For a woman in labor. "Come out of your tomb, Christ is calling you." A potsherd on the right thigh.'[58] The injunction to be written on the sherd alludes to Jesus' summoning of Lazarus from his tomb (John 11: 43), with whom the baby is here identified. In later Byzantine and medieval manuscripts one finds similar prescriptions where Christ's summoning of the baby is associated with Elizabeth giving birth to John, Mary giving birth to Jesus, or Lazarus emerging from his tomb.[59] Presumably this remedy for childbirth was already in circulation before it made its way into this particular collection, its earliest known attestation. One wonders how it came to the attention of this group of practitioners.

In addition, the first incantation in the Coptic codex has a row of eleven staurograms followed by a *beta* (line 2), placed between a row of twelve *omegas* on the line above and a row of eleven *betas* and a *delta* on the line below. The remainder of the incantation consists of names of powers, written in two columns with seven names each. The purpose of the incantation is not stated. The number of staurograms is unusual, both in this particular incantation, where one would expect twelve,[60] and in general, since staurograms or crosses typically appear at the beginning of a text singly or in sets of three or seven.[61] We cannot know what the staurograms signified for the scribe. But we should note that this device has here entered the scribal repertoire, whereas it is absent from the manuals discussed in Section 3.1.

3.2.3 A Therapeutic Miscellany

A different mode of collection is suggested by a papyrus sheet from Oxy-rhynchus, *P.Oxy.* XI 1384,[62] assigned to the fifth or sixth century.[63] It records

---

[57] Pernigotti, 'Una rilettura', 95 n. 9, with image at 101; *SM* II 97 intro., with image at Maltomini, 'I papiri greci', plate VII. See now J. H. F. Dijkstra, 'The Interplay between Image and Text on Greek Amulets Containing Christian Elements from Late Antique Egypt', in D. Boschung and J. M. Bremmer (eds), *The Materiality of Magic* (Munich: Wilhelm Fink, 2015), 271–92 at 287.

[58] *SM* II 96A.48–50.

[59] *SM* II 96 A.48–50 comm. On such narrative precedents or *historiolae*, see n. 64.

[60] Pernigotti, 'Una rilettura', 98 nn. 9 and 10.   [61] See Chapter 2 n. 149.

[62] Since *PGM* P7 republished only lines 15 to 29 (the two legends), I retain only *P.Oxy.* XI 1384 as the identifier. The papyrus has been re-edited by R. Mazza, 'P.Oxy. XI, 1384: medicina, rituali di guarigione e cristianesimi nell'Egitto tardoantico', *ASE*, 24/2 (2007), 437–62 at 438–43. However, the first edition should still be consulted to ascertain readings because the papyrus subsequently suffered loss of material.

[63] *P.Oxy.* XI 1384 intro. favours the fifth century over the sixth; Mazza, 'P.Oxy. XI, 1384', 439, argues for the fifth or sixth century. Image at <http://special.lib.gla.ac.uk/teach/papyrus/oxyrhynchus.html> (Glasgow University Library, Special Collections).

three medical recipes and two healing legends or *historiolae*. (A *historiola* is a short narrative about a mythic or heroic figure that conveys power by way of analogy to address some present need; *historiolae* often appear in incantations.[64]) The three medicinal recipes—for a laxative, for difficulty in urinating, and for healing wounds—use ingredients that, according to ancient pharmacological treatises, were reputed to have the requisite medicinal properties.[65] The scribe, therefore, was cataloguing remedies that had a basis in traditional medical practice. Alongside these remedies the scribe includes two *historiolae*:

> [...] men met us in the desert [and said to the Lord] Jesus, 'What treatment is possible for the sick?' And he says to them, '[I have] given olive oil and have poured out myrrh [for those] who believe in the [name of the] Father and the Holy [Spirit and the] Son.'

> Angels of the Lord ascended to [mid]-heaven, suffering from eye ailments and holding a sponge. The Lord says [to them], 'Why have you ascended, O holy, all-pure ones?' 'We have come up to receive healing, O Iaô Sabaôth, because you are powerful and strong.'[66]

The first narrative has peaked the interest of scholars on account of the unorthodox order of the persons of the Trinity,[67] for which parallels can be found in various ancient sources:[68] Syriac Christian texts; the *Gospel to the Hebrews*,[69] believed to issue from a Jewish Christian Egyptian milieu;[70] Sethian treatises in the Nag Hammadi corpus, such as the *Apocryphon of John* and the *Gospel of the Egyptians*;[71] and Manichaean writings.[72] Whatever the origin of these two narratives,[73] they have been received by the present scribe as effective remedies.

The writer precedes each of the remedies with a staurogram with a curl descending from the right end of the crossbar (⳨), as the first editors

---

[64] See D. Frankfurter, 'Narrating Power: The Theory and Practice of the Magical *historiola* in Ritual Spells', in Meyer and Mirecki, *Ancient Magic and Ritual Power*, 457–76; T. S. de Bruyn, 'Christian Apocryphal and Canonical Narratives in Greek Papyrus Amulets in Late Antiquity', in P. Piovanelli and T. Burke (eds), *Rediscovering the Apocryphal Continent: New Perspectives on Early Christian and Late Antique Apocryphal Texts and Traditions* (Tübingen: Mohr Siebeck, 2015), 153–74.

[65] On the ingredients for the laxative, see R. Bélanger Sarrazin, 'Le syncrétisme en Égypte dans l'Antiquité tardive: l'apport des papyrus iatromagiques grecs', MA thesis, Université d'Ottawa, Ottawa, 2015, 79 and table 7, <http://www.ruor.uottawa.ca/handle/10393/32836>. On the remedy for difficulty in urinating, see P. Mayerson, 'An Additional Note on Ascalon Wine (P. Oxy. 1384)', *IEJ*, 45 (1995), 190, <http://www.jstor.org/stable/27926389>; Bélanger Sarrazin, 'Le syncrétisme', 79. On cypress leaves in a poultice for wounds, see Dioscorides, *De materia medica* 1.74.2, ed. M. Wellmann, 3 vols (Berlin: Weidmann, 1958), 1.74.

[66] ET: *ACM*, no. 4 (modified).   [67] E.g., *P.Oxy.* XI 1384 intro.

[68] Mazza, 'P.Oxy. XI, 1384', 449–50.

[69] A. F. J. Klijn, *Jewish-Christian Gospel Traditions* (Leiden: Brill, 1992), 52–5.

[70] Klijn, *Jewish-Christian*, 30.

[71] J. D. Turner, *Sethian Gnosticism and the Platonic Tradition* (Leuven: Peters, 2001), 63–4, 70–3.

[72] T. Pettipiece, 'Towards a Manichaean Reading of the Nag Hammadi Codices', *JCSCS*, 3–4 (2012), 43–54 at 45–9.

[73] See Mazza, 'P.Oxy. XI, 1384', 444, 450.

observed. Since it was a common practice among scribes writing in a Christian milieu to precede the first line of a document with a cross or staurogram,[74] the fact that the writer uses the staurogram in this way here does not reveal a great deal about him personally. Still, it shows that he wrote in an environment where such use of the staurogram was a convention; it places him at least formally in the company of those who wrote amulets consisting of a series of biblical and liturgical passages, each preceded by a cross.[75]

3.3 COPTIC MANUALS

In Coptic manuals of procedures and incantations we see the continuing vitality of long-standing Graeco-Egyptian traditions alongside newer and diverse Christian traditions. The confluence sometimes results in elaborate syncretistic incantations of considerable length which attest, indirectly, to the ongoing exercise of individuality in the transmission of a practice.[76] A few manuals believed to have been written in the period with which this book is concerned offer some insights into the nature and context of this ongoing transmission. I have selected four examples that manifest, first, no Christian elements, then only formal Christian elements, and finally, in the last two instances, substantive Christian elements. They are roughly contemporaneous, having been assigned to the last centuries of the Roman period.

3.3.1 A Bilingual Coptic-Greek Manual

A parchment codex in the collection of the University of Michigan Library, Ms. Copt. 136, is an example of the textual transmission of Graeco-Egyptian incantations and remedies for medical concerns.[77] The codex was purchased in Medinet el-Fayum and is believed to have come from the vicinity.[78] It is written in a practiced hand,[79] which William Worrell assigned to the sixth century on account of the occurrence of a Bohairic abbreviation for 'God', ⲫ︦ϯ.[80]

---

[74] See Chapter 2 n. 143.   [75] E.g., *BKT* VI 7.1; see Section 5.2.

[76] E.g., London, British Library, Or. Ms. 6794; 6795; 6796 (2), (3), (1); 6796 (4), 6796, in *AKZ* 1, nos. E–J; ET: *ACM*, nos. 129–32.

[77] W. H. Worrell, 'Coptic Magical and Medical Texts', *Orientalia*, 4 (1935), 1–37 at 17–37, <http://www.jstor.org/stable/43581034>; ET: *ACM*, no. 43.

[78] Worrell, 'Coptic Magical', 1.

[79] Image at <http://www.lib.umich.edu/online-exhibits/exhibits/show/translating-homer-from-papyri/item/3917?exhibit=82&page=226> (University of Michigan Library Online Exhibits).

[80] Worrell, 'Coptic Magical', 17, 29 n. 3, on ⲕⲁⲧⲁⲫ︦ϯ (line 29), translated '(the condition) from God' at *ACM*, p. 84.

The Coptic, whose dialect is Sahidic, presents numerous difficulties.[81] A portion of the manual was translated into Coptic from Greek, and several portions were left untranslated. The ailments and illnesses addressed by the manual are numerous and varied: swollen eyelids, teething pains, headache, earache, chills, fevers, abdominal problems, pregnancy, constipation, mental illness, malignancy, skin disease, hip pain, and foot disease. Many of the remedies consist only of material ingredients that are to be ingested or applied topically. Some remedies are accompanied by an incantation. There are a few non-medical incantations, such as a Coptic incantation for favour (a *charitêsion*) that replicates earlier Greek versions of this type of incantation.[82] In short, the manual is an example of the continuing salience of Graeco-Egyptian incantations and remedies in a bilingual Greek and Coptic milieu. There are no Christian elements in the text.

3.3.2 The Michigan 'Hoard'

A remarkable group of Coptic manuscripts, also in the collection of the University of Michigan, reveals more about how manuals might have been copied and used. It consists of twelve manuscripts:[83] a codex of ten leaves (twenty pages) with two texts written by three practiced scribes, one tending toward a book hand (P.Mich. inv. 593);[84] a scroll (P.Mich. inv. 602) with four texts written by a practiced scribe in a more fluid, irregular hand, and fragments from two other scrolls written by that same scribe (P.Mich. inv. 600 and 601); and eight papyrus sheets written with five texts resembling parts of the previous two sources, written in a unpracticed, uncontrolled hand (P.Mich. inv. 594, 595, 596, 597, 598, 599, 603, and 1294).[85] The texts in the codex and the texts in the scrolls do not duplicate one another, but the fifth scribe appears to have copied from both of these other longer sources (or a

---

[81] Worrell, 'Coptic Magical', 17; *ACM*, p. 83.

[82] Lines 115–24; see, for a comparable incantation, *PGM* VII.1017–26, and T. S. de Bruyn, 'An Anatomy of Tradition: The Case of the *Charitêsion*', *ARG*, 16 (2015), 31–50 at 43, doi: 10.1515/arege-2014-0005.

[83] For a description of the manuscripts, see W. H. Worrell, 'A Coptic Wizard's Hoard', *AJSL*, 46 (1930), 239–62 at 239–40, <http://www.jstor.org/stable/529100>; P. Mirecki, 'The Coptic Wizard's Hoard', *HTR*, 87 (1994), 435–60 at 437–9, <http://www.jstor.org/stable/1509968>, summarized at *ACM*, pp. 294–6.

[84] ET: *ACM*, no. 133; Mirecki, 'The Coptic Wizard's Hoard', 440–50, with notes.

[85] The last of these items, inv. 1294, is not included in Worrell's inventory; it was discovered in a fragmentary state and restored by Mirecki. Selected images at <http://quod.lib.umich.edu/a/apis?page=index> (Advanced Papyrological Information System at the University of Michigan), searched by inventory number. Additional images of P.Mich. inv. 593 at <http://www.lib.umich.edu/online-exhibits/exhibits/show/puzzle-me-this–early-binding-/a-text-on-medicine—magic> (University of Michigan Library Online Exhibits).

common source).[86] Among the papyri written by the fifth scribe is an amulet (inv. 1294) that was copied either from the large scroll (inv. 602) or a common source. It indicates that collections like the one found in the large scroll were used to prepare individual applied amulets.[87] It is unclear whether all these texts were copied around the same time or whether the collection grew over time. (Opinion as to the dates of the hands has varied, ranging from the fourth to the seventh century.[88]) It is evident, however, that multiple scribes had an interest in collecting and applying these texts.

The first, longer text in the codex consists of an extended prayer, some ritual instructions, a list of thirty-two prescriptions for a broad array of physical, psychological, and daily concerns, and some concluding instructions and ritual preparations. The second, shorter text has nine lines of *voces mysticae*, an invocation, and ninety-five lines of *voces mysticae*. In the extended prayer of the first text, the speaker repeatedly identifies with 'Seth, the son of Adam'.[89] Such 'I am' statements are common in Graeco-Egyptian incantations; the speaker assumes a divine or quasi-divine status so that the adjured powers will do as they are bid.[90] The revelations Seth has received and the names he knows give him authority over the twenty-one angels who are adjured in the prayer to do the speaker's bidding. When the practitioner recites this prayer over the media named in the ensuing prescriptions, they are empowered to alleviate the specified problem. There are no explicit Christian references in this prayer, but the cosmology it evokes in appealing to God 'the almighty one' (ⲡⲡⲁⲛⲧⲟⲕⲣⲁⲧⲱⲣ), surrounded by angels or powers who do his work and service,[91] would not have been foreign to Christians. As well, the use of water and oil in many of the prescriptions indicates that customary remedies might not be all that different from those that, according to hagiographical sources, Christian monks gave out.[92] Moreover, we should note that the three components of the second text are demarcated by staurograms: seven precede the first set of *voces mysticae* (opening the text), one precedes the prayer, and three follow the second set of *voces mysticae* (closing the text).[93] We can take this as evidence that the scribe was familiar with what had become a conventional use of the staurogram in Christian milieux. But again, it tells us little about the individuality of the scribe, as we can see from the copies made by the fifth, unpracticed scribe, who replicates the staurograms.[94]

<hr/>

[86] Worrell, 'A Coptic Wizard's Hoard', 242–54, gives a reconstructed, composite text. See, however, the *caveat* at *ACM*, p. 295, on the relationship of the short texts to the texts in the codex and the scrolls.

[87] Mirecki, 'The Coptic Wizard's Hoard', 439.

[88] Worrell, 'A Coptic Wizard's Hoard', 240; Mirecki, 'The Coptic Wizard's Hoard', 435 n. 2.

[89] Lines 1.15–2.1, 3.11, 4.1–2; see Mirecki, 'The Coptic Wizard's Hoard', 455–6.

[90] H. Thyen, 'Ich-Bin-Worte', *RAC*, 17.147–213 at 205–9.

[91] Lines 1.1–12; see Mirecki, 'The Coptic Wizard's Hoard', 455–6.

[92] See Chapter 1 nn. 105–6, 119.   [93] P.Mich. inv. 593, pp. 12.6, 13.1, 20.16.

[94] P.Mich. inv. 603r.6, 13.

3.3.3 A Manual Incorporating a Sethian Invocation

The text we have just discussed does not appear to owe its personification of 'Seth, son of Adam' to the more elaborate Sethian tradition found in tractates in the Nag Hammadi codices and other writings.[95] This more elaborate Sethian tradition does, however, surface in other Coptic incantations, including an incantation in a recently edited manual in the collection of Macquarie University, *P.Macq.* I. The editors suggest that this codex was written in the seventh or eighth century.[96] Like the previous manuals, it consists of invocations or prayers, ritual instructions, a series of prescriptions, and a closing.

The text of the invocations is particularly long and complex. The editors conclude from parallels in manuscripts held in London and Berlin,[97] as well as internal evidence, that the text had an extended redaction history and probably circulated independently of the prescriptions.[98] The text exhibits a number of the most characteristic features of Sethian works,[99] but several sections of the text have undergone, in the editors' words, 'secondary Christianization'.[100] In these passages we move beyond the brief Christian references noted in the previous manuals to more substantial Christian material, as in this description of the 'perfect living Man': 'He was sent for us to the world; he gave his blood on behalf of the living and the dead, that he would redeem us from our sins.'[101] The degree of 'christianization' in the three witnesses to the text varies; it is less pronounced in the Macquarie manuscript than in the London and Berlin manuscripts.[102] The latter two also demarcate components of the text with staurograms,[103] whereas in the Macquarie manuscript the device is not used.

As the editors observe,[104] these three exemplars illustrate the shape that a particular liturgical or soteriological tradition—in this case, a Sethian tradition—could take in the course of its transmission, being subject not only to 'christianization' but also misunderstanding or garbling. The exemplars also illustrate the varied uses to which such incantations were put by practitioners, since in the London manuscript the invocations are a preamble to a short set of ritual instructions culminating in the words, 'this is the

---

[95] P. Mirecki, 'The Figure of Seth in a Coptic Magical Text', in T. Orlandi and D. W. Johnson (eds), *Acts of the Fifth International Congress of Coptic Studies, Washington, 12–15 August 1992*, 2 vols in 3 (Rome: C. I. M., 1993), 2.313–27.

[96] *P.Macq.* I, pp. 2–3.

[97] *P.Lond.Copt.* I 1008 (London, British Library, Or. Ms. 5987) and *BKU* I 23, re-edited (with English translations) in *P.Macq.* I, Appendix 1 and 2 (respectively).

[98] *P.Macq.* I, p. 9.   [99] *P.Macq.* I, pp. 31–5.

[100] *P.Macq.* I 1.13–22, 8.27–9.21, with pp. 12, 33–4.

[101] *P.Macq.* I 1.20–2; ET: *P.Macq.* I, p. 45.   [102] *P.Macq.* I, pp. 19, 21–2.

[103] *P.Lond.Copt.* I 1008.1, 134, 136, 152; *BKU* I 23.1, 5, 7.   [104] *P.Macq.* I, p. 35.

phylactery you should bind upon your right forearm',[105] while in the Berlin manuscript the invocations stand on their own.

3.3.4 A Buried Manual

We conclude this brief survey with a manual that is of interest as much for its find-spot as for its contents.[106] It was found buried in a jar in the floor of a monk's cave near the monastery Deir el-Bakhit in western Thebes,[107] one of several monasteries in the region,[108] active from the late sixth century to the early tenth century.[109] The writing has been assigned to the sixth century.[110] Like the previous manuals, it consists of an extended invocation followed by a series of prescriptions. Sections of the text are preceded by a staurogram.[111] The invocation opens with a series of angel names (to be recited three times), followed by a series of other powers and *voces mysticae* (to be recited seven times) that ends with a reference to the Christian Trinity: 'the Father, the Son, and the Holy Spirit, amen'. The collection ends with additional *voces mysticae*, a drawing of two roosters (upside down), and two *charaktêres*. In the larger of the two roosters is written the *nomen sacrum* for 'Jesus Christ' (upside right) and the word 'God' (upside down, to the left of the feet of the rooster).[112]

If this manual was among the possessions of a monk, as its find-spot suggests, it confirms that monks might own manuals consisting largely of Graeco-Egyptian recipes with few, if any, Christian references. It also reveals that the nature of the 'christianization' of this material may have been unimportant to its owner. At the same time, the fact that the manual was buried in a hermit's cave is suggestive. We do not find manuals of this sort among the remains of late antique monastic libraries, which consisted almost entirely of biblical, liturgical, homiletical, canonical, and hagiographical works, along with some educational works.[113] There is a parallel instance in a hermitage

---

[105] *P.Lond.Copt.* I 1008.158–9. ET: *P.Macq.* I, p. 112; *ACM*, no. 70.

[106] *AKZ* 1, no. K (Cairo, Egyptian Museum, Journal d'entrée, 45060); ET: *ACM*, no. 128.

[107] *AKZ* 1.50, with plate III for a photo of the jar; H. E. Winlock and W. E. Crum (eds), *The Monastery of Epiphanius at Thebes, Part I* (New York: Metropolitan Museum of Art, 1926), 21, 207, and plate I for the location of the cave.

[108] T. G. Wilfong, *Women of Jeme: Lives in a Coptic Town in Late Antique Egypt* (Ann Arbor: University of Michigan Press, 2002), 6–7.

[109] On the monastery of Deir el-Bakhit, see Winlock and Crum, *The Monastery of Epiphanius, Part I*, 21–2; R.-G. Coquin, M. Martin, and P. Grossmann, 'Dayr al-Bakhit', *CE*, 3.785–6.

[110] Winlock and Crum, *The Monastery of Epiphanius, Part I*, 207 n. 5; *AKZ* 1.xi.

[111] Lines 1, 15, 25, 80, 82. [112] Drawing at *AKZ*, 1.54; *ACM*, p. 273.

[113] For books held by monasteries, see Winlock and Crum, *The Monastery of Epiphanius, Part I*, 196–208; J. M. Robinson, *The Pachomian Monastery Library at the Chester Beatty Library and the Bibliothèque Bodmer* (Claremont: The Institute for Antiquity and Christianity, The Claremont Graduate School, 1990); T. Orlandi, 'The Library of the Monastery of Saint Shenute at Atripe', in A. Egberts, B. P. Muhs, and J. van der Vliet (eds), *Perspectives on Panopolis: An*

in the monastic complex at Naqlun in the Fayum, located about a kilometre to the north-east of the current monastery.[114] The hermitage was occupied in the second half of the fifth century by a few monks who were literate, bilingual, and of some means, to judge by the texts and objects found on the site.[115] The finds include fragments from what appears to have been a collection of healing prescriptions (most of which are written in Coptic, one in Greek), as well as texts with an aggressive purpose.[116] One of these is an incantation that invokes three great angels to bring shame and misfortune on a rival, drawing on Graeco-Egyptian astral angelology for the names and configuration of the angels.[117]

3.4 CONCLUSION

The manuals that have survived from late antique Egypt are among the most valuable sources we have for understanding the culture of the scribes who took the trouble to compile these collections, copy them, and apply the recipes contained in them. They attest to an abiding interest in some quarters in the *textual* transmission of speech that would grant the speaker authority and control over an array of spiritual powers so as to be able to empower substances and direct affairs toward a desired end. Although the incantations, inscriptions, and concoctions admit of seemingly endless variation, the structure of the practice is remarkably stable: the practitioner recites an incantation over a preparation and/or inscribes it on an object that then is ingested, applied, or worn. The practice was not rigid or fixed: the manuals themselves suggest that practitioners could improvise—and demonstrate their expertise—when reciting an incantation or assembling a preparation. Instances in the material record where a device corresponds exactly to a recipe are in fact rare.[118] Moreover, when one compares the

Egyptian Town from Alexander the Great to the Arab Conquest (Leiden: Brill, 2002), 211–31 at 225; S. Emmel, 'The Library of the Monastery of the Archangel Michael at Phantoou (al-Hamuli)', in G. Gabra (ed.), *Christianity and Monasticism in the Fayoum Oasis* (Cairo: American University in Cairo Press, 2005), 63–70 at 64–5; S. G. Richter, 'Wadi al-Natrun and Coptic Literature', in M. S. A. Mikhail and M. Moussa (eds), *Christianity and Monasticism in Wadi al-Natrun* (Cairo: American University in Cairo Press, 2009), 43–62 at 48. See also n. 3.

[114] W. Godlewski, 'Naqlun: Excavations 1997', *PAM*, 9 (1998), 77–86 at 77–83, <http://www.pcma.uw.edu.pl/en/pam-journal/spisy-tresci/pam-1998-x>. For the site as a whole, see *P.Naqlun* II, pp. 5–6, with the map after p. viii.

[115] J. van der Vliet, 'Les anges du soleil: à propos d'un texte magique copte récemment découvert à Deir en-Naqloun (N. 45/95)', in N. Bosson (ed.), *Études coptes VII: neuvième journée d'études, Montpellier 3–4 juin 1999* (Leuven: Peeters, 2000), 319–37 at 319–20.

[116] Van der Vliet, 'Les anges du soleil', 320–1.

[117] Van der Vliet, 'Les anges du soleil', 322–37.

[118] Brashear, 'Greek Magical Papyri', 3416–18.

Theban manuals with the Coptic manuals, one can see that incantations have evolved in structure and language. Thus, the manuals demonstrate both transmission and development of Graeco-Egyptian practice during the period of Christian institutional expansion.

From the manuals and related finds we also glean information about how the scribes who copied or used these collections worked. In some instances, scribes worked together or drew on one another, as in the cluster of Greek, Coptic, and Aramaic materials now held in Milan or the codex, scroll, and fragments in the collection of the University of Michigan. In other instances, there is no evidence that the scribe belonged to a group or operated out of a 'workshop'. Nevertheless, in all cases the scribes worked with pre-existing resources. In the narrowest, most concrete sense, these resources included written exemplars of procedures (as attested by multiple copies of a recipe or collection) and specific elements in a procedure (as evidenced by the identical figure with a line of *charaktêres*). In a broader sense, the resources included traditions of incantation (manifested in several versions of a Sethian incantation), forms of invocation (including, as we have seen, varying forms of Christian invocation), and typical applications (such as, for example, healing prescriptions using material concoctions).

Most relevant for our purposes is the extent to which Christian forms of invocation figure among the resources from which the compilers of these various collections drew. Christian forms of invocation are barely on the horizon of the temple scribes who compiled the large Theban manuals. This is not surprising; it is remarkable that *any* Christian elements make their way into the procedures and incantations in these manuals, given the institutional context in which they were written. The other Greek witnesses are too few and fragmentary to permit many generalizations. Nevertheless, they show that Christian forms of incantation were among the resources available to the compilers of these recipes, whose approach was in most instances syncretistic, and that there was some diversity in what entered their repertoire. We are left with many unanswered questions. Where did these elements originate? How did they circulate? How did they enter the repertoire of these particular scribes?

The Coptic manuals suggest that there was a gradient, if you will, in the extent to which Christian means of invoking power made their way into customary practice. Some manuals incorporate only formal devices, such as staurograms, whose salience is ambiguous. Others introduce snippets from Christian invocations—the names of the Trinity or the name of Jesus—into an otherwise Graeco-Egyptian incantation. Others present incantations that fall within the scope of attested Christian traditions (e.g., Sethian incantations), but outside the norms of the institutional church in Egypt in Late Antiquity. Absent from most manuals are recipes with incantations phrased in a wholly 'orthodox' Christian idiom, such as we shall see in some amulets in Chapter 4.

There is one exception to this general pattern: a late antique Coptic codex sold by Giovanni Anastasi to the National Museum of Antiquities in Leiden, Ms. AMS 9 (often referred to as Anastasy 9).[119] It contains a variety of materials, some of which, as we shall see in Chapters 5 and 6, are often found in amulets: two protective and exorcistic prayers in an 'orthodox' idiom, copies of the correspondence between Abgar and Jesus,[120] the prayer of Judas Cyriacus from the legend of empress Helena's discovery of the 'true cross',[121] the names of the seven sleepers of Ephesus, the names of the Forty Martyrs of Sebaste,[122] and the *incipits* of the canonical gospels (as well as their titles) and LXX Ps. 90.[123] It is telling that this manuscript, found in the same region of western Thebes as the roll buried in the hermit's cave,[124] was written in a formal Alexandrian majuscule hand and bound with an ornamental leather cover.[125] It would not have been out of place in a monastic library. The differences between the buried roll and the 'deluxe' codex—differences in content, appearance, and preservation—are suggestive of the diverse social locations in which traditions used in the preparation of amulets were being transmitted and preserved.

Finally, two observations bear on the incantations and amulets that we shall examine in Chapters 4 and 5. First, although we shall encounter customary elements and phraseology in those incantations, there is little evidence of direct borrowing from a manual. This is probably because many purveyors of amulets worked from individual exemplars or from memory. As we have already noted, correspondence between recipes in manuals and applied incantations is rare among Graeco-Egyptian materials. Second, the manuals that have survived remind us that much of the practice of invoking supernatural aid was *not* textual, even if the manuals themselves are. The Greek fragments

---

[119] W. Pleyte and P. A. A. Boeser, *Manuscrits coptes du Musée d'Antiquités des Pays-Bas à Leide* (Leiden: Brill, 1897), 441–79; ET: *ACM*, no. 134. J. A. Szirmai, *The Archaeology of Medieval Bookbinding* (Aldershot: Ashgate, 1999), 43 n. 6, assigns the codex to the seventh–eighth century. I have not been able to identify the source of the date of the sixth century assigned in Trismegistos, TM 100023 <http://www.trismegistos.org/text/100023>.

[120] See Section 5.4.

[121] On the prayer of Judas Cyriacus and the legend of Helena's discovery of the true cross, see J. W. Drijvers, *Helena Augusta: The Mother of Constantine the Great and the Legend of her Finding of the True Cross* (Leiden: Brill, 1992), 165–80; H. J. W. Drijvers and J. W. Drijvers, *The Finding of the True Cross: The Judas Kyriakos Legend in Syriac: Introduction, Text and Translation*, CSCO 565 (Louvain: Peeters, 1997). For a tablet bearing another Coptic version of the prayer and thought to be an amulet, see S. Pernigotti, 'Una tavoletta lignea con un testo magico in copto', *EVO*, 6 (1983), 75–92, <http://www.jstor.org/stable/24232654>.

[122] See Section 6.4.2.　　[123] See Sections 5.1–5.2.

[124] Winlock and Crum, *The Monastery of Epiphanius, Part I*, 207.

[125] Images at <http://www.rmo.nl/collectie/zoeken?object=AMS+9> (Rijksmuseum van Oudheden, Leiden, inv. AMS 9); Pleyte and Boeser, *Manuscrits coptes*. For the hand, see, e.g., R. Kasser, 'Paleography', *CE*, 8.175–84, fig. 3 (c). On the cover, see Szirmai, *The Archaeology*, chapter 3.

and the Coptic manuals consist mainly of prescriptions for material applications empowered by an incantation or some other procedure. We must assume, therefore, that the textual amulets with which this book is concerned represent only a fraction of the remedies that practitioners dispensed. Much of what practitioners and their clients did is lost to us, except for telltale clues left behind in the material and literary record.

4

Scribal Features of Customary Amulets

The emerging and eventually dominant Christian church made its presence felt in the production of amulets in a variety of ways. Sometimes, as we have seen in Chapter 3, Christian forms of invocation made their way into otherwise Graeco-Egyptian incantations without substantially altering the prevailing traditions into which they were inserted. Sometimes customary forms of incantation were modified, to a greater or lesser extent, to reflect Christian notions of divine and angelic powers and the language that Christians used to appeal to those powers. On other occasions Christian prayers or excerpts from Christian scriptures were used as amulets. Many or all of these options might be available to people in search of a remedy, as one can see, for example, from the range of amulets found at Oxyrhynchus. So we are lead to ask: who was producing these various amulets and where in a town or village might one find these producers?

In this chapter and Chapter 5, we shall examine a selection of amulets more closely in order to draw out the qualities of the people who wrote them and thereby learn more about the cultural and social location of producers of amulets in late antique Egypt. In this chapter we shall focus on amulets written with an incantation, however little or much the incantation has been modified in Christian terms. In Chapter 5, we shall focus on amulets written with one or more scriptural passages, liturgical prayers, and similar texts. Inevitably, of course, these two categories intersect; there are amulets which combine customary forms of incantation with scriptural verses or liturgical acclamations. Nevertheless, because of the volume of material and the particular features that need to be examined, it is practical to divide the examination of scribal features into two chapters.

I have chosen to organize the material in this chapter into groups of roughly comparable amulets. This allows us to distinguish among ways of formulating an incantation and to compare ways of writing a particular type of incantation. I have been selective in the material discussed in this chapter. Some material has been reserved for Chapter 6, where we shall consider the influence of Christian rituals on the formulation of amulets. (Occasionally in the present chapter it will be necessary to observe when an incantation is influenced by ritual actions of Christians, such as liturgical acclamations or appeals to saints.)

4.1 AMULETS AGAINST SNAKES AND SCORPIONS

I begin with a relatively simple type of amulet against an ever-present danger in Egyptian homes and fields: scorpions and snakes.[1] There are numerous incantations against scorpion stings and snake bites among the papyri of ancient Egypt.[2] Some of the ancient incantations are elaborate. Others are shorter and more direct, though not as brief as some amulets from Late Antiquity. The longer incantations relate the pleas of Isis to save her son Horus from a poisonous sting or bite, or describe the power of Horus to save a person who has been stung or bitten. The latter narrative, which takes various forms,[3] may lie behind the invocation of Horus in incantations against scorpions in Late Antiquity.

We have several late antique amulets against scorpions written in Greek. There is some diversity among them. A short amulet, assigned to the fourth or fifth century, consists only of *voces mysticae* and the word 'scorpion' (*SM* I 16 = *P.Wash.Univ.* II 75). The *voces mysticae* include what appears to be an angel's name, 'Ioel' or 'Ithel', and a variant of Sabaôth, 'Sbaôth'.[4] A fragmentary amulet assigned to the fifth century has *voces mysticae*, a short adjuration, and a drawing of a scorpion (*SM* I 17 [*P.Amst.* I 15]). Two recipes written on a potsherd, assigned to the fourth century, contain slightly longer, though still incomplete, adjurations against the sting of a scorpion (*SM* II 89 [*O.Ashm.Shelt.* 194]). The first of these contains a reference to 'the holy god',[5] a common appellation in incantations;[6] the editors suggest that the phrase may originally have read, 'for he is a man of the holy god'.[7]

I mention these amulets because their diversity contrasts with several amulets from Oxyrhynchus that are similar in formulation: *PGM* XXVIIIa–c (*P.Oxy.* XVI 2061–3), *PGM* P6a (*P.Oxy.* VIII 1152), and *PGM* P2 (*P.Oxy.* VII 1060). We may begin with *P.Oxy.* XVI 2061–3,[8] since they resemble one another the most. Each of these amulets consists of a short invocation, a first-person formula binding the Artemisian scorpion ('I bind you, Artemisian scorpion'),[9] and a

---

[1] On the history of such incantations in Egypt, see I. Maaßen, 'Schlangen- und Skorpion-beschwörung über die Jahrtausende', in A. Jördens (ed.), *Ägyptische Magie und ihre Umwelt* (Wiesbaden: Harrassowitz Verlag, 2015), 171–87.

[2] A representative selection can be found in *Ancient Egyptian Magical Texts*, tr. J. F. Borghouts (Leiden: Brill, 1978), 51–85 (nos. 84–123); see also A. De Buck and B. H. Stricker, 'Teksten tegen schorpioenen naar Pap. I 349', *OMRO*, 21 (1940), 53–62.

[3] E.g., Borghouts, *Ancient Egyptian Magical Texts*, nos. 102–4, 106–8, 111, 113, 123.

[4] *SM* I 16.7–8.   [5] *SM* II 89.4.

[6] E.g., *PGM* I.198, IV.2093, IV.3029, XIII.281–2; *SM* I 6.2.   [7] *SM* II 89.3–4 comm.

[8] In what follows I refer to the more precise text of the *editio princeps* in *P.Oxy.* XVI.

[9] On the association between Artemis and the scorpion in myth and astrology, and the power attributed to scorpions to protect against other animals, including poisonous ones, see S. Eitrem, 'Der Skorpion in Mythologie und Religionsgeschichte', *SO*, 7 (1928), 53–82 at 61–2, 69–71, doi: 10.1080/00397672808590206.

Fig. 4.1. *P.Oxy.* XVI 2061, 2062, and 2063. Courtesy of the Egypt Exploration Society and Imaging Papyri Project, Oxford.

date. The invocation begins with iterations, variously spelled, of the name 'Hôr Hôr Phôr Phôr',[10] probably a reference to the Egyptian god Horus,[11] since φωρ represents the name in Egyptian with the article and first letter written as a monogram (ϕωρ = ⲡϩωρ). The invocation continues with permutations of the name(s) Iaô Sabaôth Adônai,[12] and concludes with a more opaque name Salamantarchi, again with variations.[13] The three amulets are written in different hands (see Fig. 4.1). *P.Oxy.* XVI 2061 is written in an irregular semi-cursive assigned to the fifth century; *P.Oxy.* XVI 2062 and 2063 are written quickly in cursive hands assigned to the sixth century.[14] Despite variations in spelling and vocabulary, the formulation evidently remained fairly stable over time. Even the layout became standard, suited to a small amulet, since both *P.Oxy.* XVI 2062 and *P.Oxy.* XVI 2063 allocate a name per line, though there is ample space in the former to extend the lines. Only in *P.Oxy.* XVI 2063 is there an indication of Christian scribal practice. The text is headed by a row of three crosses, and the tip of a cross, barely visible, precedes the first words of the incantation. These crosses are simply prefaced to the formulation, in itself resilient to change.

Such a pattern of 'framing' a customary incantation by incorporating Christian elements at the beginning or the end can be seen in other examples

[10] *P.Oxy.* XVI 2061.1: ορ ορ φορ φορ; *P.Oxy.* XVI 2062.1–2: ωρ ωρ | φωρ φωρ; *P.Oxy.* XVI 2063.2–3: ωρ ωρ | [φ]ωρ φωρ.

[11] See *P.Oslo* I 5.2 comm. (p. 9).

[12] *P.Oxy.* XVI 2061.1–2: σαβ[α]ωθ | αδωνέ; *P.Oxy.* XVI 2062.3–5: Ἰαὼ | ἀδῳναεὶ | σαβ[α]ώθ; loss of papyrus where the name should occur in *P.Oxy.* XVI 2063.4. On the polyvalence of these names, see R. Boustan and J. E. Sanzo, 'Christian Magicians, Jewish Magical Idioms, and the Shared Magical Culture of Late Antiquity', *HTR*, 110 (forthcoming).

[13] *P.Oxy.* XVI 2061.2–3: Σαλαματαρ | χει; *P.Oxy.* XVI 2062.6: Σαλαμανταρχχει (ν corr. from ρ); *P.Oxy.* XVI 2063.5: [Σαλα]μαρθαχι. In the latter two amulets, where each name is given a line, the name is presented as a single word. 'Tarchê' appears in a group of four names in a sixth- or seventh-century amulet against snakebite written in Coptic; see G. M. Parássoglou, 'A Christian Amulet against Snakebite', *StudPap*, 13 (1974), 107–10.

[14] Images at <http://www.papyrology.ox.ac.uk/POxy/> (Oxyrhynchus Online).

of this type of amulet from Oxyrhynchus. *PGM* P6a (*P.Oxy.* VIII 1152), assigned to the fifth or sixth century, has a short version of the 'Hôr Hôr' sequence (without Salamantarchi)[15] that adds Michael and Jesus Christ to the powers invoked to protect a house and its inhabitants, ending with 'Amen'. The incantation is written hastily and sloppily in a cursive hand.[16] 'Jesus' is spelled with an *epsilon*,[17] an irregularity that, interestingly, also appears in *P.Oxy.* XI 1384,[18] the collection of recipes from Oxyrhynchus discussed in Chapter 3.[19] Both the formulation of the incantation and the manner in which it is written suggest that this 'christianized' version of the incantation had itself become customary.

The many irregularities in these texts, over and above the common phenomenon of phonetic interchanges, suggests that they were written from memory. This adds to the evidence that the incantation had become commonplace. A superfluous letter may be added or a necessary letter may be dropped.[20] Words may be misspelt.[21] The expression for the 'Artemsian scorpion' varies,[22] as does the name of the obscure power Salama(n)tarch(e)i.[23] Some scribes were clearly familiar with and faithful to what they took to be the visual format of the incantation, writing each of the powerful names on a separate line,[24] whereas other scribes ran them along in continuous text.[25] However, although the incantation had become commonplace, these particular amulets were not produced *en masse*. Several of them conclude with a date,[26] showing that they were written for individuals at a particular time. In other words, the incantation was a known remedy, familiar to both producers and clients over several centuries. This is the context in which we must consider two more elaborate versions of this amulet.

PGM P2 (*P.Oxy.* VII 1060),[27] a sixth-century amulet from Oxyrhynchus to protect a house from 'every evil creeping thing' (presumably snakes),[28] reads as follows:

---

[15] *P.Oxy.* VIII 1152.1: ωρ ωρ φωρ.

[16] Image at <http://papyri.info/hgv/64911> (Papyri.info).

[17] *P.Oxy.* VIII 1152.3: Ἰεσοῦ.   [18] *P.Oxy.* XI 1384.17.   [19] Section 3.2.3.

[20] Superfluous letter: *P.Oxy.* XVI 2062.7: δένν{ε}ω; dropped letter: *P.Oxy.* XVI 2061.3 Ἀβρα<σ>άξ.

[21] *P.Oxy.* XVI 2063.10: τέσσαρο.

[22] *P.Oxy.* XVI 2061.4: σκορπιέ Ἀρτεμισιάς; *P.Oxy.* XVI 2062.8–9: σκορπιέ Ἀρτεμίσου.

[23] See n. 13.   [24] *P.Oxy.* XVI 2062 and 2063.

[25] *P.Oxy.* VIII 1152, *P.Oxy.* XVI 2061; see also *P.Oxy.* VII 1060 below.

[26] *P.Oxy.* VIII 1152.10; *P.Oxy.* XVI 2061.6–7; *P.Oxy.* XVI 2062.9; *P.Oxy.* XVI 2063.9–10.

[27] The first edition in *P.Oxy.* VII 1060 should be consulted. The presentation in *PGM* P2 and *ACM*, no. 25, is misleading. I am grateful to the John Rylands University Library for providing me with a digital image of the papyrus, P.Ryl. inv. 452.

[28] At line 7 I read ἑρπετοῦ as an adjective, as does H. G. Liddell, R. Scott, and H. S. Jones (eds), *A Greek-English Lexicon*, 9th edn with a revised supplement (Oxford: Clarendon Press, 1996), s.v. II.2; there is no need to supply καί.

✝ The door, Aphroditên | phroditên roditên oditên | ditên itên tên tên ên. Hôr Hôr Phôr Phôr Iaô Sabaôth Adône. | I bind you, Artemisian scorpion.[29] | Deliver this house | from every evil creeping thing, quickly, quickly. | St. Phocas is here. | Phamenoth 13, third indiction. | ...

The amulet was written by a practiced scribe. He wrote the 'Aphrodite' sequence in an informal sloping majuscule hand, but then switched to a continuous cursive for the remainder of the incantation.[30] (Did he find it easier to keep track of the dropped letters of the 'Aphrodite' sequence by writing in a majuscule hand?) It is a measure of both his training and his attention to the sequence that he took the trouble to mark *iota* in 'itên' with two dots (inorganic *diairesis*).[31] He apparently did not realize that the sequence would customarily have been written as a diminishing word-shape.[32] As it happens, the Aphrodite-formula would have a long life. It appears in medieval amulets against scorpions written in Hebrew from the Cairo Genizah.[33] The manner in which it is written here—in a diminishing sequence but not a diminishing shape—may indicate that the invocation was already on its way to becoming formulaic.

The incantation is framed by two Christian elements, a cross and the mention of St Phocas. A Syrian martyr called Phocas was reputed to heal people from snake bites as soon as they reached the entrance of his tomb.[34] This text is one of the earliest witnesses to this tradition, which surfaces again in an early modern copy of a Byzantine handbook.[35] The incantation in this amulet is thus embedded in the growing Christian cult of saints.[36]

---

[29] At line 5 I read ἀρτεμήσιε rather than ἀρτερήσιε. The middle curve of *mu*, following an initial long descending stroke, is clearly visible; the ascending curve of the preceding *epsilon* (see δένο at the beginning of the line) is no longer visible.

[30] There are similarities between the cursive of the amulet and the hand in H. Harrauer, *Handbuch der griechischen Paläographie*, 2 vols (Stuttgart: Anton Hiersemann, 2010), 1.447–8 (no. 249); 2.239 (plate 235), *CPR* IX 8+32 (551 CE), image at <http://data.onb.ac.at/rec/RZ00002666> (Österreichischen Nationalbibliothek Katalog der Papyrussammlung), such as the sloped d-shaped *delta* with a long vertical and the similarly formed *gamma* and *delta*, both discussed by Harrauer at 2.448. The d-shaped *delta* intrudes into the sloping majuscule of the amulet as well.

[31] Line 3: ἴτην; inorganic *diairesis* also over initial *iota* in ϊαω (line 4) and ϊνδ(δικτίωνος) (line 10).

[32] For other instances of this phenomenon, see W. M. Brashear, 'The Greek Magical Papyri: An Introduction and Survey; Annotated Bibliography (1928–1994)', *ANRW*, 18/5.3380–684 at 3434 n. 250.

[33] G. Bohak, 'Some "Mass Produced" Scorpion-Amulets from the Cairo Genizah', in Z. Rodgers, M. Daly-Denton, and A. Fitzpatrick McKinley (eds), *A Wandering Galilean: Essays in Honour of Seán Freyne* (Leiden: Brill, 2009), 35–49.

[34] A. Papaconstantinou, *Le culte des saints en Égypte des Byzantins aux Abbassides: l'apport des inscriptions et des papyrus grecs et coptes* (Paris: CNRS Éditions, 2001), 215–16.

[35] R. Bermejo López-Muñiz, 'St. Phokas in a Spell for Snakes (Anecd. Athen., P. 83, 9, Delatte)', *ZPE*, 95 (1993), 28, <http://www.uni-koeln.de/phil-fak/ifa/zpe/downloads/1993/095pdf/095.html>.

[36] See Section 6.4.

PGM P3 (*P.Oslo* I 5),[37] an amulet of unknown provenance assigned to the fourth or fifth century,[38] is even more elaborate:[39]

XMΓ | Hôr Hôr Phôr Phôr Iaô Sabaôth Adônai Elôe Salamantarchi | I bind you, Artemisian scorpion, 315 (times). Preserve this house | with its occupants from all evil, from all bewitchment | of spirits of the air and human eye | and terrible pain [and] sting of scorpion and snake, through the | name of the most high God, naias meli, 7 (times), xoro ôro aaaaaa | Bainchooch mai êêê lênagkorê.[40] Be on guard, O Lord, son of | David according to the flesh, the one born of the holy virgin | Mary, O holy, most high God, of the Holy Spirit. Glory to you, | O heavenly king. Amen. α✝ω ✝Α✝W $\overline{ιχθυς}$.

Again the incantation is framed by Christian elements (see Fig. 4.2). The sequence *XMΓ* appears at the head of the papyrus (in heavier ink), and the final injunction turns into a Christian doxology followed by a series of Christian symbols. The scribe wrote not just one *alpha*-cross-*omega* sequence, but two. The first combines semi-cursive letter-forms with a Greek cross; the second, uncial letter-forms in the chiselled shape found in inscriptions, with a cross in the form of an Egyptian life-sign (*crux ansata*).[41] (The left, right, and lower arms of the second cross are triangular, whereas the top arm is clearly round.) The writing of the symbols thus echoes the iconography of Christian tombstones (as well as Christian gems).[42] The acrostic $\overline{ιχθυς}$ ('Ιησοῦς Χριστὸς Θεοῦ υἱὸς σωτήρ, or 'Jesus Christ, Son of God, Saviour'), too, would have been known, as its frequent occurrence in gems attests.[43]

[37] *Editio princeps*: S. Eitrem and A. Fridrichsen, 'Ein christliches Amulett auf Papyrus', *FVC*, 1 (1921), 3–22 at 3. Selected republications: S. Eitrem, 'A New Christian Amulet', *Aegyptus*, 3 (1922), 66–7, <http://www.jstor.org/stable/41213661>; *SB* III 6584. While the republication of the text at *P.Oslo* I 5 took account of prior discussion of the date of the papyrus and the reading of $\overline{τιε}$ as a number at line 2 (see n. 49), the text in the *editio princeps* is more accurate in its reading of δήγματος at line 6 (no uncertain letters) and ναιας at line 7 (second *alpha*).

[38] M. N. Tod, 'The Scorpion in Graeco-Roman Egypt', *JEA*, 25 (1939), 55–61 at 59, <http://www.jstor.org/stable/3854932>, summarizes the discussion of the date.

[39] ET: *ACM*, no. 26 (modified).

[40] See R. W. Daniel, 'Some ΦΥΛΑΚΤΗΡΙΑ', *ZPE*, 25 (1977), 145–54 at 150–3, <http://www.jstor.org/stable/20181354>, for the revised reading of lines 7–8; also *SM* I 15.1–5 comm. The digital image shows two ink marks to the left of a small hole due to loss of papyrus at the end of line 7 after the six *alphas*. The marks could be the curve of the loop and the top of the diagonal of a seventh *alpha*. As Daniel observes, a group of seven *alphas* is more common.

[41] On the use of the Egyptian life-sign by Christians in Egypt, see M. Cramer, *Das altägyptische Lebenszeichen [ankh] im christlichen (koptischen) Ägypten: Eine kultur- und religionsgeschichtliche Studie*, 3rd edn (Wiesbaden: O. Harrassowitz, 1955).

[42] For examples on Coptic tombstones, see W. E. Crum, *Catalogue général des antiquités égyptiennes du Musée du Caire (Nr. 8001/8741): Coptic Monuments* (Cairo: Institut Francais d'Archéologie Orientale, 1902), 118–23 and plates XXVI–XXXI (nos. 8550–62, 8564–70, 8573–5, 8577–81); on gemstones, J. Spier, *Late Antique and Early Christian Gems* (Wiesbaden: Reichert, 2007), 114 and plate 94 (nos. 664–5).

[43] Spier, *Late Antique and Early Christian Gems*, 34–5, with further bibliography.

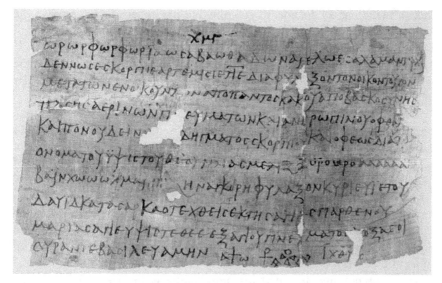

Fig. 4.2. *P.Oslo* I 5 (inv. 303). Courtesy of the University of Oslo Library Papyrus Collection.

The phrasing of the final injunction-cum-doxology is revealing. By speaking of the 'son of David according to the flesh' and the 'one born of the holy virgin Mary... of the Holy Spirit' as the 'most high God' (ὕψιστε θεέ), it would have resonated with the Alexandrian christology of the Egyptian church. Although worship of 'the most high God' (θεὸς ὕψιστος)—God who is above all other intermediaries—could be found among pagans, Jews, and Christians in the Roman period, all of whom used the phrase to refer to the supreme god,[44] in Jewish and early Christian sources the appellation is normally reserved for God the Creator; Jesus is 'the son of the most high God', as the demon-possessed man in the gospel cries out.[45] But by the fifth century 'the Son' would be identified with 'the most high God' in christology and confession, as Cyril of Alexandria's discussion of the story of the demon-possessed man reveals. Cyril explains: 'But if you really know that he is the Son of the most high God, you confess that he is God of heaven and earth and everything in

[44] S. Mitchell, 'The Cult of Theos Hypsistos between Pagans, Jews, and Christians', in P. Athanassiadi and M. Frede (eds), *Pagan Monotheism in Late Antiquity* (Oxford: Clarendon Press, 1999), 81–148; M. Choat, *Belief and Cult in Fourth-Century Papyri* (Turnhout: Brepols, 2006), 106–7; R. Cline, *Ancient Angels: Conceptualizing Angeloi in the Roman Empire* (Leiden: Brill, 2011), 53–6. For appeals to 'the most high God' in Graeco-Egyptian manuals and incantations, see *PGM* IV.1068; *PGM* V.46; *PGM* XII.63, 71; *PGM* LXII.30.

[45] Mark 5: 7 = Luke 8: 28; see also, e.g., A. Paul. et Thecl. 29, in *Acta apostolorum apocrypha post Constantinum Tischendorf*, ed. R. A. Lipsius and M. Bonnet, 2 vols in 3 (Leipzig, 1891–1903; repr. Hildesheim: G. Olms, 1990), 1.256; Aristides, *Apol.* 15.1 (SC 470.286); Eusebius, *D.e.* 4.15.42 (GCS 23.180).

them'.[46] Likewise, in documents submitted to the imperial court prior to the Council of Ephesus in 431, Cyril observes how appropriate it is that the 'son of David' is acclaimed 'Lord' and 'God', as in the doxology in our papyrus.[47] Whoever added the injunction to the customary incantation—whether the writer of the amulet or the writer of the exemplar—must have been familiar with invocations or acclamations of the Egyptian church.

The writing further distinguishes the scribe of this amulet (see Fig. 4.2). The papyrus is written in a fairly regular, informal semi-cursive hand that could have served for copying books.[48] The orthography is correct and free of phonetic spellings. The scribe has no difficulty with the vocative form of 'Adônai' or the spelling of the name 'Salamantarchi' in the 'Hôr Hôr' sequence, unlike the scribes of *PGM* XXVIIIa–c. Two numbers—315 (line 3) and 7 (line 7)—are correctly distinguished by a supralinear stroke.[49] Organic *diairesis* is used to distinguish *iota* from a preceding vowel in υἱέ (line 8) and Βαινχωωχ (line 8), and from the preceding semi-vowel in Δαυίδ (line 9); inorganic *diairesis* is used over the initial vowel in Ἰάω (line 2) and ὑψίστου (line 7, but not line 10). Perhaps most telling is the fact that the scribe reproduces a series of *voces mysticae* also found, with minor variants, in another amulet without Christian elements.[50] We can be almost certain that the scribe was copying from an exemplar. We do not know, therefore, how much of what we see is due to the exemplar and how much is due to the scribe. For instance, is the absence of *nomina sacra* due to the exemplar or the scribe?

It is a rare good fortune for our purposes that all these amulets have survived. They illustrate for us the factors that allowed for individuality in the production—or, better, reproduction—of a commonplace incantation. The individuality of these amulets is not simply a result of the qualities and circumstances of individual scribes, though evidently these are a factor in their production. It is also a consequence of the modes of transmission of this incantation. The incantation is relatively simple and, apparently, well known. The variations in the 'Hôr Hôr' sequence and the spelling of 'Salamantarchi' in several of the shorter amulets indicate that in all likelihood the incantation was

---

[46] Cyril of Alexandria, *Lc.* 8 (PG 72.633): Ἀλλὰ γὰρ εἰ οἶδας ὅλως αὐτὸν Υἱὸν ὄντα τοῦ ὑψίστου Θεοῦ, ὁμολογεῖς ὅτι Θεός ἐστιν οὐρανοῦ τε καὶ γῆς καὶ τῶν ἐν αὐτοῖς.

[47] Cyril of Alexandria, *Arcad.* 108, in E. Schwartz (ed.), *Concilium Universale Ephesenum*, ACO 1.1.1.5 (Berlin: Walter de Gruyter, 1927), 89. See also Cyril of Alexandria, *Thds.* 26, 44–5, in Schwartz, *Concilium Universale Ephesenum*, ACO 1.1.1.1, 58–9, 72, for Cyril's interpretation of the Pauline phrase 'son of David according to the flesh' (Rom. 1: 3).

[48] Image at <http://ub-prod01-imgs.uio.no/OPES/jpg/303r.jpg> (Oslo Papyri Electronic System) and fig 4.2 above. The hand bears some resemblance to G. Cavallo and H. Maehler, *Greek Bookhands of the Early Byzantine Period: A.D. 300–800* (London: Institute of Classical Studies, 1987), 46 (no. 19a), *PSI* XIV 1371 (mid-fifth century).

[49] On the eventual correct reading of these two numbers, see Tod, 'The Scorpion', 59; Daniel, 'Some ΦΥΛΑΚΤΗΡΙΑ', 151.

[50] *SM* I 15 = *P.PalauRib.Lit.* 38; see Daniel, 'Some ΦΥΛΑΚΤΗΡΙΑ', 150–3.

passed on orally or, as the line arrangement of *PGM* XXVIIIb–c suggests, recalled from memory. The manner in which these shorter amulets were written—hastily or fluidly—gives the impression that scribes wrote them out as a matter of course. Recollection of a commonplace incantation by scribes of varying degrees of skill and literacy would inevitably result in idiosyncrasies in the incantation—in other words, individuality. Yet we also have at least one and possibly two amulets that were copied from an exemplar. *PGM* P3 was almost certainly copied, given the close correspondence of the *voces mysticae* in it to those in another amulet. *PGM* P2 may well have been copied, as this would explain why the scribe wrote out the 'Aphrodite' sequence as a diminishing sequence but not a diminishing shape, reproducing the sequence as found elsewhere. If this is what happened, then the exemplars were both a resource and a constraint for the scribe. The amulets are the product of both the scribe of the exemplar and the scribe of the amulet, and we cannot be sure where the contribution of the one ended and the other began.

This group of amulets also illustrates the scope for 'christianization' in the production of amulets and the ambiguities associated with indicators of a Christian milieu. Evidence of a Christian milieu in these amulets ranges from the addition of crosses in *PGM* XXVIIIc, to the inclusion of 'Jesus' among the powers invoked in *PGM* P6a, to the appeal to St Phocas in *PGM* P2, to the numerous Christian symbols and the Christian doxology in *PGM* P3. The combination of these elements with a customary incantation exposes the manifold ways in which an incantation or a scribe might have been shaped by the surrounding Christian culture, as well as the difficulties we incur when we attempt to locate a scribe in the religious landscape of late antique Egypt. Some observations can be made with confidence. The author of *PGM* P3 must have been familiar with Christian liturgical invocations or acclamations. But what sort of formation the scribe of *PGM* XXVIIIc had, we cannot know; crosses are too formal a scribal feature to tell us much. And what we should infer from the phonetic spelling of 'Jesus' in *PGM* P6a is unclear, since scribes who clearly had a Christian formation spell 'Jesus' and 'Christ' phonetically,[51] possibly because they usually read the names only in an abbreviated form.

Furthermore, the fact that these various Christian elements are combined with a customary incantation that begins with the 'Hôr Hôr' sequence (and sometimes includes 'Salamantarchi') prompts us to wonder what significance this customary invocation held for the scribes who wrote these amulets. Did they understand the invocation to refer to Horus, or was the meaning of sequence attenuated into something one simply said to ward off scorpions and snakes? The same question could be asked of the 'Aphrodite' sequence, which, as we know from later Jewish incantations, did lose its associations with the

---

[51] E.g., *BKT* VI 7.1.8: Ἰησοῦ; P.Oslo inv. 1644.7: Χρυστοῦ. See Chapter 5 nn. 48 and 189.

goddess. We could also extend our queries to other names in the incantations. For instance, did the scribe of *PGM* P6a think of 'Elôei', 'Adônaei', 'Iaô Sabaôth', 'Michaêl', and 'Iesou Christê' as individual powers, as seems likely from the order of the first three names (which varies in all these amulets) and a tradition of appealing to them as individual entities?[52] We cannot answer these questions with certainty. But the answers are not as crucial, perhaps, as the fact that for all these scribes it was, evidently, not problematic to combine this customary incantation with crosses, an appeal to a Christian saint, or Christian signs and acclamations. Neither the incantation nor the scribe's religious affiliation or identity prevented this from happening. If we juxtapose *PGM* XXVIIIa–b (which lack any uniquely Christian element) with *PGM* P3 (which is clearly shaped by a Christian culture), we are obliged to conclude that we cannot presume that the scribes of the former did not affiliate with the Christian church, since the incantation itself was not, seemingly, unacceptable to a Christian scribe.

Finally, we would like to know if this particular incantation was confined to the region of Oxyrhynchus, the provenance of most of these amulets, or if it circulated more widely. Regrettably, the find-spot of *PGM* P3 is unknown.

4.2 AMULETS AGAINST FEVER AND ILLNESS

Amulets against sickness, especially fevers and sweats, also had a long history in Egypt,[53] as one might expect, given how widespread and menacing febrile illnesses could be in antiquity.[54] In fact, several of the fevers routinely named on these amulets—daily, tertian, quartan—can be associated with different strains of malaria.[55] Incantations against such fevers typically consisted of a series of *voces mysticae* and an invocation of divine powers by name, followed by a standard formula enjoining the powers to deliver, heal, or protect so-and-so whom so-and-so bore from various types of fevers, and ending with the routine accelerating formula, 'now, now, quickly, quickly'.[56] The powerful

---

[52] At *PGM* XXXVI.41–4 (P.*Oslo* I 1) these names, in a series, refer to 'ruling angels' (κύριοι ἄγγελοι). See also *PGM* XXXV.19–22 (*PSI* I 29).

[53] See *P.Mich.* XVIII, pp. 77–8, for an overview. For a measure of the relative abundance of such amulets in the material record, see Brashear, 'Greek Magical Papyri', 3499–501.

[54] W. Scheidel, *Death on the Nile: Disease and the Demography of Roman Egypt* (Leiden: Brill, 2001), 66–91, discusses the causes and conditions leading to deaths from typhus, typhoid, relapsing fevers, and malaria; see also J. Draycott, *Approaches to Healing in Roman Egypt* (Oxford: Archaeopress, 2012), 72–81.

[55] Scheidel, *Death on the Nile*, 75–7.

[56] M. de Haro Sanchez, 'Le vocabulaire de la pathologie et de la thérapeutique dans les papyrus iatromagiques grecs: fièvres, traumatismes et "épilepsie"', *BASP*, 47 (2010), 131–53 at 132–40, <http://hdl.handle.net/2027/spo.0599796.0047.001:13>; R. Bélanger Sarrazin, 'Le syncrétisme en

names could be written in a diminishing word-shape (a grape-cluster or a wing-shape) that was probably symbolic of the fleeing fever.[57] From the fourth century onward there was a tendency to repeat the incantation.[58]

The format of the incantation evidently lends itself to the substitution of one divine power with another in the invocation, or the addition of a divine power, which is what we see as Christian elements enter the repertoire. Some amulets juxtapose Graeco-Egyptian invocations with Christian ones. Others have a customary structure but appeal only to Christian powers. We shall discuss examples of both of these types with a view to illustrating the range of scribal culture.

4.2.1 Amulets Juxtaposing Customary and Christian Elements

We begin with a formulaic healing amulet, *SM* I 20 (see Fig. 4.3).[59] Now assigned to the end of the fourth century or beginning of the fifth,[60] it is roughly contemporary with the elaborate amulet against scorpions with which we concluded Section 4.1, *PGM* P3. The comparison is instructive. *SM* I 20 opens with seven vowels that increase in number as they are written and the names 'Ablanathamala' [*sic*] and 'Akrammachamari'. This is followed by two injunctions to heal ($\theta\epsilon\rho\acute{\alpha}\pi\epsilon\upsilon\sigma\upsilon$) a woman named Thaesa. The first injunction is addressed to 'Lord God, Lord of all gods (?)';[61] the second is addressed, implicitly, to the *charaktêres* that precede it (six *beta* shapes, two four-pointed stars, two six-pointed stars, two eight-pointed stars, and three two-pointed vertical lines with an intersecting diagonal).[62] Between the two injunctions is a further command, '...release in the name of Jesus Christ'. It is difficult to say

Égypte dans l'Antiquité tardive: l'apport des papyrus iatromagiques grecs' (MA thesis, Université d'Ottawa, 2015), 26–32 with table 1. For some examples, see *PGM* XVIIIb (*BGU* III 956); *PGM* XXXIII (*P.Tebt.* II 275); *PGM* XLIII; *PGM* XLVII; *SM* I 4 (*PUG* I 6); *SM* I 9 (*P.Michael* 27); *SM* I 11 (*P.Princ.* III 159); *SM* I 12; *SM* I 14 (*P.Erl.* 15); *SM* I 18 (*P.Leid.Inst.* 9).

[57] A. Önnerfors, 'Zaubersprüche in Texten der römischen und frühmittelalterlichen Medizin', in G. Sabbah (ed.), *Études de medecine romaine* (Saint-Étienne: Publications de l'Université de Saint-Étienne, 1988), 113–56 at 115; *SM* I, p. 5.

[58] Bélanger Sarrazin, 'Le syncrétisme', 21, 51–2, 94; e.g., *SM* I 13; *SM* I 14 (*P.Erl.* 15).

[59] ET: *SM* I, p. 56.

[60] D. Wortmann, 'Neue magische Texte', *BJ*, 168 (1968), 56–111 at 102: late fifth or early sixth century; *SM* I 20: late fourth or early fifth century.

[61] The second half of the phrase (see n. 64) is problematic; see *SM* I 20.3 comm.

[62] In K. Dzwiza, *Schriftverwendung in antiker Ritualpraxis anhand der griechischen, demotischen und koptischen Praxisanleitungen des 1.–7. Jahrhunderts*, 4 vols in 2 (Erfurt and Heidelberg, 2013), <http://www.db-thueringen.de/servlets/DocumentServlet?id=23500>, the *beta*-shape is labelled G6-03-au, and the four-pointed, six-pointed, and eight-pointed stars are labelled G1-04-ab, G1-06-ad, and G1-08-aa, respectively. G6-03-au, G1-04-ab, and G1-08-aa occur frequently in Dzwiza's catalogue; see the indices at pp. 296–7 and 642–3.

Fig. 4.3. *SM* I 20 (P.Köln inv. 2861r). Copyright Papyrussammlung Köln, Institut für Altertumskunde, University of Cologne.

if the indecipherable text prior to this command stands on its own or is subordinate to the first injunction.

The text is written in an irregular hand; many letters are awkwardly formed.[63] Whereas *PGM* P3, written by a much more accomplished scribe, does not use *nomina sacra*, *SM* I 20 does, albeit haphazardly. In the phrase 'Lord God, Lord of all gods', the first 'Lord' is written out, while the second is abbreviated without a supralinear stroke.[64] 'God' is abbreviated with a supralinear stroke—uncommon for the vocative[65]—but 'gods' is written out, as is usually the case with plural forms.[66] Later, 'Jesus Christ' is abbreviated with supralinear strokes.[67] The overall impression is of a writer whose familiarity with the conventions of incantation is greater than his knowledge of Christian scribal habits or his concern to reproduce these.

---

[63] Image at <https://papyri.uni-koeln.de/stueck/tm64875> (Kölner Papyrussammlung) and fig. 4.3 above.

[64] *SM* I 20.3: κύριε θε̄ καὶ [read: κ(ύρι)ε] θεῶ<ν> πάντω<ν>.

[65] A. H. R. E. Paap, *Nomina Sacra in the Greek Papyri of the First Five Centuries A.D.: The Sources and Some Deductions* (Leiden: Brill, 1959), 76–7, 100.

[66] Paap, *Nomina Sacra*, 100.

[67] *SM* I 20.5–6: ιην χρυ. The h-shaped *eta* of Ἰη(σο)ῦ is faintly visible on the digital image; the final *upsilon* Χρ(ιστο)ῦ, assuming it is an *upsilon*, is neither u-shaped nor y-shaped.

It is useful, at this point, to adduce *PGM* P11 as a *comparandum* to *SM* I 20, even though the purpose of this incantation is unknown.[68] (The papyrus, which cannot be securely dated, is a fragment; at least a centimetre is missing at the left edge, and an undetermined amount of papyrus is lost at the right and bottom edges.)[69] The main elements are familiar enough. The first line has a series of divine names written in an experienced but irregular semi-cursive hand: 'Jesus (?), Jesus Christ, αω, Adônai, Elôai, E[ ]leôs'(?).[70] The scribe does not observe the conventions of *nomina sacra* strictly. He adds supralinear strokes over 'Jesus Christ' (and possibly the preceding 'Jesus'), *alpha*, *omega*, 'Elôai' and 'E[ ]leôs', but not 'Adônai'. The second line has a series of vowels: εεεεεεηηηηηηηηιιιιιιοοοοοο.... Given the loss of papyrus on the left, it is likely that the series began with *alpha*. The third line, occupying the middle third of the papyrus, is taken up with *charaktêres*.[71] The remainder of the papyrus is written in irregular lines with letters and signs, some of which are hard to make out. If more of the papyrus had been preserved, we might have had a better idea of what to make of it. Nevertheless, what remains on this fragment shows that, as with *SM* I 20, the writer freely combined Christian and customary devices in his incantation: *nomina sacra*, a series of vowels, and *charaktêres*.

In *SM* I 21 (*P.Köln* VI 257)—assigned, like *SM* I 20, to the end of the fourth century or the beginning of the fifth—the juxtaposition of customary and Christian elements is visual as well as verbal (see Fig. 4.4).[72] The scribe wrote a Christian acclamation, 'One Father, one Son, one holy Spirit, amen', across the top in two lines, punctuated by three gammate crosses.[73] This is followed by 'Ablanathanabla' [*sic*] written repeatedly as a diminishing grape-cluster. Three *charaktêres* flanking the grape-cluster are enjoined to heal (θεραπεύσατε) a certain Tiron from various fevers. The last few lines are indecipherable.

---

[68] *Editio princeps*: C. Wessely, 'Neue griechische Zauberpapyri', *DAWWPh*, 42 (1893), 1–96 at 68.
[69] Image at <http://data.onb.ac.at/rec/RZ00008030> (Österreichischen Nationalbibliothek Katalog der Papyrussammlung; P.Vindob. inv. G 338).
[70] Both the *editio princeps* and *PGM* P11 omit words in the first half of the line, which I read as follows:]ις ις χς αω αδωναι ελωαι ε[ ]λεως. There have been faint traces of what may have been a supralinear stroke over the initial *iota sigma*. In the last word, ε[ ]λεως, it appears that immediately after the hole the scribe initially wrote *epsilon* and then corrected to *lambda*. The final letter in the word is clearly *sigma*; compare *iota sigma* earlier in the line. The letters after *lamba* are hard to make out from the digital image; *epsilon omega* are possible, yielding ελεως (read: ἔλεος, 'mercy'?). At line 5 both editions read ελωος, but it is difficult to verify the letter between *lambda* and *omicron* from the digital image.
[71] In Dzwiza's catalogue (see n. 62), those I have been able to match are labelled G1-02-aa, G1-02-bt (?), G1-04-ay, G1-08-aa, and (on line 4) G4-01-zi.
[72] Image at *P.Köln* VI, plate VII; <https://papyri.uni-koeln.de/stueck/tm64571> (Kölner Papyrussammlung); and fig. 4.4 below.
[73] Gammate crosses, so named because they consist of four intersecting capital Greek *gammas* (*crux gammata* or *swastika*), appear in Christian inscriptions in Rome toward the end of the third century and continuously in the fourth century; see H. Leclercq, 'Croix, crucifix', *DACL*, 3/2.3045–131 at 3119–20; H. Leclercq, 'Swastika', *DACL*, 15/2.1752–5.

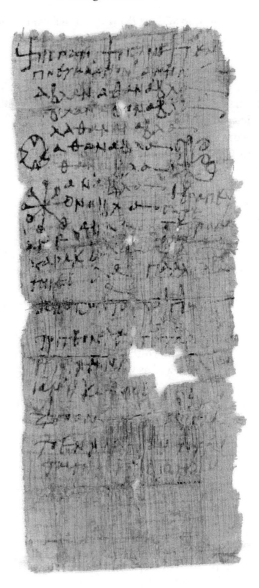

Fig. 4.4. *SM* I 21 (*P.Köln* VI 257; inv. 10266v). Copyright Papyrussammlung Köln, Institut für Altertumskunde, University of Cologne.

The configuration of the elements reveals that the scribe had a mental notion of how to compose the text or, less likely, was copying from an exemplar. The grape-cluster is formed by dropping the initial letter of the preceding line. The final *alpha* in each line ends with a horizontal stroke that extends to the edge of the papyrus in the first few lines but then stops short of the edge, leaving an increasing amount of space as the cluster diminishes. Approximately one-fifth of the way down the papyrus the grape-cluster is flanked on either side by the *charaktêres* and injunction. Slight divergences in the level of the lines reveals that the *charaktêres* and injunction were written independently of and probably after the grape-cluster. The scribe was clearly familiar with the format of this schematic amulet and had anticipated the space required for its components.

The irregular semi-cursive hand of the scribe conveys a sense of careless facility. He was not particularly attentive to the formulation of the grape-cluster, since he misspells the palindrome, switches *theta* and *nu* at line 5 ('lathananabla'), and drops a syllable at line 6 ('athanabla'). (Were these letters dropped so that the line would fit between the *charaktêres*?) The scribe also substituted the accusative for the genitive in the adjectives commonly used to name the fevers to be prevented ('tertian, quartan or every-other-day or quotidian').[74] This often occurs in formulaic injunctions against fever.[75] It indicates that the scribe adopted customary phraseology of the genre unthinkingly. We may conclude that the scribe was accustomed to writing texts like this one, and was not particularly careful in their execution.

The phrasing of the trinitarian acclamation, spelled phonetically, fits with this impression.[76] The acclamation does not correspond precisely to the response to the call to communion found in later manuscripts of the various Egyptian eucharistic liturgies ('One holy Father, one holy Son, one holy Spirit'),[77] unlike, for instance, a fragmentary conclusion of a Greek prayer (probably an amulet) assigned to the fourth or fifth century, *P.Bon.* I 9.[78] Thus, we see here a casual familiarity with a Christian acclamation in a scribe who produced an amulet in a routine fashion.

We may compare the visual presentation of *SM* I 21 with that of a later amulet, *SM* I 34 (see Fig. 4.5), now assigned to the sixth century.[79] In this amulet to heal a certain Joseph from fever, an appeal to Christ and an appeal to the white wolf (the sun god Horos-Apollo[80]) are written around a diminishing, grape-cluster sequence of the name 'Erichthonius'. Erichthonius was a mythical king of Athens who was born of the Earth of semen of Hephaistes

---

[74] *P.Köln* VI.257.14 comm.

[75] E.g., *SM* I 9.11 (*P.Michael.* 27); *SM* I 10.9; *SM* I 14.4–6 (*P.Erl.* 15); *SM* I 18.6–7 (*P.Leid.Inst.* 9); *SM* I 19.19–20 (*P.IFAO* III 50).

[76] *SM* I 21.1–2: ἷς πατήρ ἷς υἱός ἕν | πνεῦμα ἅγιον.   [77] See Section 6.1.3.

[78] *P.Bon.* I 9.5–7. The threefold 'amen' suggests it was written as an amulet; see n. 319. For instances in later Coptic incantations, see *AKZ*, 2.103 (no. XXXI.39–41), 109 (no. XXXIII.1), with 3.232; ET: *ACM*, nos. 113 and 121.

[79] D. Wortmann, 'Der weisse Wolf: Ein christliches Fieberamulett der Kölner Papyrussammlung', *Philologus*, 107 (1963), 157–61 at 158: seventh century; *SM* I 34: sixth century.

[80] For this explanation, see Wortmann, 'Der weisse Wolf', 160–1.

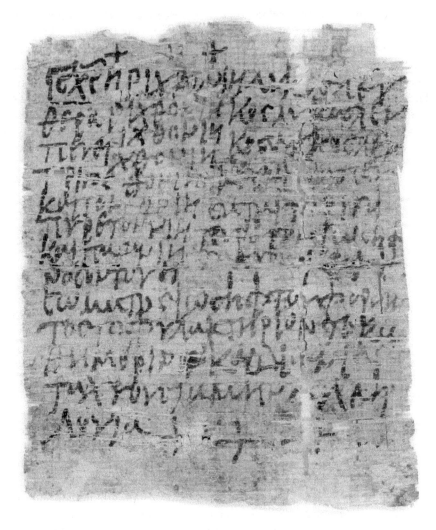

Fig. 4.5. *SM* I 34 (P.Köln inv. 851r). Copyright Papyrussammlung Köln, Institut für Altertumskunde, University of Cologne.

that fell to the ground when the latter attempted to rape Athena. Athena entrusted the infant to the daughters of Cecrops, king of Athens, on strict instruction that they not open the chest in which he lay. They disobeyed and found a child in serpent form or surrounded by serpents. They died as a consequence, from snakebite, by one account, or of terror as they leaped from the Acropolis to their death, by another. Athena gave Erichthonius two drops of the Gorgon's blood, one which healed, the other, poisoned. He was later worshipped in the form of a serpent.[81] Whether the name is included here because of Erichthonius' power to heal or because, like other mythical figures who caused death, he was fearsome to illnesses, is moot.[82]

The text fills the entire papyrus, leaving a small margin at the bottom. It is written in an irregular semi-cursive hand with some adjoining letters.[83] The scribe first penned three crosses across the top to the left of centre.[84] He then wrote the grape-cluster sequence under the crosses, dropping an initial letter from one line to the next and writing the remaining letters without error. The appeal to the white wolf—the name is repeated three times—fills the space to the right of the grape-cluster. A *charactêr* and two crosses occupy the remaining space after its last word. The appeal to Jesus Christ (written as a *nomen sacrum*[85]) fills the space to the left and below the grape-cluster. It is concludes with 'Amen, alleluia', followed by three crosses that fill out the remaining space in the bottom line. (Again, slight discrepancies in the levels of the lines show that the two appeals were written separately, after the grape-cluster had been written.) The scribe was sufficiently alert to correct the final letter of καθημερινόν ('quotidian') from *rho* to *nu* in the Christian invocation.[86] The framing of the text with three crosses along the top and the three crosses in the last line, the correct form of the *nomina sacra*, and the Christian invocation and acclamation all point to a milieu where Christian conventions were well known. This accords with the relatively late date of the papyrus. But familiarity with Christian conventions does not prevent the scribe from incorporating, as well, the powerful name of Erichthonius and the parallel appeal to Horus-Apollo. The point of the schema—whose spatial arrangement the scribe had anticipated—is to be inclusive of these three healing powers. What Jesus Christ, Erichthonius, and the white wolf signified for the scribe or the client, we cannot know.

4.2.2 Amulets in a Christian Idiom

We may compare the above 'syncretistic' examples with personalized incantations that employ customary forms of adjuration, such as the command to

---

[81] M. C. Howatson and I. Chilvers (eds), *The Concise Oxford Companion to Classical Literature* (Oxford: Oxford University Press, 1993), 212–13; for a more detailed summary, W. H. Roscher (ed.), *Ausführliches Lexikon der griechischen und römischen Mythologie*, 6 vols (Leipzig: Teubner, 1845–1923), 1.1303–8.

[82] For the former explanation, see Wortmann, 'Der weisse Wolf', 159–60. For the latter, *SM* I, pp. 4–5, 101.

[83] Image of the recto at <https://papyri.uni-koeln.de/stueck/tm65318> (Kölner Papyrussammlung).

[84] On the order of writing, see Wortmann, 'Der weisse Wolf', 158.

[85] *SM* I 34.1: ι͡ς χ͡ς.

[86] *SM* I 34.11 apparatus; Wortmann, 'Der weisse Wolf', 158, mistakenly states that the first *nu* was corrected.

heal or the command to flee, but are otherwise devoid of Graeco-Egyptian elements. We are fortunate to have two amulets that combine the acclamation 'Jesus Christ is victorious', a customary flee-formula, and an injunction prefaced by the acclamation 'Holy, holy, holy Lord Sabaôth' (one of several forms the threefold 'holy' could take[87]). This allows us to compare how two scribes executed what was evidently a familiar incantation.

SM I 25 (*P.Prag.* I 6), assigned to the fifth century, reads:

> [·ϯ· Jesus Christ] is victorious. Shivering, | [and] fever with shivering, | [and] fever, the | Son/fear (?)[88] of God | pursues you closely (σε καταδιώκει). Holy, | holy, holy, Lord | Sabaoth. Heal (ἴασαι) | Gennadia, | your servant. Jesus | Christ is victorious. ·ϯ·

BKT X 27, assigned to the sixth century, reads:

> ... | The fear of God banishes you (ἐκδιώκει σε). Holy, | holy, holy, Lord Saba<ôth>. Heal (ἴασαι) the | bearer (of this amulet). Jesus Christ is victorious. ⳨ ·ϯ· ⳨ ·ϯ·

SM I 25 is written on papyrus;[89] *BKT* X 27, on parchment.[90] Each is written in an irregular hand. The scribe of *BKT* X 27 appears to have been written at greater speed, to judge by the continuous strokes in the threefold 'holy', obviously a familiar sequence to the writer. Both writers spell phonetically, and both introduce anomalies. The scribe of *SM* I 25 employs both the genitive and the nominative when listing the fevers that are being chased away;[91] the scribe of *BKT* X 27 fails to complete words,[92] a further indication of haste, especially given how common the words of this type of incantation are. At the same time, both scribes use *nomina sacra* consistently and correctly, with supralinear strokes.[93] This, as well as their use of the cross and staurogram,[94] indicates a familiarity with basic Christian scribal conventions. (In the case of *SM* I 25, the culture of the writer is further indicated by his use of the Christian expression 'your servant'.[95]) The two scribes also employ organic *diairesis* at

---

[87] See Section 6.1.2.

[88] See now *BKT* X 27 intro. The parallel at *BKT* X 27.2 suggests that *SM* I 25.3–4 could have read ὁ φ- | ό̄βος rather than ὁ ν- | ἰός. While the new reading would fit the space better at line 4, the last letter at line 3, difficult to make out, is not *phi*.

[89] Image at *P.Prag.* I, plate XIV.

[90] Image at *BKT* X, plate XXXIV, and <http://smb.museum/berlpap/index.php/06239/>(Berliner Papyrusdatenbank).

[91] *SM* I 25.1–3 comm.; *P.Prag.* I 6.1 comm. We do not in fact know if ῥιγοπύρετος at lines 2–3 was in the nominative or the genitive, since the beginning of line 3 is missing.

[92] *BKT* X 27.3: Σαβα<ώθ>, 4: φοροῦν<τα>.

[93] *SM* I 25.4: θ̄ῡ, 9–10: ῑς̄ χ̄ς̄; *BKT* X 27.2: θ̄ῡ, 3: κ̄ς̄, 4: ῑς̄ χ̄ς̄.

[94] *SM* I 25.10, and in all likelihood also at line 1; *BKT* X 27.4.

[95] *P.Prag.* I 6.9 comm. gives parallels. The Greek word δούλη, when used in Christian contexts, is often translated 'handmaid' or 'maidservant', whereas its male equivalent, δοῦλος, is translated as 'slave' or 'servant'; see, e.g., G. H. E. Lampe (ed.), *A Greek Patristic Lexicon*

the one point it is required to indicate that a vowel is to be pronounced separately (ἴασαι).[96] All in all, these two amulets would appear to have been written by scribes in a Christian milieu accustomed to producing simple, formulaic incantations against fever. They are analogous, if you will, to the equally formulaic and quickly produced amulets against scorpions and snakes that employ the 'Hôr Hôr' sequence.

Alongside such short, formulaic amulets we can compare two sets of more developed amulets from the fifth and sixth centuries. The first set consists of amulets whose formulation and features suggests that they were written by scribes closer to the centre of institutional Christian culture. These scribes are familiar with the texts, phraseology, and rituals of the institutional church, and their use of those resources corresponds fairly closely to what we know from literary or documentary witnesses produced by the institutional church. These scribes also appear to be relatively literate as a result of their training and occupations. The formulation and features of the second set, by contrast, suggests that their writers were more on the periphery of institutional Christian culture. Their familiarity with Christian idioms seems to derive more from hearing than reading or copying, and their use of texts or phraseology associated with the institutional church is lacunose or idiosyncratic.

We begin the first set with *PGM* P5b (*P.Oxy.* VIII 1151),[97] assigned to the fifth century. It was found 'tightly folded, and tied with a string' among the Oxyrhynchus papyri.[98] It is a long oblong papyrus with writing parallel to the short edge.[99] The informal but regular upright majuscule hand likely belonged to a professional scribe.[100] This is corroborated by the ensemble of lectional signs and abbreviations the writer employs: organic and inorganic *diairesis*;[101] the compendium for καί (☧);[102] abbreviation of final *nu*;[103] and

---

(Oxford: At the Clarendon Press, 1961), *s.v.* δούλη and δοῦλος. I have chosen to render both words as 'servant', indicating the gender when it is not clear from the context.

[96] *SM* I 25.7: ϊασε; *BKT* X 27.3: ϊασε.

[97] For a revised reading of lines 39–40, see D. Hagedorn, 'Bemerkungen zu Urkunden', *ZPE*, 145 (2003), 224–7 at 226, <http://www.jstor.org/stable/20191724>. Republications of the text incorporating the revised reading, with English translations, at A. Luijendijk, 'A Gospel Amulet for Joannia (P.Oxy. VIII 1151)', in K. B. Stratton and D. S. Kalleres (eds), *Daughters of Hecate: Women and Magic in the Ancient World* (New York: Oxford University Press, 2014), 418–43 at 420 (which should, however, read 'rescue your female slave Joannia' at lines 9–11), 430–1; B. C. Jones, *New Testament Texts on Greek Amulets from Late Antiquity* (London: Bloomsbury T & T Clark, 2016), 134–5 (no. 17). These supersede the English translation at *ACM*, no. 16.

[98] *P.Oxy.* VIII 1151 intro.

[99] Image at Jones, *New Testament Texts*, 136 (plate 16), and <http://special.lib.gla.ac.uk/teach/papyrus/oxyrhynchus1151.html> (University of Glasgow Special Collections).

[100] *P.Oxy.* VIII 1151 intro.; Luijendijk, 'A Gospel Amulet', 419; Jones, *New Testament Texts*, 137.

[101] *P.Oxy.* VIII 1151.5, 11, 23, 25, 28, 30, 46, 50, 54 apparatus.

[102] *P.Oxy.* VIII 1151.20, 35, 43–50.   [103] *P.Oxy.* VIII 1151.22: γέγονε̄, 50: πάντω̄.

possibly a punctuation mark.[104] A variety of *nomina sacra* are used correctly and consistently, accompanied by supralinear strokes.[105] A cross marks the beginning of the text, as well as several sections within the text,[106] and a staurogram marks the end.[107]

The text opens with a flee-formula and an injunction similar to those we saw in the above amulets: '✝ Flee, hateful spirit! Christ pursues you (σε διώκει). The Son of God and the Holy Spirit have overtaken you. O God of the sheep-pool,[108] rescue your servant Joannia whom Anastasia, also called Euphemia, bore from every evil.'[109] From the rest of the text it is clear that the writer was well versed in the scriptures and liturgy of the church. A quotation of the beginning of the Gospel of John (John 1: 1 and 3, omitting verse 2),[110] set off by a cross,[111] follows the standard text of the gospel closely. The amulet is in fact an important witness to the wording and implied punctuation of verse 3 in the manuscript tradition of the gospel.[112] The ensuing request for healing from fever, expanding on the request already made, echoes Christian scriptural and liturgical language by appealing to the 'Son and Word of the living God, who heals every illness and every infirmity'.[113] The writer then appeals to 'the prayers and intercessions of our lady the *Theotokos* and the glorious archangels and Saint John, the glorious apostle and evangelist and theologian, and Saint Serenus and Saint Philoxenus and Saint Victor and Saint Justus and all the saints'.[114]

---

[104] *P.Oxy.* VIII 1151.3 (a high dot above the final *iota*).

[105] *P.Oxy.* VIII 1151.1: π̅ν̅α̅, 3: χ̅ς̅, 5: θ̅υ̅, 6: π̅ν̅α̅, 7: θ̅ς̅, 17: θ̅υ̅, 18: θ̅ς̅, 23: κ̅ε̅ χ̅ε̅, 24: θ̅υ̅, 52: κ̅ε̅ θ̅ς̅. The contraction of πνεῦμα when the word has a 'mundane' rather than a 'sacred' meaning, as at line 1, is common; see Paap, *Nomina Sacra*, 102.

[106] *P.Oxy.* VIII 1151.1, 15, 23. See also n. 111.

[107] *P.Oxy.* VIII 1151.56; there is a right-facing point at the top of the vertical.

[108] This is an allusion to the story of Jesus healing one of the invalids waiting at the pool by the Sheep Gate in Jerusalem (John 5: 2–9).

[109] *P.Oxy.* VIII 1151.1–14.   [110] *P.Oxy.* VIII 1151.15–22.

[111] Joseph E. Sanzo, *Scriptural Incipits on Amulets from Late Antique Egypt: Text, Typology, and Theory* (Tübingen: Mohr Siebeck, 2014), 139, rightly notes the significance of this cross in setting off the quotation. But, contrary to his description, there is no space available at the end of line 14 before the quotation, and there is no cross at the end of the quotation at line 22. The cross at line 23 (κ̅ε̅ ✝ χ̅ε̅) marks the beginning of the next section of the text.

[112] Sanzo, *Scriptural Incipits*, 98 n. 90; Jones, *New Testament Texts*, 139.

[113] *P.Oxy.* VIII 1151.23–38. For the appellation 'Son and Word of the living God', see, e.g., A. *Io.* 8, in Lipsius and Bonnet, *Acta apostolorum apocrypha*, 2/1.156, now, however, not considered part of the original work (*Acta Iohannis*, ed. E. Junod and J.-D. Kaestli, 2 vols in 1 [Turnhout: Brepols, 1983], 66–7, 840–4); Origen, *Dial.* 2 (SC 67.56), where Heracleides is speaking; Alexander Salaminus, *Cruc.* (PG 87.4036). For the phrase 'who heals every illness and every infirmity', an allusion to Matt. 4: 23, see T. S. de Bruyn, 'Appeals to Jesus as the One "Who Heals Every Illness and Every Infirmity" (Matt 4: 23, 9: 35) in Amulets in Late Antiquity', in L. DiTommaso and L. Turcescu (eds), *The Reception and Interpretation of the Bible in Late Antiquity* (Leiden: Brill, 2008), 65–81.

[114] *P.Oxy.* VIII 1151.38–51.

This closing appeal is significant for several reasons. It is among the earliest witnesses from Egypt to the practice of appealing to the intercessions of Mary.[115] Moreover, all the saints mentioned, including Mary, were honoured with churches or shrines in Oxyrhynchus.[116] In fact, Oxyrhynchus is the only city in Egypt that at this time had a church dedicated to John the Evangelist,[117] which probably explains why he, rather than John the Baptist, is named after Mary.[118] Justus, Serenus, and Philoxenus, too, were venerated locally; their cult is well documented in Oxyrhynchus but, with the exception of Serenus, not elsewhere.[119] All this suggests that the writer of the amulet not only resided in Oxyrhynchus but also was a cleric or monk who was well read in the scriptures and the liturgy. Only such a scribe would have had this accurate knowledge of the text of the gospel and the phrasing of liturgical prayers.[120] Likewise, only such a scribe would have produced the elevated wording of the final first-person declaration: 'For upon your name, Lord God, have I called, the name that is wonderful and exceedingly glorious and terrifying to your enemies. Amen.'[121] One might add that phonetic spellings are relatively infrequent.[122]

Another amulet that displays similar characteristics is *PGM* P18, assigned to the fifth or sixth century.[123] Its structure is like that of the second parts of *SM*

---

[115] T. S. de Bruyn, 'Appeals to the Intercessions of Mary in Greek Liturgical and Paraliturgical Texts from Egypt', in L. M. Peltomaa, A. Külzer, and P. Allen (eds), *Presbeia Theotokou: The Intercessory Role of Mary across Times and Places in Byzantium (4th–9th Century)* (Vienna: Verlag der Österreichischen Akademie der Wissenschaften, 2015), 115–29. For parallels in liturgical texts, see A. T. Mihálykó, 'Writing the Christian Liturgy in Egypt (3rd to 9th cent.)', PhD thesis, University of Oslo, Oslo, 2016, 231–5 at 235 (comment on *BKT* VI 7.2v.21-3).

[116] A. Papaconstantinou, 'La liturgie stationnale à Oxyrhynchos dans la première moitié du 6ᵉ siècle: réédition et commentaire du POxy XI 1357', *REB*, 54 (1996), 139–59 at 140–1, 146, doi: 10.3406/rebyz.1996.1921; A. Papaconstantinou, 'Les sanctuaires de la Vierge dans l'Égypte byzantine et omeyyade: l'apport des textes documentaires', *JJP*, 30 (2000), 81–94 at 84; Papaconstantinou, *Le culte des saints*, 62–8 (Victor), 108–9 (Justus), 115–16 (John the Evangelist), 187–8 (Serenus), 203–4 (Philoxenus). The evidence is summarized at Luijendijk, 'A Gospel Amulet', 420–1, 434–5 nn. 16–19.

[117] Papaconstantinou, *Le culte des saints*, 116.

[118] De Bruyn, 'Appeals to the Intercessions of Mary', 147–8.

[119] Papaconstantinou, *Le culte des saints*, 204. Serenus is attested in Herakleopolis and Saqqara as well; see n. 116.

[120] Luijendijk, 'A Gospel Amulet', 426–7.

[121] P.Oxy. VIII 1151.51-6: ὅτι τὸ ὄνομά σου, κ(ύρι)ε ὁ θ(εό)s, ἐπικαλεσά[μ]ην, τὸ θαυμαστὸν καὶ ὑπερένδοξον καὶ φοβερὸν τοῖς ὑπεναντίοις, ἀμήν. See, e.g., John of Thessalonica, *Dorm. B M V* A.1 (PO 19/3.375): Τῇ θαυμαστῇ καὶ ὑπερενδόξῳ καὶ ὄντως μεγάλη τοῦ παντὸς κόσμου δεσποίνῃ, τῇ ἀειπαρθένῳ μητρὶ τοῦ σωτῆρος ἡμῶν καὶ Θεοῦ Ἰησοῦ Χριστοῦ καὶ ἀληθῶς θεοτόκῳ; *Metaphrasis martyrii sanctae Tatianae* 6, in F. Halkin (ed.), *Légendes grecques de 'Martyres romaines'* (Brussels: Société des Bollandistes, 1973), 56–81 at 61: εὐλογητὸν γὰρ ὑπάρχει τὸ ὄνομα τῆς σῆς δόξης τὸ μέγα καὶ ἔνδοξον καὶ φοβερὸν τοῖς ὑπεναντίοις.

[122] To those noted in the apparatus to *P.Oxy.* VIII 1151, and Jones, *New Testament Texts*, 135, add at line 20 χωρείς [read: χωρίς] (mentioned by Jones at p. 139); line 39 πρεσβίαις [read: πρεσβείαις] (mentioned by Jones at p. 137); lines 52–3 ἐπεκαλεσά[μ]ην [read: ἐπικαλεσά[μ]ην].

[123] For a diplomatic transcription including lectional signs, see M. Naldini, 'Due papiri cristiani della collezione fiorentina', *SIFC*, 33 (1961), 212–18 at 216–18. For a revised reading of lines 1–3, see F. Maltomini, 'Osservazioni al testo di alcuni papiri magici greci. (III.)', *SCO*, 32

I 25 and *BKT* X 27: a threefold 'holy' followed by an injunction. But, as with *PGM* P5b, this structure is considerably developed in a Christian idiom. The threefold 'holy' with which the text opens—'Holy, holy, holy, Lord | Sabaôth, full are the heaven and | the earth of glory'[124]—is taken from the *Sanctus* of liturgy of the Eucharist.[125] Because of a lacuna at line 3, which could read 'your' or 'his' glory,[126] it is not possible to ascertain exactly which form of the liturgy the amulet echoes.[127] The *Sanctus* does not lead directly to an injunction to heal. Instead we have a *historiola* recounting healings performed by Jesus, the first two lines of which are indecipherable: '... and who has healed again, who has raised Lazarus from the dead even on the fourth day, who has healed Peter's mother-in-law, who has also performed many unmentioned healings in addition to those they report in the sacred gospels: heal her who wears this divine amulet of the disease afflicting her, through the prayers and intercession [*sic*] of the ever-virgin mother, the *Theotokos*, and all...'[128] The text then again becomes indecipherable.

The amulet is written in an informal but regular sloping majuscule hand with some adjoining letter-forms.[129] As in the case of *PGM* P5b, the scribe employs organic *diairesis* and the compendium for καί.[130] The scribe did not, it appears, use *nomina sacra*; the reconstruction of line 1 requires the full form of κύριος. Only a few words have irregular spellings,[131] which suggests that the scribe was reasonably familiar with 'standard' Greek. In short, this amulet was produced by someone who was able to write the *Sanctus*, compose the *historiola* with its various allusions, and phrase the appeal to the intercessions of Mary in accordance with standard liturgical and biblical usage in a practiced but informal hand. As with *PGM* P5b, this combination of qualities suggests that the writer was a Christian cleric or monk. These competencies might be found among nuns as well: among Coptic prayers of thanks for the annual filling of a reservoir, written by nuns living behind the temple of Seti in Abydos in, probably, the seventh

(1982), 235–41 at 239, <http://www.jstor.org/stable/24181825>; P. J. Sijpesteijn, 'Ein Vorschlag zu PGM II 18', *ZPE*, 52 (1982), 246, <http://www.jstor.org/stable/20183891>.

[124] *PGM* P18.1–3 (Maltomini, 'Osservazioni', 239): ✝ ἅγιος ἅγι[ος ἅ]γιος κύριος | Σαβαωθ πλήρ[ης ὁ] οὐρα[νὸς κ]αὶ | ἡ γῆ τῆς δόξης [...

[125] As both Sijpesteijn and Maltomini observed (n. 123).

[126] Maltomini, 'Osservazioni', 246.

[127] See de Bruyn, 'Appeals to the Intercessions of Mary', 123. See also Section 6.1.2.

[128] ET: *ACM*, no. 13 (modified).

[129] Image at Naldini, 'Due papiri cristiani', 215.

[130] *Diairesis*: *PGM* P18.6, 8, 10–12 (as transcribed at Naldini, 'Due papiri cristiani', 217; so too for subsequent references). Compendium: *PGM* P18.6, 10, 12, 15, 17.

[131] *PGM* P18.12: ε[ὐα]γγαλίοις for εὐαγγελίοις (vocalic interchange), 16: ἐαιπαρθένου for ἀειπαρθένου (metathesis).

century, one prayer incorporates a pre-*Sanctus* and *Sanctus* along with other Christian liturgical expressions.[132]

Our final example in this set, *SM* I 31 (*P.Turner* 49) = *BKT* IX 134,[133] assigned to the end of the fifth century or the beginning of the sixth, is similar in structure to the one we have just discussed. It consists of a declaration, a *historiola*, a petition, and a closing doxology, all of which are formulated in a wholly Christian idiom.[134] The amulet begins with a declarative summary of the career of Christ (a version of the so-called second article of the creed): '[·|· Christ was born of the] virgin Mary, and was crucified by Pontius Pilate, and was buried in a grave, and rose on the third day, and was taken up into the heavens, and . . .'[135] As we shall see in Chapter 6, this is one of several amulets that begin with a summary of Christ's career, influenced, it seems, by Christian exorcistic rituals. Two scribal features of the declaration should be mentioned. First, the scribe devotes the entire first long line of the papyrus to it. In all probability, the width of the papyrus was determined by this line, a way of setting off the declaration. Second, the scribe abbreviates ἐστ(αυ)ρ(ώ)θη ('was crucified') by using the staurogram (or *tau-rho* ligature). William Brashear, the first editor of the papyrus, described these letters as 'not so much a tau-rho monogram as a cross with a circle on it—almost a pictorial representation of the crucifixion'.[136] This would support the argument that the abbreviation functioned as a visual reference to Jesus' crucifixion.[137]

The *historiola* that follows speaks of Jesus healing 'every infirmity of the people and every illness' (another allusion to Matt. 4: 23) and of Jesus healing Peter's mother-in-law (Matt. 8: 14–15): '[We believe,] Jesus, that you were healing then every infirmity of the people and every illness. Savior Jesus, we believe that you went then into the house of Peter's mother-in-law, who was feverish, [and you touched her hand and] the fever left her.'[138] Even if one ignores the plausible reconstruction of the missing portions at the end of line 2 and the beginning of line 3 supplied by the editors in *SM* I 31, it is clear that the scribe was paraphrasing the biblical text and thus familiar with it.

---

[132] A. Delattre, 'Les graffitis coptes d'Abydos et la crue du Nil', in C. Cannuyer (ed.), *Etudes coptes VIII: dixième journée d'études, Lille 14–16 juin 2001* (Lille: Association francophone de coptologie, 2003), 133–45 at 143–5; cf. M. A. Murray, J. G. Milne, and W. E. Crum, *The Osireion at Abydos* (London: B. Quaritch, 1904), 38–42.

[133] Republished in Jones, *New Testament Texts*, 71 (no. 3). Image at *BKT* IX, plate 61; Jones, *New Testament Texts*, 72 (plate 3); and <http://smb.museum/berlpap/index.php/04427/> (Berliner Papyrusdatenbank). My examination of the images leads me to accept the reading μέγα (*SM* I 31; *BKT* IX 134) over ἄγ[ιον] (*P.Turner* 49; Jones) at line 3, and the reading π(ατ)ρός (*P.Turner* 49; *BKT* IX 134; Jones) over π(ατ)ρ(ό)ς (*SM* I 31) at line 4. The image is too indistinct for me to offer an opinion on the final πν(εύμ)α(τος)/πν(εύμα τ)ος in line 4; cf. *SM* I 31.4 comm.

[134] ET: *SM* I, pp. 87–8 (which I follow below); Jones, *New Testament Texts*, 71–3. These supersede *ACM*, no. 14.

[135] *SM* I 31.1; the first portion is a suggested restoration.

[136] *P.Turner* 49.1 comm.   [137] See Chapter 2 n. 140.

[138] *SM* I 31.2–3 (translation modified).

Moreover, the scribe cast the narrative into a confessional mode, twice employing the construction 'we believe that'.[139] This not only underlines the justificatory function of the *historiola*; it also echoes stories in the gospels, such as the one of the woman with chronic menstrual bleeding,[140] in which people are healed as a result of their faith in Jesus' power to heal.[141] The request that follows, with its repeated 'now', draws Jesus' power to heal into the present: 'And now we beseech you, Jesus, also now heal your servant [a woman], who wears your great name, from every illness and from … fever and from fever with shivering and from headache and from every malignity and from every evil spirit.'[142] The amulet concludes with the common trinitarian invocation 'in the name of the Father and the Son and the Holy Spirit'.

The hand, described as 'a small cursive, sloping to the right',[143] is that of a practiced writer who writes with evident facility, maintaining straight lines across the long papyrus. The scribe uses the compendium for καί through-out.[144] There are relatively few phonetic spellings. The *nomina sacra* for 'Father' and 'Spirit' in the last line are unusual,[145] but otherwise the scribe employs common forms.[146] In sum, we again have an amulet written by a practiced writer who was familiar with Christian symbols, scripture, and liturgy—in all likelihood, a cleric or monk. What distinguishes this amulet from the previous one (and others like it) is the confessional mode of the *historiola*. It is a specifically Christian way of relating the healings that Jesus performed during his lifetime to the healing he is being asked to perform now.

The contrast with amulets in our second set of examples is marked. We begin with *SM* I 29 (*P.Princ.* II 107),[147] now assigned to the fifth or sixth century.[148] This amulet against fever recites an adjuration addressed to the archangel Michaêl by the authority of almighty Sabaôth, the opening verses of LXX Ps. 90, several verses of the Lord's Prayer, and the threefold 'holy'. Since the syntax is problematic and the citations are lacunose, it is best to quote the text in its entirety:[149]

---

[139] Notwithstanding the reservations expressed by the editors at *SM* I 31.2 comm. about the reconstruction of πιστεύομεν in the middle of line 2, their proposed reconstruction of πιστεύομεν at the beginning and the middle of the line is supported by ὅτι that follows in both instances.

[140] Matt. 9: 20–2; Mark 5: 25–34; Luke 8: 43–8.

[141] E.g., Matt. 15: 21–8; Mark 10: 46–52; Luke 17: 11–19.   [142] *SM* I 31.3–4.

[143] *BKT* IX, p. 174; W. M. Brashear, 'Vier Berliner Zaubertexte', *ZPE*, 17 (1975), 25–33 at 31, <http://www.jstor.org/stable/20180832>. The frequent adjoining and ligatured letters are more in keeping with a cursive hand than a semi-cursive hand, *pace* Jones, *New Testament Texts*, 75.

[144] *SM* I 31.1–4.   [145] See n. 133.   [146] *SM* I 31.2: ̅τ̅υ̅ (twice), 3: ̅τ̅υ̅, 4: ̅υ̅υ̅.

[147] Republished, with English translations, in T. J. Kraus, 'Manuscripts with the *Lord's Prayer*— They Are More Than Simply Witnesses to That Text Itself', in T. J. Kraus and T. Nicklas (eds), *New Testament Manuscripts: Their Texts and their World* (Leiden: Brill, 2006), 227–66 at 254–66; Jones, *New Testament Texts*, 80–1 (no. 5).

[148] *P.Princ.* II 107: fourth to fifth century. *SM* I 29; Jones, *New Testament Texts*, 81–3: fifth to sixth century.

[149] ET: *SM* I, pp. 79–80 (modified).

·|· [3 lines] | fever with shivering—I adjure you, Michaêl, ar- | changel of the earth—
quotidian or nocturnal | or quartan; by the almighty | Sabaôth, no longer fasten to
the soul of the | wearer (of this amulet) nor to his whole body. | I adjure you and the
dead, deliver | Taiolles, daughter of Isidoros... | 'He who dwells in the help of the
Most High | will reside in the shelter of the God of heaven. He will say | to God, and
my refuge and my helper, | I put my trust in him.' 'Our father in | heaven, hallowed
be your will, | our daily bread.' 'Holy, | holy, Lord Sabaôth, heaven | and earth are full
of your holy glory. *Aniaadaii* | *a*, Michaêl, the Lord of Abraham, Isaac | (and) Jacob,
Elôei, Ele, Saba- | ôth, Ôêl.

The hand, an informal sloping semi-cursive with cursive features,[150] is that of
a practiced writer.[151] But the writing is more hurried and less controlled than,
for instance, in *PGM* P18. The lines slope increasingly to the right as the text
progresses; the writing becomes more cramped; continuous strokes between
letter-forms are more frequent. Spelling is phonetic and syntax is irregular,[152]
but *nomina sacra* are used consistently and correctly.[153]

What especially distinguishes this amulet from those in the previous set is
its confusing syntax and inaccurate citations. The adjuration does not progress, as is customary, from invocation to command; it mixes up the fevers to
be dispelled with the powers to do the dispelling. The citation of LXX Ps. 90:
1–2 omits several phrases.[154] The citation of the Lord's Prayer alters its
meaning (cf. Matt. 6: 9–13) by conflating the first and third petitions ('hallowed be your will'), skipping from the first petition (verse 9c) to the fourth
petition (verse 11), and omitting the remaining verses (verses 12–13).[155] And
the threefold 'holy', which in referring to 'your holy glory' is clearly derived
from the *Sanctus* of the Egyptian eucharistic liturgy,[156] is also defective,
lacking one 'holy' and several articles.[157]

Where, then, should we place this writer? I agree with recent editors who
regard the idiom of the incantation to be 'conventionally Christian'.[158]

---

[150] So too Jones, *New Testament Texts*, 81. Although APIS (quoted by Kraus, 'Manuscripts',
255) describes the hand as a 'fluent cursive', the letter-forms, cursively written, are mostly
detached, as in other informal sloping hands, with occasional continuous strokes between
letter-forms (as in καί). See, e.g., Harrauer, *Handbuch*, 1.462–3 (no. 263), 2.253 (plate 249),
CPR XXV 28 (sixth or seventh century), a more regular hand; Cavallo and Maehler, *Greek
Bookhands*, 116–17 (no. 53b), BKT VIII 16 (seventh or eighth century).
[151] Image at Kraus, 'Manuscripts', 239; Jones, *New Testament Texts*, 82 (plate 5).
[152] *SM* I 29 apparatus.   [153] *SM* I 29.11: $\overline{θυ}$, 12: $\overline{θυ}$, 16: $\overline{κς}$, 18: $\overline{κυ}$.
[154] *SM* I 29.12 comm.; Kraus, 'Manuscripts', 261.
[155] *SM* I 29.13–15 comm.; Kraus, 'Manuscripts', 262. Jones, *New Testament Texts*, 86, notes a
parallel for the reading 'hallowed be your will' in Cyril of Alexandria, *Ador.* 17 (PG 68.1072). But
this reading is anomalous in the works of Cyril; elsewhere he cites the standard text, as, for
instance, at *Ador.* 8 and 13 (PG 68.569, 876). The reading may be an editorial error; one would
have to consult the manuscripts.
[156] See Section 6.1.2.   [157] *SM* I 29.15–17 comm.; Kraus, 'Manuscripts', 262–3.
[158] *SM* I 29 intro.; Kraus, 'Manuscripts', 256, 265–6.

Whether one considers it to be 'syncretistic', as has been suggested,[159] depends on what one means by 'syncretism', as Thomas Kraus has observed.[160] Unlike other amulets we have already discussed, such as *PGM* P3 or *SM* I 20, this amulet does not in fact juxtapose customary elements with Christian ones. Its idiosyncrasy appears to derive from the writer's attenuated knowledge of the structure of adjurations and the formulation of Christian material. Since this Christian material is so often cited in amulets, but more completely or accurately,[161] the writer of this amulet must be placed at the periphery of institutional Christian culture—which is not to say, however, that the writer would not have identified as a Christian.

We encounter something similar in another amulet assigned to the fifth or sixth century, *SM* I 32.[162] The wide oblong papyrus is densely written in cramped lines in a rough, irregular semi-cursive hand.[163] The text is complete, though in places the ink has faded or been rubbed away, such that parts of lines are indecipherable. The amulet consists in a series of adjurations and commands to stop the discharge from a rheumy or infected eye. What the scribe copied was in fact a recipe for an incantation, since he included phrases that properly belong to the recipe rather than the amulet: a generic phrase indicating the purpose of the incantation ('...for what you wish') and a generic phrase identifying the beneficiary of the incantation ('a certain man or a certain woman').[164] There are many phonetic spellings,[165] revealing the influence of an oral culture on the transmission of the recipe and/or the writing of the scribe. Also, the scribe is not consistent in his use of *nomina sacra*; he writes κύριος both in full and in an abbreviated form.[166]

The adjurations and commands are intriguing, to the extent that we can decipher them. The first adjuration orders the discharge to stop by appealing to the angel 'Toumêêl Êl', possibly meaning the angel Toumiel.[167] The second adjuration orders the discharge to stop by appealing to 'those who say "Holy, holy, holy, Lord Sabaôth, the God, the God Adonai Aoth"'; 'those who say' probably refers to the four archangels named at the end of the incantation

---

[159] R. Kotansky, in *GMPT*, 300: 'the character of the spell shows it is syncretistic rather than distinctively Christian'.

[160] Kraus, 'Manuscripts', 266.   [161] See Sections 5.5 and 5.6.

[162] The *editio princeps*, F. Maltomini, 'Cristo all'Eufrate. P.Heid.G.1101: amuleto cristiano', *ZPE*, 48 (1982), 149–70, <http://www.jstor.org/stable/20183648>, gives extensive discussion and commentary.

[163] Maltomini, 'Cristo all'Eufrate', 150, with plate II. Image at <http://www.rzuser.uni-heidelberg.de/~gv0/Papyri/SB/12719/12719%28150%29.html> (Heidelberger Papyrussammlung; *SB* XVI 12719).

[164] *SM* I 32.1–2, with line 1 comm.   [165] *SM* I 32 apparatus.

[166] *SM* I 32.6: θ̄ς (twice), [κ̄ς], 8: κύριος, 10: κ̄υ. At line 6 the space allows only for the abbreviated form.

[167] *SM* I 32.2–3, with line 3 comm.; Maltomini, 'Cristo all'Eufrate', 159.

rather than the seraphim mentioned at Isa. 6: 3.[168] After a *historiola* about Jesus is recited as precedent, the discharge is commanded to stop: 'For our Lord was pursued by the Jews, and he came to the Euphrates river and stuck in his staff, and the water stood still. Also you, discharge, stand still from head to toe-nails in the name of our Lord, who was crucified.'[169] Finally, the four archangels Michaêl, Gabriêl, Ouriêl, and Raphaêl are told, 'Undo, undo the pains, undo, now, now, quickly'.[170]

The threefold 'holy' and the *historiola*, along with their sequels, are what brings this amulet into our purview. If the amulet were lacking these elements, the rest of the incantation could be thought to derive from the broader Graeco-Egyptian repertoire. Even the threefold 'holy' is ambiguous, since it is common to both Jewish and Christian traditions, though amulets with some form of the threefold 'holy' usually have other Christian elements.[171] The configuration of this amulet (as well as others) reminds us that elements that at one time might have been distinctive and specific to a particular cultural group can be taken up by other cultural groups or become part of a transcultural vocabulary, so that, once they are 'naturalized' within those cultural systems,[172] they become weak or polyvalent indicators of identity.[173]

A good example of an amulet that eludes easy characterization (and also reflects on the threefold 'holy' in *SM* I 32) is *PGM* XXVc (*P.Cair.Cat.* 10434). Written in a 'large, rude uncial' assigned to the sixth century,[174] it reads, simply: '✝ Holy Lord Zabaôt'. This amulet has been described as 'Jewish'.[175] The presence of a cross would seem to undercut such a characterization. However, since both the cross and Sabaôth had wide currency, neither is a strong indicator of cultural identity or difference. My guess is that *PGM* XXVc issued from a Christian milieu,[176] but I readily acknowledge that cultural idioms flowed across group boundaries.

One wonders how we might view *SM* I 32 if it lacked the *historiola* and ensuing command. How would we interpret the threefold 'holy' with its sequel 'the God, the God Adonai Aoth'? Since the name 'Aôth' occurs in

---

[168] *SM* I 32.5–6 comm.; Maltomini, 'Cristo all'Eufrate', 161.

[169] *SM* I 32.8–11 (translation, p. 92).   [170] *SM* I 32.11–12.

[171] See Section 6.1.2.

[172] On 'naturalization' of foreign cultural elements, see G. Bohak, *Ancient Jewish Magic: A History* (Cambridge: Cambridge University Press, 2008), 229–30.

[173] Boustan and Sanzo, 'Christian Magicians'.

[174] *P.Cairo.Cat.* 10434 intro.

[175] *PGM* XXVc intro.; TM Magic (TM 65022), <http://www.trismegistos.org/magic/detail.php?tm=65022>, accessed 16 October 2015.

[176] For a comparable artefact, a pendant inscribed on the obverse with *Ιαωθ Σαβαθ Αδοναει* with one cross above and three below, and on the reverse with *ο ω ν* (i.e., ὁ ὤν) with a cross above and below, see S. Michel, *Magischen Gemmen im Britischen Museum*, 2 vols (London: British Museum Press, 2001), 1.283 (no. 456), 2 plate 69; C. Bonner, *Studies in Magical Amulets, Chiefly Graeco-Egyptian* (Ann Arbor: University of Michigan, 1950), 225.

Graeco-Egyptian incantations in connection with other names for the God of the Jews, as well as other contexts,[177] we might well read this amulet as another instance of the modulation of such names in Graeco-Egyptian practice. The accelerating formula at the end of the last adjuration, followed by *charaktêres* (that possibly filled out the line but now leave only traces), would reinforce this impression, as would the absence of any crosses or staurograms.

But here we must read the threefold 'holy' in conjunction with the *historiola*. The scribe (or his source) is evidently familiar with an otherwise unattested legend about Jesus that may derive from the tradition that Abgar, king of Edessa, offered Jesus a haven from the hostility of the Jews.[178] The correspondence was well known in Christian circles in Egypt.[179] Both Greek and Coptic versions survive in many formats, including amulets,[180] where it is accorded a status akin to the canonical gospels.[181] In some versions the description of the Jews' animosity toward Jesus is especially vehement;[182] the tradition served to differentiate Christians from Jews notionally if not socially.[183] Even if the legend in our amulet was not an extension of this tradition, it nevertheless expresses a Christian identity in speaking of 'our Lord' twice.[184] In the second instance the appellation is combined with an epithet commonly used by Christian writers when describing Jesus' power over demons: 'our Lord, who was crucified'.[185] But at same time the incantation incorporates a version of the threefold 'holy' that is several removes from the liturgical form of this acclamation in the *Sanctus*, suggesting that the scribe was on the periphery of institutional Christian culture. The amulet is thus an example of how customary and Christian traditions might be combined by scribes working in an increasingly Christian milieu but not necessarily close to the centre of the institutional church.

---

[177] *P.Mich.* XVI, p. 100; Maltomini, 'Cristo all'Eufrate', 162.

[178] G. Fiaccadori, 'Cristo all'Eufrate (P. Heid. G. 1101, 8 ss.)', *PP*, 41 (1986), 59–63. See also *SM* I 32 intro., and Maltomini, 'Cristo all'Eufrate', 152–3, for parallels in *historiolae* that speak of Elijah or Jesus stopping the flow of the Jordan River.

[179] See Section 5.4.

[180] T. S. de Bruyn, 'Christian Apocryphal and Canonical Narratives in Greek Papyrus Amulets in Late Antiquity', in P. Piovanelli and T. Burke (eds), *Rediscovering the Apocryphal Continent: New Perspectives on Early Christian and Late Antique Apocryphal Texts and Traditions* (Tübingen: Mohr Siebeck, 2015), 153–74 at 158–60.

[181] J. E. Sanzo, 'Brit. Lib. Or. 4919(2): An Unpublished Coptic Amulet in the British Library', *ZPE*, 183 (2012), 98–9, <http://www.jstor.org/stable/23849875>; Sanzo, *Scriptural Incipits*, 153–4.

[182] Boustan and Sanzo, 'Christian Magicians'.

[183] For further discussion, see J. E. Sanzo, '"For our Lord was pursued by the Jews...": The (Ab)Use of the Motif of "Jewish" Violence against Jesus on a Greek Amulet (P. Heid. 1101)', in D. Matson and K. C. Richardson (eds), *One in Christ Jesus: Essays on Early Christianity and 'All that Jazz,' in Honor of S. Scott Bartchy* (Eugene: Pickwick Publications, 2014), 86–98.

[184] *SM* I 32.8, 10.   [185] *SM* I 32.10 comm.

It can be tricky, however, to place a scribe within a putative range of Christian culture, as we see from a third amulet, *P.Köln* VIII 340.[186] It, too, is assigned to the fifth or sixth century.[187] It consists of a long oblong papyrus, now in two fragments (fr. A, 3.5 cm w × 15.8 cm h; fr. B, 3.4 cm w × 5.1 cm h), written on both sides (a and b).[188] According to its editor, Franco Maltomini, it is the product of two scribes.[189] One was responsible for a long incantation (side a);[190] the other, for two figures accompanied by some writing (side b).

The long incantation is written by a practiced writer in an irregular semi-cursive hand that becomes rapid and cramped toward the end of the text, with many compressed and adjoining letter-forms.[191] In the first line the scribe wrote seven staurograms followed by some letters that may have read 'One God'.[192] He then wrote out John 1: 1–11—the longest citation of the opening of a gospel among extant amulets.[193] This is followed by an appeal to God the Father and Mary the *Theotokos* to send the angel in charge of cures to chase 'every illness and every infirmity' from 'the one who wears this adjuration'.[194] After several fragmentary lines, the incantation concludes with a lacunose adjuration banishing various threats including the evil eye and insidious plots (the text is lacunose due to damage) in 'the glorious name of the Lord ... for ever and ever, amen, amen, amen'.[195] In the remaining space the scribe wrote a *charaktêr* accompanied by *alpha* and *omega* and two crosses, along with a series of letters in a rectangular scheme.

The scribe's experience is evident not only from the speed of his writing, but also from his use of *nomina sacra*,[196] the compendium (as well as the full form) for καί,[197] inorganic *diairesis*, and a supralinear stroke for final *nu*.[198] However, the writing is characterized by a certain inattentiveness, possibly the result of routine production of amulets like this one. (The incantation is, in fact, generic; it does not name a specific individual, but refers simply to the wearer, as noted above.) Although the citation from John follows the standard text of the gospel quite closely,[199] there are two omissions and a few instances

---

[186] Jones, *New Testament Texts*, 140–2 (no. 18).   [187] *P.Köln* VIII 340 intro.

[188] Image at *P.Köln* VIII, plate VII; J. H. F. Dijkstra, 'The Interplay between Image and Text on Greek Amulets Containing Christian Elements from Late Antique Egypt', in D. Boschung and J. M. Bremmer (eds), *The Materiality of Magic* (Munich: Wilhelm Fink, 2015), 271–92 at 283; Jones, *New Testament Texts*, 143 (plate 17); and <https://papyri.uni-koeln.de/stueck/tm61663> (Kölner Papyrussammlung).

[189] *P.Köln* VIII 340 intro.   [190] ET: Jones, *New Testament Texts*, 142.

[191] *P.Köln* VIII 340 intro.   [192] *P.Köln* VIII 340, side *a*, fr. A.1 comm.

[193] Sanzo, *Scriptural Incipits*, 140–1.

[194] *P.Köln* VIII 340, side *a*, fr. A.41–3: τὸν φρ. [] | τα τὸν ὁρκισμὸ(ν) | τοῦτον, with comm. For instances of ὁρκισμός used to refer to an adjuration, see *PGM* IV.3018–19, 3079; *PGM* P10.22–3.

[195] *P.Köln* VIII 340, side *a*, fr. B.4–13. The Italian translation of Maltomini at *P.Köln* VIII, p. 95, is more precise than that of Jones.

[196] Side *a*, fr. A.3: θ̄ν̄, θ̄ς̄; 5: θ̄ν̄; 12: θ̄ῡ; 13: θ̄ῡ; 36: κ̄ῡ; 37: ῑ̄ῡ χ̄ῡ. Side *a*, fr. B.9: κυ (with a supralinear stroke over the first letter of the next word).

[197] Compendium: side *a*, fr. A.6, 10, 43.   [198] *P.Köln* VIII 340 intro.

[199] See Jones, *New Testament Texts*, 146.

of dittography, which also occurs in the ensuing invocation.[200] The invocation, which like other amulets uses a standard form of address for God ('the Father of our Lord Jesus Christ/our Lord and Saviour Jesus Christ'),[201] is here irregular in several ways: 'I call upon you, God—and Mary the *Theotokos*—Father of our Lord {Lord} <and> Saviour Jesus Christ...'[202] First, the scribe misconstrues the opening verb.[203] Next, the appeal to Mary is interjected. Then, the scribe writes 'Lord' twice as a *nomen sacrum*, the second time without a supralinear stroke. (It may be that the scribe's exemplar had the compendium for *καί*—which Maltomini supplies—and that scribe misread the compendium in haste.) Finally, the scribe adds supralinear strokes above 'Mary', '[Theo]tokos', and 'Saviour', as well as several others words written in full.[204] ('Saviour' is occasionally abbreviated as a *nomen sacrum*.[205] The addition of the lines above 'Mary' and '[Theo]tokos' may be an indication of her status. But the lines about the other words are harder to explain,[206] except insofar as supralinear strokes appear above, for example, *voces mysticae* in customary incantations.[207]) In short, although the scribe is working with typically Christian material, phraseology, and conventions, he is not particularly scrupulous in his execution, whether in copying from an exemplar or in writing from memory. Still, later on he is sufficiently alert to correct an error in the closing formula, replacing the incorrect accusative form of the second 'ever' with the correct genitive form.[208] Moreover, the speed with which he writes the closing formula shows that he is quite familiar with it.

On the other side of the papyrus are two figures with hands raised in prayer (*orantes*). (Maltomini saw three figures, two *orantes* and the head of a woman surmounting the lower *orans*, but recent examination has corrected this impression.[209]) The upper *orans* is a man; the lower *orans*, a woman. The figures would have allowed the amulet to be applied to either a man or a woman.

---

[200] Omissions: side a, fr. A.11 (the second half of verse 5 and the first two words of verse 6); side a, fr. A.19 (two words of verse 8—*o*<*ὐκ ἦν*>—probably as a result of parablepsis). Dittography: side a, fr. A.13, 29; cf. also side a, fr. A.36, 41.

[201] Compare, e.g., MPER N.S. XVII 10 Ir.2–5 (see Section 5.3); PGM P9.2–3. For early witnesses of this common formulation in Greek and Coptic liturgical texts, see Mihálykó, 'Writing the Christian Liturgy', 204 (comment on *O.Frangé* 730.3–4).

[202] *P.Köln* VIII 340, side a, fr. A.33–7: ἐ[πικαλοῦ-] | μέν [read: ἐπικαλοῦμαί; cf. lines 33–4 comm.] σε, θ[(εό)ν, καὶ τὴν θεο-] | τόκον Μαρία, π[(ατέ)ρα] | τοῦ κ(υρίο)υ {κυ} <καὶ> σωτῆρ[ος] | [ἡ]μῶν Ἰ(ησο)ῦ Χ(ριστο)ῦ.

[203] *P.Köln* VIII 340, side a, fr. A.33–4 comm. Jones, *New Testament Texts*, 145–6, argues against Maltomini's correction of ἐ[πικαλοῦ]μέν to ἐπικαλοῦμαί. But ἐπικαλέω + σε in the sense of 'call upon' is commonly in the middle voice. There are no instances of the construction in the active voice in *Thesaurus Linguae Graecae*.

[204] *P.Köln* VIII 340, side a, fr. A.38: ἐ]κ̄σαοστιλης; side a, fr. A.40: ῑματο̄ῡ.

[205] Paap, *Nomina Sacra*, 97, 112.   [206] *P.Köln* VIII 340, side a, fr. A.38 comm.

[207] E.g., *SM* I 19.9–13 (*P.IFAO* III 50).

[208] *P.Köln* VIII, 340 side a, fr. B.10–12: εἰς τοὺς | αἰῶνας τῶν αἰώ- | νας {τῶν αἰών[ων]}.

[209] Dijkstra, 'The Interplay', 283–5; Jones, *New Testament Texts*, 144. The lower figure in the line drawing at *P.Köln* VIII, p. 86, is in fact the mirror image of the lower figure on the papyrus.

Around the upper *orans* is an invocation for healing that can be only partially reconstructed. It may have contained a name, but we cannot be certain.[210] The incantation on the other side does not name the client, as we have already noted. It employs only a generic masculine participial phrase, 'the one who wears'.[211] This does not necessarily mean that the amulet was meant for a man, since the masculine construction can be used for a woman, as one sees in *SM* I 29.[212] However, even if the client was not named in the missing text, the folds in the papyrus suggest that it was in fact applied as an amulet.[213]

The generic participial phrase and the two figures indicate that the amulet was prepared on the basis of a non-specific model. The instances of dittography in the long incantation suggest that the text was in fact copied from an exemplar. The appeal to Mary between 'God' and 'Father' is also easier to explain as a phrase inserted as some point into an exemplar than as a natural manner of speaking. Thus, the amulet could have been one of many routinely produced from a model. We do not know how much of the formulation of the amulet was the work of the scribes, but we can attribute its transmission to them, particularly the idiosyncrasies of the invocation. That the scribe of the incantation did not notice these idiosyncrasies, but either produced or reproduced them, places him some distance from the scribes we discussed in the first set of amulets. Nevertheless, the scribe's familiarity with the scriptural and liturgical material of the incantation also places him some distance from, for instance, the scribe of *SM* I 32 (though not perhaps as much from the scribe of *SM* I 29).

4.2.3 Summary

In amulets against fever and illness, the individuality of the scribe expresses itself around traditional injunctions and adjurations. The basic form of these injunctions and adjurations remains stable, expressed in customary phrases commanding fever to flee, declaring that a greater power pursues it, or adjuring a greater power to heal or deliver or protect the client. The scribe (or the scribe's sources) could develop or modify this structure, in the invocation, the names of the powers, or the *historiolae*, all of which could be modulated in the language of traditions deemed to be powerful or authoritative for the scribe or the client. Longer incantations obviously offer the scribe more scope for individuality.

We can differentiate among longer amulets with Christian elements by the manner in which the scribe develops the structure. Some amulets echo or cite the language of the Christian liturgy and scriptures fairly closely, whereas

---

[210] *P.Köln* VIII 340, side b, fr. A.10 comm.   [211] See n. 194.

[212] *SM* I 29.6–8, with Kraus, 'Manuscripts', 260; Jones, *New Testament Texts*, 144–5.

[213] *P.Köln* VIII 340 intro. identifies two vertical and two horizontal folds in fr. B and seven horizontal folds in fr. A.

others appear to recollect Christian material at some removes from its use in the liturgy of the church. In the two sets of amulets we just reviewed, this difference in formulation correlates, roughly, with a difference in scribal skill and execution. Amulets in the first set are written in more regular hands by scribes familiar with abbreviations and lectional signs. Amulets in the second set are written in less regular or skilled hands. Several *caveats* are immediately in order. First, this is a small sample. Second, we are dealing with found materials; we have no idea how representative these particular amulets are of the many that were made but subsequently perished. Third, an amulet such as *P.Köln* VIII 340 has qualities in common with amulets in either set: it cites scripture closely but incorporates a garbled invocation; the scribe is familiar with *nomina sacra*, but adds supralinear strokes to words written in full. So the correlation between formulation and writing may be contradicted in some instances. Nevertheless, the formulation and writing of these particular amulets suggest that they were written by scribes whose relation to places of scribal training and liturgical performance was different. Some were closer to the centre of institutional Christian culture, others were further from the centre.

It is important to recall that scribes of various types of amulets could be found in the same town or region. The short formulaic amulets against scorpions with which we began this chapter and the long amulet to heal Joannia from fever were both found at Oxyrhynchus, and we shall encounter other amulets from Oxyrhynchus as we continue with this study. Thus, we must think of scribes of varying skills and culture working in the same locale. A scribe's familiarity with institutional Christian culture was more likely to be an expression of social rather than spatial location. So, though we often do not know the provenance of amulets, we should imagine a scenario in which various types of amulets—short formulaic amulets against scorpions or fevers, amulets juxtaposing customary and Christian elements in a visual scheme, and amulets developed in a Christian idiom—were on offer from different scribes, some of whom produced these devices in a perfunctory manner, others of whom took some care.

4.3 BINDING INCANTATIONS AND PRAYERS FOR JUSTICE

In the competitive face-to-face societies of the ancient Mediterranean it was not uncommon for people to try to handicap a competitor and gain an advantage by what are called curses or 'binding spells'.[214] Other terms for

---

[214] For overviews, see C. A. Faraone, 'The Agonistic Context of Early Greek Binding Spells', in C. A. Faraone and D. Obbink (eds), *Magika Hiera: Ancient Greek Magic and Religion* (New York: Oxford University Press, 1991), 3–32; J. G. Gager, 'Introduction', in J. G. Gager (ed.), *Curse*

this type of incantation in scholarly discussions are *katadesmos* (plural: *kate-desmoi*), from the action of binding (καταδεῖν) often mentioned in these incantations,[215] and *defixio* (plural: *defixiones*), a word rarely used in connection with these incantations in antiquity.[216] Over fifteen hundred binding incantations have been found throughout the ancient Graeco-Roman world, spanning a millennium from the sixth century BCE to the sixth century CE.[217] They are concerned mostly with one of four areas of competition or conflict: commercial activities; theatrical and circus contests (especially chariot races); erotic or amatory affairs; and legal and political disputes.[218] The text of the incantation could take several forms: (1) a binding formula expressed in the first person whereby the person commissioning the incantation acts on the target in a direct way ('I bind so-and-so'); (2) a prayer formula addressed to local or underworld deities, asking them to bind the target ('O Hermes, restrain so-and-so'); or (3) a *similia similibus* formula, whereby the target is hindered by analogy to some thing, such as the corpse with which it could be buried ('Just as you [the corpse] are powerless, so may so-and-so be powerless').[219] The preferred medium for these incantations was a thin sheet of lead, lead alloys, or other metals—more for practical reasons, initially, than ritual ones[220]—though pottery sherds, limestone, gems, and papyrus were also used. The inscribed object was then deposited close to the underworld deities or untimely dead being summoned to help— in a chthonic sanctuary, a grave, or an underground body of water (a well, a fountain, baths). The object might also be buried close to the target being hindered—in the hippodrome or the stadium, for incantations against competitors; near the home or place of work of an adversary.[221]

The various types of binding incantations are not of equal interest to us, since Christian elements have been found only in some types of incantations. I shall discuss them under two headings, amatory incantations and 'prayers for justice'.

Tablets and Binding Spells from the Ancient World (New York: Oxford University Press, 1992), 3–41; D. Ogden, 'Binding Spells: Curse Tablets and Voodoo Dolls in the Greek and Roman Worlds', in B. Ankarloo and S. Clark (eds), *Witchcraft and Magic in Europe: Ancient Greece and Rome* (Philadelphia: University of Pennsylvania Press, 1999), 1–90.

[215] Ogden, 'Binding Spells', 26–7.

[216] On this terminology, see Faraone, 'Agonistic Context', 21 n. 3; Gager, 'Introduction', 30 n. 1; Ogden, 'Binding Spells', 5.

[217] The main collections are: R. Wünsch, 'Defixionum tabellae Atticae', in W. Dittenberger and R. Wünsch (eds), *Inscriptiones Atticae aetatis romanae*, Inscriptiones Graecae 3/3 (Berlin: G. Reimer, 1897), Appendix; A. Audollent, *Defixionum tabellae* (Paris: A. Fontemoing, 1904); D. R. Jordan, 'A Survey of Greek Defixiones Not Included in the Special Corpora', *GRBS*, 26 (1985), 151–97, <http://grbs.library.duke.edu/issue/view/1131>; D. R. Jordan, 'New Greek Curse Tablets (1985–2000)', *GRBS*, 41 (2000), 5–46, <http://grbs.library.duke.edu/issue/view/321>.

[218] Faraone, 'Agonistic Context', 10–17; Gager, *Curse Tablets*, chapters 1 to 4; Ogden, 'Binding Spells', 31–7.

[219] Faraone, 'Agonistic Context', 4–10; Gager, 'Introduction', 13.

[220] Gager, 'Introduction', 3–4.

[221] Faraone, 'Agonistic Context', 3, 22–3 nn. 7–9; Ogden, 'Binding Spells', 15–25.

4.3.1 Amatory Incantations

Approximately one-quarter of the binding incantations that have survived from the ancient world deal with erotic or amatory affairs.[222] Such incantations typically fall into two categories: attraction spells, which seek to constrain the beloved to fall in love with or have sex with the person commissioning the incantation,[223] and separation spells, which seek to inhibit amorous relations between the beloved and a rival lover.[224] A single incantation might act both to separate and to attract.[225] (There are also many recipes for aphrodisiacal compounds, which technically are not incantations.) Amatory incantations are, of course, prevalent among the materials from Roman Egypt.[226] But amatory incantations with Christian elements are quite rare. There is none among the Greek materials from Egypt.[227] There are a number among the Coptic materials,[228] some of which belong to the period after the Arab conquest and the introduction of paper.[229] Rarely are the targets named.[230] The most common Christian element is a cross.[231] Several incantations refer in a legendary manner to 'the crown of stars upon the head of Jesus'[232] or the binding of Christ upon the wood of the cross,[233] and one includes an adjuration by 'the right hand of the Father [...] the Son and the authority of the Holy Spirit, and Gabriel [who] went to Joseph (and) caused him to take Mary for himself as a [wife]'.[234] These materials deserve more study than can be given them here.

The relative paucity of Greek amatory incantations with Christian elements does not mean that Christian did not have recourse to such incantations. In an innovative study of the names of persons commissioning incantations, Walter Shandruk found six amatory incantations where the name was possibly that of a Christian.[235] However, there are weaknesses in Shandruk's method. First, there are lingering uncertainties when identifying names that are typically Christian. Shandruk took as his point of departure Roger Bagnall's

---

[222] Gager, *Curse Tablets*, 78.

[223] E.g., *PGM* XV, XVI, XVIIa, XXXII, XXXIIa, XXXIX, LXVIII; *SM* I 37, 39, 40, 41, 42, 43, 44, 45, 50, 51.

[224] E.g., *PGM* O2 (*P.Oslo* II 15); *SM* I 38.   [225] E.g., *PGM* XIXa; *SM* I 46, 47, 48, 49.

[226] See Brashear, 'Greek Magical Papyri', 3502, for a list of recipes and applied incantations.

[227] De Bruyn and Dijkstra, 'Greek Amulets', 178.

[228] *ACM*, nos. 75, 76, 77, 78, 79, 80, 82, 84.   [229] *ACM*, nos. 73, 85, 86, 87.

[230] *ACM*, no. 84 (Phello son of Maure), no. 85 (Pharaouo son of Kiranpales); no. 87 (Shinte son of Tanheu), which does not have a Christian element. *ACM*, nos. 85–7, are incantations to render a man impotent so that he may not be able to 'release the virginity' of a woman.

[231] *ACM*, nos. 75, 76, 79, 80, 82, 84.   [232] *ACM*, no. 75.28–9.

[233] *ACM*, nos. 85.3; 86.23–5.   [234] *ACM*, no. 78.7–9 (slightly modified).

[235] See W. M. Shandruk, 'Christian Use of Magic in Late Antique Egypt', *JECS*, 20 (2012), 31–57, doi: 10.1353/earl.2012.0003, at table 4, nos. 8–10 (one person), 23, 24, 35, 38, 69; table 5, col. 3.

groundbreaking study of onomastic data from Egypt.[236] The categories of names proposed by Bagnall have now been revised by Mark Depauw and Willy Clarysse on the basis of an analysis of data held in a database of names and individuals from ancient Egypt (Trismegistos People).[237] Depauw and Clarysse retain many of Bagnall's names, but eliminate others. Of the people Shandruk classifies as Christian, I would query Theodorus of Techosis (late second or early third century),[238] since the evidence for the popularity of Theodorus among Christians emerges in the fourth century and later,[239] not the second and third centuries when the incantations naming him are now believed to have been written;[240] and Zoel of Droser (third or fourth century),[241] since the name is attested nowhere else and could be Jewish.[242] So the number of amatory incantations commissioned by someone bearing a Christian name may be fewer than Shandruk supposes (four rather than six).[243]

Second, since Christians had non-Christian or religiously neutral names not only in the third century before the Constantinian change but also in the fourth and fifth centuries when the Christian affiliation increased,[244] some of the people with non-Christian or religiously neutral names who commissioned amatory incantations in that period could have been Christian. To arrive at a more accurate estimate of the percentage of Christians in Egypt in a given century, Bagnall initially argued that one needed to multiply the number of persons with Christian names by a coefficient of approximately 1.5,[245] a number he subsequently revised to 1.7.[246] The revised data and coefficient resulted in a more gradual rate of conversion to Christianity from approximately 12 per cent of the population in 278 to 88 per cent of the population in 428.[247] Depauw and Clarysse have arrived at a slightly slower but similarly gradual rate of conversion by a different method, corroborating Bagnall's estimates.[248] Shandruk applied

---

[236] R. S. Bagnall, 'Religious Conversion and Onomastic Change in Early Byzantine Egypt', *BASP*, 19 (1982), 105–24, <http://hdl.handle.net/2027/spo.0599796.0019.003:02>; R. S. Bagnall, 'Conversion and Onomastics: A Reply', *ZPE* 69 (1987), 243–50, <http://www.jstor.org/stable/20186672>; R. S. Bagnall, *Reading Papyri, Writing Ancient History* (London: Routledge, 1995), 85–9.

[237] M. Depauw and W. Clarysse, 'How Christian was Fourth Century Egypt? Onomastic Perspectives on Conversion', *VigChr*, 67 (2013), 407–35, doi: 10.1163/15700720-12341144. Trimegistos People available at <http://www.trismegistos.org/ref/index.php>.

[238] Shandruk, 'Christian Use of Magic', table 2, nos. 8–10.

[239] Depauw and Clarysse, 'How Christian was Fourth Century Egypt?', 416 and table 5.

[240] *SM* I, p. 193, on the date of *SM* I 49, 50, and 51.

[241] Shandruk, 'Christian Use of Magic', table 2, no. 23.

[242] See *SM* I 41.11–12 comm. No instance of either name was found in Trismegistos People.

[243] Shandruk, 'Christian Use of Magic', 50–1 and table 5.

[244] On the data in letters from Oxyrhynchus, see L. H. Blumell, *Lettered Christians: Christians, Letters, and Late Antique Oxyrhynchus* (Leiden: Brill, 2012), 275–7 and tables 1 and 26.

[245] Bagnall, 'Religious Conversion', 117–21.

[246] Bagnall, 'Conversion and Onomastics', 248–9.

[247] Bagnall, 'Conversion and Onomastics', 249.

[248] Depauw and Clarysse, 'How Christian was Fourth Century Egypt?', 431–4.

Bagnall's coefficient of 1.5 to arrive at an estimate of the ratio of Christians who commissioned an incantation in successive periods, as the proportion of Christians in the population increased.[249] But Shandruk did not take the coefficient into account later in his article when he analysed the rates of use of different types of incantations (amulets, amatory *defixiones*, non-amatory *defixiones*) by persons with Christian and non-Christian names.[250] The actual number of Christians who commissioned the types of incantations listed by Shandruk would therefore have been greater than the number of incantations bearing what are thought to be Christian names.

Still, despite these methodological problems, it seems reasonable to assume that Christians (or at least some Christians) continued to make use of amatory incantations, since in other areas of social conduct, such as entertainment, many Christians often did what everyone else did.[251] Thus, the relative paucity of Greek amatory incantations with Christian elements probably reflects more a pattern of supply than of demand, as Shandruk concluded.[252] It seems unlikely that scribes close to the centre of institutional Christian culture would have provided such incantations, since they contravened not only Christian moral norms but also Christian ascetic values. For Christian authorities, as we saw in Chapter 1, amatory incantations are instances of the worst aspects of 'magic' for which no substitute or accommodation could be entertained. Purveyors of such incantations would therefore have operated on the periphery of institutional Christian culture or outside the purview of that culture. As well, the resources available to purveyors of such incantations— recipes, models, and customary phraseology—would have been relatively untouched by Christian influences, unlike the resources available to purveyors of amulets against fever and illness, for example.

4.3.2 Prayers for Justice

People seeking to avenge an injury, redress a wrong, or recover what was taken from them account for another large body of binding incantations in the Graeco-Roman world.[253] Henk Versnel has argued that such incantations constitute a distinct class, different from the various types of binding incantations discussed at the beginning of Section 4.3 in a number of important

[249] Shandruk, 'Christian Use of Magic', 36 n. 20, 45–6, and table 3.

[250] Shandruk, 'Christian Use of Magic', 50–1 and table 5.

[251] See, e.g., R. A. Markus, *The End of Ancient Christianity* (Cambridge: Cambridge University Press, 1990), chapter 8.

[252] Shandruk, 'Christian Use of Magic', 53–7.

[253] See Gager, *Curse Tablets*, chapter 5; Ogden, 'Binding Spells', 37–44.

ways.[254] Of the various phrases he and others have used to refer to this class of incantations—'judicial prayers', 'prayers for justice', 'pleas for justice and revenge'—'prayers for justice' has become the settled term.[255] The distinctiveness and boundaries of this class of incantations has been the subject of some discussion, but most scholars recognize the characteristics that are typical of the class. In recent publications on the subject, Versnel summarizes these characteristics as follows:

> I define 'prayers for justice' as pleas addressed to a god or gods to punish a (mostly unknown) person who has wronged the author (by theft, slander, false accusations or magical action), often with the additional request to redress the harm suffered by the author (e.g. by forcing a thief to return a stolen object, or to publicly confess guilt). The great majority of *defixiones* as brought together in the standard collections...lack such appeals to divine justice and are clearly of a different nature, most conspicuously in that 1: the submissive and deferential tone of the prayer is lacking, and 2: no explicit motive is advanced in justification. Whenever prayers for justice are found in some concentration, the site is not a grave, as it so often is in the case of *defixiones*, but a sanctuary of a (mostly but not invariably) chthonic deity.[256]

Versnel identified seven formal characteristics that according to him distinguish prayers for justice from *defixiones*.[257] Those most relevant for our purposes are that the petitioner states his or her name; some grounds for the appeal are offered; the deity is addressed with a flattering epithet or superior title; expressions of supplication (e.g., ἱκετεύω, βοήθει μοι, βοήθησον αὐτῷ) and direct, personal invocations are employed; and the appeal uses language referring to (in)justice and punishment (e.g., ἐκδικέω, ἀδικέω, κολάζω, and κόλασις). In addition, as Versnel and others have observed,[258] the tone of the appeal is emotional, and the terms of abuse are harsh. The objective is not merely to neutralize the opponent (as, for instance, in binding incantations directed at athletic competitors), but to make the adversary suffer. The petitioner is happy to publicize the complaint, as well as the intervention that is being requested.

---

[254] The most commonly cited early study is H. S. Versnel, 'Beyond Cursing: The Appeal to Justice in Judicial Prayers', in Faraone and Obbink, *Magika Hiera*, 60–106. For prior and subsequent publications, see H. S. Versnel, 'Prayers for Justice, East and West: Recent Finds and Publications since 1990', in R. Gordon and F. M. Simón (eds), *Magical Practice in the Latin West* (Boston: Brill, 2010), 275–354 at 275.

[255] Versnel, 'Prayers for Justice', 275–7.

[256] Versnel, 'Prayers for Justice', 278–9; reproduced in H. S. Versnel, 'Response to a Critique', in M. Piranomonte and F. M. Simón (eds), *Contesti magici = Contextos mágicos* (Rome: De Luca editori d'arte, 2012), 33–45 at 34.

[257] Versnel, 'Beyond Cursing', 68; Versnel, 'Prayers for Justice', 279–80.

[258] Versnel, 'Prayers for Justice', 280–2; Ogden, 'Binding Spells', 38–9.

Quite a few incantations with Christian elements from Egypt issue from such conflicts,[259] drawing on both Egyptian techniques and biblical idioms.[260] We have examples in Coptic as well as Greek.[261] I shall focus on the scribal features of the incantations written in Greek, and draw on Coptic texts at relevant points.

We begin with a short curse, *SM* II 62, assigned to the fifth or sixth century on the basis of the practiced cursive on the other side of the papyrus:[262] '☧ *XMΓ* Above all, bad times for punishable Theodorus; for he is bad.'[263] As Adam Łukaszewicz pointed out after this papyrus was first published, the phraseology of this text echoes that of stylized chants against rival teams in the circus.[264] In all likelihood the person whom Theodorus had wronged wrote the text. The hand is that of a 'slow writer' who wrote capitals separately and deliberately and could not write evenly across the papyrus despite the shortness of the lines.[265] The only Christian elements in the curse are the staurogram and the sequence *XMΓ*. These could have been familiar to the writer from their appearance at the head of letters and documents in the fifth and sixth centuries.[266] By that time, as well, the name Theodorus had become popular among Christians.[267] So we may safely regard this curse as having issued from a Christian milieu.

The next incantation, *SM* II 61, now also assigned to the sixth century,[268] is closer to a prayer for justice in its appeal for pity, though it does not state the grounds for its appeal: '⳨⳨⳨ Holy God, Gabriêl, Michaêl, give me, Megas (?), satisfaction. Great (?) | Lord God, strike down Philadelphê; and her children, | Lord Lord Lord God God, strike them down with her. | Jesus Christ, pity me

---

[259] Many were already noted in G. Björck, *Der Fluch des Christen Sabinus: Papyrus Upsaliensis 8* (Uppsala: Almquist and Wiksells, 1938) [= *P.Ups.8*], an exhaustive study that informed the work of Versnel ('Prayers for Justice', 275 n. 3).

[260] R. K. Ritner, 'Curses: Introduction', in *ACM*, pp. 183–6; see also R. K. Ritner, 'The Religious, Social, and Legal Parameters of Traditional Egyptian Magic', in M. Meyer and P. Mirecki (eds), *Ancient Magic and Ritual Power* (Leiden: Brill, 1995), 43–60 at 53–4.

[261] The Coptic texts are conveniently collected in *AKZ* 2.223–47 (nos. LXVI–LXXV); *P.Ups.8*, pp. 49–60; *ACM*, pp. 183–225 (nos. 88–112).

[262] H. Harrauer, 'Strafaufschub', *ZPE*, 30 (1978), 209–10 at 209, <http://www.jstor.org/stable/20181621>; *SM* II 62 intro.

[263] The English translation at *SM* II, p. 56, follows Łukaszewicz (see n. 264) rather than Harrauer in its interpretation of the text.

[264] A. Łukaszewicz, 'Christlicher Fluchtext (Notiuncula ad P.Vindob. G 16685)', *ZPE*, 73 (1988), 61–2, <http://www.uni-koeln.de/phil-fak/ifa/zpe/downloads/1988/073pdf/073.html>; *SM* II 62.4–5 comm.

[265] Harrauer, 'Strafaufschub', 209, with plate V b; H. Förster, 'Alltag und Kirche', in J. Henner, H. Förster, and U. Horak (eds), *Christliches mit Feder und Faden: Christliches in Texten, Textilien und Alltagsgegenständen aus Ägypten* (Vienna: Österreichische Verlagsgesellschaft, 1999), 40–51 at 49 (no. 39).

[266] See, e.g., the instances given at *CPR* XXIII 34.1 comm.

[267] Depauw and Clarysse, 'How Christian was Fourth Century Egypt?', 416 and table 5.

[268] L. Barry, 'Deux documents concernant l'archéologie chrétienne', *BIFAO*, 6 (1908), 61–9 at 61, <http://www.ifao.egnet.net/bifao/6/>: fourth century; *SM* II 61: sixth century.

and hear me, Lord.'[269] It is not clear from the end of the first line whether the writer was referring to the petitioner by name—'Megas' ($M\acute{\epsilon}\gamma a\langle s\rangle$)[270]—or to God by an epithet—'great Lord God' ($\mu\acute{\epsilon}\gamma a$ $\kappa\acute{\upsilon}\rho\iota\epsilon$ $\acute{o}$ $\theta\epsilon\acute{o}s$).[271] I incline toward the former reading, since the appellation $\kappa\acute{\upsilon}\rho\iota\epsilon$ $\acute{o}$ $\theta\epsilon\acute{o}s$, with which the second line then begins, parallels the appellation $\acute{a}\gamma\iota os$ $\acute{o}$ $\theta\epsilon\acute{o}s$, with which the first line begins. These appellations would have been familiar to the scribe from the scriptures and liturgy of the church. Moreover, the expression the scribe uses for the desired retribution—'strike down' ($\pi\acute{a}\tau a\xi ov$), common in Greek and Coptic curses with Christian elements[272]—echoes the language of the Septuagint.[273]

The prayer is written by a practiced scribe in a fluent hand that combines discrete letter-forms with continuous, adjoining letter-forms.[274] From the phonetic spellings, morphological variants, and grammatical irregularities it appears that the scribe composed the prayer as he wrote.[275] This would be consistent with the combination of the predictable and the idiosyncratic in this text: on the one hand, the formulaic phrasing and typical patterns (three crosses, threefold 'Lord');[276] on the other hand, the incomplete sequences (twofold 'God') and the expunged or superfluous letters.[277] The scribe does not use *nomina sacra*.[278] The phonetic spelling of 'Christ' (with an *eta*) is unusual in the sixth century:[279] a study of phonetic interchanges in the spelling of $X\rho\iota\sigma\tau\acute{o}s$ and $\chi\rho\iota\sigma\tau\iota a\nu\acute{o}s$ found that instances of 'Christ' spelled with an *eta* are relatively infrequent, confined mostly to letters from the fourth century.[280] At the very least, the spelling indicates that the scribe was not governed by biblical and liturgical reading, and was perhaps also not familiar with official documents.

A comparable short prayer for justice, also assigned to the sixth century, is *PGM* P15c: '✝ O Lord, master of the world, | avenge ($\grave{\epsilon}\kappa\delta\acute{\iota}\kappa\eta\sigma ov$) me | on the one who opposes | me and on the one who | has driven me | from my place, | and pay him back | at once, Lord, | so that he may fall into hands | harder than his own.'[281] The prayer displays several of the characteristics listed by Versnel,

---

[269] ET: *SM* II, p. 53 (slightly modified).

[270] There are a number of instances of Megas as a man's name from the fourth to the seventh century in Trismegistos People, <http://www.trismegistos.org/name/4059>.

[271] *SM* II 61.1 comm. The top right-hand corner of papyrus is lost, but the descending diagonal of *alpha* at the end of the line would seem to rule out a final *sigma*.

[272] *P.Ups.8*, pp. 19–20 and 49–53 (nos. 26, 27, 31); ET: *ACM*, nos. 89, 91, and 90, respectively.

[273] E.g., LXX Exod. 3: 20, 9: 15; see H. Seesemann, $\pi a\tau\acute{a}\sigma\sigma\omega$, *TDNT*, 5.939–40.

[274] *SM* II, plate III.   [275] *SM* II 61 apparatus and comments.

[276] See *PGM* P16.25–6 (*P.Ross.Georg.* I 23), discussed below.

[277] *SM* II 61.3, 3–4 comm.   [278] *SM* II 61.3 comm.   [279] *SM* II 61.4.

[280] W. M. Shandruk, 'The Interchange of ι and η in Spelling $\chi\rho\iota\sigma\tau$- in Documentary Papyri', *BASP*, 47 (2010), 205–19 at 211, <http://hdl.handle.net/2027/spo.0599796.0047.001:16>, where, however, the parenthetical reference should be A30 rather than A29.

[281] ET: *ACM*, no. 28 (slightly modified); see below on the uncertain antecedent of 'harder'.

particularly the phrasing of the invocation, the use of the verb ἐκδικέω, and the explanation of the reason for the petition. The prayer is almost certainly addressed to Christ.[282] Formulaic invocations introduced into documents by the decree of the emperor Maurice at the end of the sixth century routinely refer to Christ as 'our lord and master',[283] and in these formulae the Greek word for 'master' is typically abbreviated, as it is here: δεσπ(ότου). The scribe also writes 'Lord' in the invocation as a *nomen sacrum*,[284] which sometimes occurs in these formulae. (Later the scribe writes 'Lord' in full.)

The cursive hand with frequent continuous strokes and occasional ligatures between letter-forms,[285] assigned to the sixth century,[286] could be that of a scribe accustomed to writing letters or documents. The text is preceded by a cross in the left margin, as was common in letters and documents.[287] The writing is rapid and not particularly careful, but is relatively correct.[288] The writing expands about two-thirds of the way down the papyrus, and then becomes compressed as the scribe crams the last two lines into the remaining space at the bottom of the papyrus. This may be why he deleted the word 'and' (καί) at the end of line 8. Rather than continue with another clause parallel to 'and pay him back', the scribe instead turns to the desired outcome: 'so that he may fall into hands harder than his own'.

Although the scribe omits the case ending that would tell us exactly what or who should be 'harder',[289] one cannot escape the echo of LXX Ps. 34: 10, as others have observed:[290] 'All my bones will say, O Lord, who is like you, who saves the poor man from the hand of those who are harder than he?'[291] The allusion is apt in the circumstance, since the petitioner appears to have lost his land, or possibly his position, because of what his opponent did.[292] The naturalness of the allusion suggests that the petition was composed, not

---

[282] *Pace* Förster, 'Alltag und Kirche', 48, who suggests that the invocation could refer to the Devil, who was also addressed as δεσπότης, since the petitioner makes a vengeful request. But as we have already seen, Christians were not above exacting vengeance. The epithet 'master of the world' was also applied to the emperor, but it is unlikely that he is intended here.

[283] R. S. Bagnall and K. A. Worp, 'Christian Invocations in the Papyri', *CdE*, 56 (1981), 112–33 at 112–15 (Types 1, 4A, and 4B): ἐν ὀνόματι τοῦ κυρίου καὶ δεσπότου Ἰησοῦ Χριστοῦ κτλ.

[284] *PGM* P15c.1: κε̄.

[285] Image at <http://data.onb.ac.at/rec/RZ00009628> (Österreichischen Nationalbibliothek Katalog der Papyrussammlung); Förster, 'Alltag und Kirche', 47.

[286] C. Wessely (ed.), 'Les plus anciens monuments du christianisme écrits sur papyrus II', in PO 18/3 (1924), 341–509 at 440.

[287] See Chapter 2 n. 144.

[288] Two irregularities: ἐκβαλότος for ἐκβαλόντος (line 5); στεραιωτέρ for στερεωτέρ(ας or -ων or -ου) (line 10).

[289] See n. 288.

[290] *PGM* P15c.10 apparatus; *P.Ups.8*, p. 46; Förster, 'Alltag und Kirche', 47–8.

[291] A. Rahlfs (ed.), *Psalmi cum Odis*, 3rd edn (Göttingen: Vandenhoek and Ruprecht, 1979), 132: πάντα τὰ ὀστᾶ μου ἐροῦσιν Κύριε, τίς ὅμοιός σοι; ῥυόμενος πτωχὸν ἐκ χειρὸς στερεωτέρων αὐτοῦ. See also LXX Jer. 38: 11.

[292] *PGM* P15c.4–6: μετὰ τοῦ ἐκβαλό<ν>τος με ἀπὸ τοῦ τόπου μου.

copied, by the scribe. If so, the scribe came from a milieu where he would have absorbed the cadence of this particular psalm. (From a transcription of the psalm that someone wrote on the back of a documentary papyrus from Arsinoe in the sixth or seventh century,[293] we know that it was a favourite of at least one person.)

An echo of the phraseology of LXX Ps. 34: 10 (and similar passages in the Septuagint) also appears in the final line of another prayer for justice, *SM* II 59 (*P.Ups.8*).[294] This remarkable text from Panopolis, exhaustively studied by Gudmund Björck,[295] comprises three parts: a prayer written in prose (lines 1–8), a subscription also written in prose but indented by a wide margin (lines 9–12), and an invocation written in hexameters (lines 13–18). In the prayer a certain Sabinus appeals to God to judge and punish his daughter Severine and Didymus (probably her husband) for the injuries and dishonour they showed toward him—dishonour that apparently resulted in him wasting away from shame.[296] Sabinus also asks God to protect his other children from Severine and Didymus. The text, more than any we have considered thus far, evinces characteristics Versnel associates with prayers for justice.[297] It merits quoting in its entirety:

> ...Lord...God...let all know | that the Lord God will assist me. Let | Didymus and Severine, my daughter, be pursued, they who pursued me | in the past. Let her body wither up in bed, just as | you beheld how mine (withered up) due to them who covered my dignity with dishonor. Lord, show | them quickly your might. Nullify the contrivances of their hearts | against my dearest children. | Let them come before the tribunal, o lord and master, wherever you judge. |
>
> I Sabinus, crying and wailing night and | day, have submitted my case to God, the master of all, | for vindication of the injuries which | I have suffered from Severine and Didymus. |
>
> Son of the great God, whom man never beheld, | you who granted the blind to see the light of the sun, | show as before your godlike wonders. | Pay memorable compensation for the sufferings | which I suffered, which I endured on account of my only daughter, | striking down my enemies with your firm hands.[298]

In all likelihood this prayer and invocation was buried with Sabinus;[299] the papyrus was folded twelve times from left to right to that end.[300] On the outer visible panel an epitome of the petition was written, in the fashion of a

---

[293] K. Niederwimmer, 'Zwei Psalmenfragmente aus der Sammlung Erzherzog Rainer', *JOB*, 35 (1985), 123–30 at 123–7 (P.Vindob. inv. G 26205 [published in MPER N.S. IV 9] + P.Vindob. inv. G 26607).

[294] *SM* II 59.18: ἐχθροὺς ἡμετέρο[υ]ς στερεαῖς ἐνὶ χερς[ὶ] πατάσσων (translation below).

[295] *P.Ups.8*; see n. 259.   [296] *P.Ups.8*, p. 72 n. 1.

[297] As one might expect; see n. 259.   [298] ET: *SM* II 59 (slightly modified).

[299] *SM* II, p. 49.   [300] *P.Ups.8*, p. 9.

document:[301] 'Vindicate (ἐκδίκησον) ·ϝ·ϝ·ϝ· ·ϝ·ϝ·ϝ· Emmanuel, vindicate'.[302] The metrical invocation was reproduced, with halting alterations, on another papyrus, *SM* II 60 (*P.Hamb*. I 22),[303] that, as the opening lines make clear, was intended to serve as the template for Sabinus' grave stele. The alterations awkwardly reduce the length of the invocation and, after the first attempt at revising the final line was scratched out, replace the reference to Severine with a more oblique request:[304]

> The stele of the ill-fated, miserable Sabinus, | who endured many evils on account of his only daughter. | Son of the great God, whom man never beheld, | you who granted to the blind to see the light of the sun, | show among the people and straightway punish everywhere | my enemies, striking them down with your firm hands.[305]

It is possible, but not certain, that the same scribe wrote both papyri.[306]

SM II 59 was written by a practiced writer in a sixth-century cursive hand commonly found in letters and documents.[307] The writing becomes more compressed and less distinct toward the end of the text. There are few phonetic spellings and no grammatical anomalies. In the metrical section the scribe employs both organic and inorganic *diairesis* (there is no occasion earlier in the text),[308] as well as an apostrophe twice to mark elision between words.[309] The education of the writer is apparent not only from the relative correctness of the writing but also the literary quality of the text. The metrical invocation is replete with Homeric and epic phraseology, though the description refers to Christ.[310] Only in the last line of the invocation does biblical usage intrude.[311] Moreover, when the prayer calls upon God to show his might and nullify Severine's and Didymus' contrivances, it anticipates language used in the Liturgy of St Mark to pray for the church and the thwarting of her enemies.[312] Thus, the writer was relatively literate and Christian. It is worth noting that there are no *nomina sacra*, since this shows that a writer with these qualities

---

[301] *P.Ups.8*, p. 100. Image of *SM* II 59r at *P.Ups.8*, plate I; images of *SM* II 59v and *SM* II 60 at *P.Ups.8*, plate II.

[302] *SM* II 59v.1.

[303] See *P.Ups.8*, pp. 12–14, for a discussion of the sequence in which the two papyri were produced.

[304] *P.Ups.8*, pp. 13–14; W. Crönert, 'De critici arte in papyris exercenda', in *Raccolta di scritti in onore di Giacomo Lumbroso (1844–1925)* (Milan: Cisalpino-La Goliardica, 1925), 439–534 at 496–7.

[305] ET: *SM* II 60 (slightly modified).

[306] *P.Ups.8*, p. 12, reports the opinion of Wilhelm Schubart.

[307] *P.Ups.8*, p. 8, where Wilhelm Schubart is quoted as saying: 'Schrift der Alltags, in Briefen und Geschäftsurkunden nicht selten, aber nicht Hand eines Berufsschreibers'.

[308] *SM* II 59.14, 16, 17.   [309] *SM* II 59.13, 15.   [310] *P.Ups.8*, pp. 15–19.

[311] *P.Ups.8*, p. 19.

[312] Compare *SM* II 59.5–7 and G. J. Cuming, *The Liturgy of St Mark* (Rome: Pontificium Institutum Studiorum Orientalium, 1990), 34–5; see *P.Ups.8*, p. 74.

might choose not to use the abbreviations or, less likely, might not have been familiar with them.

We may compare *SM* II 59 with *PGM* P16 (*P.Ross.Georg.* I 23). Though it falls within the class of prayers for justice and, like *SM* II 59, looks to God as judge, it appeals more for help than for retribution. The appeal—which, if one accepts the first editor's reconstruction, uses the vocabulary of prayer[313]—is directed to the Lord through the holy martyrs.[314] The petitioner bewails the suffering that he or she has borne at the hands of a certain Theodosius: 'Nothing but hostilities have I suffered from his tyrannical behavior...Such wrong has he done to me!'[315] The petitioner's only hope is 'the power of God and the testimony for us through the saints', presumably referring to God's vindication of the martyrs asked to mediate the appeal. Some of the phrasing echoes language found in Christian hymns.[316] The Christian culture of the scribe is in fact readily apparent from the threefold acclamation written across the top of the papyrus—'Holy Trinity, holy Trinity, holy Trinity'[317]—and the confession at the end of the appeal: 'For there is only one Lord, [only one] God, in the Son [and] in the Father and the Holy Spirit, for ever and ever, amen.'[318] (We shall return to the order of the three persons of the Trinity in this confession.) The scribe also employs a visual pattern found in incantations with Christian elements: at the end of his appeal he writes, on three successive lines, three amens,[319] three staurograms, and threefold 'Lord'. (The cross that the first editor noted in the left margin before the first line of the text is not visible in the digital image of the papyrus, and there does not appear to have been any loss of papyrus after that edition was published.)

The scribe wrote in an irregular hand with mostly upright letters with frequent continuous strokes and occasional ligatures between letter-forms.[320] The hand is somewhat less regular than the hand in *SM* II 59. The

---

[313] *P.Ross.Georg.* I 23.2–3: διὰ τῶν ἁγίων μαρτύρω[ν εὔχομαι τῷ | κ(υρί)ῳ. The scribe's writing would have had to be compact (as in line 1) for the proposed reconstruction to fit in the remaining space, assuming that the right edge of the papyrus originally extended at least as far as it does at line 5. Image at <http://papyri.info/apis/hermitage.apis.21> (Papyri.info).

[314] For prayers to or through the martyrs, see *PGM* P5c (*P.Cairo.Cat.* 10696); W. H. Worrell, 'Coptic Magical and Medical Texts', *Orientalia*, 4 (1935), 1–37 at 3–4, <http://www.jstor.org/stable/43581034>, (*ACM*, no. 108).

[315] ET: *ACM*, no. 27.

[316] E.g., *P.Ross.Georg.* I 23.10: προσφεύγω [σοι], which one finds in Byzantine hymns; see, e.g., *Analecta hymnica graeca e codicibus eruta Italiae inferioris*, vol. 11: *Canones iulii*, ed. A. A. Longo (Rome: Istituto di Studi Bizantini e Neoellenici, Università di Roma, 1978), 78 (day 5, canon 7, ode 6, line 17.A).

[317] *P.Ross.Georg.* I 23.1.

[318] *P.Ross.Georg.* I 23.19–23, but reading ἐν πατρί rather than ἐν τῷ πατρί at line 21; all three persons are named without the article.

[319] For three amens written in a row in an amulet, see *P.Bon.* I 9.8; *P.Köln* IV 171.8; *P.Köln* VIII 340, side a, fr. B.13. For three amens written in a column, see *PGM* P15a.29–31 (*P.Ross. Georg.* I 24).

[320] Image at n. 313.

first editor assigned it to the fourth century.[321] The scribe's phonetic spelling betrays the influence of Egyptian speech.[322] He employs inorganic and organic *diairesis*,[323] and what appears to be one accent.[324] He uses a *nomen sacrum* once near the beginning of the text,[325] but never again thereafter.

In his confession of 'one Lord, one God', the scribe inverts the usual order of Father and Son. The theology and liturgy of the church would lead one to expect 'in the Father and in the Son and in the Holy Spirit',[326] not 'in the Son and in the Father and in the Holy Spirit'. The inverted order is unusual even among amulets with trinitarian invocations and acclamations.[327] It seems unlikely that this was just a slip of the pen. Could it be an inadvertent holdover of a form of Christian doxology prior to the Arian controversy, whereby praise was offered through the Son to the Father in the Holy Spirit?[328] This older form of doxology can be found in the mid-fourth-century Euchologion attributed to Sarapion.[329] In any case, the phraseology of the papyrus reflects the individuality of this particular writer.

Near the beginning of the prayer—after the invocation and before the complaint—there is an intriguing line: 'For the angel is not ignorant of our [suffering].'[330] While the scribe might be referring to Christ as an angel (an older way of understanding Christ's role that fell out of favour in the fourth century),[331] it is more likely that he is referring to the spirit of some deceased person who is to relay the petitioner's miseries to God.[332] The papyrus was folded; there are five horizontal creases and one vertical crease. It could have been buried in or near the grave of an intermediary. A longer seventh-century Coptic prayer for justice—in which, incidentally, a widow and her children 'appeal to the Father and the Son and the Holy Spirit and the consubstantial Trinity, that he may hear and bring judgment'—ends with an instruction to

---

[321] *P.Ross.Georg.* I, p. 161; see, e.g., Cavallo and Maehler, *Greek Bookhands*, 26–7 (no. 9a) P.Cornell inv. II 38 (388 CE), which, however, does not use the h-form for *eta*.

[322] *P.Ross.Georg.* I 23 apparatus and p. 163, noting particularly δ > τ and σ > σσ.

[323] *P.Ross.Georg.* I 23.9, 20.   [324] *P.Ross.Georg.* I 23.16: παρώρα.

[325] *P.Ross.Georg.* I 23.3: κῷ.

[326] See, e.g., Theodoret of Cyr, *Exp. rect. fid.* 2, 7, in *Corpus apologetarum Christianorum saeculi secundi*, ed. J. C. T. Otto, 9 vols in 7, 3rd edn of vols 1–5 (Jena: In libraria Maukii, 1851–1881), 4.4–6, 26.

[327] For amulets with the regular trinitarian sequence, see, e.g., *BKT* VI 7.1.1; *PGM* P5d.1–2 (*P.Lond.Lit.* 231); *PGM* P10.40–1; *PGM* P15a.17–22 (*P.Ross.Georg.* I 24); *PGM* P19.5–6 (*PSI* VI 719); *SM* I 21.1–2 (*P.Köln* VI 257); *SM* I 31.4 (*P.Turner* 49) = *BKT* IX 134; *SM* I 36.1.

[328] A. Stuiber, 'Doxologie', *RAC*, 4.210–26 at 222–3.

[329] M. E. Johnson, *The Prayers of Sarapion of Thmuis: A Literary, Liturgical, and Theological Analysis* (Rome: Pontificio Istituto Orientale, 1995), 46–81; see J. A. Jungmann, *The Place of Christ in Liturgical Prayer*, 2nd edn, tr. A. Peeler (Staten Island: Alba House, 1965), 23–4, 150–1.

[330] *P.Ross.Georg.* I 23.3–4.

[331] J. Barbel, *Christos Angelos: Die Anschauung von Christus als Bote und Engel in der gelehrten and volkstümlichen Literatur des christlichen Altertums* (Bonn: Peter Hanstein, 1964).

[332] On angels as the escorts and spirits of the dead, see R. Cline, *Ancient Angels: Conceptualizing Angeloi in the Roman Empire* (Leiden: Brill, 2011), 77–104.

the mummy with whom the papyrus is to be buried: it must call out night and day, together with the other mummies lying around its grave, until God hears and renders judgement on the widow's behalf.[333] But was the intermediary among the 'ordinary' or the 'special' dead? Since the prayer is addressed to the Lord 'through the holy martyrs', the papyrus could have been buried in or near the shrine of a martyr sought out by the petitioner to relay the prayer to God.

Although we cannot discuss Coptic prayers for justice in detail, those that have been preserved from Late Antiquity offer some depth of field to the Greek examples we have discussed. First, the Coptic materials confirm what we have already seen in the Greek materials, namely, that Christians thought it appropriate—indeed just—to appeal to heaven for vindication when they were wronged. Among Coptic prayers for justice we have one from a priest or monk, Apa Victor, who calls upon God to curse a certain woman, Alo, and her companion Phibamon,[334] and another from a woman, Theodora, who appeals to the holy martyrs against a certain man, Joor, and his wife.[335] Second, as these and other examples show, writers could be quite specific about the torments they wanted the adversary to suffer. For instance, a mother whose son has abandoned her for a woman named Tnoute asks God to make Tnoute barren, to make her eat the fruit of her womb, to bring illness and affliction upon her, worms and blood coming out of her all the days of her life.[336] The unnamed mother, who refers to herself in monastic parlance as 'a miserable, wretched sinner', calls upon all those present in the heavenly throne-room to execute this judgement—the cherubim and seraphim, Michael and other archangels, the twenty-four elders, the four creatures. Third, the manner of appealing to God in his role as judge and of invoking punishments upon the opponent could be elaborate. Thus, a prayer for justice assigned to the fourth or fifth century opens with a description of God in the heavenly throne-room and then invokes biblical precedent for the punishments it repeatedly adjures.[337] The appeal of the widow in the prayer mentioned above likewise recalls God's mercy toward prominent biblical heroes (Abel, Noah, Lot, Job, Daniel, Stephen), evokes the heavenly throne-room thronging with angels, and cites biblical precedent and language for the fate that will befall the offender.[338]

Two curses—characteristic features of prayers for justice are absent—are of particular interest for our purposes because they were written by the same scribe. One of them is invoked by a woman named Mary against a woman

---

[333] *ACM*, no. 89. See also Ritner, 'Curses: Introduction', 184.
[334] Worrell, 'Coptic Magical and Medical Texts', 13–16; *ACM*, no. 104.
[335] Worrell, 'Coptic Magical and Medical Texts', 3–4; *ACM*, no. 108.
[336] *P.Lond.Copt.* I 1223; *ACM*, no. 93.   [337] *ACM*, no. 90.
[338] *ACM*, no. 89; see n. 333.

named Martha.[339] The other is invoked by a man named Jacob against, possibly, someone named Hetiere.[340] It is clear from the handwriting, spelling, and dialect of these two texts that they were written by the same scribe.[341] The dialect—Akhmimic mixed with Subakhmimic (now termed Lycopolitan) or Sahidic[342]—flourished in the area around Panopolis (Akhmim) in the fourth and fifth centuries and then fell out of use.[343] The two texts have been assigned to that period.

The two curses display several similarities. First, in each case the desired retribution is the same, an ulcerous eruption or tumour.[344] One wonders whether this punishment was a particular favourite of the scribe or a common curse in the region. Second, both curses invoke the archangels 'Michaêl, Gabriêl, Souleêl' and call upon 'my Lord Jesus (Christ)' to bring about the punishment. Third, like other writers of amulets,[345] this scribe was in the habit of writing crosses in series of three: at the end of Mary's curse and at the beginning and near the end of Jacob's curse. Finally, the two papyri were folded in the same way—six times vertically and three times horizontally.[346]

Jacob's curse invokes more figures than Mary's curse: the fifty-four hundred martyrs (possibly a reference to a massacre that was believed to have occurred in Panopolis);[347] Mary, the mother of Jesus; and 'my holy father Zachariah' (probably a reference to the prophet who, in the version of the Septuagint [LXX Zach. 5: 1–4], had a vision of a flying sickle that brings a curse on the land, to which the second line of Jacob's curse alludes).[348] Why was the scribe

---

[339] W. E. Crum, 'La magie copte: nouveaux textes', in *Recueil d'études égyptologiques dédiées à la mémoire de Jean-François Champollion* (Paris: E. Champion, 1922), 539–40; ET: *ACM*, no. 100.

[340] R. Rémondon, 'Un papyrus magique copte', *BIFAO*, 52 (1953), 157–61, <http://www.ifao.egnet.net/bifao/52/>; ET: *ACM*, no. 101. I follow *ACM*, p. 208, rather than Rémondon, p. 159, line 1 comm., in taking Jacob to be the petitioner, given that Jacob is named at the beginning of this text, just as Mary is named at the beginning of the text edited by Crum (with the Greek genitive case ending, indicating, perhaps, for whom the curse was written?). The role and identity of Hetiere is obscure; see *ACM*, pp. 208 and 372, line 4 comm., with Rémondon, p. 160, line 4 comm.

[341] Rémondon, 'Un papyrus magique copte', 157–8; see the plates accompanying the editions of Crum and Rémondon.

[342] Rémondon, 'Un papyrus magique copte', 158.

[343] P. Nagel, 'Akhmimic', *CE*, 8.19–27 at 19.

[344] *ACM*, no. 101, translates ⲙⲁϣⲡⲱⲛⲉ 'ulcerous tumor'; see W. E. Crum, *A Coptic Dictionary* (Oxford: At the Clarendon Press, 1939), *s.v.* ⲙⲉϫⲡⲱⲛⲉ (p. 213b).

[345] See Chapter 2 n. 149.

[346] Crum, 'La magie copte', 539, and Rémondon, 'Un papyrus magique copte', 157, both state 'plié autrefois... en sept et en quatre'. Six vertical creases and three horizontal creases are visible in the plate accompanying Crum's edition. The vertical creases are harder to see in the plate accompanying Rémondon's edition, but the three horizontal creases are obvious.

[347] Rémondon, 'Un papyrus magique copte', 160–1, line 5 comm.

[348] Rémondon, 'Un papyrus magique copte', 159, line 2 comm.; see Papaconstantinou, *Le culte des saints*, 88–9. For instances when ⲉⲓⲱⲧ refers to a biblical prophet, see Crum, *A Coptic Dictionary*, *s.v.* ⲉⲓⲱⲧ (p. 87a). For later Greek exorcisms that invoke 'the sickle of Zacharias', see

more generous in his invocations in Jacob's curse? Was he paid more for a longer curse?

The role of the figures named above is ambiguous, since the scribe does not employ the customary formula of adjuring demons or spirits by some higher power. It is not clear whether these figures are enjoined directly or by means of a spirit of the dead. Since Jacob's curse appears to call upon the spirit of the father of Hetiere—'who is in the Father', i.e., dead—to bring about the tortured end,[349] the implicit second-person agent in Mary's curse may also be a spirit of the dead.[350] The fact that the two papyri were folded supports this interpretation, as they were probably buried in or near a grave.[351]

In short, these two curses written by a single scribe reveal how habitual the writing of an incantation might be. The angels invoked, the punishment sought, carelessness in the use of personal suffixes,[352] the formal device of crosses, and the manner of folding—all these suggest that the preparation of these incantations was a routine affair. Nevertheless, routine production did not preclude specificity or personalization.

4.3.3 Summary

The amatory incantations and prayers for justice that we have discussed are, like all of our materials, chance finds. We cannot be certain that they are representative of the habits of the population. Nevertheless, they allow us to advance a number of inferences or observations.

The relative paucity of Greek incantations with Christian elements that address amatory rivalries or athletic competitions is probably not the result of chance, since we have a number of Greek prayers for justice with Christian elements. Some types of adversarial incantations appear to have been more acceptable than others to scribes operating in a Christian milieu, especially those closer to the centre of institutional Christian culture.

The two Coptic curses written for Mary and Jacob reveal that a scribe could have a more or less standard way of composing a curse, one that could be expanded at will, either at the request of the client or the inclination of the scribe. The customary phraseology of *SM* II 61 and *PGM* P15c suggests that they were written by scribes familiar with the form. Some scribes, however, were more eloquent than others, as one sees from *PGM* P15c, which draws on the language of the Psalms.

A. A. Barb, 'St. Zacharias the Prophet and Martyr: A Study in Charms and Incantations', *JWI*, 11 (1948), 35–67 at 60–2, doi: 10.2307/750461.

[349] *ACM*, pp. 208 and 372, line 6 comm.   [350] Lines 2–5.   [351] *ACM*, p. 207.
[352] Rémondon, 'Un papyrus magique copte', 158; *ACM*, p. 208.

Who composed the prose prayer and metrical incantation of Sabinus? Was this the work of a scribe or was it the work of Sabinus? Sabinus clearly wanted his grievance against his daughter to be known, even if the inscription for the stele is more circumspect about naming her than the incantation accompanying the prayer. (This is one of the distinguishing features of prayers for justice, which were often, if not always, publicized, whereas binding incantations were not.[353]) Sabinus also wanted to display a degree of literary culture, insofar as his appeal for justice is set in hexameters. If this incantation was not composed by Sabinus, it would have had to have been composed by a relatively literate scribe. (We are reminded of Dioscorus of Aphrodite, poet and notary, who invested his petitions with literary qualities,[354] though any association with our incantation is more a matter of rhetorical culture than verbal echoes.[355]) Would such technique have been within the scope of the writers of more formulaic incantations or prayers for justice? The phraseology and orthography of, for example, *SM* II 61 suggests not.

We do not know whether the stele was ever erected over Sabinus' grave. If it was, it would presumably have been placed, and possibly commissioned, by his other children. This act would have had social repercussions for Sabinus, his daughter, and his other children; their honour and reputations would have been vindicated or diminished in the eyes of those who knew them or knew of them. The revision of the last line in the inscription for the stele is, therefore, telling. The individuality of this incantation is conditioned by its social context, both in its literary pretensions, which align Sabinus with a particular segment of his society, and in its circumspection, which veils the details of his shame from public eyes.

4.4 CONCLUSION

Customary amulets are, by definition, more or less traditional. They are comprised of incantations that in their entirety or in parts are recognizable to both purveyor and client as effective remedies. In fact, it is precisely because the amulets examined in this chapter are more or less traditional that we are able to observe similarities and differences in the culture of the scribes and their use of the resources available to them.

---

[353] Versnel, 'Prayers for Justice', 281 n. 22.

[354] L. S. B. MacCoull, *Dioscorus of Aphrodito: His Work and his World* (Berkeley: University of California Press, 1988), 16–19, 149–51; A. B. Kovelman, 'From Logos to Myth: Egyptian Petitions of the 5th–7th Centuries', *BASP*, 28 (1991), 135–52, <http://hdl.handle.net/2027/spo.0599796.0028.003:03>.

[355] *P.Ups.8*, pp. 22, 101–6, esp. 105.

Simple commonplace incantations like those against scorpion stings were evidently reproduced without much adaptation on the part of the scribe. The central adjuration was relatively stable and resistant to change. It is telling that when Christian elements are introduced, they tend to frame the traditional adjuration rather than modify it. The examples we have of this type of amulet suggest that they were written in a perfunctory manner from memory by various types of scribes, some of whom followed what was apparently a known layout for the incantation. Consequently, the one instance of this type of amulet that is carefully written, and that concludes with a fairly nuanced Christian doxology, stands out as something of an exception to the norm. The amulet is distinguished by the qualities and culture of the scribe.

If the amulets against scorpions are of interest because they reveal various instances of a commonplace incantation, the two curses written by the same scribe, one for Mary and the other for Jacob, are valuable because they show how an individual scribe might modulate a customary form and habitual phraseology when formulating a specific incantation. Although the retribution sought and the principal agents of retribution are the same, the two curses are far from identical. While working with a certain set of resources, a scribe could expand or shrink the manner in which those resources were used, though limitations imposed by level of literacy remain constant.

Other amulets we examined did not present us with a commonplace incantation reproduced by various scribes over time or multiple incantations written by a single scribe. Nevertheless, they allowed us to compare incantations that are similar in purpose and length. In fact, longer incantations are particularly useful, since they give their writers more scope for individuality in how they work with the resources available to them, both customary and Christian. The two sets of amulets against fever and illness that we examined suggest that some producers of amulets were closer to the institutional centre of the Egyptian church, and others further from the institutional centre. The former reproduce the normal wording of passages from the scriptures and the liturgy. They incorporate opening or closing formulae from Christian prayers. For the most part, they are familiar with the conventions of the system of *nomina sacra*. The latter, further from the institutional centre, are less concerned with or capable of replicating liturgical elements, and combine them with elements that are not derived from the liturgy of the church. Moreover, if one were to locate the scribes of these two sets of amulets along a continuum of scribal qualities, the most deliberately written amulet, *PGM* P5b, is the product of a writer close to the institutional centre, whereas the least regularly written amulet, *SM* I 32, is the product of a writer further from the institutional centre. Most of the writers are practiced; they are accustomed to writing. But there are more orthographical and syntactical irregularities in amulets written by those further from the institutional centre.

As I have already suggested, we should probably think of a scribe's proximity to or distance from the institutional centre of the Egyptian church in social rather than spatial terms. That is to say, in a given town or village, there would have been various purveyors of remedies, some of whom would have benefited from clerical or monastic formation, others not. The social distance between some scribes and the institutional centre of the Egyptian church raises interesting questions about the nature and range of Christian identity or religious affiliation in Egypt at this time. We should not assume that a scribe whose cultural horizon does not coincide with that of the institutional Christian centre was not a Christian or less of a Christian, since Christian identity can be more a function of affiliation (participation in rituals) than formation (knowledge of rituals). We cannot know, of course, how the scribes of our materials would have identified themselves. But how we describe them depends on the criteria that we ourselves employ. In this regard, the materials we have reviewed in this chapter confirm what the literary and legal sources in Chapter 1 inadvertently disclosed: the scope for individuality and modulation of Christian elements in the production of incantations is far greater than that envisioned by ecclesiastical norms.

At the same time, the production of incantations is not unaffected by ecclesiastical norms. In this regard, the relative scarcity of incantations having to do with amorous or athletic competitions among materials with Christian elements is probably not a mere happenstance. These sorts of incantations typify practices that Christian writers and leaders routinely demonized and condemned. They are the least likely to have been expressed in Christian terms, however remotely. Certainly it would be highly surprising for such an incantation to be the work of a scribe close to the institutional Christian centre. By contrast, it is not surprising that prayers for justice continued to be produced, since the retribution sought by the petitioner is assumed to be in a just cause and is not without precedent in the Christian tradition.

5

Scribal Features of Scriptural Amulets

One of the ways that Christian devotion makes its influence felt in the production of amulets is through the use of scripture, as we saw on occasion in Chapter 4. The array of scriptures found in amulets is both broader and narrower than what became the scriptural canon of the Christian church—broader in that amulets drew on selected extra-canonical works related to Jesus, such as his legendary correspondence with Abgar,[1] and narrower in that amulets drew mainly on gospels and psalms from within the canon. There are three principal ways in which scriptures appear in amulets: through their titles or opening words, through recitation or quotation, and through retelling (*historiolae*).[2] In Chapter 4 we noted instances of retelling, as when, for example, healings performed by Jesus are recalled as the basis of the adjuration or petition in an incantation.[3] In this chapter we shall focus on the two other ways in which scriptures come into play. What can we learn from amulets that simply refer to or recite scripture about the people who wrote these artefacts?

In considering artefacts written with a scriptural passage, we are immediately confronted with the question: was this artefact used or meant to be used as an amulet?[4] There are other possible reasons for writing a short scriptural passage: scripture was used, for example, in school exercises.[5] And there are

---

[1] T. S. de Bruyn, 'Christian Apocryphal and Canonical Narratives in Greek Amulets and Formularies in Late Antiquity', in P. Piovanelli and T. Burke (eds), *Rediscovering the Apocryphal Continent: New Perspectives on Early Christian and Late Antique Apocryphal Texts and Traditions* (Tübingen: Mohr Siebeck, 2015), 153–74 at 155–60.

[2] My approach is more restrictive than that of A. Biondi, 'Le citazioni bibliche nei papiri magici cristiani greci', *StudPap*, 20 (1981), 93–127, which registers any allusion to a biblical passage in an incantation.

[3] See also de Bruyn, 'Christian Apocryphal', 160–8.

[4] For detailed discussion of this question, see T. S. de Bruyn, 'Papyri, Parchments, Ostraca, and Tablets Written with Biblical Texts in Greek and Used as Amulets: A Preliminary List', in T. J. Kraus and T. Nicklas (eds), *Early Christian Manuscripts: Examples of Applied Method and Approach* (Leiden: Brill, 2010), 145–89.

[5] E.g., R. Cribiore, *Writing, Teachers, and Students in Graeco-Roman Egypt* (Atlanta: Scholars Press, 1996), 244 (no. 295), 245 (no. 297), 246 (no. 302), 248 (no. 307), 251 (no. 317), 252 (no. 321), 252–3 (no. 322). On no. 302, see A. Luijendijk, 'A New Testament Papyrus and its Documentary Context: An Early Christian Writing Exercise from the Archive of Leonides

other possible sources for a fragment of papyrus or parchment written with a scriptural passage: it could have come from a liturgical manual or a biblical manuscript. In some cases the text or the material of the artefact offers a clue to its intended use. The text may be a passage often used in amulets, such as the opening words of a gospel or LXX Ps. 90, or the material may retain traces of having been worn or affixed, such as folds, holes used for hanging or posting, and remains of thread. In this chapter we shall limit ourselves for the most part to cases where the text was certainly or probably written to be used as an amulet or subsequently put to such a use.[6]

The use of scripture in amulets has been the subject of a number of studies in recent years. In addition to several articles on the use of LXX Ps. 90 and the Lord's Prayer in amulets,[7] we now have Joseph Sanzo's exhaustive study of scriptural *incipits* in amulets and Brice Jones' systematic investigation of the value of scriptural citations in amulets for New Testament textual criticism.[8] I shall draw on these studies throughout this chapter.

In what follows I examine artefacts in groups according to the manner in which they cite scripture (such as titles and opening words or a short excerpt) or the passages they cite (such the correspondence between Abgar and Jesus, the Lord's Prayer, and LXX Ps. 90). I seek to observe what conventions governed the use of scripture in amulets, how the passages were known to or conveyed to the scribe, and what range of skill can be found in the writing of the amulets.

(*P.Oxy.* II 209/𝔓[10])', *JBL*, 129 (2010), 575–96, <http://www.jstor.org/stable/25765953>. On differentiating exercises from amulets, see N. Carlig and M. de Haro Sanchez, 'Amulettes ou exercises scolaires: sur les difficultés de la catégorisation des papyrus chrétiens', in M. de Haro Sanchez (ed.), *Écrire la magie dans l'antiquité: actes du colloque international (Liège, 13–15 octobre 2011)* (Liège: Presses Universitaires de Liège, 2015), 69–83.

[6] T. S. De Bruyn and J. H. F. Dijkstra, 'Greek Amulets and Formularies from Egypt Containing Christian Elements: A Checklist of Papyri, Parchments, Ostraka, and Tablets', *BASP*, 48 (2011), 163–216 at 184–203 (tables 1 and 2), <http://hdl.handle.net/2027/spo.0599796.0048.001:14>.

[7] T. J. Kraus, 'Septuaginta-Psalm 90 in apotropäischer Verwendung: Vorüberlegungen für eine kritische Edition und (bisheriges) Datenmaterial', *BN*, n.f. 125 (2005), 39–73; J. Chapa, 'Su demoni e angeli: il Salmo 90 nel suo contesto', in G. Bastianini and A. Casanova (eds), *I papiri letterari cristiani: atti del convegno internazionale di studi in memoria di Mario Naldini, Firenze, 10–11 Giugno 2010* (Florence: Istituto Papirologico 'G. Vitelli', 2011), 59–90; T. J. Kraus, 'Manuscripts with the Lord's Prayer—They Are More Than Simply Witnesses to That Text Itself', in T. J. Kraus and T. Nicklas (eds), *New Testament Manuscripts: Their Texts and their World* (Leiden: Brill, 2006), 227–66. Earlier studies include Biondi, 'Le citazioni bibliche'; E. A. Judge, 'The Magical Use of Scripture in the Papyri', in E. W. Conrad and E. G. Newing (eds), *Perspectives on Language and Text: Essays and Poems in Honor of Francis I. Andersen's Sixtieth Birthday, 28 July 1985* (Winona Lake: Eisenbrauns, 1987), 339–49.

[8] J. E. Sanzo, *Scriptural Incipits on Amulets from Late Antique Egypt: Text, Typology, and Theory* (Tübingen: Mohr Siebeck, 2014); B. C. Jones, *New Testament Texts on Greek Amulets from Late Antiquity* (London: Bloomsbury T. & T. Clark, 2016).

5.1 TITLES AND OPENING WORDS

Of the three principal ways of referring to scripture just mentioned—titles and opening words, recitation, and retelling—titles and opening words comprise the narrowest set of references. They consist almost exclusively of the titles of the canonical gospels and the opening words of a small set of texts: the canonical gospels, LXX Ps. 90, the Lord's Prayer, and, in one Coptic amulet,[9] the letter of Jesus to Abgar. In his study of this way of referring to scripture, Sanzo documents each instance of the title or the opening words of a text and weighs the extent to which the words quoted may be considered an *incipit*— that is, an abbreviated reference to a larger text or narrative.[10] The titles or opening words of the canonical gospels—usually all four gospels; occasionally three, two, or one—occur most often, with the opening words of LXX Ps. 90 in second position, followed by the opening words of Matthew's version of the Lord's Prayer (Matt. 6: 9–13).

That protective and healing power was attributed to the gospels is evident not only from admonitions of bishops, who tolerated the wearing of a 'gospel' as a substitute for pagan practices,[11] but also from amulets that have survived from Late Antiquity. Since it was obviously impractical to wear an entire gospel as an amulet (notwithstanding the small formats that books could take), scribes typically wrote only the opening words of the gospel or gospels. Likewise, LXX Ps. 90, which is the most frequently cited biblical text in amulets with Christian elements in Late Antiquity,[12] is usually represented by its first verse or its first two verses. One finds opening words of these texts written on papyrus, parchment, potsherds, wood tablets, and, in the case of LXX Ps. 90, medallions and pendants.[13] In fact, the practice extended beyond portable artefacts to, for example, inscriptions on walls and texts in large codices.[14] The great majority of Egyptian materials, written in Greek and Coptic, have been assigned dates from the fourth to the eighth centuries.

Several interesting observations emerge from these materials. First, scribes did not have a set notion as to where the opening words of a gospel or LXX Ps. 90 ended. The texts vary in length.[15] Second, the Greek and Coptic materials differ in the number of gospels that might be cited by a title or opening words and in the order in which they are cited. Whereas all but one of the Coptic artefacts refer to all four of the gospels, the Greek artefacts

---

[9] See n. 52.   [10] Sanzo, *Scriptural Incipits*, chapter 5.
[11] See Section 1.2.1.   [12] See Section 5.6.
[13] For the range of materials with verses from LXX Ps. 90, see Kraus, 'Septuaginta-Psalm 90', 49–58; Sanzo, *Scriptural Incipits*, 106–20.
[14] E.g., Sanzo, *Scriptural Incipits*, 77–8 (no.1, wall), 78–80 (no. 2, limestone), 82–3 (no. 5, codex), 90–1 (no. 14, wall), 116–18 (nos. 38–41, armbands/bracelets consisting of medallions).
[15] Sanzo, *Scriptural Incipits*, 102–3, 134.

refer to four, three, two, or one of the gospels.[16] Third, whereas almost all the Coptic artefacts refer to the gospels in their canonical order (Matthew, Mark, Luke, John), the order of the gospels in Greek artefacts can vary. Since the dates assigned to the Coptic materials are on the whole later than those assigned to the Greek materials, it would appear that the practice became more standard over time, reflecting the order and number of the canonical gospels.

One of the objectives of Sanzo's study was to distinguish between opening words that stand in for a larger whole (*incipits*) and opening words that are quoted for themselves only (independent textual units). According to Sanzo, when there is limited or inconclusive evidence to support the conclusion that opening words refer to a larger whole, they should be taken as an independent textual unit.[17] Another objective of Sanzo's study was to determine the extent of the larger whole to which *incipits* refer.[18] In the case of short texts, such as LXX Ps. 90, the Lord's Prayer, or Jesus' letter to Abgar, it is likely that the *incipit* stood in for the entire text. Indeed, one amulet, *PGM* P19 (*PSI* VI 719), explicitly indicates as much when it concludes LXX Ps. 90: 1 and Matt. 6: 9 with the phrase 'and so forth' ($\kappa\alpha\grave{\iota}\ \tau\grave{\alpha}\ \dot{\epsilon}\xi\hat{\eta}s$).[19] In the case of longer texts, such as the gospels, the referent is less clear. It has often been assumed that *incipits* were used to refer, as a part for the whole, to scripture in general or to an entire gospel, both which are deemed to have power to protect or heal.[20] But Sanzo argues on the basis of both ancient practice and current theory that gospel *incipits* would have been understood to refer not to an entire gospel, but rather to certain stories or sayings from the gospels that narrate Jesus' divine status or power over sickness and demons.[21] Even the *incipits* of shorter texts may have been understood to refer only to a portion of those texts, according to Sanzo.[22]

Sanzo's study has refined our notion of how opening words may have functioned as sources of power and has reminded us that certain stories from the gospels or motifs in the psalms would have figured more prominently than others in the minds of ancient writers and audiences. However, it is impossible to know what a scribe was thinking of when he (or she) wrote the opening words of a gospel or psalm, particularly when the words are not cited in the context of an incantation. Moreover, the opening words of a gospel or psalm may well have had more than one referent or resonance, and that referent or resonance may have been more experiential than textual. Nevertheless, it may be interesting to see if there are significant differences between amulets with scriptural passages functioning as *incipits* and amulets with scriptural passages

---

[16] Sanzo, *Scriptural Incipits*, 147–8, table 2: four (nos. 3, 8, 10, 12), three (no. 16), two (no. 15), one (nos. 18–22; also no. 17 in Latin).

[17] Sanzo, *Scriptural Incipits*, 143–4.   [18] Sanzo, *Scriptural Incipits*, 9–10, 14, 16.

[19] Sanzo, *Scriptural Incipits*, 136–7; further discussion of this amulet below.

[20] Sanzo, *Scriptural Incipits*, 3–6.   [21] Sanzo, *Scriptural Incipits*, chapters 2 and 6.

[22] Sanzo, *Scriptural Incipits*, 39–51, 165–8.

functioning as independent textual units (e.g., 'gospel' amulets), since the latter may offer more clues as to why they were selected.

5.2 AMULETS CONSISTING (MAINLY) OF *INCIPITS*

In many amulets the *incipits* of one or more gospels or LXX Ps. 90 are combined with an incantation or with a longer scriptural passage.[23] Relatively few amulets consist only (or mostly) of *incipits*. One which does is *PGM* P19 (*PSI* VI 719),[24] to which we referred in Section 5.1.[25] This papyrus, assigned to the sixth century on account of the *protokollon* written on the other side,[26] recites a series of *incipits* and ends with a trinitarian doxology.[27] The *incipits* belong to the canonical gospels (John, Matthew, Mark, and Luke), LXX Ps. 90, and the Matthean version of the Lord's Prayer. The scribe has less command of the *incipit* of the Gospel of Mark than of the other gospels (which match the standard text),[28] introducing into it phrases from the Gospel of John and the Gospel of Matthew.[29] As Sanzo suggests, this was probably a result of the relative 'unpopularity' of the Gospel of Mark in Egypt.[30] As we have already noted, the *incipits* of LXX Ps. 90 and the Lord's Prayer end with the words 'and so on' (καὶ τὰ ἑξῆς),[31] indicating that the entire psalm and the entire Lord's Prayer were being invoked.[32]

---

[23] With or in an incantation: *BKT* VI 7.1; *PGM* P5b (*P.Oxy.* VIII 1151); *PGM* P5c (*P.Cairo. Cat.* 10696); *PGM* P9 (*BGU* III 954); *PGM* P17 (*P.Iand.* I 6) = *P.Giss.Lit* 5.4; *P.Köln* VIII 340; *SM* I 26 = *BKT* IX 206; *SM* I 29 (*P.Princ.* II 107); *SM* I 36; and several tablets with a Βους-formula and opening words from LXX Ps. 90 (Sanzo, *Scriptural Incipits*, 115–16, 119–20 [nos. 37, 42–3]). With a longer scriptural passage: *P.Oxy.* XVI 1928v; R. W. Daniel, 'A Christian Amulet on Papyrus', *VigChr*, 37 (1983), 400–4, doi: 10.2307/1583548 (P.Vindob. inv. G 348); C. A. La'da and A. Papathomas, 'A Greek Papyrus Amulet from the Duke Collection with Biblical Excerpts', *BASP*, 41 (2004), 93–113, <http://hdl.handle.net/2027/spo.0599796.0041.001:06> (P.Duke inv. 778).

[24] Jones, *New Testament Texts*, 77 (no. 4), with 79 for a corrected reading in the doxology at line 6.

[25] See n. 19.

[26] R. Pintaudi, 'Per la datazione di PSI VI 719', *AnalPap*, 2 (1990), 27–8; see Section 2.2.1.

[27] ET: Jones, *New Testament Texts*, 77.

[28] By 'standard text' I mean a text that is attested by a group of manuscripts in current critical editions of the Septuagint and the New Testament, not only the text that is supported by the best or the majority of witnesses. I use the expression for convenience, acknowledging that what might have been the standard text for a given scribe does not necessarily correspond to what has become the standard text in a critical edition.

[29] See the discussion at Sanzo, *Scriptural Incipits*, 87 n. 55.

[30] In addition to Sanzo's discussion, see D. Limongi, 'La diffusione dei Vangeli in Egitto (secc. I–VIII): osservazioni sul *Vangelo secondo Marco*', *AnalPap*, 7 (1995), 49–62.

[31] The reconstruction κα[ὶ τὰ ἑξῆς] at line 5 is supported both by the precedent at lines 4–5 and the space for six or seven letters in the gap.

[32] Sanzo, *Scriptural Incipits*, 168–71.

The scribe wrote in an informal, upright semi-cursive hand. It is roughly bilinear (β, ζ, κ, ξ, φ, and occasionally ι are enlarged, and λ, υ, and χ have long descenders).[33] There are occasional resemblances to Alexandrian majuscule script.[34] The passages are written as *scriptio continua* in well-spaced lines across the long width of the oblong papyrus. There are a few phonetic spellings.[35] The scribe employed organic *diairesis* consistently throughout.[36] The first line begins with a cross, several cursive letters that should probably be read as $\chi\mu\gamma$ surmounted by a supralinear stroke, and a cross appended to the final cursive letter.[37] The last line ends with a *nomen sacrum* for 'Christ' ($\overline{\chi\rho}$),[38] followed by three crosses, with the last horizontal filling out the line. Otherwise, the scribe does not use *nomina sacra*.

All in all, this is the work of a practiced writer who, evidently, was familiar not only with the practice of referring to texts by their *incipits* but also with the types of texts that were commonly referenced in this fashion—the gospels, LXX Ps. 90, and the Lord's Prayer—even if he was not as well acquainted with the Gospel of Mark as with the other gospels, a peculiarity that, as we have said, may reveal as much about his milieu as about him.

BKT VI 7.1,[39] a parchment with writing that should probably be assigned to the sixth or seventh century,[40] is illustrative of a different form of presentation.[41] The text opens with a trinitarian invocation: 'In the name of the Father and

---

[33] Jones, *New Testament Texts*, 78. Image at Kraus, 'Manuscripts', 244; Jones, *New Testament Texts*, 78 (plate 4); and <http://www.psi-online.it/documents/psi;6;719> (PSIonline).

[34] G. Cavallo and H. Maehler, *Greek Bookhands of the Early Byzantine Period: A.D. 300–800* (London: Institute of Classical Studies, 1987), 52–3 (no. 22a), P.Berol. inv. 13418 (mid-fifth century).

[35] Jones, *New Testament Texts*, 77, apparatus.

[36] These are noted in the text of *PSI* VI 719.

[37] *PSI* VI 719.1 comm. suggested $X\rho\iota\sigma\tau\grave{\epsilon}$ $\sigma\hat{\omega}\tau\epsilon\rho$ ('Christ Saviour') with reservation, but $\chi\mu\gamma$ is more likely, as Arthur Hunt noted in his copy of *PSI* VI: '$\overline{\chi\mu\gamma}$?' (The volume, now held in the Sackler Library in the University of Oxford, has written on the first page, 'A.S. Hunt, from G.V., Jan. 1921.') For a parallel instance of $\chi\mu\gamma$ preceded and followed by crosses formed in ligature with *chi* and *gamma*, respectively, see *PGMP*8a.v1 (*P.Oxy.* XVI 1926), image at <http://www.papyrology.ox.ac.uk/> (Oxyrhynchus Online). I am grateful to Juan Chapa for advising on the reading of these letters, observing Hunt's notation, and adducing the parallel.

[38] Traces of letters are visible after *chi*.

[39] Jones, *New Testament Texts*, 65–6 (no. 2).

[40] Most scholars have assigned the hand to the sixth or seventh century; see Sanzo, *Scriptural Incipits*, 80 n. 23. Jones, *New Testament Texts*, 68–9, argues for the fifth or sixth century, citing as a *comparandum* Cavallo and Maehler, *Greek Bookhands,* 42 (no. 17a), *P.Oxy.* XI 1373 (middle or second half of the fifth century). Cavallo and Maehler, *Greek Bookhands*, 92–3 (no. 42c), *BKT* V.1 (fifth or sixth century; see now <http://smb.museum/berlpap/index.php/03653/>), is arguably a better *comparandum* for, e.g., *mu* with a middle curve, rounded *pi*, and sweeping *chi*. In any case, the hand in *BKT* VI 7.1 is much less regular and formal, making precise assignment difficult.

[41] Image at Jones, *New Testament Texts*, 67 (plate 2), and <http://smb.museum/berlpap/index.php/01656/> (Berliner Papyrusdatenbank). I am grateful to Marius Gerhardt of the Ägyptisches Museum und Papyrussammlung for providing me with an image for study prior to its posting on the museum's site.

the Son and the Holy Spirit'. A series of passages ensues: the *incipits* of LXX Ps. 90 and the canonical gospels (John, Matthew, Mark, and Luke), LXX Ps. 117: 6–7, LXX Ps. 17: 3a, and Matt. 4: 23.[42] The text closes with an appeal: 'The body and blood of Christ spare your servant who wears this amulet. Amen. Alleluia',[43] followed by three crosses interspersed with *alpha* (written in the form of two intersecting *chi* letter-forms) and *omega*.[44] The parchment was almost certainly worn as an amulet; it was folded and is stained from moisture (possibly from sweat).[45]

The scribe clearly wanted to set off the passages. He began each of the passages and the closing appeal with a new line. The opening invocation, each of the passages except LXX Ps. 90: 1 (presumably because it follows immediately on the invocation), and the closing appeal are all preceded by a cross. As the writing progresses, the first lines of passages are projected into the left margin (*ekthesis*).[46] As well, when there is space at the end of a passage, it is filled by a *diple obelismene* (a forked horizontal line used to mark a section of verse or prose).[47] It is not surprising that the *incipits* of LXX Ps. 90 and the gospels take precedence in this series, but it is still significant, as it attests to the customary power accorded these passages. The verses from LXX Pss. 117 and 17 have obviously been chosen for their protective value, and Matt. 4: 23, as we shall see in other amulets, was cited for its healing promise.

The scribe wrote in an irregular, sloping semi-cursive hand. He did not maintain even lines across the parchment. The lines slope downward for the most part, but also upward, becoming compressed toward the end. The scribe employed *nomina sacra* throughout. However, in the phrase 'Jesus Christ, son of God' in the *incipit* of the Gospel of Mark, he wrote 'Jesus' in full, spelling it, presumably, as he pronounced it ($Y\iota\sigma o\hat{v}$).[48] Is it possible that the scribe was unfamiliar with the spelling of the name because he normally wrote it as a *nomen sacrum*? There are many phonetic spellings and other orthographical irregularities,[49] which suggest that the scribe was recalling the passages from memory. Other features, such as the speed of the writing and the fact that the

---

[42] ET: *ACM*, no. 9; Jones, *New Testament Texts*, 66.

[43] Although *BKT* VI 7.1 (following the *editio princeps* of F. Krebs, 'Altchristliche Texte im Berliner Museum', *NAWG*, 4 [1892], 114–20 at 118–20), reads $\delta\epsilon\mu a$ at line 21 and supplies $a\hat{\iota}\mu a$ in the apparatus, the first letter resembles *alpha* in $\beta a\sigma\iota\lambda\epsilon\hat{\iota}[as]$ at line 19 and $\dot{a}\mu\dot{\eta}\nu$ at line 23 and the second letter is a thick vertical that could be mistaken for *epsilon* because of the downward stroke adjoining *mu*; thus $a\hat{\iota}\mu a$, with Jones, *New Testament Texts*, 66.

[44] On such forms of *alpha*, see Section 2.4.6.

[45] Krebs, 'Altchristliche Texte', 119; Jones, *New Testament Texts*, 66.

[46] Lines 9, 11, 13, 15, and 17.

[47] Lines 6, 10, 14, and 16, at the ends of the *incipits* of John and Luke, LXX Ps. 117: 7, and LXX Ps. 17: 3a. The *diple obelismene* at line 6 is very short, beginning over the *nu* of the *nomen sacrum* $\overline{\theta\nu}$ and extending about a letter-space to the right.

[48] Line 8: $\dot{a}\rho\chi\dot{\eta}$ $\tau o\hat{v}$ $\epsilon\dot{v}a\gamma\gamma\epsilon\lambda\acute{\iota}ov$ $Y\iota\sigma o\hat{v}$ $X(\rho\iota\sigma\tau o)\hat{v}$ $v(\iota o)\hat{v}$ $\tau o\hat{v}$ $\theta(\epsilon o\hat{v})$.

[49] Jones, *New Testament Texts*, 66, apparatus.

scribe used both the compendium and the full form for καί, support this impression. However, the passages cited correspond, with a few exceptions, to the text as attested by other witnesses.[50]

In short, this amulet, like the previous one, was written by a scribe familiar with the convention of referring to certain passages of scripture by their *incipits*. In this instance, however, the layout of the text calls attention to the passages cited, and the sequence of the passages reflects the priority given to LXX Ps. 90 and the gospels. The passages themselves were, not surprisingly, recalled from hearing or speaking them rather than from reading them.

Two other Greek amulets recite the titles or *incipits* of all four gospels along with much of the text of LXX Ps. 90: *P.Oxy.* XVI 1928v and P.Vindob. inv. G 348. We shall discuss them in the context of other amulets that recite the psalm. Otherwise, Greek amulets recite titles or opening words from fewer than four gospels, usually in association with an incantation of some kind.[51] By contrast, as we noted in Section 5.1, Coptic amulets consisting of gospel *incipits* typically recite all four *incipits* in their canonical order, indicating that it had become customary to do so. The one exception to this pattern, *P.Lond.Copt.* I 317, is noteworthy not only because its *incipits* do not follow the canonical order (Matthew, Luke, John, Mark), but also because the *incipits* of the gospels are preceded by the *incipit* of the letter of Jesus to Abgar.[52] This adds to our evidence of the status accorded this letter and its promise of protection, believed to have originated from Jesus, as we shall see in Section 5.4.

5.3 'GOSPEL' AMULETS

Some amulets draw on the power of a gospel not by its title or *incipit*, but rather by a short passage (an independent textual unit). These amulets illustrate what Christian writers may have been referring to when they spoke of gospels as substitutes for pagan remedies.

---

[50] Line 3: κ(υρίο)υ instead of θεοῦ (LXX Ps. 90: 1). Line 5: omission of θεόν (John 1: 1); see Jones, *New Testament Texts*, 70. Line 11: addition of κ(αί) (LXX Ps. 117: 6), attested by some manuscripts; see A. Rahlfs (ed.), *Psalmi cum Odis*, 3rd edn (Göttingen: Vandenhoek and Ruprecht, 1979), 285. Line 8: addition of τοῦ, attested by some manuscripts; see NA[28] and Limongi, 'La diffusione', 58. Line 17: ὁ κ(ύριο)ς Ἰ(ησοῦ)ς ὅλην τὴν Γαλλείαν [read: Γαλιλαίαν] (Matt. 4: 23), attested by some manuscripts (apart from addition of κύριος); see NA[28] and Jones, *New Testament Texts*, 70.

[51] See Sanzo, *Scriptural Incipits*, 91–9 (nos. 15–16, 18–19, 21–2).

[52] J. E. Sanzo, 'Brit. Lib. Or. 4919(2): An Unpublished Coptic Amulet in the British Library', *ZPE*, 183 (2012), 98–9, <http://www.jstor.org/stable/23849875>.

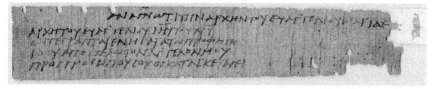

Fig. 5.1. *P.Oxy.* LXXVI 5073. Courtesy of the Egypt Exploration Society and Imaging Papyri Project, Oxford.

One of the earliest examples, *P.Oxy.* LXXVI 5073,[53] consists of an instruction and the opening words of the Gospel of Mark:

> Read the beginning of the gospel, and see: | 'The beginning of the gospel of Jesus the Christ. | As it is written in Isaiah the prophet, | "Behold, I shall send my angel | before your face, who will prepare"'. (Mark 1: 1–2)

The instruction was, presumably, directed at the malevolent spirit the amulet was meant to ward off. It is clearly set off from the quotation (see Fig. 5.1): the first line (the instruction) is indented some distance from the left edge and runs the length of the long oblong papyrus, whereas the remaining lines (the quotation) have a more conventional narrow margin and run about two-thirds the length of the papyrus.[54] (The scribe appears to have used a different stylus to write the instruction and may have added it later.[55]) The quotation breaks off in mid-sentence, as is often the case with biblical citations in amulets.[56] The scribe could have written more of the opening verses of Mark, including the last few words of verse 2, but evidently did not think it necessary to do so.[57] (The scribe's use of the imperative ἴδε, 'see', a form that occurs frequently in the Gospel of Mark, suggests that he knew the gospel well.[58]) The value of the quoted passage lay in its promise of angelic protection, as the editors observe.[59] The passage was cited for that reason, and not as a substitute for the gospel as a whole or for certain parts of the gospel.[60]

The scribe wrote in a fairly regular sloping majuscule hand that has been assigned to the third or fourth century.[61] To the arguments adduced for this date one may add that three-letter *nomina sacra*, like those used by

---

[53] Jones, *New Testament Texts*, 130 (no. 16).

[54] Image at *P.Oxy.* LXXVI, plate 1; Jones, *New Testament Texts*, 131 (plate 15); <http://www.papyrology.ox.ac.uk/> (Oxyrhynchus Online); and fig. 5.1 above.

[55] *P.Oxy.* LXXVI 5073 intro., p. 20.   [56] Jones, *New Testament Texts*, 182.

[57] Jones, *New Testament Texts*, 132.   [58] *P.Oxy.* LXXVI 5073.1 comm.

[59] *P.Oxy.* LXXVI 5073 intro., p. 20. I am not persuaded, however, by the suggestion that the angel was invoked to handle preparations needed to render the amulet effective, since the point at which the quotation ends may not have been significant; it is more likely that the angel would have afforded protection or favour, as in the next example, MPER N.S. XVII 10.

[60] Sanzo, *Scriptural Incipits*, 141–2; Jones, *New Testament Texts*, 132.

[61] *P.Oxy.* LXXVI intro., p. 21; Jones, *New Testament Texts*, 131.

the scribe,[62] are more common in the third and fourth centuries than they are later.[63] The scribe's competence is evident from the practiced hand (despite some variability) and the roughly bilinear writing, as well as the use of apostrophes (to separate double consonants), organic and inorganic *diairesis*, and *nomina sacra*. The quotation from Mark diverges at points from the standard text.[64] The most interesting variation, for our purposes, is the replacement, probably inadvertent, of 'Jesus Christ' with 'Jesus the Christ',[65] an expression Christian writers of the second and third centuries used to assert Jesus' messianic identity.[66] Thus, the amulet manifests not only the writer's professional scribal competence, but also a particular reception of the opening words of the gospel.

We may compare this amulet with MPER N.S. XVII 10,[67] a small parchment bifolium (6.5 cm w × 4.2 cm h), where verses from the Gospel of John are preceded by an invocation:

> I call upon you, God, the Father of our Lord Jesus Christ, to send out your angel upon the one who wears this. The light shines in the darkness and the darkness did not overcome it. There was a man sent from.   (John 1: 5–6)

In this case the request for angelic protection is explicit, and the ensuing quotation confirms the power of God's emissary to resist 'darkness'. The scribe wrote in a formal biblical majuscule script that has been assigned to the sixth or seventh century.[68] There are a few phonetic spellings in the invocation,[69] but the verses from the gospel do not vary from the standard text.[70] The scribe employed *nomina sacra* correctly and consistently in both the invocation and the verses.[71] The parchment's first editors, Kurt Treu and Johannes Diethart, designated it an amulet. G. H. R. Horsley subsequently argued that the bifolium was initially written to be part of a miniature codex of the Gospel of John, but was then discarded because the scribe made a mistake by writing the verses on the wrong side of a sheet of parchment.[72] (As classified by Eric

---

[62] Line 2: $\overline{\iota\eta\upsilon}$ τοῦ $\overline{\chi\rho\upsilon}$.

[63] A. H. R. E. Paap, *Nomina Sacra in the Greek Papyri of the First Five Centuries A.D.: The Sources and Some Deductions* (Leiden: Brill, 1959), 108–11.

[64] Jones, *New Testament Texts*, 133.   [65] See n. 62.

[66] *P.Oxy.* LXXVI 5073.2 comm.

[67] Jones, *New Testament Texts*, 147 (no. 19), with 151 for the corrected reading ἐξαποστίλης. Image at MPER N.S. XVII, Tafelband, plate VI; Jones, *New Testament Texts*, 148 (plate 18); and <http://data.onb.ac.at/rec/RZ00000868> (Österreichischen Nationalbibliothek Katalog der Papyrussammlung; P.Vindob. inv. G 29831).

[68] MPER N.S. XVII 10; Jones, *New Testament Texts*, 147–9.

[69] Jones, *New Testament Texts*, 147, apparatus.

[70] Jones, *New Testament Texts*, 151.

[71] Fol. Ir.2: $\overline{\theta\varsigma}$, 3: $\overline{\pi\eta\rho}$, 4: $\overline{\kappa\upsilon}$, 5: $\overline{\iota\upsilon}$ $\overline{\chi\upsilon}$; fol. IIv: $\overline{\alpha\upsilon\varsigma}$.

[72] G. H. R. Horsley, 'Reconstructing a Biblical Codex: The Prehistory of MPER *n.s.* XVII. 10 (*P.Vindob.* G 29 831)', in B. Kramer et al. (eds), *Akten des 21. Internationalen Papyrologenkongresses, Berlin, 13.–19.8.1995* (Stuttgart: Teubner, 1997), 473–81.

Turner in his study of early codices, a miniature codex has a breadth of less than 10 cm.[73]) But one of Horsley's arguments—the fact that the citation from John breaks off in mid-sentence—is now less compelling in light of examples of this practice in other amulets, such as the one we just considered, *P.Oxy.* LXXVI 5073.[74] Treu and Diethart were right to call the bifolium an amulet—an amulet, we should note, prepared by a scribe capable of writing a formal script.

A third example of this type of amulet is *PGM* P4 (*P.Oxy.* VIII 1077).[75] It consists of a free citation of Matt. 4: 23–4,[76] a passage that is often cited or echoed in amulets,[77] as we have already seen with *BKT* VI 7.1.[78] The amulet reads:

> Curative gospel according to Matthew. 'And Jesus went around all of Galilee teaching and preaching the gospel of the kingdom and healing every illness and every illness [*sic*] and every infirmity among the people. And a report about him went out into all of Syria and they brought to him all who were sick and Jesus healed them.'[79]

The heading—'curative gospel according to Matthew'—shows that short passages from a gospel, such as those we have been considering, were referred to as a 'gospel', illustrating what it might have meant for people to wear the 'gospel' as an amulet. The heading also states explicitly what can be inferred from citations of Matt. 4: 23–4 in other amulets, namely, that the passage itself was believed to have the power to heal or protect from sickness.

The design of the amulet is unique.[80] The text is written in the shape of fourteen crosses spaced out over five columns in three rows. In the outside columns (the first and fifth ones), each of the three crosses is delineated by a border. The scribe gave the fifteen sections of the amulet an octagonal shape by cutting out diamond-shaped spaces between the rows and columns in the interior of the parchment and notches around the edge of the parchment. In the middle of the third column—the centre of the amulet—is a human bust. The figure has more verisimilitude than cruder depictions on the other

---

[73] E. G. Turner, *The Typology of the Early Codex* (Philadelphia: University of Pennsylvania, 1977), 22, 29–30.

[74] Jones, *New Testament Texts*, 150–1.   [75] Jones, *New Testament Texts*, 60 (no. 1).

[76] Jones, *New Testament Texts*, 63–5.

[77] T. S. de Bruyn, 'Appeals to Jesus as the One "Who Heals Every Illness and Every Infirmity" (Matt 4: 23, 9: 35) in Amulets in Late Antiquity', in L. DiTommaso and L. Turcescu (eds), *The Reception and Interpretation of the Bible in Late Antiquity* (Leiden: Brill, 2008), 65–81 at 66–9.

[78] *BKT* VI 7.1.17–20.

[79] ET: *ACM*, no. 7; Jones, *New Testament Texts*, 60.

[80] Image at *P.Oxy.* VIII, plate I; J. H. F. Dijkstra, 'The Interplay between Image and Text on Greek Amulets Containing Christian Elements from Late Antique Egypt', in D. Boschung and J. M. Bremmer (eds), *The Materiality of Magic* (Munich: Wilhelm Fink, 2015), 271–92 at 285; Jones, *New Testament Texts*, 61 (plate 1). The image in the *editio princeps* is the clearest, as Jones observes (p. 62).

amulets with Christian elements.[81] Scholars disagree on whether it is a man or a woman.[82] The hairstyle of a woman in a late antique tapestry from Akhmim,[83] adduced by Brice Jones,[84] is comparable to the hairstyle in the image, suggesting that the figure is that of a woman. In any event, the amulet was designed by its shape to focus the text, imagery, and symbolism of the amulet on the figure, who is no doubt the beneficiary of its healing power. It has been suggested that the octagonal pattern was used to resonate with the resurrection of Jesus, just as the crosses would resonate with his crucifixion.[85]

The scribe evidently took some care in the preparation of this amulet. He wrote in a fairly regular Alexandrian majuscule script that probably should be assigned to the sixth century, as the first editor suggested.[86] Since he had to anticipate how his text would form the fourteen crosses and fit within the spaces created by his ornamental cuts, it is likely that he made a draft or copied from an exemplar. The verses from Matthew are modified to suit the purpose. In verse 23 the amulet omits to say that Jesus taught 'in their synagogues'[87]—an inadvertent or deliberate elimination of Jewish specificity[88]—and in verse 24 it skips over the various types of illness from which people suffered,[89] a further loss of specificity.[90] In addition, the scribe used both the compendium and the full form of καί so as to be able to fit portions of the text within the allotted space. Yet he wrote the phrase 'every illness' twice[91]—an odd mistake, if it was a mistake, given the calculation that an amulet in this format would require. It could be that the dittography was meant to focus the healing power of the text on the illness surrounding the client.[92]

---

[81] For comparable skill in the depiction of a face, see U. Horak (ed.), *Illuminierte Papyri, Pergamente und Papiere I* (Vienna: A. Holzhausens, 1992), plate 15 (no. 1 recto). For cruder figures, see, e.g., *PGM* XXXV (*PSI* I 29) and *P.Köln* VIII 340, discussed at Dijkstra, 'The Interplay', 280–5.

[82] Woman: Horak, *Illuminierte Papyri*, 247 (no. 206); Jones, *New Testament Texts*, 63. Man: Dijkstra, 'The Interplay', 286.

[83] 'Tabula (Square) with the Head of Spring', Metropolitan Museum of Art, New York, Accession no. 90.5.848, <http://www.metmuseum.org/art/collection/search/444327>. For additional images of women with long and short hair, see Horak, *Illuminierte Papyri*, 150, plate 9 (no. 48), and 124–5, plate 48 (no. 31), with 117, plate 24 (no. 27).

[84] Jones, *New Testament Texts*, 63, with a line drawing based on the image in *P.Oxy.* VIII.

[85] J. E. Sanzo, 'Wrapped Up in the Bible: The Multifaceted Ritual on a Late Antique Amulet (P. Oxy. VIII 1077)', *JECS*, 24 (2016), 569–97 at 588–93.

[86] Jones, *New Testament Texts*, 62–3, would assign the hand to the sixth or seventh century. Although it is difficult to compare the hand of the amulet with more formal Alexandrian majuscule hands, it seems to me to resemble more the simpler, less mannered examples of the sixth century. See Cavallo and Maehler, *Greek Bookhands*, nos. 37, 51, and 52, with discussion.

[87] *P.Oxy* VIII 1077.16–18 comm.

[88] R. Mazza, 'P.Oxy. XI, 1384: medicina, rituali di guarigione e cristianesimi nell'Egitto tardoantico', *ASE*, 24/2 (2007), 437–62 at 456–8; Sanzo, 'Wrapped Up in the Bible', 581–3.

[89] *P.Oxy.* VIII 1077.64 comm.   [90] Sanzo, 'Wrapped Up in the Bible', 581–3.

[91] *PGM* P4, col. iii, 2–5, 12–14.   [92] Sanzo, 'Wrapped Up in the Bible', 583–4.

These three amulets are exceptional in that they were written in formal hands by what were probably professional scribes. While the hands are not executed with perfect consistency, they nevertheless display the qualities of an identifiable style. Both the text and the execution of these amulets suggests that their writers would not be out of place in the offices of a church or a monastery, or some other setting occupied with writing documents or copying books. In the case of the last two amulets—MPER N.S. XVII 10 and *PGM* P4— one wonders whether the writing in the amulet was meant to look like the writing in a biblical codex, so that the amulet would evoke not only the words of the gospel but also its appearance. The amulet would thereby become a 'gospel' in every sense of the word. Yet the 'gospel' as recited in such amulets may nevertheless be mediated by the scribe and the scribe's milieu, as the telling variants in the first and the third of these amulets show.

The contrast in text and execution with the final artefact we shall consider in this section, P.Berol. inv. 11710,[93] could not be more marked. These two leaves from a small papyrus codex (approximately 6.5 cm w × 7.5 cm h) have enjoyed repeated scrutiny in recent years as scholars have queried whether the leaves served as an amulet and whether the text they preserved came from an apocryphal gospel, as the first editor claimed. Scholarly opinion is moving away from the view that the text preserves an excerpt from an apocryphal gospel,[94] and toward the view that it is a reworking of biblical material for an amulet or some apotropaic purpose.[95] The text on the first three leaves reads as follows:

He [answered] Jesus and said: 'Rabbi, Lord, you are the son of God.' The rabbi [answered him] and said: 'Nathanael, walk in the sun (?).'[96] Nathaniel answered him and said, 'Rabbi, Lord, you are the lamb of God who takes away the sins of the world.' The rabbi answered him and said [two letters or *charaktêres*].[97]

---

[93] H. Lietzmann, 'Notizen', *ZNW*, 22 (1923), 150–60 at 153–4. Re-editions: T. J. Kraus, '*P.Berol.* 11710', in T. Nicklas, M. J. Kruger, and T. J. Kraus (eds), *Gospel Fragments* (Oxford: Oxford University Press, 2009), 227–39; Jones, *New Testament Texts*, 151–2 (no. 20); J. E. Sanzo and L. Zelyck, 'The Text and Function of P. Berol: 11710 Revisited', *JTS* (forthcoming). I follow the edition of Sanzo and Zelyck, which improves on prior editions.

[94] See Sanzo and Zelyck, 'Text and Function', for prior discussions and translations of P.Berol. inv. 11710.

[95] Kraus, '*P.Berol.* 11710', 238: an amulet that may have 'preserved passages from a gospel that became apocryphal later on'; Jones, *New Testament Texts*, 159: 'a kind of patchwork of Gospel texts, as we find in many amulets'; Sanzo and Zelyck, 'Text and Function': an original text 'designed to play a role in an apotropaic or curative ritual'.

[96] Most interpreters have read ἐν τ | ῷ ἡλίο as 'in the sun' (ἐν τῷ ἡλίῳ); see Jones, *New Testament Texts*, 158–9 (whose reading, however, of a final *iota* in ἡλίοι [p. 151] is not supported by the papyrus). Sanzo and Zelyck, 'Text and Function', suggest 'in the "Eli"' (ἐν τῷ Ἡλι), an allusion to Jesus' words on the cross, often cited in amulets.

[97] Jones, *New Testament Texts*, 155; Sanzo and Zelyck, 'Text and Function'.

The last word on the third leaf, 'said' ($\epsilon \hat{\iota} \pi \epsilon \nu$), is underlined, confirming that the text ends on this leaf.[98] The fourth leaf has the words 'Jesus Christ God' written in Coptic,[99] preceded by a staurogram with a curl descending from the right tip of the crossbar (⳨).[100] At the bottom of the page, inverted, is a staurogram (without the curl) and the *nomen sacrum* for 'God'.[101] We do not have the complete codex, which must have included at least one additional leaf, since the first extant leaf begins mid-word. The holes used to thread the leaves together are visible, and a bit of thread has survived on the first leaf.

We need not discuss the allusions in this text, or its interpretation, since these aspects are amply treated in recent studies.[102] The presence of what appear to be *charaktêres* strengthens the argument that this codex served some amuletic purpose. Of particular interest for us is the hand of the writer.[103] It is the coarse, clumsy, and belaboured hand of an inexperienced writer who cannot reproduce letter-forms consistently. The semi-cursive capitals are written individually with effort; some are overwritten; their shapes are awkward and erratic; their spacing is uneven. The lines, short as they are, slope downward to the right. Spelling is phonetic, and the name 'Nathanael' is spelled two different ways.[104] *Nomina sacra* are not used consistently.[105] *Diairesis* is used once redundantly.[106] In short, this writer is aware of scribal conventions, but his knowledge is imperfect and his execution is erratic.

Clearly, the writer wrote from memory, not an exemplar, conveying a narrative recalled orally. The repeated use of the phrase 'answered and said'— a favourite of the Gospel of John,[107] on which the narrative draws[108]—is what one might expect when a narrative is fashioned or recalled orally. The writer could have written these leaves for himself. If so, it indicates that a person might

---

[98] Jones, *New Testament Texts*, 155.

[99] Sanzo and Zelyck, 'The Text and Function', adduce Cairo, Egyptian Museum, Journal d'entrée, 45060, a manual we discussed in Section 3.3.4 as a *comparandum*.

[100] De Bruyn, 'Christian Apocryphal', 157 n. 22; Jones, *New Testament Texts*, 154.

[101] Sanzo and Zelyck, 'The Text and Function', line 24 comm., observe a faint *sigma* after the *theta*.

[102] Kraus, 'P.Berol. 11710', 234–7; Jones, *New Testament Texts*, 158–60; Sanzo and Zelyck, 'The Text and Function'.

[103] Image at Kraus, 'P.Berol. 11710', plate 11; Jones, *New Testament Texts*, 153 (plate 19); Sanzo and Zelyck, 'The Text and Function'; and <http://smb.museum/berlpap/index.php/03270/> (Berliner Papyrusdatenbank).

[104] Lines 6–7: $N\eta\theta\alpha\nu\alpha\dot{\eta}\lambda$; lines 10–11: $N\alpha\theta\alpha\nu\alpha\dot{\eta}\lambda$.

[105] Lines 1: ιεσου, 3: κ̄ε (dot above *kappa*), 3–4: ϋϊος, 4: θεου, 13: κ̄ε (the supralinear stroke continues over next letter), 15: θ̄υ (a triangle is superimposed on the supralinear stroke), 22: ιc xc. The triangular supralinear stroke was observed by Jones, *New Testament Texts*, 156, who adduces an instance in another amulet, *PGM* P17.9–10 (*P.Iand.* I 6) = *P.Giss.Lit.* 5.4.

[106] Lines 3–4 (see n. 105).

[107] E.g., John 1: 48, 50; 2: 19; 3: 3, 9, 10, 27; 4: 10, 13, 17; 6: 26, 29, 43; 7: 16, 21; 8: 14; 9: 30, 36; 12: 30; 13: 7; 14: 23; 20: 28. The phrase is often used in the Septuagint as well.

[108] Kraus, 'P.Berol. 11710', 234–5; Jones, *New Testament Texts*, 159–60; Sanzo and Zelyck, 'The Text and Function'.

want to extend the role or power of a narrative that he or she already knew into the material realm—into something one could read or wear—by writing it down. In effect, this writer was doing what the writers of the previous three amulets were doing: mediating an authoritative tradition associated with the appearing of Jesus and transferring it to a concrete, physical medium. Nevertheless, the particular tradition that is conveyed and the manner in which it is written reveals a cultural and social location for this scribe that is different from that of the previous three scribes.

5.4 JESUS' CORRESPONDENCE WITH ABGAR

We turn next to the legendary exchange between Abgar, king of Edessa, and Jesus.[109] This exchange had a protective power because of what Jesus was reported and believed to have said in his reply to Abgar. It had a value in antiquity equivalent to narratives from the canonical gospels, as its use in amulets (as well as other formats) attests.

Several versions of this legendary exchange circulated in antiquity.[110] In Eusebius of Caesarea's account, Abgar asks in his letter to be healed from an illness, and Jesus replies in writing that he cannot come himself, but will send one of his disciples after his ascension to heal Abgar's disease.[111] In the account in the *Teaching of Addai*, Jesus replies orally to the king's emissary, promising not only to heal the king but also to bless the city: 'As for your city may it be blessed and may no enemy ever again rule over it.'[112] In another version, present in Coptic manuscripts, Abgar asks for healing not for himself but for the sick in his city, and Jesus grants healing directly in his written reply.[113] In the Coptic version, as in other versions but not Eusebius', Jesus promises that wherever his letter is displayed the place will be protected against the adversary and impure spirits.[114] These promises explain why inscriptions

---

[109] On the legend, see K. E. McVey, 'Abgar, Epistle of Christ to', *ABD*, 1.12–13; H. J. W. Drijvers, 'The Abgar Legend', in *New Testament Apocrypha*, ed. W. Schneemelcher, tr. R. McL. Wilson, 2 vols (Louisville: Westminster/John Knox, 1991), 1.492–500.

[110] What follows draws on de Bruyn, 'Christian Apocryphal', 158, with permission from the publisher (see n. 1).

[111] Eusebius of Caesarea, *H.e.* 1.13.1–10 (GCS NF 6/1.82–8).

[112] *The Teaching of Addai*, tr. G. Howard (Chico: Scholars, 1981), 8–9, reprinting the text of *The Doctrine of Addai the Apostle*, ed. and tr. G. Phillips (London: Trübner, 1876).

[113] E. Drioton, 'Un apocryphe anti-arien: la version copte de la correspondence d'Abgar, roi d'Édesse, avec Notre-Seigneur', *ROC*, 20 (1915–17), 306–26 and 337–73 at 310–17.

[114] Drioton, 'Un apocryphe anti-arien', 318–25; E. von Dobschütz, 'Der Briefwechsel zwischen Abgar und Jesus', *ZWT*, 43 (1900), 422–86 at 442.

of the letter have been found, for instance, at a grave near Edessa, by a gate to the city of Philippi, and above a door of a house in Ephesus.[115]

There are numerous copies of the correspondence, or parts thereof, from Egypt, written in Greek and Coptic on papyrus, parchment, potsherds, and stone.[116] In many cases we can be certain or almost certain that the artefact served as an amulet. For instance, two fifth-century transcriptions—one of the letter from Abgar, written in Greek;[117] the other, of Jesus' reply, written in Coptic[118]—include an injunction for Jesus to heal a certain individual 'quickly, quickly'. Several Coptic transcriptions of the letter from Jesus to Abgar were folded,[119] suggesting that they were used as amulets. For other witnesses we cannot be certain that they were used as amulets, but such an application is highly likely, given the promise made in Jesus' letter.[120] (A potsherd written with only the blessing promised to Edessa indicates the power attributed to this portion of the text.[121]) In some cases, as in a Coptic text of Jesus' letter written on a tablet, use as an amulet may have been secondary to some other prior purpose.[122] All in all, the relatively high number of copies indicates that

---

[115] J. B. Segal, *Edessa 'The Blessed City'* (Oxford: The Clarendon Press, 1970), 75. See also von Dobschütz, 'Der Briefwechsel', 423–6; C. Picard, 'Un texte nouveau de la correspondance entre Abgar d'Osroène et Jésus-Christ gravé sur une porte de ville, à Philippes (Macédoine)', *BCH*, 44 (1920), 41–69.

[116] For materials written in Greek, see *P.Oxy.* LXV 4469 intro. For materials written in Coptic, see, in addition to items listed at Drioton, 'Un apocryphe anti-arien', 307–9, Y. Åbd Al-Masīh, 'An Unedited Bohairic Letter of Abgar', *BIFAO*, 45 (1947), 65–80, <http://www.ifao.egnet.net/bifao/45/>, and 54 (1954), 13–43, <http://www.ifao.egnet.net/bifao/54/>; S. Giversen, 'Ad Abgarum: The Sahidic Version of the Letter to Abgar on a Wooden Tablet', *AcOr*, 24 (1958), 71–82; K. P. Sullivan and T. G. Wilfong, 'The Reply of Jesus to King Abgar: A Coptic New Testament Apocryphon Reconsidered (P. Mich. Inv. 6213)', *BASP*, 42 (2005), 107–23, <http://hdl.handle.net/2027/spo.0599796.0042.001:09>. In the list of Drioton, the editions of J. Krall, 'Koptische Amulete', *MPER*, 5 (1892), 115–22, are superseded by V. Stegemann, *Die koptischen Zaubertexte der Sammlung Papyrus Erzherzog Rainer in Wien* (Heidelberg: Carl Winters Universitätsbuchhandlung, 1934), nos. XXVI, L, and XLVI (Drioton, Regn. 55, 78, 3151, respectively).

[117] *P.Oxy.* LXV 4469.

[118] Stegemann, *Die koptischen Zaubertexte*, 21, 45–9 (no. XXVI).

[119] *P.Lond.Copt.* I 316; Stegemann, *Die koptischen Zaubertexte*, 28, 45–9 (no. L), with plate III, where folds are visible; Sullivan and Wilfong, 'The Reply of Jesus', 112, 115–16.

[120] E.g., *P.Got.* 21 has the promise of protection, and *P.Cair.Cat.* 10736 + Bodl. Ms. gr. th. b. 1 (P), lacunose at this point, resembles the version of the correspondence in the *Teaching of Addai*, which has the promise. On the former, see H. C. Youtie, 'A Gothenburg Papyrus and the Letter to Abgar', *HTR*, 23 (1930), 299–302, <http://www.jstor.org/stable/1507889>, and 'Gothenburg Papyrus 21 and the Coptic Version of the Letter to Abgar', *HTR*, 24 (1931), 61–5, <http://www.jstor.org/stable/1507898>, both reprinted in H. C. Youtie, *Scriptiunculae*, 2 vols (Amsterdam: Adolf M. Hakkert, 1973), 1.455–66. On the latter, see R. Peppermüller, 'Griechische Papyrusfragmente der *Doctrina Addai*', *VigChr*, 25 (1971), 289–301, doi: 10.2307/1583048.

[121] W. E. Crum and H. G. Evelyn White (eds), *The Monastery of Epiphanius at Thebes, Part II* (New York: The Metropolitan Museum of Art, 1926), 11 and 162 (no. 50).

[122] See now A. Delattre and K. A. Worp, 'Trois tablettes de bois du Musée de Leyde', *CdE*, 87 (2012), 361–82 at 379–82, doi: 10.1484/J.CDE.1.103137, on the orientation of the writing in relation to the holes in the tablet (their no. 9), which Giversen, 'Ad Abgarum', 78, took as evidence that the tablet had been fixed somewhere. The two holes along the length of the tablet

in Egypt—as elsewhere[123]—the letter of Jesus to Abgar was valued for its promise of healing and protection, no doubt because it was attributed directly to Jesus, written by his own hand, no less.[124]

We shall limit our remarks to the two amulets that include an injunction to heal a particular individual, *P.Oxy.* LXV 4469 and P.Vindob. inv. K 8636, mentioned earlier.[125] They differ in a number of ways. *P.Oxy.* LXV 4469 is written in an irregular, informal hand in small, thick semi-cursive letters (see Fig. 5.2).[126] The lines slope markedly downwards to the right with little space between lines. There are numerous phonetic spellings, but *nomina sacra* are for the most part used correctly and consistently.[127] The Greek text of Abgar's letter converges with several of the literary sources, but is not aligned with any of them.[128] It is interrupted at the point where Abgar asks for Jesus to come and heal him with a customary injunction written twice in Coptic: 'heal Epimachus, son of [...], quickly quickly quickly'.[129] A few lines later the text again diverges as Abgar begins to describe his city. Shortly thereafter the letter breaks off and the customary injunction recurs in Greek—'Heal quickly quickly quickly'[130]—followed by three crosses, several lines of *charaktêres*, and a citation of LXX Ps. 28: 7. The sequence is repeated in the indicative—'Iaô Sabaôth Elôe Adônai, you heal quickly quickly quickly'[131]—flanked by two configurations of words and symbols in cross-formation (which includes what appears to be [α] ⨮ ω).[132] The entire text is preceded and followed by three crosses.

P.Vindob. inv. K 8636,[133] by contrast, is written in a formal book hand.[134] The text of the letter is transcribed without interruption to its closing salutation, 'Fare well in the holy Trinity, amen',[135] a formulation used in monastic letters.[136] A customary injunction follows: 'God, Jesus Christ, you

---

along the bottom were most likely made so that the tablet could be bound with other tablets in a codex. Nevertheless, the tablet could have been displayed in a niche.

[123] E.g., *P.Ness.* II 7, found at Nessana, Palestine.

[124] This detail of the tradition can be found at, e.g., *P.Got.* 21.5; Giversen, 'Ad Abgarum', 74–5, line 8; Stegemann, *Die koptischen Zaubertexte*, 46 (no. XXVI.24–6); Sullivan and Wilfong, 'The Reply of Jesus', 113, lines 4–5.

[125] See nn. 117–18.

[126] Image at *P.Oxy.* LXV, plate XIV; <http://www.papyrology.ox.ac.uk/POxy/> (Oxyrhynchus Online); and fig. 5.2 below.

[127] The one unusual abbreviation is π̄ατ̄α for π(νεύμ)ατα at line 9.

[128] *P.Oxy.* LXV 4469 intro., p. 124.   [129] *P.Oxy.* LXV 4469.21–5.

[130] *P.Oxy.* LXV 4469.34–5.   [131] *P.Oxy.* LXV 4469.39–42.

[132] *P.Oxy.* LXV 4469.41 comm.

[133] Stegemann, *Die koptischen Zaubertexte*, 45–9 (no. XXVI).

[134] Stegemann, *Die koptischen Zaubertexte*, 21. Image at <http://data.onb.ac.at/rec/RZ00004842> (Österreichischen Nationalbibliothek Katalog der Papyrussammlung).

[135] Stegemann, *Die koptischen Zaubertexte*, no. XXVI.35–6.

[136] E.g., Crum and White, *The Monastery of Epiphanius*, 55 and 206 (no. 198.11).

Fig. 5.2. *P.Oxy.* LXV 4469. Courtesy of the Egypt Exploration Society and Imaging Papyri Project, Oxford.

shall give healing for Christodora, the daughter of Gabriel. Amen, it shall be, quickly quickly'.[137] The form of the *nomen sacrum* for Christ in the injunction ($\overline{\text{xpc}}$) is less common than that in the superscription to the letter

---

[137] Stegemann, *Die koptischen Zaubertexte*, no. XXVI.37–41.

($\overline{xc}$),[138] perhaps reflecting the habit of the scribe, since he is here no longer transcribing a text. There are no other customary elements, such as the *charaktêres* we saw in the preceding amulet.

Both of these scribes were, evidently, familiar with the Abgar tradition and had access to a text of the letters they transcribed. But they differ in the character of their scribal training and their reception of customary forms of incantation. In the second amulet, a more professional scribal training correlates with a more restrained use of customary elements, just as we saw in the more formally written 'gospel' amulets. At the same time, the way in which customary elements are configured in the first amulet indicates that they were deemed to be entirely appropriate as resources for healing incantations; the sequence of crosses, *charaktêres*, and psalm verse is uninterrupted.[139] Thus, the two amulets reveal cultural horizons that are slightly different, while nevertheless overlapping. They are yet one more example of the variegated Christian culture of Egypt in Late Antiquity.

5.5 THE LORD'S PRAYER

The text of the Lord's Prayer would have been more familiar to a greater number of Christians than the text of the Abgar correspondence, since the Lord's Prayer was a staple of Christian catechetical instruction and was said in daily prayer services,[140] as well as in the liturgy of the Eucharist.[141] In fact, in several amulets we can see that the prayer was recalled from its use in liturgical settings. First, the vocative 'Lord' is inserted between 'and lead us not into temptation' and 'but deliver us from evil' (Matt. 6: 13),[142] as was the custom in the inaudible prayer spoken by the priest (the *embolismos*) after the congregational recitation of the Lord's Prayer prior to the Prayer of Inclination.[143] Second, the final petition is followed by a

---

[138] Compare line 37 with lines 2–3. For instances in documents, see M. R. M. Hasitzka (ed.), *Koptisches Sammelbuch I–IV* (Vienna: Brüder Hollinek, 1993–2012), 1.323, 2.280, 4.244.

[139] *P.Oxy.* LXV 4469.35–9.

[140] *Can. Hipp.* 21 (PO 31/2.386–7), quoted in Section 6.2, mentions 'the prayer' as part of the daily service of morning prayer, on which see R. F. Taft, *The Liturgy of the Hours in East and West: The Origins of the Divine Office and its Meaning for Today*, 2nd edn (Collegeville: Liturgical Press, 1993), 34–5.

[141] On the recitation of the Lord's Prayer prior to communion, see P. F. Bradshaw and M. E. Johnson, *The Eucharistic Liturgies: Their Evolution and Interpretation* (Collegeville: Liturgical Press, 2012), 171 with table 5.3.

[142] *P.Bad.* IV 60.8; P.Duke inv. 778v.20 (n. 23, this chapter); *PGM* P9.23 (*BGU* III 954).

[143] For medieval witnesses to the *embolismos* in the Liturgy of St Mark, see G. J. Cuming, *The Liturgy of St Mark* (Rome: Pontificium Institutum Studiorum Orientalium, 1990), 50–1 (texts and variants at line 23). An early witness to the *embolismos* in Egypt may be found in a seventh-century Sahidic manuscript of the Liturgy of St Basil (Louvain-la-Neuve, Université Catholique

doxology.[144] We therefore should expect to see a greater diversity in scribal formation in amulets (and other artefacts) that recite the Lord's Prayer.[145] We are not disappointed.

The Lord's Prayer could have been copied for various reasons, not only liturgical but also pedagogical.[146] In many instances the entire Matthean version of the prayer is written.[147] Sometimes only a portion of the prayer was used or only a fragment of what was presumably the entire prayer remains.[148] Where the prayer, or a portion thereof, is recited in the context of a petition or adjuration, the protective purpose of the text is clear.[149] So too when it is combined with LXX Ps. 90.[150] But when the prayer is copied without these elements or other clues[151]—which occurs more frequently with the Lord's Prayer than with LXX Ps. 90—its purpose is more ambiguous. Nevertheless, it is telling that a wax tablet with a copy of the prayer written as a dictation exercise accompanied a body to its grave[152]—possibly as an amulet?[153]

In what follows we shall consider amulets (or what may have been amulets) in groups according to their hands, since we encounter hands along the spectrum from formal book hands to 'slow writers'. An exquisite example of a biblical majuscule hand, assigned to the fifth century, is found in *P.Col.* XI 293.[154] This damaged parchment leaf from a codex preserves verses from Matthew leading up to the Lord's Prayer (Matt. 6: 4–6) on the recto and verses from the Lord's Prayer (Matt. 6: 8–10) on the verso. The ragged left edge of the

de Louvain, Ms. Lefort copte 28A), published in J. Doresse and E. Lanne, *Un témoin archaïque de la liturgie copte de S. Basile* (Louvain: Publications Universitaires, 1960), 32–3. I am indebted to Ágnes Mihálykó for this reference.

[144] A long form of the doxology appears in *P.Bad.* IV 60.9–12 and P.Duke inv. 778v.22–5; a short form of the doxology appears in *PGM* P9.24–5 (*BGU* III 954); *PGM* P19.4 (*P.Iand.* I 6) = *P.Giss.Lit.* 5.4, col. IIIb; and P.Oslo inv. 1644.6–7. See also *P.Köln* IV 171.6–7. On the addition of the doxology to the prayer early on in its use in Christian worship, see F. H. Chase, *The Lord's Prayer in the Early Church* (Cambridge: Cambridge University Press, 1891), 168–76.

[145] These have been conveniently collected and discussed in Kraus, 'Manuscripts'; Jones, *New Testamjent Texts*, 77–127 (nos. 4–14). For English translations, the reader is referred to Jones.

[146] See, e.g., the proposals as to purpose in Kraus, 'Manuscripts', 234–5, 238–9, 247–50 (nos. 1, 5, 14, 15, 16).

[147] *P.Bad.* IV 60; P.Duke inv. 778; *PGM* P9 (*BGU* III 954); *PGM* P17 (*P.Iand.* I 6) = *P.Giss.Lit.* 5.4; P.Oslo inv. 1644 + *P.Schøyen* I 16; *P.Oxy.* LX 4010.

[148] *P.Ant.* II 54; *P.Köln* IV 171 (portion); *P.Köln* VIII 336 (fragment).

[149] *PGM* P9 (*BGU* III 954); *PGM* P17 (*P.Iand.* I 6) = *P.Giss.Lit.* 5.4; *SM* I 29 (*P.Princ.* II 107).

[150] P.Duke inv. 778; *PGM* P19 (*PSI* VI 719); P.Oslo inv. 1644 + *P.Schøyen* I 16; *SM* I 29 (*P.Princ.* II 107).

[151] E.g., the threefold 'amen' and 'holy' at *P.Köln* IV 171.8–9.

[152] *P.Bad.* IV, pp. 46–7, regarding *P.Bad.* IV 60; E. Feucht (ed.), *Vom Nil zum Neckar: Kunstschätze Ägyptens aus pharaonischer und koptischer Zeit an der Universität Heidelberg* (Berlin: Springer, 1986), 214 (no. 647).

[153] *Pace* Kraus, 'Manuscripts', 250.

[154] Jones, *New Testament Texts*, 100 (no. 8). Image at *P.Col.* XI, plate 1; Jones, *New Testament Texts*, 101 (plate 8); and <http://papyri.info/apis/columbia.apis.p1812/images> (Papyri.info)

leaf suggests that it was torn out of its codex.[155] In all likelihood the leaf was removed for its protective power,[156] though the petitions that are most explicit in that regard—'lead us not into temptation, but deliver us from evil' (Matt. 6: 13)—would have appeared on the next leaf of the codex. It is worth noting that the scribe's use of *nomina sacra* is inconsistent; he abbreviates a 'mundane' instance of 'people' ($\dot{\alpha}\nu\theta\rho\dot{\omega}\pi\omega\varsigma$) in the preamble,[157] but not 'Father' or 'heaven' in the prayer. Thus, professional training as a copier of biblical manuscripts does not correlate with perfect consistency in this particular technique, as has been observed elsewhere.[158]

P.Duke inv. 778[159] presents an amulet written by an experienced but careless writer in an irregular, informal, upright semi-cursive hand with frequent continuous strokes between letter-forms, assigned to the sixth or possibly seventh century.[160] The text consists of LXX Ps. 90, the heading of LXX Ps. 91, the Lord's Prayer, and a doxology, written in fairly evenly spaced lines of *scriptio continua* along the fibres on both the recto and the verso of a long rectangular papyrus. The text begins with three staurograms, and there is a line of three crosses after it ends. The text is riddled with phonetic spellings and textual variants,[161] more than one often finds in amulets citing LXX Ps. 90 or the Lord's Prayer. The scribe also omits sense-units or clauses in both LXX Ps. 90 and the Lord's Prayer, omitting, in the latter text, verse 10b—'your will be done'—and verse 12b—'as we also forgive our debtors'.[162] These omissions were most likely due to the carelessness of the scribe, not the poor quality of his exemplar.[163] *Nomina sacra* are also not applied consistently.[164] In short, although the scribe was clearly practiced, able to write quickly in fairly regular lines across the papyrus, he was not particularly concerned about the correctness of the passages he transcribed.

---

[155] *P.Col.* XI 293 intro.

[156] De Bruyn and Dijkstra, 'Greek Amulets', 198–9 (no. 105); Jones, *New Testament Texts*, 102.

[157] *P.Col.* XI 293.9 with comm.: $\alpha\nu\omega\iota\varsigma$. The supralinear stroke is missing, perhaps due to fading.

[158] Paap, *Nomina Sacra*, 117–18.

[159] La'da and Papathomas, 'A Greek Papyrus Amulet'; Jones, *New Testament Texts*, 94–5 (no. 7).

[160] Image at Jones, *New Testament Texts*, 96 (plate 7), and <http://library.duke.edu/rubenstein/scriptorium/papyrus/records/778.html> (Duke Papyrus Archive). See the descriptions of the hand at La'da and Papathomas, 'A Greek Papyrus Amulet', 96, and Jones, *New Testament Texts*, 98. On this type of hand during the transition to Byzantine cursive writing, see G. Cavallo, *La scrittura greca e latina dei papiri: una introduzione* (Pisa: Fabrizio Serra, 2008), 127–32.

[161] La'da and Papathomas, 'A Greek Papyrus Amulet', 99, apparatus.

[162] P.Duke inv. 778v.16, 19.

[163] La'da and Papathomas, 'A Greek Papyrus Amulet', 95; see also Section 5.6.

[164] P.Duke inv. 778r.1: $\theta\epsilon\circ\hat{\upsilon}$, $\kappa\upsilon\rho\acute{\iota}\upsilon\upsilon$; r.2: $\overline{\theta\varsigma}$; v.20: $\overline{\kappa\epsilon}$. Other words that might be abbreviated, such as $\pi\alpha\tau\acute{\eta}\rho$ and $\upsilon\dot{\upsilon}\rho\alpha\nu\acute{\upsilon}\varsigma$, are written in full (lines r.1, v.15).

The scribe of a somewhat later copy of the Lord's Prayer, P.CtYBR inv. 4600,[165] was arguably better trained; the execution is more refined than in the previous example. The scribe wrote in an informal sloping hand that combines majuscule and miniscule letter-forms.[166] It has a parallel in a mid-seventh-century document,[167] and resembles hands of the late seventh and early eighth centuries.[168] Even though the transcription corresponds for the most part to the standard text,[169] the scribe transcribed the prayer as it was heard or said, not as it was read. The spelling is phonetic. *Upsilon* is substituted for *eta* in all the first-person plural pronouns (e.g., $\dot{\upsilon}\mu\hat{\omega}\nu$ for $\dot{\eta}\mu\hat{\omega}\nu$),[170] which makes sense only if one allows for the interchange in daily speech. In the fifth petition the scribe wrote $o\varphi\eta\tau\eta s$ for $\dot{o}\varphi\epsilon\iota\lambda\acute{\epsilon}\tau\alpha\iota s$ ('debtors'),[171] a syllable lost either through carelessness or manner of speech.[172] And the vocative 'Lord' appears to have been interjected between the last two petitions,[173] as one would have done when reciting the prayer in the liturgy.[174] Thus, the papyrus preserves for us the oral-scribal culture of the writer, conveying the prayer as it was recalled from having been prayed aloud. The latter half of every line of the text must be reconstructed due to loss of papyrus. The words after 'our Father'—are problematic,[175] as is the reference to 'the Lord' in the last line of the text after the final petition.[176]

The writers of our next two examples, *P.Köln* IV 171[177] and P.Oslo inv. 1644 + *P.Schøyen* I 16,[178] were less practiced than the previous two scribes.

[165] B. Nongbri, 'The Lord's Prayer and *XMГ*: Two Christian Papyrus Amulets', *HTR*, 104 (2011), 59–68 at 59–64; N. Gonis, 'An "Our Father" with Problems', *ZPE*, 181 (2012), 46–7, <http://www.jstor.org/stable/41616956> (correcting the *editio princeps*); Jones, *New Testament Texts*, 104 (no. 9).

[166] Image at Nongbri, 'The Lord's Prayer', 61; Jones, *New Testament Texts*, 105 (plate 9); and <http://brbl-legacy.library.yale.edu/papyrus/oneSET.asp?pid=4600> (Beinecke Rare Book and Manuscript Library, Papyrus Collection).

[167] Nongbri, 'The Lord's Prayer', 60–1, referring to Cavallo and Maehler, *Greek Bookhands*, 94, 96–7 (no. 43c), P.Vindob. inv. G 39726 (643 CE).

[168] Gonis, 'An "Our Father"', 46.

[169] Jones, *New Testament Texts*, 107, qualified by the unresolved reading of line 1 and the anomalous $o\varphi\eta\tau\eta s$ in line 7.

[170] On this common interchange, see F. T. Gignac, *A Grammar of the Greek Papyri of the Roman and Byzantine Periods*, 2 vols (Milan: Istituto Editoriale Cisalpino-La Goliardica, 1976–1981), 1.284.

[171] P.CtYBR inv. 4600.7.

[172] On loss of a syllable, see Gignac, *A Grammar*, 1.312–13.

[173] P.CtYBR inv. 4600.8: $\kappa[\acute{\upsilon}\rho\iota\epsilon]$, as suggested by Gonis, 'An "Our Father"', 46–7.

[174] See n. 143.   [175] Gonis, 'An "Our Father"', 46.

[176] Gonis, 'An "Our Father"', 47.   [177] Jones, *New Testament Texts*, 124 (no. 14).

[178] L. Amundsen, 'Christian Papyri from the Oslo Collection', *SO*, 24 (1945), 121–47 at 141–7, 10.1080/00397674508590389 (P.Oslo inv. 1644), published the top two fragments of this papyrus. Rosario Pintaudi then published an additional fragment in 2005 (*P.Schøyen* I 16). The entire text is republished in Jones, *New Testament Texts*, 112–13 (no. 11).

Fig. 5.3. *P.Köln* IV 171 (inv. 3302r). Copyright Papyrussammlung Köln, Institut für Altertumskunde, University of Cologne.

Both wrote in an irregular, upright semi-cursive hand,[179] the former assigned to the fifth century,[180] the latter to the fourth or fifth century.[181] The letter-forms are large; their shapes, variable; their slopes, erratic. This is the sort of hand one would expect of someone who could write, but was not routinely employed as a scribe.

P.Köln IV 171 preserves the bottom half of what was probably the entire Lord's Prayer (see Fig. 5.3).[182] What remains corresponds closely to the standard text of the prayer,[183] apart from a few phonetic spellings. The writer was evidently familiar with liturgical prayers of the Egyptian church. The short doxology with which the prayer concludes—'through your only-begotten Jesus Christ'—echoes phrasing found in prayers in the Euchologion attributed to Sarapion.[184] Below the doxology is a line with threefold 'amen' and a

---

[179] See the descriptions at Amundsen, 'Christian Papyri', 142; *P.Köln* IV 171 intro.; Jones, *New Testament Texts*, 115, 126. Images at Jones, *New Testament Texts*, 125 (plate 13), and <https://papyri.uni-koeln.de/stueck/tm64737> (Kölner Papyrussammlung); *P.Schøyen* I, plate XI, and Jones, *New Testament Texts*, 114 (plate 10).

[180] Jones, *New Testament Texts*, 126.   [181] Jones, *New Testament Texts*, 115–16.

[182] *P.Köln* IV 171 intro.   [183] Jones, *New Testament Texts*, 126.

[184] *P.Köln* IV 171.6–7 comm.; see now M. E. Johnson, *The Prayers of Sarapion of Thmuis: A Literary, Liturgical, and Theological Analysis* (Rome: Pontificio Istituto Orientale, 1995), 46–81.

line with threefold 'holy', the words separated by three short diagonal lines. These reinforcing acclamations make it likely that the papyrus functioned as an amulet.[185]

P.Oslo inv. 1644 preserves two fragments from the top of a sheet of a papyrus with the Lord's Prayer and a doxology, which was followed by LXX Ps. 90, a fragment of which is preserved in *P.Schøyen* I 16. Although the spelling is phonetic, the transcription of the Lord's Prayer, again, corresponds closely to the standard text, apart from what was probably an accidental omission of the final phrase of the prayer, 'from evil'.[186] (What little we have of LXX Ps. 90 in this papyrus also corresponds fairly closely to the standard text.[187]) The scribe employs a *nomen sacrum* for 'Lord',[188] but spells 'Christ' in full, with *upsilon* rather than *iota* (Χρυστοῦ),[189] a further instance of phonetic spelling of the name by scribes whose cultural formation was evidently Christian.[190] The editors of these fragments took them to be the remains of an amulet, but this interpretation has recently been questioned by Carlig and de Haro Sanchez, who argue that the papyrus may have been a writing exercise.[191] The presence of an ornamented line between the doxology and the psalm may tip the balance in favour of their view, since such lines appear on occasion in writing exercises.[192]

A more formal but still developing hand appears in *P.Ant.* II 54,[193] a small papyrus bifolium whose leaves (four pages) are written recto and verso with a few verses of the Lord's Prayer.[194] When folded, the bifolium would have been the size of a large postage stamp (2.6 cm w × 4 cm h); it is the smallest example in Eric Turner's lists of miniature codices.[195] The scribe wrote somewhat laboriously but fairly consistently in a formal sloping majuscule hand belonging to the transition between the 'severe style' and sloping ogival majuscule.[196] It has been assigned to the third century,[197] but one should perhaps not rule

---

[185] *P.Köln* IV 171.8–9 comm. [186] Jones, *New Testament Texts*, 116.

[187] Jones, *New Testament Texts*, 112–13, apparatus, and 116 n. 170. The addition of βοηθός μου at verse 2 is common in amulets; see n. 256. The other irregularities are orthographic.

[188] P.Oslo inv. 1644.9; *P.Schøyen* I 16.6. [189] P.Oslo inv. 1644.7. [190] See n. 48.

[191] Carlig and de Haro Sanchez, 'Amulettes ou exercises scolaires', 76–7.

[192] Cribiore, *Writing, Teachers, and Students*, 79.

[193] Jones, *New Testament Texts*, 117 (no. 12). For bibliography and discussion, see Kraus, 'Manuscripts', 234–5.

[194] Image at *P.Ant.* II, plate IV (verso only); Kraus, 'Manuscripts', 233 (recto and verso); Jones, *New Testament Texts*, 118 (plate 11).

[195] Turner, *Typology*, 22, 29–30.

[196] On this transition, see P. Orsini and W. Clarysse, 'Early New Testament Manuscripts and their Dates: A Critique of Theological Palaeography', *ETL*, 88 (2012), 443–74 at 453–4, doi: 10.2143/ETL.88.4.2957937. Jones, *New Testament Texts*, 119, regards the hand as an example of the 'severe style'. Some characteristics fit the 'severe style'—triangular middle part of *phi*, flat-based *omega*; others, less so—*alpha* with a slightly rounded loop, *nu* with the two verticals on the same plane, variable *omicron*, y-shaped *upsilon*.

[197] *P.Ant.* II 54.

out the fourth.[198] In her study of students' exercises, Raffaella Cribiore characterized the hand as 'evolving':[199] the hand of someone who writes regularly and is moderately fluent, but which may still seem clumsy and uneven and may not be perfectly aligned.[200] There are several irregularities (not only phonetic spellings) in the short text,[201] which suggest that the prayer was recalled from memory.[202]

The writing begins in the middle of verse 10 at the top of one page and ends abruptly in the middle of verse 12 in the middle of another, despite space remaining on that page and the following one, which is blank. In the middle of the papyrus, where it would have been folded to form two leaves, there are slits, one descending from the top and another ascending from the bottom. These could have been used to bind this bifolium with another (or others) whose leaves could have been written with the preceding verses of the prayer, as the first editor suggested.[203] If the writer began at the beginning of the prayer (verse 9b), the additional writing (without abbreviations) would have filled approximately 2.5 additional pages, based on the number of letters on the two pages that are fully written.[204] If the writer began at the beginning of verse 9—unusual in an amulet—the writing would have filled three pages. It would have taken the writer approximately three pages to complete the prayer.[205] If only two bifolia were used and gathered one on top of the other, the writer must have begun at the beginning of the prayer, writing somewhat more closely (as the first editor suggested),[206] since only then would the verses fit into the available space.[207] The remaining pages at the end of the codex would have been sufficient to complete the prayer. If three bifolio were used, there would have been ample room for the missing text, wherever it began, while leaving the first page unwritten as an outer cover.

The purpose of this papyrus remains enigmatic. Why did the writer choose such a small format, and why did the writer not complete the prayer? Although scriptural passages in amulets often end abruptly in mid-verse, this does not usually occur in amulets with the Lord's Prayer. Moreover, the writer stops in the middle of a word, and the last letter is at the beginning of a

---

[198] Jones, *New Testament Texts*, 119; Cavallo and Maehler, *Greek Bookhands*, 10 (no. 2b).

[199] Cribiore, *Writing, Teachers, and Students*, 273 (no. 387).

[200] Cribiore, *Writing, Teachers, and Students*, 112.

[201] *P.Ant.* II 54.10: ἡμᾶς for ἡμῖν; 13: ἄφεις for ἄφες; 14: τό for τά. Jones, *New Testament Texts*, 119.

[202] On memorization for writing exercises, see Cribiore, *Writing, Teachers, and Students*, 46–7.

[203] *P.Ant.* II 54 intro.

[204] Fol. 1 recto and verso each have thirty-three characters. Verse 9 has sixty-seven letters from the beginning of the verse and forty-three letters from πάτερ onward. Verse 10 has thirty-four letters prior to σου ὡς.

[205] There are 101 letters in the text missing to the end of verse 13.

[206] *P.Ant.* II 54 intro.   [207] I.e., seventy-seven letters over two pages.

line rather than the end.[208] It looks as if the writer simply abandoned the project. If we knew that the writer had intended to complete the prayer (which obviously we cannot know), we might be more confident in thinking it was meant to be an amulet, given how portable it would have been. As it is, we cannot be certain that this papyrus was written to serve as an amulet,[209] just as we cannot exclude that possibility.[210] Still, the papyrus is valuable because it is an early instance of a writer copying the prayer for some personal reason and attempting to do so in a formal hand.

We conclude with one of the few examples in our materials of a 'slow writer', that is, a writer who could only write individual letter-forms separately and laboriously.[211] This particular writer also could not read what he was writing. The amulet in question, *PGM* P17 (*P.Iand.* I 6) = *P.Giss.Lit.* 5.4,[212] has been assigned to the fifth or sixth century on the basis of affinities to other amulets with Christian elements rather than the character of the hand, which is not easily dated.[213] It is written in irregular capitals (some of which are semi-cursive) varying in size and angle, formed separately and deliberately in lines that run across the length of a large rectangular papyrus (30 cm w × 15.5 cm h).[214] The letter-forms become smaller and the writing more compressed as the writer proceeds down the papyrus.

The text, written in *scriptio continua*, is jumbled. The first editor discerned the cause of the confusion.[215] The amulet was copied from an exemplar that consisted of a preamble (conflating passages from the Gospel of Luke), the Matthean version of Lord's Prayer, a Solomonic exorcism (with a citation of LXX Ps. 90: 13), and an adjuration. In the exemplar, the text was written in six columns of four lines each that were to be read downwards, one column after the other.[216] When copying the text, the writer followed each line of the exemplar across all the columns, thereby mixing up the text,[217] even while preserving sense-markers from his exemplar.[218] Thus, as originally constructed, the amulet differs from artefacts comprising the Lord's Prayer alone or together with LXX Ps. 90. It is more akin to *SM* I 29 (*P.Princ.* II 107), which we discussed in Chapter 4. Nevertheless, the amulet as it was copied is a useful foil to those we discuss in this section.

---

[208] *P.Ant.* II 54.15–16: ὀφειλή | μ.   [209] *Pace* Jones, *New Testament Texts*, 118–19.

[210] *Pace* Carlig and de Haro Sanchez, 'Amulettes ou exercises scolaires', 80.

[211] Cribiore, *Writing, Teachers, and Students*, 116–17.

[212] Jones, *New Testament Texts*, 87 (no. 6).   [213] *P.Giss.Lit.* 5.4 intro, p. 171.

[214] Image at *P.Iand.* I 6, plate IV, and <http://bibd.uni-giessen.de/papyri/images/piand-inv014 recto.jpg> (Giessener Papyri- und Ostrakadatenbank).

[215] *P.Iand.* I 6, p. 30 with inserted, folded page.

[216] See now *P.Giss.Lit.* 5.4 intro., pp. 175–6; ET: Jones, *New Testament Texts*, 90.

[217] See now *P.Giss.Lit.* 5.4 intro., pp. 172–4; ET: *ACM*, no. 21.

[218] E.g., dicola at the ends of Matt. 6: 9b and 9c in line 2.

In the transcription of the Lord's Prayer, as in the rest of the amulet, there are two types of orthographical irregularities: phonetic spellings that the writer appears to have replicated from the exemplar, and nonsense readings that the writer introduced by transposing letters or by misidentifying letter-forms.[219] If the copier was familiar with the prayer (which is certainly possible), that oral knowledge does not help him here. Nevertheless, what this illiterate copier was doing is not very different from what more skilled and literate writers were doing when they composed amulets with the Lord's Prayer, transferring into writing a text that would have been known to many, as it was to them, in its oral form. All the amulets illustrate the value attached to the written word—to an incantation written down rather than merely spoken—even when, as in the present instance, the written word is unintelligible to the writer.

5.5.1 Summary

The Lord's Prayer had an inherent authority as the prayer taught by Jesus to his disciples, an authority that was sustained by its recurring recitation in the liturgy of the church. The prayer as recited or recalled could vary from the text in a biblical manuscript. Among the papyri and parchments we reviewed above, the only instance of a text of the prayer that follows the standard text without variants, omissions, or phonetic spellings is *P.Col.* XI 293, and it was not originally written to be an amulet. Most of the variants in the other amulets reflect the way Greek was spoken and the prayer was said. It was the prayer— not, first of all, a passage of scripture—that was being transferred to writing in amulets, with, on occasion, liturgical features such as the insertion of 'Lord' between the last two petitions and the addition of a doxology at the end.

As a resource for purveyors of amulets, the prayer was both accessible and restrictive. It was accessible in that it would have been widely known. Many a writer would have been able to write an amulet with a copy of the prayer. One would not have needed expertise in the customary formulation of incantations. Thus, examples of amulets written with the Lord's Prayer display a wide range of hands and skill. At the same time, the prayer was restrictive. Writers reproduced it by and large as it was commonly recited. It was not a vehicle for improvisation. Still, the transcriptions of the prayer are not without traces of individuality, each of them unique products of the oral-scribal culture of the writer.

---

[219] *P.Giss.Lit.* 5.4 intro., p. 171; *P.Iand.* I 6 intro., pp. 20–1. One should consult the diplomatic transcriptions at *P.Iand.* I 6, p. 22, and *P.Giss.Lit.* 5.4, p. 175, alongside the transcription at Jones, *New Testament Texts*, 87, to observe all the irregularities. For those occurring in the text of the prayer: line 2: $\epsilon > \dot{\epsilon}\nu$; $o\dot{v}\rho\alpha\nu os > o\dot{v}\rho\alpha\nu o\hat{\iota}s$; $\dot{\alpha}\gamma\iota\alpha\sigma\theta\nu\tau\omega > \dot{\alpha}\gamma\iota\alpha\sigma\theta\dot{\eta}\tau\omega$; $\dot{\epsilon}\lambda\theta\dot{\alpha}\tau\omega > \dot{\epsilon}\lambda\theta\dot{\epsilon}\tau\omega$; line 14: $\dot{\eta}\mu\hat{\omega} > \dot{\eta}\mu\hat{\omega}\nu$; $\dot{\alpha}\sigma\pi\dot{\iota}s$ (with *P.Iand.* I 6; *P.Giss.Lit.* 5.4) $> \ddot{\alpha}\phi\epsilon s$; line 17: $\dot{\eta}\mu\hat{\iota}\nu$ *om.*; $o\dot{v}\phi\lambda\dot{\eta}\mu\alpha\tau\alpha > \dot{o}\phi\epsilon\iota\lambda\dot{\eta}\mu\alpha\tau\alpha$; line 18: $\omega\nu$ (with *P.Iand.* I 6; *P.Giss.Lit.* 5.4) $> \dot{\omega}s$; $\dot{\alpha}\phi\kappa\alpha\mu\epsilon > \dot{\alpha}\phi\dot{\eta}\kappa\alpha\mu\epsilon\nu$; $\dot{o}\phi\iota\lambda\dot{\epsilon}\tau\alpha o\iota$ (with *P.Iand.* I 6) $> \dot{o}\phi\epsilon\iota\lambda\dot{\epsilon}\tau\alpha\iota s$.

5.6 LXX PSALM 90

The protective value of LXX Ps. 90 (Hebrew Ps. 91), a psalm of deliverance, is readily apparent from its text.[220] The psalm was used in Jewish contexts to deflect or expel demons from the period of the Second Temple to the Middle Ages, as we know from a scroll from Qumran,[221] the witness of the Mishnah and the Talmuds,[222] and documents from the Cairo Genizah.[223] Its widespread use in Christian contexts almost certainly grew out of Jewish practice. The psalm is quoted in an array of objects or settings from around the ancient world: armbands, medallions, rings, tablets, and inscriptions on door frames, houses, and graves.[224] In smaller objects only the opening verse(s) or a portion thereof may be cited: 'He who lives by the help of the Most High, in a shelter of the God of the sky he will lodge. He will say to the Lord, "My supporter you are and my refuge; my God, I shall hope in him."'[225] In texts on papyrus or parchment,[226] which afford more space than medallions or rings, either the opening verses or the entire psalm may be transcribed. These may be combined, as we have already seen, with gospel *incipits*, the Lord's Prayer, and liturgical acclamations—all of which suggest that the artefact had an apotropaic purpose.[227] The opening verses of the psalm may also accompany specific adjurations or petitions.[228]

We shall consider papyri and parchments that recite all or a good part of LXX Ps. 90, including those that add the titles or *incipits* of the gospels, the Lord's Prayer, or other scriptural passages.[229] In some cases only a fragment remains of what is thought to have been a complete text.

---

[220] ET: A. Pietersma and B. G. Wright (eds), *A New English Translation of the Septuagint and the Other Greek Translations Traditionally Included under That Title* (Oxford: Oxford University Press, 2007), 593.

[221] 11Q11. See G. Bohak, *Ancient Jewish Magic: A History* (Cambridge: Cambridge University Press, 2008), 108–11, with bibliography at 108 n. 111; Chapa, 'Su demoni e angeli', 76–7.

[222] D. C. Duling, 'Solomon, Exorcism, and the Son of David', *HTR*, 68 (1975), 235–52 at 239, <http://www.jstor.org/stable/1509184>; Kraus, 'Septuaginta-Psalm 90', 43; Bohak, *Ancient Jewish Magic*, 378–80.

[223] P. Schäfer and S. Shaked (eds), *Magische Texte aus der Kairoer Geniza*, 3 vols (Tübingen: J. C. B. Mohr, 1994–9), 2.199, 201 (T.-S. NS 153.162, fol. 1b.17, which gives the instruction to recite the entire psalm), 3.3 n. 17, 18–19, with 475 (index to multiple references).

[224] Kraus, 'Septuaginta-Psalm 90', 52–8.

[225] ET: *A New English Translation of the Septuagint*, 593.

[226] Kraus, 'Septuaginta-Psalm 90', 49–52.

[227] Chapa, 'Su demoni e angeli', 14–15, 27–8 (nos. 9–15).

[228] Chapa, 'Su demoni e angeli', 15–16, 28–9 (nos. 16, 17, and 19).

[229] LXX Ps. 90 alone: *BKT* VIII 12: *BKT* VIII 13; *P.Bodl.* I 4; *P.Leid.Inst.* 10; *P.Oxy.* XVII 2065; *P.Oxy.* LXXIII 4931; *P.Oxy.* LXXVIII 5127; *P.Ryl.* I 3. With gospel titles or *incipits*: *P.Oxy.* XVI 1928v; Daniel, 'A Christian Amulet' (P.Vindob. inv. G 348). With, *inter alia*, the Lord's Prayer: P. Duke inv. 778 (n. 23, this chapter); P.Oslo inv. 1644 (n. 178, this chapter) + *P.Schøyen* I 16. See Chapa, 'Su demoni e angeli', Appendix, nos. 8–9, 13–14, 24–30; *P.Oxy.* LXXIII 4931 intro., pp. 3–5 (table I).

Scribes typically chose one of two formats for the text: a sheet or a miniature codex. The sheets are of a size that would have had to have been folded in order to be worn.[230] Those that were folded or rolled were probably used as amulets.[231] The use to which other sheets were put is less clear; they may have been affixed to a place, since the text of the psalm would serve equally well to protect a home, shop, or monastic cell.[232] The codices would have been portable.[233] A few of them have one or more creases running down the leaves in addition to the medial fold,[234] showing that the codex was folded to form a small packet. It may be significant that among the codices and sheets that were certainly (or almost certainly) used as amulets, three whose beginning is intact precede the text with one or more staurograms.[235]

Since artefacts with the Lord's Prayer have already introduced us to the range of hands one finds in instances of a commonly cited text, we shall review the hands in artefacts with LXX Ps. 90 in a more summary fashion. A parchment fragment assigned to the seventh or eighth century, *BKT* VIII 12, is written in a somewhat irregular Alexandrian majuscule script,[236] but there are few clues as to its purpose.[237] A few of the miniature codices are written in irregular sloping majuscule hands: *P.Oxy.* LXXIII 4931, assigned to the late fifth century,[238] and *P.Oxy.* XVII 2065, assigned to the fifth or sixth century.[239] Another such codex, *P.Leid.Inst.* 10, assigned to the fifth century, is written in a documentary cursive hand.[240] Several sheets are fluently written

---

[230] *BKT* VIII 12, originally 33 cm w × 20 cm h; *BKT* VIII 13, originally 8 cm w × 32 cm h; *P.Bodl.* I 4, fragment 9.1 cm w × 14 cm h; *P.Oxy.* XVI 1928v, 30 cm w × 21.5 cm h; *P.Ryl.* I 3, fragment 10 cm w × 10.4 cm h.

[231] There are visible creases in the papyrus of *P.Oxy.* XVI 1928; image at <http://www.papyrology.ox.ac.uk/> (Oxyrhynchus Online). It is possible that *BKT* VIII 12 was once rolled up, but the damage the parchment has suffered over time makes it difficult to be sure; image at <http://smb.museum/berlpap/index.php/01135/> (Berliner Papyrusdatenbank).

[232] LXX Ps. 90: 1, 5–6.

[233] *P.Leid.Inst.* 10, a bifolium from a codex approximately 4–5 cm w × 6 cm h; *P.Oxy.* XVII 2065, a bifolium from a codex approximately 3 cm w × 4 cm h; *P.Oxy.* LXXIII 4931, a codex leaf 5.8 cm w × 8.5 cm h; *P.Oxy.* LXXVIII 5127, a bifolium from a codex 4.3 cm w × 3.8 cm h.

[234] *P.Leid.Inst.* 10 intro.; *P.Oxy.* LXXVIII 5127 intro.

[235] P.Duke inv. 778r.1 (three staurograms); *P.Leid.Inst.* 10, page 2.1 (one); *P.Oxy.* XVI 1928v.1 (one).

[236] Image at <http://smb.museum/berlpap/index.php/01130/> (Berliner Papyrusdatenbank). Compare, e.g., Cavallo and Maehler, *Greek Bookhands*, 104–5 (no. 47b), *P.Köln* V 215 (663?); 112–13 (no. 51), now *P.Louvre Hag.*, pp. 71–2 (Codex 2, second half of seventh century).

[237] Cf., e.g., *BKT* VIII 13, whose narrow format makes its designation as an amulet more likely.

[238] *P.Oxy.* LXXIII 4931 intro. The *alpha* with the narrow wedge is typical of the 'severe' style from which this hand is derived, but *mu* with the deep central curve and the y-shaped *upsilon* are typical of sloping ogival majuscule; see, e.g., Cavallo and Maehler, *Greek Bookhands*, 40–1 (no. 16a), *P.Oxy.* XI 1371 (first half or middle of the fifth century).

[239] *P.Oxy.* XVII 2065 intro.; image at <http://www.papyrology.ox.ac.uk/> (Oxyrhynchus Online).

[240] *P.Leid.Inst.* 10, plate IV; C. E. Römer, 'Christliche Texte (1989–August 1996)', *APF*, 43 (1997), 107–45 at 112, doi: 10.1515/apf.1997.43.1.78. Cf., e.g., H. Harrauer, *Handbuch der*

by practiced writers in informal semi-cursive hands of quite different aspects: *P.Oxy.* XVI 1928v,[241] written in the sixth century or later;[242] P.Duke inv. 778, which we have already discussed, assigned to the sixth or possibly seventh century;[243] P.Vindob. inv. G 348, assigned to the sixth or seventh century;[244] and *BKT* VIII 13, assigned to the seventh or eighth century.[245] In the first two, the scribes maintain fairly evenly spaced lines (not strictly bilinear) across the breadth of the wide rectangular papyrus; in the third, the lines are more compressed. (The current condition of *BKT* VIII 13 does not allow for easy comparison.) *P.Oxy.* LXXVIII 5127, a bifolium assigned to the late fifth century, is written fluently in an irregular semi-cursive.[246] *P.Ryl.* I 3, a sheet assigned to the fifth or early sixth century,[247] is written rather deliberately in an upright semi-cursive. P.Oslo inv. 1644 + *P.Schøyen* I 16, a sheet we have already examined,[248] is less practiced in its execution.[249]

The extent to which the text of LXX Ps. 90 corresponds to the standard text in these artefacts varies, as one might expect. The small excerpt cut from what appears to have been a parchment codex, *BKT* VIII 12, has no phonetic spellings or textual irregularities; the two instances of *nomina sacra* are also correct.[250] In three other codices and one sheet there are relatively few phonetic spellings,[251] which may indicate that the scribe was copying from an exemplar. However, in other cases, mostly sheets but also one codex, the text is full of phonetic spellings and other types of errors,[252] which suggests that the scribe was copying from memory or from a phonetically spelled exemplar. The use of *nomina sacra* in these texts can be inconsistent,[253] though this occurs as well in texts that are relatively free of phonetic

---

griechischen Paläographie, 2 vols (Stuttgart: Anton Hiersemann, 2010), 1.437–8 (no. 241), 2.229 (plate 226; *P.Prag.* II 158, first hand); Harrauer assigns the second hand to the fifth century.

[241] *P.Oxy.* XVI 1928 intro.; for the image, see n. 231.

[242] The psalm was written on the back of a document dated 5 October 533; see *P.Oxy.* XVI 1928 intro., with *BL* 7.142, 8.252, 9.192, 10.145, 11.156 = *SB* XXII 15581.

[243] See n. 159.

[244] Daniel, 'A Christian Amulet', 400; image at <http://data.onb.ac.at/rec/RZ00001340> (Österreichischen Nationalbibliothek Katalog der Papyrussammlung).

[245] *BKT* VIII 13 intro.; image at <http://smb.museum/berlpap/index.php/01135/> (Berliner Papyrusdatenbank).

[246] *P.Oxy.* LXXVIII 5127 intro.; image at <http://www.papyrology.ox.ac.uk/> (Oxyrhynchus Online).

[247] *P.Ryl.* I 3 intro.; image at <http://enriqueta.man.ac.uk:8180/luna/servlet/ManchesterDev~93~3> (Rylands Papyri Collection, image no. JRL040027tr).

[248] See n. 178.   [249] *P.Schøyen* I, plate XI.   [250] *BKT* VIII 12.1.

[251] Codices: *P.Leid.Inst.* 10; *P.Oxy.* XVII 2065; *P.Oxy.* LXXIII 4931. Sheet: P.Vindob. inv. G 348.

[252] *BKT* VIII 13; *P.Bodl.* I 4 (possibly an amulet, originally from a roll); P.Duke inv. 778; P.Oslo inv. 1644 + *P.Schøyen* I 16; *P.Oxy.* XVI 1928v; *P.Oxy.* LXXVIII 5127 (a codex); *P.Ryl.* I 3 (possibly an amulet).

[253] *BKT* VIII 13.3–5, 7; P.Duke inv. 778r.1–2; *P.Oxy.* XVI 1928v.1–2; but not P.Oslo inv. 1644 + *P.Schøyen* I 16.

spellings.[254] Phonetic spellings and other irregularities aside, all of the texts vary at points from the text printed in Rahlfs' critical edition.[255] However, several of the recurring variants are supported by other witnesses,[256] indicating that the scribes were reproducing what was for them (or their exemplars) the standard text. For instance, almost all of them add the words 'my help' after 'my God' in verse 2,[257] a variant found in some manuscripts believed to transmit Lucian of Antioch's revision of the Septuagint.[258] Lucian's version of the Septuagint was widely used in the East, including, as it happens, by an anchorite at the monastery at Naqlun who, in the second half of the sixth century or the first half of the seventh, wrote out a list of psalm *incipits* and copied out several psalms.[259] We shall return to this set of texts below.

Portions of the standard text are omitted or rearranged in several amulets. This occurs in amulets that are relatively free of phonetic spellings as well as those that are replete with them. Some omissions may have occurred because the scribe (or the scribe's exemplar) skipped over text between words that are the same or similar. This may explain, for instance, why the text in *P.Oxy.* LXXVIII 5127 jumps from the middle of verse 7c to the middle of verse 10a and from the end of verse 8 to the beginning of verse 11.[260] (It does not explain, however, why the text jumps back from the middle of verse 10b to the beginning of verse 8.[261]) Other omissions may have occurred because the scribe (or the scribe's exemplar) omitted one or more *stichoi*—parts of verses (sense-units) that in liturgical manuscripts might be marked by reading aids (single dots, double dots, or oblique slashes) or written as individual lines. For example, P.Vindob. inv. G 348 lacks verses 7c–8b, an omission that coincides with the end of a *stichos* in some ancient witnesses.[262] The text in P.Duke inv. 778 omits two sense-units of the psalm (verses 7c and 9a), and misplaces another of a similar length (verse 14b). In the latter instance the scribe appears to have been misled by the preceding word, which is the same where the clause should have occurred and where it does occur (αὐτῷ).[263] As this last remark

---

[254] *P.Leid.Inst.* 10 employs *nomina sacra* only for θεός, writing οὐρανοῦ (verse 1) and κύριε (verse 9) in full. P.Vindob. inv. G 348.16 also appears to have written κύριε (verse 9) in full.

[255] Rahlfs, *Psalmi cum Odis*, 239–41.

[256] E.g., verse 2: θεός μου βοηθός μου and καὶ ἐλπιῶ; verse 6: ἐν σκότει διαπορευομένου; verse 7: κλίτου σου. See *P.Leid.Inst.* 10, page 3, lines 3–4, 4 comm.; *P.Oxy.* LXXIII 4931.↓1–2, 6 comm.; *P.Oxy.* LXXVIII 5127.12–15 comm.; Daniel, 'A Christian Amulet', 403 (P.Vindob. inv. G 348.7, 15 comm.).

[257] *P.Leid.Inst.* 10, page 3, lines 3–4 comm.

[258] *P.Leid.Inst.* 10 intro. On Lucian's revision of the Septuagint, see B. M. Metzger, *Chapters in the History of New Testament Textual Criticism* (Grand Rapids: Eerdmans, 1963), 1–41 at 24–7; M. H. K. Peters, 'Septuagint', *ABD*, 5.1098–100.

[259] *P.Naqlun* I 1–6. For the date, see *P.Naqlun* I, pp. 41–2; for the version of the psalms, see *P.Naqlun* I, pp. 54–5.

[260] *P.Oxy.* LXXVIII 5127.22–9 comm.   [261] *P.Oxy.* LXXVIII 5127.24–8.

[262] Daniel, 'A Christian Amulet', 403 (P.Vindob. inv. G 348.15f comm.).

[263] La'da and Papathomas, 'A Greek Papyrus Amulet', 102 (P.Duke inv. 778r.11–13 comm.).

illustrates, when *stichoi* begin or end with the same or similar phraseology, the two possible explanations for an omission coincide. For example, the text in *P.Oxy.* LXXIII 4931 skips from verse 5b to verse 6b, probably because both parts of verse 6 begin with the same word (ἀπό);[264] there are other indications that the scribe was registering the ends of *stichoi*.[265] Likewise, the text of *P.Ryl.* I 3 omits verse 16a, probably because the scribe mistook the word that ended verse 15b (αὐτῶν for αὐτόν) with the word that ended verse 16a (presumably, αὐτῶν for αὐτόν).

In all these examples there is no consistent pattern of verses (or parts of verses) omitted. The most plausible explanation is that the scribe (or the scribe's exemplar) omitted text through some oversight in copying or recollection. This itself is significant, as it tells us that the practice of writing down the psalm for protective purposes did not entail exact copying or recollection. It is puzzling, at first glance, when a scribe spells phonetically but skips or rearranges verses in ways that suggest that the scribe was copying rather than recollecting the psalm, as in P.Duke inv. 778 or *P.Oxy.* LXXVIII 5127. But we see this as well in the texts written out by the anchorite at Naqlun. That this particular monk recalled psalms from memory is clear from his list of psalm *incipits*, which are replete with phonetic spellings and other mistakes.[266] He also appears to have relied on his memory when copying out several other psalms, since they also have phonetic spellings.[267] Yet at some points he corrects what he wrote in a way that, according to the editor of the papyri, suggests that he referred to a codex of the Psalter.[268] One cannot rule out the possibility that the monk noticed these errors from memory, since elsewhere he fails to recognize and correct mistakes;[269] if he did consult an exemplar, he did not do so systematically. Nevertheless, it remains true that phenomena associated with writing from memory and phenomena associated with writing from an exemplar occur in the same text. Moreover, the monk preserved the stichometry of the psalms he wrote down, sometimes employing dicola to do so.[270] Incidentally, the work of this monk reminds us that copies of individual psalms spelled phonetically, like those found at Naqlun, could have served as exemplars for subsequent copies—something that is quite possible in the case of LXX Ps. 90, a text of known protective value.

Finally, it is intriguing that several of the above examples depart from the standard text at verse 7c. In two other artefacts, *BKT* VIII 13 and *P.Gen.* 6 (a text of the psalm appended to an agricultural account written on a tablet), the text in fact skips from verse 7b to verse 10a.[271] Although the omission could be

---

[264] *P.Oxy.* LXXIII 4931.↓1–2 comm.   [265] *P.Oxy.* LXXIII 4931 intro., p. 2.
[266] *P.Naqlun* I 1.   [267] *P.Naqlun* I, pp. 53–4.
[268] *P.Naqlun* I 4.17 comm.; *P.Naqlun* I 5.22 comm.; see also *P.Naqlun* I, p. 54 n. 65.
[269] *P.Naqlun* I 5.7 comm.   [270] *P.Naqlun* I, p. 54.
[271] *BKT* VIII 13.32–4; *P.Gen.* [hors série] 6.10.

due to the similarity in wording at these junctures,[272] one wonders whether a text of the psalm without verses 7c–9b had come to be used for protective purposes. By way of contrast, although the text of *P.Oxy.* LXXVIII 5127 jumps from the middle of verse 7c to the middle of verse 10a, the scribe corrected the omission by inserting verse 8 (but not verse 9).[273] Thus, here the omission, whether originating with the scribe or the scribe's exemplar, was not intentional.

5.6.1 Summary

The value of LXX Ps. 90 as a protective text is evident from the many artefacts that cite it.[274] The opening words would have been familiar to many purveyors of amulets,[275] though they may not always have been aware of what they were evoking, as the phrasing of several βους-amulets shows.[276] Fewer purveyors would have known the entire text of the psalm. Even so, the material record from late antique Egypt includes more artefacts written with all or most of this psalm than with any other psalm. It is possible that habits of prayer and habits of amulet production reinforced one another.[277] Basil of Caesarea reports that the psalm was prayed by ascetics in Pontus at midday and before going to bed, undoubtedly because it promised protection from the 'noonday demon' (verse 6b) and 'nocturnal fright' (verse 5a).[278] Reciting the psalm in daily prayer would not only have reinforced its value as a protective text; it would also have led to its being learned in its entirety, certainly by clerics and monks and possibly by lay Christians. But we have no explicit evidence that LXX Ps. 90 was routinely recited at these (or other) hours in Egypt. The psalm is not mentioned in early literary accounts of daily prayer in Egypt,[279] and it is not included in early lists of the daytime and night-time hours,[280] one of which comes from the anchorite at Naqlun.[281]

As with artefacts written with the Lord's Prayer, we find a range of hands in artefacts written with LXX Ps. 90: more or less regular book hands, practiced

---

[272] Verse 7b–7c: σου | πρὸς; verse 9b–10a: σου | οὐ προσελεύσεται.

[273] See nn. 260–1.   [274] See n. 13.

[275] Sanzo, *Scriptural Incipits*, 106–20, with 134 nn. 140–2.

[276] T. J. Kraus, 'Βους, Βαινχωωχ und Septuaginta-Psalm 90? Überlegungen zu den sogenannten "Bous"-Amuletten und dem beliebtesten Bibeltext für apotropäische Zwecke', *ZAC*, 11 (2008), 479–91 at 482–3, doi: 10.1515/ZAC.2007.025.

[277] Chapa, 'Su demoni e angeli', 61–7.

[278] Basil of Caesarea, *Reg. fus.* 37.4–5 (PG 31.1013–16); Taft, *The Liturgy of the Hours*, 84–7.

[279] Taft, *The Liturgy of the Hours*, 57–66.

[280] *P.Naqlun*, pp. 88–95; see also S. S. R. Frøyshov, 'The Cathedral-Monastic Distinction Revisited. Part I: Was Egyptian Desert Liturgy a Pure Monastic Office?', *StudLit*, 37 (2007), 198–216 at 209–11.

[281] *P.Naqlun* I 6.

but informal hands, and less practiced and more laborious hands. This is not surprising; we would expect a well-known text to be copied or written out by writers of every level of skill. Some writers either copied or recalled the psalm as it might have appeared in a biblical or liturgical manuscript, with few or no phonetic spellings or textual irregularities. More often, however, the texts are replete with phonetic spellings and other irregularities. If such texts were copied from an exemplar rather than recalled from memory, they were nevertheless products of oral-scribal transmission. They illustrate that what counted was the writing of the psalm, however it was known, not the reproduction of the text from, for example, a Psalter, though such biblical and liturgical manuscripts still influence the oral-scribal transmission of the psalm through their presentation of the text in *stichoi*.

5.7 OTHER PSALMS

The passages we have considered thus far—titles and *incipits*, short verses from the gospels, the correspondence with Abgar, the Lord's Prayer, and LXX Ps. 90—were frequently recited in amulets, in various configurations, with or without injunctions or adjurations. But other, less commonly cited passages from scripture were also written down and worn for protective purposes. However, when we turn to materials written with such passages, we face the difficulty of determining whether they were written down primarily for some protective purpose. Evidence that the papyrus or parchment was folded into a size small enough to be worn is often a starting point, as is the fact that the papyrus or parchment was written with isolated discrete verses from scripture. Even so, distinguishing between something that was written to serve as an amulet and something that was written for some other purpose is often moot, since scriptural passages might have been recalled, recited, written down, and carried about for more than one purpose.

Often it is the presence of verses from one or more psalms that leads to the suggestion that the artefact may have been an amulet. This is to be expected. The Psalms afford a wealth of passages expressing in rich imagery and memorable cadences how God is the refuge, protector, helper, restorer, and vindicator of those who call upon him. The Psalms were also a staple of daily prayer, and some, if not all, of them were committed to memory by clergy, monks, and indeed lay Christians.[282] The repertoire of possible passages is, therefore, large. Among artefacts thought probably or possibly to have been used as amulets we find verses from LXX Pss. 1, 2, 3, 4, 7, 8, 9, 12, 19, 20, 24, 26,

---

[282] E. Wipszycka, *The Alexandrian Church: People and Institutions* (Warsaw: Journal of Juristic Papyrology, 2015), 326.

30, 31, 36, 40, 43, 44, 49, 50, 53, 62, 64, 72, 73, 80, 86, 91, 106, 109, 111, 114, 117, 118, 120, 132, 135, 140, 148, 149, and 150.[283]

Other psalms were no doubt also used. Often only a fragment of a sheet of papyrus or parchment has survived, written with a few partial verses from a psalm; the original sheet would have contained much more of the psalm. Sometimes the scribe wrote out the entire psalm.[284] Sometimes the scribe intended to write only part of the psalm.[285] Typically, verses are written in continuous lines, though some scribes marked the ending of verse-units with punctuation and/or a space.[286]

5.7.1 LXX Pss. 3 and 62

Among this array of artefacts written with verses from psalms we find several that are written with verses from LXX Ps. 3 or LXX Ps. 62, or both these psalms. The repeated use of these psalms invites further investigation, since it allows us to compare the scribal features of such artefacts with those of amulets written with more common, well attested texts (the Lord's Prayer, LXX Ps. 90). Moreover, the repeated use of these psalms prompts us to consider the role of daily prayer in the production of amulets, a subject we shall explore in more detail in Chapter 6. We begin with artefacts that were written for some personal use, and then turn to artefacts that appear, at least originally, to have had a liturgical use.

MPER N.S. IV 11 has been labelled an amulet.[287] This small papyrus sheet (9 cm w × 8 cm h) was folded diagonally. A hole in the centre of the papyrus, made after it was written, may have been used to thread a string.[288] Letters are

---

[283] See De Bruyn and Dijkstra, 'Greek Amulets and Formularies', tables 2 and 3.

[284] E.g., MPER N.S. XVII 3, written with LXX Ps. 53.

[285] E.g., *P.Ross.Georg.* I 1; the papyrus ends at LXX Ps. 49: 7 though space remains for more writing. This item was mislabeled *PGM* P16 in de Bruyn and Dijkstra, 'Greek Amulets and Formularies', table 2 (no. 112).

[286] E.g., *P.Köln* X 405; C. E. Römer, 'Psalm 40, 3–6 auf einem Wiener Papyrus (P. Vindob. G 14289)', *ZPE*, 114 (1996), 56, <http://www.uni-koeln.de/phil-fak/ifa/zpe/downloads/1996/114pdf/114.html>; C. La'da and A. Papathomas, 'Ein neues Papyrusamulett mit dem Septuaginta-Psalm 30, 3d–4a', *Aegyptus*, 81 (2001), 37–46 at 40, <http://www.jstor.org/stable/41217732> (P.Vindob. inv. G 40580). One can also observe a horizontal and an oblique stroke in the space after με at P.Vindob. inv. G 40580.2; image at <http://data.onb.ac.at/rec/RZ00010385> (Österreichischen Nationalbibliothek Katalog der Papyrussammlung; P.Vindob. inv. G 40580).

[287] MPER N.S. IV 11 title and intro.; H. Harrauer and C. Gastgeber, 'Bibeltexte im Alltag: Schutzamulette', in H. Froschauer, C. Gastgeber, and H. Harrauer (eds), *Ein Buch verändert die Welt: Älteste Zeugnisse der Heiligen Schrift aus der Zeit des frühen Christentums in Ägypten* (Vienna: Phoibos, 2003), 35–43 at 38; image at plate 3 and <http://data.onb.ac.at/rec/RZ00001887> (Österreichischen Nationalbibliothek Katalog der Papyrussammlung; P.Vindob. inv. G 26166).

[288] MPER N.S. IV 11 intro.

lost from wear. The scribe wrote in an irregular, informal semi-cursive hand with some cursive features; it has been assigned to the fifth or sixth century.[289] The letter-forms are more irregular on the verso than on the recto, indicating that the scribe's care or control in executing the hand declined as he wrote. The scribe first wrote LXX Ps. 62: 2–3 on one side of the papyrus, preceded by the sequence χμγ with a supralinear stroke, and then LXX Ps. 3: 5–6 on the other—both passages that appeal to God for help.[290] The many phonetic spellings suggest that the scribe wrote from memory.[291] *Nomina sacra* are used correctly and consistently. Each of the passages is preceded by a cross.

MPER N.S. IV 20 has also been labelled an amulet.[292] This small parchment bifolium (10.5 cm w × 6.5 cm h), evidently meant to be folded vertically in the middle, has LXX Ps. 118: 155–60 on the first two pages and LXX Ps. 3: 2–4 on the second two pages. (There are two diagonal folds across the sheet, but it is not clear when and why they were incurred, since the bifolium would have been just as portable once folded in half.) The two passages express the steadfastness of the psalmist in the face of numerous enemies.[293] The scribe wrote in a very irregular but nevertheless fluid hand, a mixture of semi-cursive and cursive, with continuous strokes and occasional ligatures between some letter-forms.[294] It has been assigned to the fifth or sixth century,[295] though the sixth or seventh century is possible in view of certain letter-forms (e.g., *delta*, *mu*, and *pi*).[296] *Nomina sacra* are used correctly and consistently. As with the previous amulet, the many phonetic spellings and orthographical irregularities suggest that the scribe recalled the verses from memory.[297] Nevertheless, the scribe preserves the stichometry of LXX Ps. 118, which he apparently recalled from recitation or reading (or both), by marking the ends of verse-units (with some omissions),[298] an oral-scribal habit we have already observed with LXX Ps. 90. For some reason the scribe does not bother to mark verse-units in LXX Ps. 3.

The passage from LXX Ps. 118 concludes with 'Alleluia' and an ornamental cross. LXX Ps. 118 was in fact one of the so-called 'Alleluia' psalms—psalms bearing the title 'Alleluia' and constituting a separate group in some early

---

[289] MPER N.S. IV 11 intro.

[290] ET: *A New English Translation of the Septuagint*, 548, 577.

[291] MPER N.S. IV 11 intro.

[292] MPER N.S. IV 20 title; Harrauer and Gastgeber, 'Bibeltexte im Alltag', 38–9.

[293] ET: *A New English Translation of the Septuagint*, 609–10.

[294] On such hands, though more regular, see Cavallo, *La scrittura greca*, 131–3.

[295] MPER N.S. IV 20 intro.; image at Harrauer and Gastgeber, 'Bibeltexte im Alltag', plate 3, and <http://data.onb.ac.at/rec/RZ00001889> (Österreichischen Nationalbibliothek Katalog der Papyrussammlung; P.Vindob. inv. G 26786).

[296] See, e.g., MPER N.S XVII 3, assigned to the sixth or seventh century.

[297] MPER N.S. IV 20 intro.

[298] To the markings noted by Sanz in his transcription of LXX Ps. 118, one may add a curved line after εδηγομην at the end of verse 158a (hair side, left column, line 2).

Christian classifications of the Psalms.[299] This may account for the addition of 'Alleluia', since according to John Cassian the monks of Egypt concluded only 'Alleluia' psalms with this response.[300] However, John Cassian's testimony is contradicted by John of Gaza's, who reports that the monks of Scetis concluded every psalm with 'Alleluia'.[301] The last page (the left half of the flesh side) has only a few lines of text, the conclusion of LXX Ps. 3: 4. About half of the remaining space is empty,[302] apart from the letters $\kappa\epsilon$ read upside down (without a supralinear stroke), and about half the space is filled with a scale-like pattern. Could it be that the bifolium, having been folded vertically in half, was meant to be folded over twice horizontally, such that the text on the last page was not exposed? Does $\kappa\epsilon$ stand for $\kappa(\acute{v}\rho\iota)\epsilon$, the addressee of the amulet, as in a letter?

Our next two examples, unlike the previous two, were not written in a small format. P.Vindob. inv. G 14197 consists of the top corner of a sheet of papyrus written on both sides.[303] The sheet was repeatedly folded, which no doubt accounts for its current fragmentary state.[304] Approximately one-quarter of the sheet survives (a fragment 6.9 cm w × 9.8 cm h from a sheet about 15 cm w × 20 cm h).[305] The sheet originally contained LXX Ps. 3: 4–9 and some verses from another psalm, quite possibly LXX Ps. 62, which begins with the words $\acute{o}$ $\theta\epsilon\acute{o}\varsigma$, as does the first line of the second psalm on the fragment.[306] The scribe wrote in an irregular, informal semi-cursive hand that sometimes slopes slightly to the right.[307] The hand has been assigned to the seventh or early eighth century.[308] The scribe did not employ *nomina sacra* or punctuation, and did not mark verse-units. He troubled to correct himself at a few points.[309] There are a few phonetic spellings, but too little of the text survives to determine how prevalent such spellings were. The scribe was in the habit of beginning a page of writing with a cross, since he wrote a cross at the outset of the verso before continuing with the remainder of LXX Ps. 3.[310] Further down the page he also preceded the first words of the second text with a cross.[311]

---

[299] *P.Naqlun* I, pp. 83–6.

[300] John Cassian, *Inst. coen.* 2.5.5, 2.11.3 (SC 109.68, 78).

[301] John of Gaza, *Ep.* 143 (SC 427.522); see Frøyshov, 'The Cathedral-Monastic Distinction', 202–3, 207.

[302] The writing from the other side of the leaf (hair side, right half) shines through.

[303] A. Papathomas, 'Ein griechisches Papyrusamulett mit Teilen aus zwei Septuaginta Psalmen', *Tyche*, 27 (2012), 113–18, <http://dx.doi.org/10.15661/tyche.2012.027.05>. Image at plate 3 and <http://data.onb.ac.at/rec/RZ00009696> (Österreichischen Nationalbibliothek Katalog der Papyrussammlung; P.Vindob. inv. G 14197).

[304] Papathomas, 'Ein griechisches Papyrusamulett', 113.

[305] Papathomas, 'Ein griechisches Papyrusamulett', 113.

[306] But see Papathomas, 'Ein griechisches Papyrusamulett', 118 (lines 19–21 comm.).

[307] See the image at n. 303.

[308] Papathomas, 'Ein griechisches Papyrusamulett', 116. Of the two *comparanda* given by Papathomas, MPER N.S. XVII 27 and 57, the former is the better fit.

[309] P.Vindob. inv G 14197.6, 16.

[310] P.Vindob. inv G 14197.14.   [311] P.Vindob. inv G 14197.19.

P.Ryl. III 461, likewise, consists of fragments of a sheet of parchment written with verses from LXX Ps. 3 and LXX Ps. 62. The original sheet, which would have measured at least 15 cm in width and over 30 cm in height,[312] probably contained all or much of both psalms written in two columns. Portions of only the first column remain.[313] The bottom fragment is pierced from holes due to stitching (some thread still remained when the piece was edited), but the reason for the stitching is uncertain. Colin Roberts, the parchment's editor, suggested that the thread might have been used to stitch up the ends of the sheet after it had been rolled up or, alternatively, that the sheet was later used as binding material.[314] To be worn or carried, the sheet would have had to have been folded vertically in half and then rolled up. At some later date the other side of the parchment was written over.[315] This would appear to tell against its having been rolled up.

The scribe of this parchment was more accomplished than the previous writers. He writes in a regular, formal sloping ogival majuscule hand belonging to the sixth century.[316] He marks the ends of verses that occur in the middle of a line with high stop and a space.[317] He uses *nomina sacra* correctly and consistently, and marks initial *upsilon* twice with inorganic *diairesis* (a short curve).[318] There are some phonetic spellings, but no other orthographical irregularities. When transcribing LXX Ps. 3, the scribe skipped from verse 5 to verse 7, perhaps because verses 5 and 6 each end with the letters *omicron upsilon*. He wrote verse 6 after the last verse of the psalm before turning to LXX Ps. 62, separating the two psalms by a horizontal line.

Finally, we should note *P.Mich.* III 132, a nearly complete leaf (5 cm w × 7.5 cm h) of a miniature parchment codex written with LXX Ps. 3: 4–9 in a regular, formal biblical majuscule script by a professional scribe.[319] The parchment's editor assigned it to the fifth century. It is a foil to the above examples in much the same way that *P.Col.* XI 293 and *BKT* VIII 12 were to amulets reciting the Lord's Prayer and LXX Ps. 90. All the qualities one typically finds in a professionally copied biblical manuscript are present. Verse-units are marked by dicola. The expression διάψαλμα is transcribed between verses 5 and 6. There are a few omissions and irregularities,[320] but otherwise the transcription agrees with other witnesses. Since what remains

---

[312] *P.Ryl.* III 461 intro., which gives 7 cm for a full line in the extant column (e.g., line 20 in fragment c) and estimates the height at over 30 cm.

[313] Image at <http://enriqueta.man.ac.uk:8180/luna/servlet/ManchesterDev~93~3> (Rylands Papyri Collection, image no. JRL030615tr).

[314] *P.Ryl.* III 461 intro.   [315] *P.Ryl.* III 461 intro.

[316] See, e.g., Cavallo and Maehler, *Greek Bookhands*, 86–7 (no. 39a), P.Berol. inv. 11754 + 21187 (second half of the sixth century).

[317] *P.Ryl.* III 461.3, 12, 21, 27.   [318] *P.Ryl.* III 461.2, 17.

[319] Image at <http://papyri.info/apis/michigan.apis.1472> (Papyri.info).

[320] Verse 6: ὕπνωσαι; verse 7: κύκλων; verse 8: omission of πάντας.

begins and ends in mid-verse, this leaf was once part of a codex. What the codex originally contained and how the leaf came to be separated, we do not know. But, as with the detached parchment leaf bearing the text of the Lord's Prayer, if this leaf was removed from its original setting to be used as an amulet, it is unlikely that this happened by chance. The leaf has been folded,[321] which would have allowed it to be carried as an amulet, but again, we do not know when this occurred.

5.7.2 Summary

To sum up, several features of these artefacts are relevant for our larger discussion of how scribes drew on scripture for some personal use, especially, though not necessarily, as an amulet. First of all, we see a predilection for certain psalms, in this case LXX Pss. 3 and 62, which evidently had a protective value. The fact that various scribes at different times availed themselves of these psalms suggests that their selection is not simply a matter of individual choice but also the result of a collective habit. We shall return to this point in Chapter 6, when we consider how the practice of prayer, particularly in daily services, influenced the production of amulets. Second, several of these artefacts were written or manipulated so as to be portable. However, as we see with P.Vindob. inv. G 14197, scribes of artefacts meant to be portable did not necessarily resort to a small format, but rather relied on folding to render the object portable. Third, when we compare the leaf that was torn out of a codex (*P.Mich.* III 132) with artefacts that were written for some personal use (MPER N.S. IV 11, MPER N.S. IV 20, P.Vindob. inv. G 14197), it is apparent that the scribes of the latter were operating under different norms than the former. Even if their texts echo features of the texts of biblical and liturgical manuscripts (such as verse-units and dicola) or are corrected by consulting or recollecting such texts, they do not replicate the presentation of those texts. Only the scribe of *P.Mich.* III 132, for example, reproduces the expression διάψαλμα. The frequency of phonetic spellings confirms, in fact, that writers of the less formal artefacts were recalling the texts from memory. Finally, scribes could exercise some freedom in selecting verses. But verses are cited in full; the text does not stop in the middle of a sense-unit, as we saw in amulets citing verses from the gospels.

Which of these artefacts were in fact used as amulets? Perhaps the strongest case can be made for secondary use as an amulet of the leaf with verses from LXX Ps. 3 taken from what could well have been a Psalter or a liturgical book, *P.Mich.* III 132. By contrast, if *P.Ryl.* III 461 indeed originally contained the full text of

---

[321] Two horizontal creases, two vertical creases, and one diagonal crease are visible on the digital image.

LXX Pss. 3 and 62, as seems likely, then it is more likely to have been written for some liturgical use rather than as an amulet. The fact that the three other artefacts were written more informally, contain selected verses of these psalms, and were constructed or folded so as to be portable increases the likelihood that they were intended to be used as amulets. Even so, one cannot be certain.

5.8 OTHER NEW TESTAMENT PASSAGES

Amulets comprising one or more passages from the New Testament other than gospel *incipits* or the Lord's Prayer are not as common as amulets citing verses from psalms other than LXX Ps. 90. Moreover, once one moves beyond the commonly cited New Testament passages, the intended purpose of an artefact can be ambiguous.

For example, P.Berol. inv. 13977,[322] a small parchment biofolium (11.5 cm w × 7.5 cm h), now damaged, is written on one side only with 1 Tim. 1: 15–16:

> The saying is sure and worthy of full acceptance, that Christ Jesus [came] into the [world to save sinners]—of whom I am the foremost. But for that very reason I received mercy, so that in me, as the foremost, Christ [Jesus] might display the [utmost patience].   (NRSV, slightly modified)[323]

The small triangular hole in the middle of the parchment could have been used to thread a string for it to be worn. The passage was evidently recalled from memory, since there are a number of phonetic spellings and several other irregularities,[324] though the wording itself conforms to the standard text.[325] What is especially striking about this amulet is the writing, which belongs to the seventh century.[326] The scribe wrote the first column in an informal sloping majuscule hand, and then carried on in the second column in an irregular miniscule cursive hand that at one point reverts to sloping majuscule.[327] The writer was capable but careless: his use of *nomina sacra* is inconsistent.[328] The first column is headed by a cross, and two lines in that column end in a

---

[322] K. Treu, 'Neue neutestamentliche Fragmente der Berliner Papyrussammlung', *APF*, 18 (1966), 23–38 at 36–7, doi: 10.1515/apf.1966.1966.18.23; Jones, *New Testament Texts*, 171 (no. 23). Image at Treu, 'Neue neutestamentliche Fragmente', plate 3, and <http://smb.museum/berlpap/index.php/03978/> (Berliner Papyrusdatenbank).

[323] Text presumed to be in the original, where parchment is now missing, is enclosed in square brackets.

[324] Jones, *New Testament Texts*, 171, apparatus.

[325] Jones, *New Testament Texts*, 174–5.   [326] Jones, *New Testament Texts*, 172.

[327] Treu, 'Neue neutestamentliche Fragmente', 36; Jones, *New Testament Texts*, 171–2. The scribe reverts to majuscule letter-forms for ἐλεήθην at line 10.

[328] Line 3: Χριστὸς $\overline{Ἰς}$; line 11: $\overline{Χς}$ $\overline{Χ}$ (?) $\overline{[Ἰς]}$ (?). As Treu observed (line 11, apparatus), there appears to have been a *chi* after $\overline{Χς}$. The letters after *chi* are no longer visible, though traces of a supralinear stroke remain.

staurogram.[329] While the cross and staurograms could have been written as protective signs, the text itself is more an expression of humility: referring to oneself as 'a sinner' was typical of monastic piety. This parchment, then, may have been worn as a perpetual expression of humility. If so, it reminds us that scribal features associated with amulets are not unique to amulets but are manifestations of a broader scribal culture.

The protective value of P.Vindob. inv. G 26034 + G 30453 is more apparent.[330] The papyrus, now in fragments, was evidently folded.[331] It is not so much a recital of scriptural passages as a declaration that draws on biblical language. Echoing phrases from Paul's letters (italicized below),[332] the scribe expresses his intention to take up spiritual armour and asks to be granted the victory that Christ has achieved over evil:

> *The weapons of warfare are not fleshly but have divine power* (2 Cor. 10: 4). I shall take up *the breastplate of faith and for a helmet the hope of salvation* (1 Thess. 5: 8).[333] My Lord, give [me] as one who knows you the transformation that you have manifested:[334] you have conquered the tyrant, you have taken the crown. Son, have mercy on us all.[335]

The scribe writes evenly spaced lines in an informal sloping majuscule hand assigned to the sixth century.[336] He spells phonetically, uses *nomina sacra* inconsistently,[337] and presents several ungrammatical readings.[338] The way in which the text is composed, using the first person, and the manner in which it is written suggests that the writer wrote it for himself (or herself) as a prayer *cum* amulet.[339]

---

[329] Jones, *New Testament Texts*, 172–3, figures 6 and 7.

[330] H. Hunger, 'Zwei unbekannte neutestamentliche Papyrusfragmente der Österreichischen Nationalbibliothek', *Biblos*, 8 (1959), 7–12 at 11–12; H. Hunger, 'Ergänzungen zu zwei neutestamentlichen Papyrusfragmenten der Österreichischen Nationalbibliothek', *Biblos*, 19 (1970), 71–5 at 72–5; Jones, *New Testament Texts*, 167 (no. 22). Image at Hunger, 'Ergänzungen', 73 (printed upside down); Jones, *New Testament Texts*, 168 (plate 21); and <http://data.onb.ac.at/rec/RZ00003765> (Österreichischen Nationalbibliothek Katalog der Papyrussammlung).

[331] De Bruyn and Dijkstra, 'Greek Amulets and Formularies', 196 n. 161.

[332] Hunger noted an echo of Eph. 6: 16 when reconstructing ἀνα[λάβ]ω at line 3, which led me, as well as others, to include the reference when discussing this papyrus. Since I deal here with citations rather than echoes, I omit the reference now.

[333] On the futuristic use of the aorist subjunctive, see Hunger, 'Ergänzungen', 72, line 3 comm.; F. Blass and A. Debrunner, *A Greek Grammar of the New Testament and Other Early Christian Literature*, tr. R. W. Funk (Chicago: Chicago University Press, 1961), 183–4 (§§363–4).

[334] For ἐναλλαγή in the sense of 'change of life', see G. H. E. Lampe (ed.), *A Greek Patristic Lexicon* (Oxford: At the Clarendon Press, 1961), *s.v.* 2.

[335] For the Greek text, see Hunger, 'Ergänzungen', 72 with 74–5. Jones, *New Testament Texts*, 167, observes the *nu* corrected to *lambda* at line 8.

[336] Hunger, 'Zwei unbekannte neutestamentliche Papyrusfragmente', 11; Jones, *New Testament Texts*, 169.

[337] Line 2: [θ(ε)ῷ]; line 5: κ[ύρι]<ε>; line 9 υἱό[s]; see Jones, *New Testament Texts*, 169.

[338] Line 8: ἔ[[ν]]λαβεν for ἔλαβες; line 9: ἐλεήθηνη for ἐλεήθητι.

[339] Jones, *New Testament Texts*, 170, argues that the papyrus was certainly an amulet.

One certain instance of an amulet is *SPP* XX 294.[340] The papyrus, which had been folded to form a packet approximately 2 cm by 2.5 cm square,[341] comprises three biblical passages: LXX Ps. 90: 1–2, Rom. 12: 1–2, and John 2: 1–2. The passages are preceded by a line of seven seven-pointed stars—far less common in amulets than six- or eight-pointed stars[342]—and followed by a line of *charaktêres* accompanying the names 'Adonai', 'Lord' written as a *nomen sacrum*, and 'Sabaoth'.[343] The verses are written in a fairly regular, bilinear sloping majuscule hand that has now been assigned to the fifth or sixth century.[344] The scribe uses *nomina sacra* correctly and consistently.[345] There are a few phonetic spellings.[346] While the wording of the verses for the most part follows the standard text, the transcription is 'free' rather than 'strict'.[347] By means of several ellipses, the scribe compresses the thought of Rom. 12: 1–2 and focuses the attention on Jesus in John 2: 1–2. Since the passage from John is the beginning of the story of the miracle at the wedding at Cana (John 2: 1–11), scholars have suggested that the amulet was intended for newly-weds. But Joseph Sanzo has argued on several grounds that the amulet had a more general protective and curative purpose; the importance of the miracle at Cana lies in the fact that it is the first of Jesus' signs, manifesting his glory (John 2: 11).[348]

The combination of *charaktêres* and *voces mysticae*—elements more commonly associated with customary incantations—with scriptural passages

---

[340] C. F. G. Heinrici, *Die Leipziger Papyrusfragmente der Psalmen* (Leipzig: Dürr, 1903), 31–2; C. Wessely (ed.), *Catalogus Papyrorum Raineri. Series Graeca. Pars I: Textus graeci papyrorum, qui in libro 'Papyrus Erzherzog Rainer-Führer durch die Ausstellung Wien 1894' descripti sunt* (Leipzig, 1921; repr. Amsterdam: A. M. Hakkert, 1969), 141 (no. 294), abbreviated as *SPP* XX 294; C. Wessely, 'Les plus anciens monuments du christianisme écrits sur papyrus II', PO 18/3 (1924), 341–509 at 411; Jones, *New Testament Texts*, 161 (no. 21). Image at H. Förster, 'Alltag und Kirche', in J. Henner, H. Förster, and U. Horak (eds), *Christliches mit Feder und Faden: Christliches in Texten, Textilien und Alltagsgegenständen aus Ägypten* (Vienna: Österreichische Verlagsgesellschaft, 1999), 40–51 at 48 (no. 38); Jones, *New Testament Texts*, 162 (plate 20); and <http://data.onb.ac.at/rec/RZ00001822> (Österreichischen Nationalbibliothek Katalog der Papyrussammlung; P.Vindob. inv. G 2312).

[341] Wessely, 'Les plus anciens monuments II', 411.

[342] I have found a few other examples at *GMA* I 34.7, 41.10 (?), 49 D.22. K. Dzwiza, *Schriftverwendung in antiker Ritualpraxis anhand der griechischen, demotischen und koptischen Praxisanleitungen des 1.–7. Jahrhunderts*, 4 vols in 2 (Erfurt and Heidelberg, 2013), <http://www.db-thueringen.de/servlets/DocumentServlet?id=23500>, found none in her study of Demotic, Greek, and Coptic manuals and individual recipes; see the indices at 2.296, 642, 881.

[343] Jones, *New Testament Texts*, 163. Compare also *SM* I 48 J.26–7 (*P.Mich.* XVI), which includes *charaktêres* in the shape of Coptic *fei* (ϥ) and Greek *rho*.

[344] Jones, *New Testament Texts*, 162–3.

[345] Line 1: $[\overline{\theta}]\underline{\nu}$; line 2: $ου\overline{\nu}ου$, $\overline{\kappa\omega}$; line 3: $\overline{\theta}\varsigma$; line 4: $\overline{\theta\nu}$; line 8: $\overline{\iota\varsigma}$; line 9: $\overline{\kappa\varsigma}$.

[346] Jones, *New Testament Texts*, 161, apparatus.

[347] S. R. Pickering, 'The Significance of Non-continuous New Testament Textual Materials in Papyri', in D. G. K. Taylor (ed.), *Studies in the Early Text of the Gospels and Acts: The Papers of the First Birmingham Colloquium on the Textual Criticism of the New Testament* (Atlanta: Society of Biblical Literature, 1999), 121–41 at 126–9; Jones, *New Testament Texts*, 165–7.

[348] Sanzo, *Scriptural Incipits*, 166–8, followed by Jones.

refashioned to suit the purposes of the scribe makes this a remarkable and valuable artefact among Greek amulets with Christian elements. Although in Chapter 4 we saw that writers of incantations might incorporate both customary elements and scriptural passages in their incantations, the materials reviewed in this chapter suggest that scribes of amulets consisting primarily of scriptural passages tended not to incorporate such elements. The present artefact shows that at least some writers of scriptural amulets were familiar with customary elements. Were the other writers not familiar with such elements? Did they deliberately avoid them as unsuitable? It is hard to say. But at least this amulet shows that a scribe could be aware of them and could think them suitable. It is a fitting piece to conclude the review in this chapter, since it encompasses the scriptural repertoire covered in this chapter but also crosses over into the repertoire of Chapter 4.

5.9 CONCLUSION

With regard to the resources available to writers of amulets, the materials discussed in this chapter both overlap with and diverge from the materials discussed in Chapter 4. In both chapters we find amulets that incorporate scriptural passages such as the opening words of the gospels or LXX Ps. 90 or some other short passage as a means to invest the amulet with protective or healing power. Furthermore, in this chapter we have seen writers combine a scriptural passage with an invocation or adjuration typical of customary incantations discussed in Chapter 4. But the materials discussed in this chapter reveal that for some writers of amulets scripture was the principal source of protection and that the passages drawn from it for protective purposes could be more diverse than what we typically encounter in customary incantations, particularly with regard to the Psalms. We cannot know whether writers of amulets consisting only of a scriptural passage are aware of customary techniques and deliberately choose not to use them, or are simply conditioned culturally to recite scriptural passages on their own without being aware of or giving thought to adding, say, an adjuration. However, there is a small but revealing difference in how they recite scriptural passages, which may tip the balance in favour of the latter of these two interpretations. Whereas *incipits* or similar scriptural passages recited in the context of an incantation or along with an instruction or command often end in mid-sentence, verses from the Lord's Prayer or a psalm are typically recited in full.

In one sense, it is a misnomer to refer to these resources as 'scriptural'. They issue not from a practice of reading and referring to scriptural books, but from a practice of meditating upon and praying with the scriptures. This is evident from the liturgical form of the Lord's Prayer found in amulets, from the frequency of certain fixed psalms in what appear to have been amulets, and from the wide range of verses from the Psalms that were written down for some personal reason. It might be better to call these resources 'devotional'. They are all products of collective and individual habits of prayer. Even so, habits of prayer are layered. They echo habits of reading (whether private or public), as one sees from the particular version of LXX Ps. 90 recited in amulets, the verse structure preserved in psalms recalled from memory, and corrections made to psalm verses recalled from memory.

The devotional nature of the scriptural resources found in amulets is reflected not only in the texts that are recited but in the manner in which they are inscribed. This is particularly apparent in amulets that consist simply of the Lord's Prayer or verses from the Psalms. They are the product of an oral-scribal culture: they are written down from memory, and the memory is more oral than visual, as the frequent phonetic spellings show. (It is telling that in the two instances when leaves of a biblical codex appear to have been used as an amulet—in one case, a leaf with verses of the Lord's Prayer (*P.Col.* XI 293); in another, a leaf with verses of LXX Ps. 3 (*P.Mich.* III 132)—phonetic spellings and other scribal irregularities are absent.) Moreover, as a consequence of how widely the Lord's Prayer and the Psalms were learned, the range of writers who would have been able to write them down in the form of an amulet (or for some other devotional purpose) is also relatively broad. We see this reflected especially in the range of hands and the relative 'accuracy' of the text in amulets comprising the Lord's Prayer and/or LXX Ps. 90.

In some amulets comprising the Lord's Prayer or verses from the Psalms, it is possible (or indeed likely) that the writer wrote down the passage for him or herself. We must think of amulets, therefore, as not only something prepared by a 'specialist' for a 'client', but also as something prepared by people for themselves. It is easy to see how, for instance, writing down the Lord's Prayer or verses of a psalm would be an extension of the devotional habits of a cleric or a monk, who not only recited these passages daily but also believed them to protect against evils wrought by demons. We should include laity in our purview as well, since they too would have known and recited the Lord's Prayer or the fixed psalms of the daily services. In the case of the Lord's Prayer, a passage set by regular collective recitation, the scope for individuality is relatively limited. In the case of the Psalter, an almost boundless resource, the scope for individuality is much greater, at least in the selection of verses to be written down.

One aspect of practice that amulets comprising only the Lord's Prayer or verses from a psalm have in common with amulets comprising an incantation (whether or not the incantation incorporates scriptural material) is that they are written down. Even when the passage is known from memory and recited in prayer, as with the Lord's Prayer, it takes on an additional value when it is written down and worn. It is a form of perpetual protection, derivative of collective or individual ritual habits, but able to operate continuously. The amulet was something more than the rituals from which it was derived— whether those were rituals accompanying the writing of the amulet or rituals authorizing the text written on the amulet—because of its materiality, which made it durable, tactile, and visible. We should thus allow for scenarios in which people obtained amulets without an accompanying ritual: the inscribed object was all that they needed or wanted.

Nevertheless, amulets cannot be entirely disassociated from the ritual practices that empowered the text written on it, if only indirectly. In Chapter 6 we shall consider some of the ritual practices that generated or authorized Christian elements.

6

Christian Ritual Contexts

The incantations and amulets we discussed in Chapters 4 and 5 were part of a constellation of practices that mediated relations between mundane and divine realms. That constellation would have included rituals performed on a regular basis in Graeco-Egyptian temples (for as long as the cults were maintained) and Christian churches; services provided at these sites as well as other sanctuaries, such as responding to requests for an oracle or for healing; and ad hoc consultations with a priest or cleric or holy man or woman. It would also have encompassed rituals observed in the home, in a workshop, in the fields, and along roads or paths: placement of an image or symbol of the deity in a niche or shrine; devotions or gestures before the image or symbol of the deity; actions upon rising from sleep or going to bed; and rituals associated with the life cycle, particularly birth and death.[1] Within this constellation, the symbolism, language, and actions of institutionally based or authorized rituals would have informed domestic and unofficial rituals. But the latter, while echoing institutional rituals, would have had their own vibrancy and autonomy. People are capable of replicating or reworking institutionally based idioms to serve the occasion or need at hand. They are also capable of generating new idioms.

In this chapter we shall explore some of the ways in which Christian elements in incantations were informed by rituals of the Christian church in Egypt. The incantations themselves point to a symbiotic relationship with institutional rituals. Incantations incorporate acclamations found in the liturgy of the Eucharist and other services. They draw on biblical passages recited daily during the services of morning and evening prayer. They recite texts learned and repeated by Christians for devotional and educational purposes, such as the Lord's Prayer. They appeal to the intercessions or help of saints who were honoured at local sanctuaries and on specific days in the

---

[1] For an evocative description and analysis of the rituals and practices associated with Graeco-Egyptian cults in Egypt during the period of the Roman Empire, see D. Frankfurter, *Religion in Roman Egypt: Assimilation and Resistance* (Princeton: Princeton University Press, 1998), chapters 2 to 4.

liturgical calendar. They echo doxological traditions favoured in particular communities or at particular times in the evolution of the Christian movement, broadly conceived. We shall explore these various types of connections with a view to understanding not only how incantations might be indebted to institutional rituals, but also how they rework aspects of those rituals with a degree of freedom and individuality.

6.1 LITURGICAL ACCLAMATIONS

Among the papyri in the collection of the Austrian National Library is an amulet from Krokodilopolis, now assigned to the sixth century, that consists of a series of adjurations commanding all manner of evil spirits not to harm the wearer, *PGM* P10.[2] Each adjuration begins with the formula 'I adjure you' (in the plural: ὁρκίζω ὑμᾶς).[3] The language of the adjurations, particularly the use of the verb ἀναχωρεῖν to command the evil spirits to depart,[4] is also found in later Byzantine liturgical exorcisms.[5] These later liturgical texts in fact help to fill in lacunae in the first lines of the papyrus.[6] The amulet was written by a practiced scribe in a regular, informal sloping majuscule hand that becomes more rapid in the second half, with more ligatures between letter-forms.[7] His professional training is apparent not only from his hand but also his use of *nomina sacra* (whose range is greater than one usually sees in amulets),[8] *diairesis* (both organic and inorganic),[9] and the compendium for καί.[10] It could well be that he regularly produced amulets like this one, since it is generic, designed to protect the wearer without naming her or him.[11]

---

[2] C. Wessely, 'Neue griechische Zauberpapyri', *DAWWPh*, 42 (1893), 1–96 at 65–7. Wessely assigned the hand to the fourth century, but Hans Gestinger, who prepared the transcription published in *PGM*, assigned it to the sixth. One unusual feature of the hand is the form of *delta*, which resembles the Latin uncial D.

[3] ET: *ACM*, no. 20. The first line of the text is missing due to loss of papyrus, but can confidently be reconstructed from the subsequent adjurations.

[4] *PGM* P10.5, 23–4, 45.

[5] R. Kotansky, 'Excursus: Liturgical Exorcism, Solomon, and Magic *Lamellae*', in *GMA* I, pp. 174–80.

[6] *PGM* P10.1, 3 apparatus.

[7] Image at H. Förster, 'Alltag und Kirche', in J. Henner, H. Förster, and U. Horak (eds), *Christliches mit Feder und Faden: Christliches in Texten, Textilien und Alltagsgegenständen aus Ägypten* (Vienna: Österreichische Verlagsgesellschaft, 1999), 40–51 at 46 (no. 36), and <http://data.onb.ac.at/rec/RZ00010485> (Österreichischen Nationalbibliothek Katalog der Papyrussammlung; P.Vindob. inv. G 337).

[8] Lines 6: θ̄ς, ιστραηλ (not abbreviated); 7: αν̄ο; 8: πν̄α (referring to an evil spirit); 14: ουνου; 20: πν̄α (referring to unclean spirits), κ̄ν; 30: αν̄ον; 33: κ̄ν; 34: αν̄ους; 35: πν̄α (referring to an evil spirit); 37: αν̄ον; 41: πρ̄α, [υ]ν̄; 46: κ̄ς ῑς.

[9] Lines 1, 15, 23–8, 39–40.   [10] Lines 41–2.   [11] Lines 22–3.

Two features of this litany are of particular interest. One is the description of demons and their activity: they bring fevers, as we have come to expect (lines 2–4); they lurk about the house, under bed, window, door, firewood, utensil, or pit (lines 24–9);[12] they make people weep or laugh hysterically, send troubling and frightening dreams, dim their vision, deprive them of their wits, and confuse their minds (lines 36–40). If we enter imaginatively into such terrors, we can see why people would have sought out amulets to protect themselves and their homes. The other instructive feature of the litany are the sources of power used to compel these demons: the 'gospels of the Son' (lines 1–2); the seven heavenly spheres, each identified with a metal or precious stone (lines 15–20); the oath sworn before Solomon (lines 29–30)— an allusion to one of the means by which Solomon constrained demons to do his bidding;[13] 'the "amen" and the "alleluia" and the gospel of the Lord who suffered for the sake of us people' (lines 32–5); and the Father and the Son and the Holy Spirit and the angels who stand in the divine presence (lines 41–3).[14] In effect, the litany invokes many of the sources of power that operated to compel or dispel evil spirits in amulets discussed in Chapters 4 and 5. In so doing, however, it draws our attention to the role of ritual in vesting certain expressions with power—'amen', 'alleluia', and 'the gospel of the Lord'.

Acclamations—collective shouts and chants, both spontaneous and stylized—were a regular feature of public gatherings in antiquity.[15] They were used formally to honour emperors and authorities. They were a means to indicate assent or opposition when appointing candidates or approving proceedings, and were used for that purpose in meetings of Christian bishops. They could be heard in the theatre and the circus, as audiences cheered or booed performers and competitors. They served to express the displeasure of the

---

[12] The plural form δοκούς at line 27 suggests 'firewood' rather than 'beams'; see H. G. Liddell, R. Scott, and H. S. Jones, *A Greek-English Lexicon*, 9th edn, with a revised supplement (Oxford: Clarendon Press, 1996), *s.v.* δοκός.

[13] See K. Preisendanz, 'Salomo', *PWSup*, 8.660–704 at 671–2. *SM* I 24, fr. B3–4, a fragmentary fourth-century exorcism, also alludes to this oath. More complete renderings of exorcisms invoking the legend of Solomon, the means by which he constrained demons, and the oath they swore before him are found in later Byzantine liturgical manuscripts; see, e.g., F. Pradel, *Griechische und süditalienische Gebete, Beschwörungen und Rezepte des Mittelalters* (Giessen: Alfred Töpelmann, 1907), 273, lines 1–7; A. Delatte, *Anecdota Atheniensia. Tome I. Textes grecs inédits relatifs à l'histoire des religions* (Liège and Paris: H. Vaillant-Carmanne and Édouard Champion, 1927), 232, lines 15–25.

[14] *PGM* P10.42–3 reads τοὺς ἁγίους ἀγγέλ[ους] τοὺς [ἑσ-] | τῶτας ἐνώπιον τῆ[ς δεσποίνης ἡμῶν]. There is space for about ten letters in the lacuna after τῆ[. . .]. In Greek manuscripts of Tobit 12: 15 the seven archangels are said to go in and out before 'the glory of the Holy One' (ἐνώπιον τῆς δόξης τοῦ ἁγίου) or 'the glory of the Lord' (ἐνώπιον τῆς δόξης κυρίου). Thus the line might have read ἐνώπιον τῆ[ς δόξης κ(υρίο)υ] or ἐνώπιον τῆ[ς δόξης θ(εο)ῦ]. The use of *nomina sacra*, evident throughout the text, would result in a line that falls short of the right edge, but this is not unprecedented; see line 39.

[15] T. Klauser, 'Akklamation', *RAC*, 1.215–33; C. Roueché, 'Acclamations in the Later Roman Empire: New Evidence from Aphrodisias', *JRS*, 74 (1984), 181–99, doi: 10.2307/299014.

crowd in public protests. Most importantly for our purposes, they were one of the ways that the laity actively participated in weekly services, giving voice to their presence in formal responses during the liturgy as well as in impromptu reactions during the sermon.

Several of the acclamations one finds in amulets with Christian elements were also proclaimed by the laity during the liturgy of the Eucharist of the Egyptian church (as well as eucharistic liturgies in other regions). I do not believe this to be a mere coincidence. The repeated ritualized voicing of acclamations during the liturgy would have vested these expressions with an authority and power beyond that of everyday human speech.[16] This is one of the outcomes of stylized, collective, participatory, and embodied ritual performance. Moreover, the structure of the liturgy, rising to points of high significance, would have amplified the power of certain acclamations. It would also have rendered them relatively stable. Regular chanting of such acclamations in the liturgy would therefore have yielded formulae that were both powerful and well known—qualities that would have favoured their use in unofficial or private contexts, including amulets.

Before we consider a few of the more common acclamations from the Eucharist of the Egyptian church, a brief introduction to liturgies used in Egypt in Late Antiquity may be helpful. The principal 'named' traditions are the Liturgy of St Mark or St Cyril,[17] the Liturgy of St Basil,[18] and the Liturgy of St Gregory.[19] In what follows we are concerned mainly with the central eucharistic prayer associated with these liturgies, the anaphora or 'canon of the mass'. The anaphora of St Mark/St Cyril originated in the Alexandrian patriarchate.[20] Numerous ancient Greek fragments of the anaphora have survived, the earliest being assigned to the fourth or fifth century.[21] The

---

[16] In what follows I have benefited from reflections on the nature and effects of ritual in R. A. Rappaport, *Ritual and Religion in the Making of Humanity* (Cambridge: Cambridge University Press, 1999), 32–50, 317–24.

[17] For the Greek text of the Liturgy of St Mark, see G. J. Cuming, *The Liturgy of St Mark* (Rome: Pontificium Institutum Studiorum Orientalium, 1990). For an English translation of the Coptic Liturgy of St Cyril, see F. E. Brightman (ed.), *Liturgies Eastern and Western*, vol. 1: *Eastern Liturgies* (Oxford: Clarendon Press, 1896), 144–88.

[18] For the Byzantine text of the Liturgy of St Basil, see Brightman, *Liturgies Eastern and Western*, 309–44. For the Greek text of the Egyptian Liturgy of St Basil, see E. Renaudot (ed.), *Liturgiarum orientalium collectio*, 2 vols, 2nd edn (Paris, 1716; repr. Frankfurt am Main and London: Joseph Baer and John Leslie Bibliopolam, 1847), 1.57–85. But see further below.

[19] For the Greek text of the Liturgy of St Gregory, see Renaudot, *Liturgiarum orientalium collectio*, 1.85–115. A more recent critical edition of the anaphora of this liturgy can be found in A. Gerhards, *Die griechische Gregoriosanaphora: Ein Beitrag zur Geschichte des eucharistischen Hochgebets* (Münster: Aschendorff, 1984), 21–49.

[20] For an overview, with relevant bibliography, see H. Brakmann, 'Das Alexandrinische Eucharistiegebet auf Wiener Papyrusfragmenten', *JAC*, 39 (1996), 149–64 at 151–5; J. Henner, *Fragmenta Liturgica Copta* (Tübingen: Mohr Siebeck, 2000), 20–6.

[21] These are conveniently presented in J. Hammerstaedt, *Griechische Anaphorenfragmente aus Ägypten und Nubien* (Opladen: Westdeutscher Verlag, 1999), 22–134 (nos. 1–8). See also Cuming, *The Liturgy of St Mark*, xxiii–xxxiv; Henner, *Fragmenta Liturgica Copta*, 23–4 n. 102.

anaphora of St Basil, most scholars agree, was introduced into Egypt from
Syria sometime in the sixth or (at the latest) seventh century, as the Egyptian
church looked to Syria for liturgical models after the breach with the Chalce-
donian church.[22] This anaphora exists in a shorter Egyptian form preserved in
Sahidic, Bohairic, Greek, and Ethiopic versions, and in a longer form preserved in Armenian, Syrian, and Byzantine versions.[23] It is generally agreed,
with some qualifications, that the shorter Egyptian form originated earlier
than, and developed independently of, the longer form.[24] The anaphora of St
Gregory was also introduced into Egypt from Syria.[25] This anaphora, composed in Greek, is believed to have originated in the early fifth century.[26]
A Sahidic fragment is evidence of its presence in Egypt by the second half of
the sixth century.[27] Witnesses to anaphoral texts that do not belong to one of
these 'named' traditions have also been found,[28] indicating that other liturgies
were known, available, or used. Today the Liturgy of St Mark/St Cyril is rarely
used in the Coptic Church. The Liturgy of St Basil is the normal liturgy, and
the Liturgy of St Gregory is used on Christmas, Epiphany, and Easter.

6.1.1 Amen

The most frequently occurring acclamation in amulets with Christian elements is 'amen', an acclamation that entered the Christian repertoire from
Jewish practice.[29] Jews responded to prayers and blessings with 'amen' in
domestic contexts and in communal worship. The response was in fact their

---

[22] H. Brakmann, 'Zwischen Pharos und Wüste: Die Erforschung der alexandrinisch-ägyptischen
Liturgie durch und nach Anton Baumstark', in R. F. Taft and G. Winkler (eds), *Comparative Liturgy
Fifty Years after Anton Baumstark (1872–1948)* (Rome: Pontificio Istituto Orientale, 2001), 323–76
at 357–8; A. Budde, *Die ägyptische Basilios-Anaphora: Text—Kommentar—Geschichte* (Münster:
Aschendorff, 2004), 578–82.

[23] On the transmission of the anaphora of St Basil, see G. Winkler, *Die Basilius-Anaphora:
Edition der beiden armenischen Redaktionen und der relevanten Fragmente, Übersetzung und
Zusammenschau aller Versionen im Licht der orientalischen Überlieferungen* (Rome: Pontificio
Istituto Orientale, 2005), 9–21. For a critical edition of the Egyptian anaphora of St Basil, see
Budde, *Die ägyptische Basilios-Anaphora*, with the remarks of Winkler, *Die Basilius-Anaphora*,
30–7.

[24] Winkler, *Die Basilius-Anaphora*, 15, 876–7.

[25] For an overview, see Henner, *Fragmenta Liturgica Copta*, 32–5.

[26] Gerhards, *Die griechische Gregoriosanaphora*, 244–7.

[27] See now Henner, *Fragmenta Liturgica Copta*, 36–79, with discussion of the date at 40, 75–6.

[28] P. F. Bradshaw and M. E. Johnson, *The Eucharistic Liturgies: Their Evolution and Interpretation* (Collegeville: Liturgical Press, 2012), 75. For selected Greek texts, see Hammerstaedt,
Griechische Anaphorenfragmente, 135–218 (nos. 9–19). Henner, *Fragmenta Liturgica Copta*,
4–20, reviews the Sahidic witnesses.

[29] For an overview of Jewish practice, see H. Avenary, 'Amen', *Encyclopaedia Judaica*, 2nd
edn, 2 (2007), 38–9. For an overview of Christian practice, see A. Stuiber, 'Amen', *RAC*,
Supplement 1.310–23.

principal form of participation in the liturgy of the synagogue, since in communal worship the leader spoke and the congregation responded. Indeed, some rabbinic sources regarded the saying of 'amen' to be superior to the saying of the benediction to which it responded.[30] It became Christian practice to respond to doxologies with 'amen' as well, as one sees, for example, in the Euchologion attributed to Sarapion.[31] But Christians departed from Jewish practice by concluding every prayer with 'amen', regardless of whether the prayer ended with a benediction or doxology. According to the catechetical sermons delivered by Cyril or John of Jerusalem,[32] the Lord's Prayer recited in the course of the Eucharist ended with 'amen' but no doxology.[33] Christians uttered 'amen' at other significant moments as well. Several fragmentary witnesses to the anaphora of St Mark/St Cyril from the fifth and sixth centuries suggest that in Egypt the faithful uttered 'amen' during the epiclesis in response to the request that the bread and wine become the body and blood of Christ,[34] as is the case in later manuscripts of the Liturgy of St Mark/ St Cyril.[35] It also appears that at that time they received the bread and wine at communion with the response 'amen',[36] a custom attested elsewhere by several late fourth- and early fifth-century sources,[37] as well as later Coptic manuscripts of the Liturgy of St Mark/St Cyril.[38] The faithful probably responded with 'amen' to the doxology that concluded the eucharistic liturgy.[39] It goes without saying, moreover, that there would have been many

---

[30] *b. Ber.* 53b.

[31] M. E. Johnson, *The Prayers of Sarapion of Thmuis: A Literary, Liturgical, and Theological Analysis* (Rome: Pontificio Istituto Orientale, 1995), 50–81.

[32] The authorship and date of the *Mystagogical Catecheses*, attributed both to Cyril, bishop of Jerusalem from approximately 351 to 387 CE, and to his successor John, is still disputed. See, most recently, A. J. Doval, *Cyril of Jerusalem, Mystagogue: The Authorship of the Mystagogic Catecheses* (Washington, D.C.: The Catholic University of America Press, 2001), arguing for Cyril, and J. Day, *The Baptismal Liturgy of Jerusalem: Fourth- and Fifth-century Evidence from Palestine, Syria and Egypt* (Aldershot: Ashgate, 2007), arguing for John.

[33] *Catech. myst.* 5.18 (SC 126 *bis*.168).

[34] P.Ryl. III 465v.3 and P.Vindob. inv. G 26134r.6, in Hammerstaedt, *Griechische Anaphorenfragmente*, 80 and 97.

[35] Cuming, *The Liturgy of St Mark*, 46–8; Brightman, *Liturgies Eastern and Western*, 179.

[36] The response is found in an Ethiopic sermon for the newly baptized, thought to originate in Alexandria (or Egypt) in the fifth century. See *Le synaxaire éthiopien: mois de terr*, 28 terr (PO 45/1.228–9), with H. Brakmann, 'Le déroulement de la messe copte: structure et histoire', in A. M. Triacca and A. Pistoia (eds), *L'Eucharistie: célébrations, rites, piétés* (Rome: C.L.V.-Edizioni liturgiche, 1995), 107–32 at 109. I am indebted to Ágnes Mihálykó for bringing this source to my attention.

[37] Ambrose of Milan, *Sacr.* 4.25 (SC 25 *bis*.116); Cyril or John of Jerusalem, *Catech. myst.* 5.21–2 (SC 126 *bis*.170–2); Theodore of Mopsuestia, *Catechetical Homilies* 16.27 in *Les homélies catéchétiques de Théodore de Mopsueste*, tr. R. Tonneau and R. Devreesse (Vatican: Biblioteca apostolica vaticana, 1949), 578–9.

[38] Brightman, *Liturgies Eastern and Western*, 186.

[39] Cuming, *The Liturgy of St Mark*, 70, 74, reconstructing the anaphora of St Mark around 350 CE and 450 CE, respectively.

more occasions that Christians responded with 'amen' in formal services, not only during the Eucharist, but also during morning and evening prayer.

In amulets 'amen' concludes doxologies and prayers.[40] It punctuates other acclamations.[41] It stands on its own, usually repeated three times.[42] And it appears together with 'alleluia'.[43] Since it had become customary to conclude prayers with 'amen' by the time most of these amulets were produced, we cannot attribute this usage specifically to one or another instance in the liturgy of the Egyptian church. But neither, I would argue, should we regard this usage as a textual habit without reference to ritual enactment. For most Christians, 'amen' was a word they said and heard during prayer and worship, not a word they read or wrote. Thus, the significance the word acquired as an acclamation, particularly as the congregation's responses during the liturgy, would explain why it was written (and possibly uttered) repeatedly in some amulets.

We should note that 'amen' rarely occurs in customary Graeco-Egyptian incantations. Two incantations in which it does appear are, significantly, replete with Jewish elements. *PGM* VII.260–71, an incantation that calls upon the one 'established over the abyss' and the one 'who sits over the cherubim' to return a wandering womb to its proper place, ends by adjuring the womb to stay put by 'the one who in the beginning made heaven and earth and all that is therein. Alleluia! Amen!'[44] The so-called 'Prayer of Jacob', *PGM* XXIIb, also reinforces its appeal to the Jewish God by twice uttering a twofold 'amen'.[45] The fact that 'amen' is associated in these incantations with Jewish elements suggests that here too the incantation echoes a ritual practice—in this case, the Jewish practice of responding to benedictions with 'amen'.

---

[40] *PGM* P3.11 (*P.Oslo* I 5); *PGM* P5b.56 (*P.Oxy.* VIII 1151); *PGM* P15b.10; *PGM* P19.6 (*PSI* VI 719); *PGM* P21.49; William M. Brashear, *Magica Varia* (Brussels: Fondation Égyptologique Reine Élisabeth 1991), 63–70 at 64, line 18 (*SB* XVIII 13602); C. A. La'da and A. Papathomas, 'A Greek Papyrus Amulet from the Duke Collection with Biblical Excerpts', *BASP*, 41 (2004), 93–113, <http://hdl.handle.net/2027/spo.0599796.0041.001:06> (P.Duke inv. 778v.25).

[41] *P.Oxy.* LXXXII 5313.2; *SM* I 21.1–2 (*P.Köln* VI 257); *SM* I 23.1–4 (*P.Haun.* III 51).

[42] *P.Bon.* I 9.8; *PGM* P15a.29–31 (*P.Ross.-Georg.* I 24); *P.Köln* IV 171.8; *P.Köln* VIII 340, side a, fr. B.13.

[43] *BKT* VI 7.1.23; *SM* I 34.12–13; see also *PGM* VII.271.

[44] On this incantation, see R. Kotansky, 'Greek Exorcistic Amulets', in M. Meyer and P. Mirecki (eds), *Ancient Magic and Ritual Power* (Leiden: Brill, 1995), 243–77 at 266–7; H. D. Betz, 'Jewish Magic in the Greek Magical Papyri (*PGM* VII.260–71)', in P. Schäfer and H. G. Kippenberg (eds), *Envisioning Magic: A Princeton Seminar and Symposium* (Leiden: Brill, 1997), 45–63; C. A. Faraone, 'New Light on Ancient Greek Exorcisms of the Wandering Womb', *ZPE*, 144 (2003), 189–200 at 190–1, <http://www.jstor.org/stable/20191675>.

[45] *PGM* XXIIb.21, 25; R. Merkelbach (ed.), *Abrasax: Ausgewählte Papyri religiösen und magischen Inhalts*, vol. 4: *Exorzismen und jüdisch/christlich beeinflusste Texte* (Cologne: Westdeutscher, 1996), 105–10. See also the Hebrew 'Prayer of Jacob' in P. Schäfer and S. Shaked (eds), *Magische Texte aus der Kairoer Geniza*, 3 vols (Tübingen: J. C. B. Mohr, 1994–9), 2.31–2, 50–1 (no. 22; fol. 2a.1–17). On the complex transmission of this Hebrew version, which echoes the Christian form of the *Sanctus* and concludes with 'amen' (fol. 2a.17) contrary to Jewish practice, see R. Leicht, '*Qedushah* and Prayer to Helios: A New Hebrew Version of an Apocryphal Prayer of Jacob', *JSQ*, 6 (1999), 140–76, esp. 152 n. 29, <http://www.jstor.org/stable/40727701>.

6.1.2 The *Sanctus* and Related Acclamations

In the liturgy of the Eucharist, the preface with which the anaphora begins culminates in the *Sanctus*, accompanied by the Hosanna and *Benedictus* in many liturgical traditions (but not in Egypt). The *Sanctus* brings the angelic hosts and the earthly faithful together in a united act of worship; Christians were taught to imagine entering the ranks of angels in heaven, into whose company the liturgy brought them, or, alternatively, to imagine the angelic host watching their progress and descending to attend the mysteries on earth.[46] After the *Sanctus* is chanted, the priest continues with the prayer of consecration, whose elements can vary from one liturgical tradition to another. Two fourth-century Egyptian witnesses, a Euchologion or collection of liturgical prayers now held in Montserrat (previously Barcelona)[47] and the Euchologion attributed to Sarapion,[48] are among the earliest witnesses to the *Sanctus* in an anaphora. (The ongoing debate as to whether evidence of the earliest use of the *Sanctus* in an anaphora is to be found in Egypt or Syria is not directly relevant;[49] it suffices simply that there are early Egyptian witnesses.) In these early Egyptian anaphoras and in the later Liturgy of St Mark/St Cyril, the *Sanctus* is chanted without the Hosanna and *Benedictus*, and the priest repeats part of the *Sanctus* in the Post-*Sanctus* as he asks God to fill the faithful with glory or the sacrifice with blessings.[50] The wording varies in the early witnesses,[51] but the structure is clear. Geoffrey Cuming's reconstruction of the text of the anaphora of St Mark/St Cyril in the mid-fourth century is illustrative:

> [The people chant:] 'Holy, holy, holy, Lord of Sabaoth; heaven and earth are full of your glory'. [The priest continues:] Full in truth are heaven and earth of your glory through our Lord and Saviour Jesus Christ: fill, O God, this sacrifice also with the blessings from you through your holy Spirit.[52]

---

[46] E. Muehlberger, *Angels in Late Ancient Christianity* (Oxford: Oxford University Press, 2013), 183–200.

[47] R. Roca-Puig, *Anàfora de Barcelona i altres pregàries (Missa del segle IV)*, 2nd edn (Barcelona: Grafos, 1996), 11 (P.Monts.Roca inv. 154b–155a); S. Janeras, 'Sanctus et Post-Sanctus dans l'anaphore du *P.Monts.Roca inv. no 154b–155a*', *SOC*, 11 (2007), 9–13; M. Zheltov, 'The Anaphora and Thanksgiving Prayer from the Barcelona Papyrus: An Under-estimated Testimony to the Anaphoral History in the Fourth Century', *VigChr*, 62 (2008), 467–504, <http://www.jstor.org/stable/20474889>.

[48] Johnson, *The Prayers of Sarapion*, 46–7.

[49] For a summary, with bibliography, of the considerable discussion as to when, where, how, and why the *Sanctus* was introduced into the anaphora, see Bradshaw and Johnson, *The Eucharistic Liturgies*, 111–21.

[50] Cuming, *The Liturgy of St Mark*, 120–2.

[51] The texts of the main witnesses can be conveniently compared in A. Hänggi and I. Pahl (eds), *Prex eucharistica: textus e variis liturgiis antiquioribus selecti*, 2nd edn (Fribourg: Editions universitaires, 1968), 101–42.

[52] Cuming, *The Liturgy of St Mark*, 70.

Although the earliest Egyptian witnesses do not state explicitly that the faithful proclaimed the *Sanctus*, it is likely that they did, given the testimony of late fourth- and early fifth-century sources elsewhere.[53]

As is well known, the *Sanctus* of the anaphora is comparable to the *Qedushah* of the synagogue liturgy in that both draw on Isa. 6: 3. In texts of the *shema'* and the *'amidah* from the gaonic period (ninth century and later),[54] the *Qedushah* follows the wording of Isaiah closely: 'Holy, holy, holy, is the Lord of Hosts; the whole earth is full of his glory'.[55] This wording is altered in the *Sanctus* in two ways.[56] First, heaven as well as earth are said to be full of God's glory, a change found already in the earliest East Syrian witnesses.[57] Second, in some early witnesses (including those from Egypt) but not others (such as those from East Syria, Antioch, and Cappadocia) 'of his glory' is replaced by 'of your glory'. Over the past several decades, scholars have examined Jewish pseudepigraphical writings and Hekhalot literature with a view to charting what routes the acclamation may have taken in moving from Jewish to Christian usage.[58] Whatever those routes may have been, it is significant, for our purposes, that all the incantations that incorporate some form of the acclamation have Christian elements. To put this negatively, we do not find even a minimal version of the acclamation—a threefold 'holy'—in customary Graeco-Egyptian incantations.[59] This suggests the acclamation's incorporation as a powerful expression in late antique amulets is primarily an extension of its incorporation into the liturgy of the Christian church. (We might note that in medieval Jewish incantations from the Cairo Genizah the acclamation, analogously, follows the wording of the *Qedushah*.[60])

As we have already seen in preceding chapters, the acclamation could take several forms in amulets. It could consist simply in repeating 'holy' three times, as in the last line of an amulet that recites the Lord's Prayer.[61] It could

---

[53] *Const. apost.* 8.12.27 (SC 336.192); *Catech. myst.* 5.6 (SC 126 *bis*.154).

[54] On the emergence and evolution of the first Jewish prayer-books, see S. C. Reif, *Judaism and Hebrew Prayer: New Perspectives on Jewish Liturgical History* (Cambridge: Cambridge University Press, 1993), 124–31.

[55] On the *Qedushah* in early Judaism, see B. D. Spinks, *The Sanctus in the Eucharistic Prayer* (Cambridge: Cambridge University Press, 1991), 25–45; L. I. Levine, *The Ancient Synagogue: The First Thousand Years*, 2nd edn (New Haven: Yale University Press, 2005), 571–6.

[56] The evidence is conveniently presented in Spinks, *The Sanctus*, 116–21; R. F. Taft, 'The Interpolation of the Sanctus into the Anaphora: When and Where? A Review of the Dossier. Part II', *OCP*, 58 (1992), 83–121 at 84–106.

[57] G. Winkler, *Das Sanctus: Über den Ursprung und die Anfänge des Sanctus und sein Fortwirken* (Rome: Pontificio Istituto Orientale, 2002), 133.

[58] Spinks, *The Sanctus*, 25–54, 104–16; C. Böttrich, 'Das "Sanctus" in der Liturgie der hellenistischen Synagoge', *JLH*, 35 (1994–1995), 10–36, <http://www.jstor.org/stable/24200623>; Winkler, *Das Sanctus*, 69–123.

[59] A search of texts included under the heading 'Magica' in *Thesaurus Linguae Graecae* yielded no instances.

[60] Schäfer and Shaked, *Magische Texte*, 1.194–5; 2.198, 201.

[61] *P.Köln* IV 171.9. See Section 5.5.

consist in the acclamation 'Holy, holy, holy, Lord Sabaôth'—common to Isa. 6: 3, the *Qedushah*, and the *Sanctus*—as we saw in several amulets against fever.[62] It could consist in the *Sanctus* proper from the eucharistic liturgy.[63] Sometimes it stands on its own;[64] other times it precedes an injunction.[65] The wording of the acclamation in the amulet may not necessarily conform to the standard form of the acclamation, both in instances of 'Holy, holy, holy, Lord Sabaôth'[66] and in instances of the *Sanctus*.[67] Variances from the standard form, considered in light of other textual and scribal features of the amulet, can lead to the conclusion that the scribe was operating at some distance from the institutional centre of the Egyptian church, as we suggested when discussing such cases in Chapter 4. Nevertheless, both standard and non-standard forms are evidence of the significance the acclamation had acquired because of where and how it was proclaimed in institutional liturgies. This is clearest in the case of the *Sanctus*, which, as we have seen, was acclaimed by the faithful at the culmination of the preamble to the prayer of consecration. Even when the form of the acclamation is briefer than the *Sanctus* (one of the shorter forms of the threefold 'holy'), it is likely that the continual repetition of the *Sanctus* in the liturgy helped to maintain and convey the value of the briefer form.[68]

Two papyri we have not yet discussed offer further evidence to support this claim. P.Vindob. inv. G 19887r,[69] written in an irregular, informal sloping majuscule hand assigned to the fifth or sixth century,[70] simply repeats the *Sanctus* three times. From its wording we know that the writer was recalling the acclamation as recited in the anaphora of St Mark/St Cyril or, possibly, the anaphora of St Basil, both of which have 'of your holy glory',[71] as does the papyrus. The irregular spelling of $\pi\lambda\eta\rho s$ for $\pi\lambda\acute{\eta}\rho\eta s$ and of ϵ for $\acute{\eta}$ (in $\acute{\eta}\,\gamma\hat{\eta}$) tells us

---

[62] *BKT* X 27.2–3; *SM* I 25.4–6 (*P.Prag.* I 6). See Section 4.2.2.

[63] *PGM* P18.1–3, as revised by F. Maltomini, 'Osservazioni al testo di alcuni papiri magici greci. (III.)', *SCO*, 32 (1982), 235–41 at 239, <http://www.jstor.org/stable/24181825>; *SM* I 29.15–17 (*P.Princ.* II 107). See Section 4.2.2.

[64] *P.Köln* IV 171.9; *SM* I 29.15–17.

[65] *BKT* X 27.3–4; *PGM* P18.12–15; *SM* I 25.6–9; *SM* I 32.6–8.

[66] E.g., *BKT* X 27.2–3.   [67] E.g., *SM* I 29.15–17; *SM* I 32.6.

[68] T. S. de Bruyn, 'The Use of the Sanctus in Christian Greek Papyrus Amulets', *StudPatr*, 40 (2006), 15–20 at 18–19.

[69] C. Wessely (ed.), 'Les plus anciens monuments du christianisme écrits sur papyrus II', in PO 18/3 (1924), 341–509 at 437.

[70] Image at <http://data.onb.ac.at/rec/RZ00009623> (Österreichischen Nationalbibliothek Katalog der Papyrussammlung). There are traces of writing on the other side of the papyrus.

[71] Cuming, *The Liturgy of St Mark*, 37–9, 120–1; Budde, *Die ägyptische Basilios-Anaphora*, 146–7, 263–5. The adjective is present in a fragmentary sixth-century Greek witness to the Post-*Sanctus*, MPER N.S. XVII 36, republished in Hammerstaedt, *Griechische Anaphorenfragmente*, 156–60 (P.Vindob. inv. G 41043v); in an inscription dated 7 May 735, republished in Hammerstaedt, *Griechische Anaphorenfragmente*, 186–99 at 188 (Cairo, Coptic Museum, inv. 753); and in a tablet from the seventh or eighth century that preserves a portion of the anaphora of St Mark from the Post-*Sanctus* to the Epiclesis, published in H. Quecke, 'Ein saïdischer Zeuge der Markusliturgie (Brit. Mus. Nr. 54 036)', *OCP*, 37 (1971), 40–57.

that the scribe was recalling the acclamation from memory,[72] as one would expect. Although the papyrus was published among liturgical and prayer fragments by its first editor, the repetition of the *Sanctus*, framed each time by a cross at the beginning and the end, suggests that it was meant to serve as an amulet.[73]

Even more interesting is a rare Latin amulet said to have been found in Babylon (Fustat), *SM* I 36.[74] Eventually purchased by the University Library in Heidelberg,[75] the papyrus was stolen or destroyed at the end of World War II.[76] The present edition is based on a typescript copy made by Karl Preisendanz, with some revisions, of the transcription prepared by O. Guérard.[77] The amulet consists of a trinitarian invocation, a free rendering of the opening words of the Gospel of John, a request for healing followed by verses from Ps. 20 and Ps. 15, and finally an adjuration of the 'heavenly doctor' that invokes seven named archangels, the twenty-four elders who stand before the throne of God, and the four creatures who bear the throne of God and say, 'Holy, holy, holy Lord God Sabaoth. Blessed is he who comes in the name of the Lord, the king of Israel. Hosanna in the highest to God, peace to all people of good will.' The amulet also included *charaktêres*, but their location in the text was not recorded.[78]

This papyrus was a remarkable find, as Preisendanz and others were quick to note.[79] It is the only known instance of an amulet from Egypt written in Latin. It is a rare example of the written expression of spoken late Latin, manifesting numerous vocal phenomena.[80] The verses from Ps. 20 reflect a north Italian-African tradition of the Psalter, introduced into Africa from Italy by Augustine.[81] And the free rendition of the *Sanctus*, Hosanna, and *Benedictus* is an early witness to the presence of these elements in western eucharistic liturgies. The *Sanctus* entered the Roman rite not long before the pontificate of Leo (440–461 CE), having been introduced into the West from the East.[82] The

---

[72] P.Vindob. inv. G 19887r.2–3, 6–7, 10.

[73] *P.Köln* IV 171.9 comm. identifies it as an amulet.

[74] For valuable discussion and commentary, see the *editio princeps*: R. W. Daniel and F. Maltomini, 'From the African Psalter and Liturgy', *ZPE*, 74 (1988), 253–65, <http://www.uni-koeln.de/phil-fak/ifa/zpe/downloads/1988/074pdf/074.html>.

[75] R. Seider, 'Aus der Arbeit der Universitätsinstitute die Universitäts-Papyrussammlung', *HeidJahr*, 8 (1964), 142–203 at 164.

[76] Daniel and Maltomini, 'From the African Psalter', 254.

[77] Image of Preisendanz's copy at Daniel and Maltomini, 'From the African Psalter', plate XII.

[78] Daniel and Maltomini, 'From the African Psalter', 254.

[79] Daniel and Maltomini, 'From the African Psalter', 253–4.

[80] Daniel and Maltomini, 'From the African Psalter', 261–2; J. Kramer, 'A Linguistic Commentary on Heidelberg's Latin Papyrus Amulet', *ZPE*, 74 (1988), 267–72, <http://www.uni-koeln.de/phil-fak/ifa/zpe/downloads/1988/074pdf/074.html>.

[81] Daniel and Maltomini, 'From the African Psalter', 257–9.

[82] E. Mazza, *The Eucharistic Prayers of the Roman Rite*, tr. M. J. O'Connell (New York: Pueblo, 1986), 47–8; Spinks, *The Sanctus*, 95–6; additional literature at Daniel and Maltomini, 'From the African Psalter', 260 n. 16.

text of the Roman *Sanctus* is the same as that in the anaphoras of St Basil, St Chrysostom, and St James, all of which add the Hosanna and *Benedictus*. The earliest attestation of the *Benedictus* in the West is, otherwise, in a sermon of Caesarius of Arles.[83] So this amulet is a precious witness not only to the culture of the scribe but also to the evolving liturgy of the church in the West. Whether the amulet was composed in Italy, Africa, or Egypt is difficult to say.

Of immediate relevance to our present discussion is the fact that the writer echoes a *Sanctus* that is, once again, specific to a particular liturgy, as is the case with several of the amulets we have already discussed.[84] This confirms the role of the liturgy not only in establishing the value of the acclamation but also in determining its wording.

6.1.3 One Holy Father, One Holy Son, One Holy Spirit

Another high point in the eucharistic liturgy came after the anaphora when the priest prepared and presented the elements to the faithful for their communion—actions that came to include lifting up the bread (the elevation), mixing some bread with the wine in the chalice (the commixture), and breaking the bread (the fraction).[85] By the second half of the fourth century the presentation of the elements to the faithful was accompanied throughout the East by the proclamation 'Holy things for holy ones' (τὰ ἅγια τοῖς ἁγίοις), at once summoning the faithful to communion and warning off the unworthy.[86] The sequence of prayers following the anaphoral prayer in the Euchologion attributed to Sarapion suggests that by the mid-fourth century the structure that we see later in the Liturgy of St Mark/St Cyril was already in place.[87] In all the later Egyptian eucharistic liturgies—St Mark/St Cyril, St Basil, and St Gregory—the response of the faithful is 'One holy Father, one holy Son, one holy Spirit'.[88] In the earliest witnesses to the liturgies of Jerusalem and Antioch, however, the response is 'One holy, one Lord, Jesus Christ',[89] which was retained in the later Liturgy of St James and the Byzantine Liturgies

---

[83] Caesarius of Arles, *Serm.* 73.2 (CCSL 103.307). Caesarius does not cite the Hosanna. But since his reference to the *Sanctus* is abbreviated, his reference to the *Benedictus* may be abbreviated as well.

[84] *PGM* P18; *SM* I 29 (*P.Princ.* II 107); P.Vindob. inv. G 19887r.

[85] The earliest sources vary on these actions; see Bradshaw and Johnson, *The Eucharistic Liturgies*, 171–2.

[86] R. F. Taft, '"Holy Things for the Saints": The Ancient Call to Communion and its Response', in G. Austin (ed.), *Fountain of Life: In Memory of Niels K. Rasmussen* (Washington, D.C.: Pastoral Press, 1991), 87–102; R. F. Taft, *A History of the Liturgy of St. John Chrysostom*, vol. 5: *The Precommunion Rites* (Rome: Pontificio Istituto Orientale, 2000), 230–40.

[87] M. E. Johnson, *Liturgy in Early Christian Egypt* (Cambridge: Grove Books, 1995), 32–3; Johnson, *The Prayers of Sarapion*, 114–17.

[88] Cuming, *The Liturgy of St Mark*, 140. [89] Taft, *History of the Liturgy*, 5.240–1.

of St Basil and St Chrysostom.[90] Geoffrey Cuming held that the trinitarian response in the Liturgy of St Mark/St Cyril was part of the original nucleus of this section of the liturgy.[91] Robert Taft, on the contrary, has argued that the trinitarian response was an innovation, a reaction to subordinationist views of the relation of the Son and the Holy Spirit to the Father.[92] The earliest Egyptian sources are not decisive. 'One holy, one Lord, Jesus Christ' is attested in a treatise on the Trinity attributed to Didymus the Blind, but the attribution is not secure.[93] Cyril of Alexandria cites the invitation 'Holy things for holy ones' in his *Commentary on John* when he describes how only the baptized who have received the Holy Spirit are invited to partake of the divine mysteries, but he does not record the response.[94] The earliest extant witness from Egypt to the actions accompanying the invitation to communion, two leaves from a seventh- or eighth-century liturgical codex preserving a tradition going back to Alexandria in the fifth century,[95] records the priest's acclamation, but the people's response has been lost to damage.[96] However, there is indirect evidence that the trinitarian response was in place by the fifth century. It is recorded in the Ethiopic sermon believed to have originated in Alexandria in the fifth century,[97] as well as in an Ethiopic redaction of the *Apostolic Tradition* that incorporates portions of a fifth-century prayer book from Alexandria.[98]

The trinitarian response appears as an acclamation in two Greek amulets, *SM* I 21 (*P.Köln* VI 257) and *P.Bon.* I 9, both of which we discussed in Chapter 4. As we noted there, the wording of the acclamation in *P.Bon.* I 9 corresponds exactly to the eucharistic response,[99] whereas in *SM* I 21 the writer drops the adjective 'holy' when referring to the Father and the Son ('One Father, one Son, one holy Spirit, amen').[100] In *P.Bon.* I 9 the acclamation follows a conventional Christian conclusion to a prayer: '[in the most blessed name] of the holy *Theotokos* and ever-virgin Mary and the holy Longinus, the centurion, one holy Father, one holy Son, one holy Spirit. Amen, amen, amen.'[101] Although the beginning of the text is lost, what is left (the prayer formula, the trinitarian acclamation, and the threefold 'amen') suggests that the writer was familiar with Christian liturgical phraseology. *SM* I 21, on the

---

[90] Brightman, *Liturgies Eastern and Western*, 62, 341.

[91] Cuming, *The Liturgy of St Mark*, 140.   [92] Taft, *History of the Liturgy*, 5.242–3.

[93] Taft, *History of the Liturgy*, 5.240–1.

[94] Cyril of Alexandria, *Jo.* 12 (on John 20: 17), in *Sancti patris nostri Cyrilli archiepiscopi Alexandrini in d. Joannis evangelium*, ed. E. P. Pusey, 3 vols (Oxford, 1872; repr. Brussels: Culture et Civilisation, 1965), 3.119.

[95] *P.Bad.* IV 58; re-edited in A. T. Mihálykó, 'Writing the Christian Liturgy in Egypt (3rd to 9th cent.)', PhD thesis, University of Oslo, Oslo, 2016, 237–42.

[96] *P.Bad.* IV 58r.21–6.

[97] *Le synaxaire éthiopien*, 28 terr (PO 45/1.228–9); see n. 36.

[98] Hugo Duensing (ed.), *Der aethiopische Text der Kirchenordnung des Hippolyt* (Göttingen: Vandenhoeck & Ruprecht, 1946), 29, with Brakmann, 'Le déroulement de la messe copte', 109 n. 13.

[99] *P.Bon.* I 9.5–7.   [100] *SM* I 21.1–2.   [101] *P.Bon.* I 9.1–8.

other hand, is a customary adjuration written in a somewhat careless fashion, as we observed when we reviewed the papyrus. That the acclamation would appear at the head of the text, however freely recalled, reveals that its reach as a known and powerful invocation extended to people less formally versed in the liturgy of the church. We should note that the trinitarian acclamation also appears in a few Coptic amulets.[102] However, to my knowledge, no amulet from Egypt incorporates the christological acclamation used in Jerusalem and Antioch. If this is so, it once again demonstrates the influence that the liturgy (or liturgies) customarily used in Egypt had in shaping the language of invocation and adjuration, since all the later Egyptian liturgies employ the trinitarian acclamation.

6.2 DAILY PRAYER

Daily prayer was enjoined upon all Christians in antiquity. In the fourth century numerous sources attest to organized arrangements for daily prayer—known in liturgical parlance as the 'daily office'—in the major regions of the East—Egypt, Palestine, Syria, and Cappadocia.[103] In liturgical scholarship it has become customary to distinguish between the 'cathedral office' and the 'monastic office'.[104] The former refers to daily services led by clergy in churches under the direction of the bishop that used a selected set of psalms (or parts of psalms) and incorporated responsorial or alternating forms of chant. The latter refers to daily forms of prayer—both individual and communal—practiced by monks in which, over a given period, all the psalms were recited meditatively according to their sequence in the Bible ('in course'). The distinction has been the subject of some debate, with some scholars questioning whether continuous, individual recitation of the Psalms by monks constituted a distinct form of the monastic office.[105] I shall

---

[102] *AKZ*, 2.103 (no. XXXI.39–41), 109 (no. XXXIII.1). The latter, first published as *BKU* I 8, was republished by W. Beltz, 'Die koptischen Zauberpapyri der Papyrus-Sammlung der Staatlichen Museen zu Berlin', *APF*, 29 (1983), 59–86 at 68–70, doi: 10.1515/apf.1983.1983.29.59, who assigned it to the eighth century. ET: *ACM*, nos. 113, 121.

[103] For what follows I rely primarily on R. F. Taft, *The Liturgy of the Hours in East and West: The Origins of the Divine Office and its Meaning for Today*, 2nd edn (Collegeville: Liturgical Press, 1993).

[104] Taft, *The Liturgy of the Hours*, 32–3; R. F. Taft, 'Christian Liturgical Psalmody: Origins, Development, Decomposition, Collapse', in H. W. Attridge and M. E. Fassler (eds), *Psalms in Community: Jewish and Christian Textual, Liturgical, and Artistic Traditions* (Atlanta: Society of Biblical Literature, 2003), 7–32 at 9–23.

[105] See, e.g., R. F. Taft, 'Cathedral vs. Monastic Liturgy in the Christian East: Vindicating a Distinction', *BBGG*, III series, 2 (2005), 173–219; S. S. R. Frøyshov, 'The Cathedral-Monastic Distinction Revisited. Part I: Was Egyptian Desert Liturgy a Pure Monastic Office?', *StudLit*, 37 (2007), 198–216.

return to an aspect of this debate shortly, when I discuss the monastic office in Egypt.

A number of Egyptian sources reveal that in the fourth century, daily services led by the clergy were held in the morning and the evening (the cathedral office).[106] The services included prayer, psalmody, and scripture reading. For Lower Egypt we have the testimony of the *Canons of Hippolytus*, which preserves the practice of the Patriarchate of Alexandria in the mid-fourth century:

> *Canon 21. Concerning the gathering of all the priests and people in the church every day.* Let the priests gather in the church every day, and the deacons, subdeacons, readers, and all the people, at cockcrow. They shall do the prayer, the psalms, and the reading of the books and the prayers.[107]

For Upper Egypt we have the report in the Coptic *Life of Aaron*,[108] a work narrating events set in the late fourth and early fifth centuries,[109] of two monks from Aswan who 'would go to church every day, morning and evening, and listen to the holy scriptures being read'.[110] Other Coptic hagiographic and homiletic sources either describe or recommend attending daily services in the morning and the evening.[111] These sources, obviously, promote an ideal. We do not know whether daily services were observed in every church, and we may wonder how many Christians in fact attended them. But we must take such services into consideration when we think about how scriptures made their way into amulets, what scriptures were selected, and who may have recalled or written them.

Monks in Egypt also observed two daily services, one beginning in the small hours of the morning and continuing until dawn, the other coming at the end of the day.[112] Semi-anchorite monks in the desert south-west of Alexandria (Nitria, Kellia, and Sketis) performed these services in their cells from Monday to Friday, gathering together in a common assembly for prayer (as well as the Eucharist) only on Saturday and Sunday. Cenobitic monks in the communities

---

[106] Taft, *The Liturgy of the Hours*, 34–6. The duty to hold these services was in fact stipulated in contracts the clergy entered into upon their ordination; see E. Wipszycka, *The Alexandrian Church: People and Institutions* (Warsaw: Journal of Juristic Papyrology, 2015), 310–18, esp. 316–17 with reference to *O.Crum* 31.

[107] *Can. Hipp.* 21 (PO 31/2.386–7); ET: Taft, *The Liturgy of the Hours*, 34–5.

[108] On this work, which E. A. Wallis Budge titled 'Histories of the Monks of the Egyptian Desert' and Tim Vivian titled 'Histories of the Monks of Upper Egypt', see now J. H. F. Dijkstra, 'Monasticism on the Southern Egyptian Frontier in Late Antiquity: Towards a New Critical Edition of the Coptic *Life of Aaron*', *JCSCS*, 5 (2013), 31–47, doi: 10.1163/15700720-12341209.

[109] Dijkstra, 'Monasticism', 36.

[110] *Life of Aaron* 12, in *Miscellaneous Coptic Texts in the Dialect of Upper Egypt*, ed. E. A. Wallis Budge (London: British Museum, 1915), 437 (fol. 6a), 953 (translation). A new edition and translation by Professors Dijkstra and van der Vliet is in preparation.

[111] H. Quecke, *Untersuchungen zum koptischen Stundengebet* (Louvain: Université catholique de Louvain, Institut Orientaliste, 1970), 10–11.

[112] Taft, *The Liturgy of the Hours*, 57–66.

founded by Pachomius in the Nile valley came together for prayer daily, meeting in a common assembly in the morning and in their houses in the evening. Alongside these services, however, monks were enjoined to recall and recite scripture as they went about their various tasks,[113] since meditating on the scriptures was at the heart of monastic spirituality.[114] The scriptures not only schooled monks in the virtues of the contemplative life; they were the principal means of deflecting the taunts and temptations of demons.[115]

The question of what psalms the monks of Egypt regularly recited in their daily services is a complex one. The principal literary sources—John Cassian's account in the *Institutes* of the daily services of the monks of Scetis;[116] Palladius' account in the *Lausiac History* of the rule established by the visit of an angel;[117] John of Gaza's description of the practice at Scetis—speak of twelve psalms in the morning service and twelve psalms in the evening service.[118] (John Cassian adds that the monks of Scetis did not recite a psalm without interruption to its end in their services; rather, the chanter sang a few verses, and then the monks prayed silently.[119]) According to Taft, the psalms recited in these services followed the sequence of the Psalter.[120] Frøyshov, however, argues that the psalms were selected and set, originating in an older tradition of reciting a psalm at each hour of the day—the 'Rule of the Angel' attested by Palladius and, secondarily, Cassian.[121] While we cannot settle this debate, we must bear it in mind as we turn to amulets (or possible amulets) written with verses from the Psalms.

As we noted in Chapter 5, there are numerous papyri and parchments from Egypt written with a few verses from one or more psalms.[122] Often there is no pattern to the selection of verses. They are many and varied. This is what one would expect of monks continuously meditating and drawing upon the

[113] Taft, *The Liturgy of the Hours*, 66–72.

[114] C. Rapp, 'Christians and their Manuscripts in the Greek East in the Fourth Century', in G. Cavallo, G. de Gregori, and M. Maniaci (eds), *Scritture, libri e testi nelle aree provinciali di Bisanzio*, 2 vols (Spoleto: Centro italiano di studi sull'alto Medioevo, 1991), 1.127–48 at 136–9; D. Burton-Christie, *The Word in the Desert: Scripture and the Quest for Holiness in Early Christian Monasticism* (New York: Oxford University Press, 1993), 122–3.

[115] Burton-Christie, *The Word in the* Desert, 123–6; D. Brakke, 'Introduction', in Evagrius of Pontus, *Talking Back: A Monastic Handbook for Combating Demons*, tr. D. Brakke (Collegeville: Liturgical Press, 2009), 1–40 at 14–23.

[116] John Cassian, *Inst. coen.* 2.4–12 (SC 109.64–80).

[117] Palladius, *Laus. hist.* 32, in *The Lausiac History of Palladius*, ed. C. Butler, Texts and Studies 6/2 (Cambridge: Cambridge University Press, 1898–1904), 99.

[118] John of Gaza, *Ep.* 143 (SC 427.522–24).

[119] John Cassian, *Inst. coen.* 2.11.1–2 (SC 109.76–8).

[120] J. Mateos, 'The Origins of the Divine Office', *Worship*, 41 (1967), 477–85; Taft, *Liturgy of the Hours*, 60; Taft, 'Christian Liturgical Psalmody', 11.

[121] Frøyshov, 'The Cathedral-Monastic Distinction Revisited', 207–8.

[122] See Section 5.7.

Psalter. Sometimes, however, certain psalms recur. This suggests that the scribes—clergy, monks, or laity—were drawing on a selected set of psalms regularly recited in communal services.

As we saw in Chapter 5, two psalms that appear in several amulets are LXX Ps. 3 and LXX Ps. 62. The latter psalm, which in the Septuagint (but not the Hebrew) refers to the morning at verse 2a ('early I approach you') and verse 7b ('in the early morning I would meditate on you'), was a fixed psalm of the morning cathedral service in Palestine and Western Syria.[123] It is attested already in the fourth century by Eusebius of Caesarea,[124] John Chrysostom,[125] and the *Apostolic Constitutions*.[126] In those regions it also makes its way into the morning service in urban monastic communities.[127] Literary and liturgical sources do not assign a similar role to LXX Ps. 3 in the cycle of daily services, though today it as well as LXX Ps. 62 are among the 'Six Psalms' (*hexapsalmos*) in the Byzantine service of morning prayer and among the psalms chanted in the Coptic service of morning prayer.[128] (A late sixth- or early seventh-century account of a Saturday night vigil observed by monks in Palestine refers to the *hexapsalmos*, without, however, specifying the psalms.[129]) It seems plausible that a Christian might wish to wear throughout the day—or indeed, day and night, if one wore an amulet while one slept— psalms recited daily at dawn. Should we infer, therefore, that the morning service in Egypt included LXX Pss. 3 and 62 in the fifth and sixth centuries, the dates assigned to these amulets? Or should we infer that these amulets issued from communities in Egypt influenced by traditions of daily prayer in Palestine and Western Syria?

The influence of liturgical recitation on the production of amulets is suggested not only by the selection of the psalms in some artefacts but also by the manner of presentation. This may be illustrated by two examples, one of which is more likely to have been an amulet than the other, *PGM* P22 (*P.Rein.* II 61) and *P.Ryl.* III 462.

---

[123] Taft, *The Liturgy of the Hours*, 33, 42, 44–5. The psalm is not recited in the morning service in Eastern Syria, undoubtedly because in the Syriac text of the psalm (like the Hebrew text) verse 2a has no temporal reference and verse 7b refers to night; see G. Winkler, 'New Study of Early Development of the Divine Office', *Worship*, 56 (1982), 27–35 at 32–3.

[124] Eusebius of Caesarea, *Ps.* 142 (PG 24.49); see Taft, *The Liturgy of the Hours*, 33.

[125] John Chrysostom, *Exp. in Ps.* 140 (PG 55.427); see Taft, *The Liturgy of the Hours*, 42.

[126] *Const. apost.*, 2.59.2 (SC 320.324); see Taft, *The Liturgy of the Hours*, 44–5.

[127] Taft, *The Liturgy of the Hours*, 76–84.

[128] Taft, *The Liturgy of the Hours*, 277–82; U. Zanetti, 'La distribution des psaumes dans l'horologion Copte', *OCP*, 56 (1990), 323–69 at 338–9.

[129] A. Longo, 'Il testo integrale della *Narrazione degli abati Giovanni e Sofronio* attraverso le *Hermêneiai* di Nicone', *RSBN*, 12–13 (1965–6), 233–67 at 251–2. The account is discussed in Taft, *The Liturgy of the Hours*, 198–9.

PGM P22 (*P.Rein.* II 61),[130] assigned to the seventh or eighth century,[131] records initial words of LXX Ps. 140, a psalm of the cathedral evening service in the Byzantine and Coptic traditions.[132] It has the opening line of the psalm—'Lord, I cried to you; listen to me!' (verse 1b)—followed by words taken mostly from the beginnings of verse-units (verses 2a, 3a, 4b, 5a, 6b, 8a, 10a). The text is written in continuous lines (*scriptio continua*), with spaces before some verse *incipits* occurring in the middle of a line (verses 3a, 5a) and punctuation before others (verse 6b).[133] There are a few irregularities. Verses 7 and 9 are omitted; verse 4 is represented by a word from the middle of a line (verse 4b); and verse 8a is cited in full: 'Because to you, O Lord, O Lord, were my eyes'. The small format (12 cm w × 9.2 cm h), as well as the irregular, informal sloping majuscule hand, indicate that the psalm was recorded for some personal use. In the top right-hand corner of the papyrus one can see a cord threaded through two holes and tied,[134] but it is not obvious how this would have allowed the papyrus to be worn or affixed. The two verse-units cited in full would be consistent with use as an amulet, as would the psalm as a whole (a cry to God for deliverance from enemies and danger), but other reasons for writing down the psalm cannot be ruled out.

P.Ryl. III 462, by contrast, is clearly a textual product of liturgical recitation. It is a long narrow parchment written with the initial words of verses from LXX Pss. 148 and 149 and then the initial words (and sometimes all the words) of verse-units (*stichoi*) from LXX Ps. 150.[135] Today these psalms are recited just before dawn in the Byzantine morning office (the *Ainoi* or Lauds),[136] and in the Psalmodia of the Evening and the Psalmodia of the Night in the Coptic tradition.[137] We know that already in the fourth century these psalms were recited just before dawn in urban monastic centres in Palestine, Syria, and (probably) Cappadocia.[138] This parchment appear to derive from this practice, recording the initial words of verses as a memory-aid.

---

[130] P. Collart, 'Un papyrus Reinach inédit: Psaume 140 sur une amulette', *Aegyptus*, 13 (1933), 208–12, <http://www.jstor.org/stable/41214260>.

[131] Collart, 'Un papyrus Reinach inédit', 208 (seventh century); K. Treu, 'Referate: Christliche Papyri 1940–1967', *APF*, 19 (1969), 169–206 at 178 (eighth century).

[132] Taft, *The Liturgy of the Hours*, 33, 42, 44–5, 51, 256.

[133] Image at <http://www.papyrologie.paris-sorbonne.fr/menu1/collections/pgrec/preinach. htm> (Institut de Papyrologie de la Sorbonne).

[134] Collart, 'Un papyrus Reinach inédit', 209.

[135] There are several errors in the transcription. Line 17 should read ἐνίτε αὐτὸν η ἐν τῷ στερ[; line 25 should read [ἐ]νί'τε' αὐτὸν ἐν κυμφάλις (αὐτόν is present in the papyrus as in the LXX, contrary to the editor's note); and a line of text was omitted after line 26: [ἐν]ί'τε' αὐτὸν ἐν κυμφάλις (the first four words of LXX Ps. 150: 5b, present in the papyrus, contrary to the editor's note).

[136] Taft, *The Liturgy of the Hours*, 281, with 77 n. 2, on the terms '*Ainoi*' or 'Lauds'.

[137] Taft, *The Liturgy of the Hours*, 254–6.

[138] Taft, *The Liturgy of the Hours*, 76, 80–1, 87–9, referring to John Cassian, *Inst. coen.* 3.6 (SC 109.108); John Chrysostom, *Hom. 14 in 1 Tim.* 4 (PG 62.576); and Pseudo-Athanasius, *Virg.* 20,

The parchment is written in a fairly regular sloping majuscule hand assigned to the sixth or seventh century.[139] The scribe took some care over this piece, enlarging the first letter of each line and filling in the space at the bottom of the parchment with ornamental lines, an enlarged *alpha* and *omega* with elaborate crosses in between, and a sort of christogram (a *chi* with a long vertical up the middle topped with a small inverted triangle). He uses *nomina sacra* consistently and correctly; there is one instance of inorganic *diairesis*.[140] From the spelling it would appear that the text was written from memory.

Colin Roberts, the parchment's editor, suggested that it may have been used as an amulet on the grounds that 'any passage glorifying the power and majesty of God might be used to repel the powers of evil'. He noted, as well, the *alpha, omega*, crosses, and *chi-rho* figure at the bottom.[141] But the piece seems too elaborate for an amulet, and we do not know what might have been written on the column to the right of the text, now lost. Moreover, many long narrow sheets written with liturgical texts like this one have survived from antiquity. Their format indicates that they were meant to serve as memory-aids to be used, for instance, in services.[142] Sometimes, like *P.Ryl.* III 462, such sheets have only the beginnings of lines, as we see in two memory-aids for sung parts of the liturgy of the hours from the eighth and ninth centuries.[143] As it happens, one of these, *P.Fay.Copt.* 8, may have had a secondary use as an amulet, as a second writer completed one of the original lines and added two psalm verses of protective value in Coptic.[144]

A much later piece, *P.Bad.* V 129, assigned to the thirteenth or fourteenth century,[145] indicates how enduring the liturgical-textual habits of such memory-aids could be. When it was published by Friedrich Bilabel and Adolf Grohmann, Paul Collart immediately adduced it as a *comparandum* to *PGM* P22.[146] *P.Bad.* V 129 consists of a long narrow strip of paper (9.7 cm w × 24.3 cm h) written on front and back with the opening words (in Greek) of verses from LXX Pss. 140, 141, and 129, followed by LXX Ps. 116: 2 in full: 'Because his mercy became strong toward us, <and> the truth of the Lord endures forever'. These psalms, which are now sung at the beginning of the

---

in *De uirginitate: Eine echte Schrift des Athanasius*, ed. F. von der Goltz, TU 29/2A (Leipzig: J. C. Hinrichs, 1905), 55–6.

[139] Image at <http://luna.manchester.ac.uk/luna/servlet/ManchesterDev~93~3> (Rylands Papyri Collection, image no. JRL030616tr).

[140] *P.Ryl.* III 462.6.   [141] *P.Ryl.* III 462 intro., p. 16.

[142] See Mihálykó, 'Writing the Christian Liturgy in Egypt', 106–7, 144–5.

[143] P.Duke inv. 668, image and description at <http://library.duke.edu/rubenstein/scriptorium/papyrus/records/668.html> (Duke Papyrus Archive); *P.Fay.Copt.* 8, re-edited by Quecke, *Untersuchungen*, 449–53, with discussion at 139–45. See Mihálykó, 'Writing the Christian Liturgy in Egypt', 141.

[144] Quecke, *Untersuchungen*, 141 n. 15.   [145] *P.Bad.* V, p. 369.

[146] P. Collart, 'Psaumes et amulettes', *Aegyptus*, 14 (1934), 463–7, <http://www.jstor.org/stable/41214438>.

Byzantine cathedral service of evening prayer,[147] were at one time also sung in that service in certain monasteries of Upper Egypt, as well as in the cathedral in Cairo, as a fourteenth-century manuscript from the Monastery of St Macarius in the Wadi el-Natrun reveals.[148] (This particular liturgy has since fallen into disuse in Egypt.) The two sides of paper were written by several hands. Each line of Pss. 140 and 141, but only the first line of Ps. 129, is preceded by a cross. Verse divisions are usually, but not always, indicated by a sign (:—). The text of Pss. 140 and 141 also includes what appear to be musical notations. The verse divisions of Ps. 140 are more regular in *P.Bad.* V 129 than they are in *PGM* P22, but the divisions in the latter nevertheless correspond to the former, except for the anomalous verse 4b (see above).[149] Thus, the two artefacts, separated by at least six centuries, drew on a standard division of the psalm. The fact that *PGM* P22 preserves initial words of only Ps. 140, not a series of psalms, may support the view that it served as an amulet, as it is unclear why a memory-aid would be necessary to recall a single psalm.

We may conclude this section with an anecdote that epitomizes the inter-section of doxological, textual, therapeutic, and apotropaic practices. It is among the stories recounted in the *Miracles of Cyrus and John*, a work composed at the beginning of the seventh century by Sophronius, bishop of Jerusalem.[150] A wealthy and beautiful woman from Syria, Joannia, was poi-soned by her jealous sisters-in-law. Hearing of the miraculous healing power of the martyrs Cyrus and John, she travels from Caesarea, where she was then living, to the martyrs' sanctuary in Alexandria. The martyrs appear to her in a dream and prescribe a remedy: lentils, boiled down, eaten and applied exter-nally to her stomach. She follows their instructions, and the poison she unwittingly drunk is expelled, breaking out on her skin. After she recovers somewhat, the martyrs appear to her a second time and restore her to complete health: 'they handed her a pastille (a type of confection) to eat, gave her one of the psalms which were regularly recited to them, written on a sort of ticket, and charged her to recite it unceasingly'. She eats the confection, recovers completely, sings the hymn, and, promising the martyrs always to sing it, returns to Caesarea.[151] Although it is unclear whether Joannia was

---

[147] Taft, *The Liturgy of the Hours*, 278.

[148] U. Zanetti, 'Horologion copte et vêpres byzantines', *Le Muséon*, 102 (1989), 237–54 at 246–7, doi: 10.2143/MUS.102.3.2011385; Taft, *The Liturgy of the Hours*, 256.

[149] Collart, 'Psaumes et amulettes', 406.

[150] For a recent translation of this work, incorporating new textual readings and providing commentary, see *Sophrone de Jérusalem: miracles des saints Cyr et Jean (BHGI 477–479)*, tr. J. Gascou (Paris: De Boccard, 2006).

[151] Sophronius of Jerusalem, *Mir. Cyr. et Jo.* 68.6, in N. F. Marcos, *Los Thaumata de Sofronio: contribucion al estudio de la* incubatio *Cristiana* (Madrid: Instituto 'Antonio de Nebrija', 1975), 390–1: Ἐπιφανέντες δὲ πάλιν οἱ ἅγιοι τελείαν αὐτῇ τὴν ὑγείαν χαρίζονται, πάστελλον αὐτὴν ἐσθίειν ὀρέξαντες (εἶδος τοῦτο πλακοῦντος καθέστηκεν), καὶ ψαλμόν τινα δόντες τῶν εἰς αὐτοὺς λεγομένων γεγραμμένον ὡσεὶ εἰς πιττάκιον, καὶ λέγειν αὐτὸν συνεχῶς ἐπιτρέψαντες. Ἡ δὲ φαγοῦσα τὸν

given a specific psalm or a composed hymn—both ψαλμός and ὕμνος are used—and although we are not told exactly when and how the song was regularly recited at the sanctuary, the story reveals how a recurring liturgical act at the sanctuary yields the medium for praise and protection that is transposed into writing, taken away, and sung continually. The transfer from liturgical action to written text for a purpose that is at once doxological and apotropaic is analogous to what we observed in amulets and memory-aids written with psalms routinely chanted during morning and evening prayer.

6.3 EXORCISM

The world of the ancients was populated by a host of subordinate spiritual beings.[152] They served as assistants to higher deities; as protectors of particular places, people, and things; as messengers; and as agents in human affairs, working on behalf of higher deities or human petitioners for good or for ill. The term *daimon* (δαίμον), used in ancient sources and modern discussions to refer to such agents, encompasses a diverse array of spiritual beings—lesser deities, astral spirits, guardians of places in the heavens or the underworld, spirits of the dead. These beings could be protective and helpful to humans as well as aggressive and harmful. In rituals in the Graeco-Egyptian manuals we discussed in Chapter 3, they figure in various capacities.[153] They may be summoned as assistants (*parhedroi*) to execute the practitioner's instructions or wishes.[154] They operate as mediums of revelation in divinatory procedures. As spirits of the dead, they may be called upon in binding incantations to

---

πάστελλον, καὶ τελείας τυχοῦσα τῆς ῥώσεως, καὶ τὸν ὕμνον ὑμνήσασα, καὶ τοῦτον ἀεὶ μελῳδεῖν ὑποσχομένη τοῖς μάρτυσιν, ἐπὶ Παλαιστίνην καὶ Καισάρειαν ᾤδευσεν.

[152] The literature is vast. For overviews, see the multiple articles under the heading 'Geister (Dämonen)', *RAC*, 9.546–797; 'Demon, Demonology', *EBR*, 6.531–84 at 531–63. More specifically, see E. Sorensen, *Possession and Exorcism in the New Testament and Early Christianity* (Tübingen: Mohr Siebeck, 2002), 18–117; R. Lucarelli, 'Demonology during the Late Pharaonic and Greco-Roman Periods in Egypt', *JANER*, 11 (2011), 109–25, doi: 10.1163/156921211X603904; J. F. Quack, 'Dämonen und andere höhere Wesen in der Magie als Feinde und Helfer', in A. Jördens (ed.), *Ägyptische Magie und ihre Umwelt* (Wiesbaden: Harrassowitz Verlag, 2015), 101–18.

[153] G. S. Gasparro, 'Magie et démonologie dans les *Papyrus Graecae Magicae*', in E. Callieri and R. Gyselen (eds), *Démons et merveilles d'Orient* (Bures-sur-Yvette: Groupe pour l'étude de la civilisation du Moyen-Orient, 2001), 157–74.

[154] L. J. Ciraolo, 'Supernatural Assistants in the Greek Magical Papyri', in M. Meyer and P. Mirecki (eds), *Ancient Magic and Ritual Power* (Leiden: Brill, 1995), 279–95; A. Scibilia, 'Supernatural Assistance in the Greek Magical Papyri: The Figure of the *Parhedros*', in J. N. Bremmer and J. R. Veenstra (eds), *The Metamorphosis of Magic from Late Antiquity to the Early Modern Period* (Leuven: Peeters, 2002), 71–86.

hinder opponents, constrain lovers, or exact vengeance. They can be the cause of illness and distress, attacking or invading their human victims.

It is this last type of activity with which we are concerned here. The evils that spirits can work are conveyed in vivid terms by *PGM* P10, the incantation with which we opened this chapter. The spirits enumerated there are wholly maleficent agents—'demons' in the sense given that term in ancient Jewish and early Christian sources.[155] In incantations with Christian elements they are called 'impure' or 'wicked' spirits,[156] as in the New Testament.[157] They are identified by the harm they do:[158] 'the demon of envy and the one of evildoing and the one of enmity';[159] 'whatever demon, whether blind or deaf or dumb or toothless';[160] 'every spirit of unclean, destructive demons'.[161]

Christian rituals to ward off or expel evil spirits were a specific instance of a more general practice in antiquity. This is apparent from the arguments of Christian apologists and their pagan opponents, as we saw in Chapter 1. While the latter sought to discredit Christian exorcism by associating it with 'magic', the former sought to differentiate Christian exorcism from ambient practices. From this literature we get a general, albeit stereotypical, understanding of what Christians claimed to say and do when dealing with demons.[162] Christians cast out demons in the name of Jesus or God, accompanied by laying on of hands and signing with the cross.[163] The exorcist might expand on the

---

[155] See Kotansky, 'Greek Exorcistic Amulets', 243–5, 257–61; Sorensen, *Possession and Exorcism*, 59–74, 118–67; G. Bohak, *Ancient Jewish Magic: A History* (Cambridge: Cambridge University Press, 2008), 88–114; R. Leicht, 'Mashbia' Ani 'Alekha: Types and Patterns of Ancient Jewish and Christian Exorcism Formulae', *JSQ*, 13 (2006), 319–34 at 322–30, <http://www.jstor.org/stable/40753414>; A. T. Wright, 'Evil Spirits in Second Temple Judaism: The Watcher Tradition as Background to the Demonic Pericopes in the Gospels', *Henoch*, 28 (2006), 141–59.

[156] *PGM* P10.20: [ἀκά]θαρτα πν(εύματ)α; *PGM* P13.15 (*P.Cair.Cat.* 10263): ἀκάθαρτον πνεῦμα; *PGM* P13a.3 (*P.Cair.Masp.* II 67188 vᵒ 1–5 10263): πονηροῦ πν(εύμ)ατος; *PGM* P17.9 (*P.Iand.* I 6) = *P.Giss.Lit.* 5.4: ἀκάθαρτον πν(εῦμ)α; *SM* I 31.4 (*P.Turner* 49) = *BKT* IX 134: πν(εύμ)α(τος) πονηροῦ. It is not uncommon in the papyri for πνεῦμα to be contracted even if the sense of the word is mundane; see A. H. R. E. Paap, *Nomina Sacra in the Greek Papyri of the First Five Centuries A.D.: The Sources and Some Deductions* (Leiden: Brill, 1959), 102.

[157] See Sorensen, *Possession and Exorcism*, 120–2.

[158] See Sorensen, *Possession and Exorcism*, 121–2 n. 16.

[159] *PGM* P9.8–11 (*BGU* III 954): τὸν δαίμονα προβασκανίας καὶ τὸν κ[ακο]ε[ρ]γίας καὶ τὸν τῆς ἀηδίας.

[160] *PGM* P17.15–16 (*P.Iand.* I 6) = *P.Giss.Lit.* 5.4: ἢ ὅσα τυφλὰ δαιμόνια ἢ κω[φὰ ἢ ἄλ]αλα ἢ νωδὰ; see *P.Giss.Lit.*, p. 181. On the expression 'deaf and dumb' spirits in the gospels and later Christian usage, see *SM* II 84.6–7 comm.

[161] *PGM* P13a.3–4 (*P.Cair.Masp.* II 67188 vᵒ 1–5): πᾶν πν(εῦμ)α δαιμονίων φθειροποιούντων ἀκαθάρτων.

[162] The following summary is taken from T. S. de Bruyn, 'What Did Ancient Christians Say When They Cast Out Demons? Inferences from Spells and Amulets', in W. Mayer and G. D. Dunn (eds), *Christians Shaping Identity from the Roman Empire to Byzantium: Studies Inspired by Pauline Allen* (Leiden: Brill, 2015), 64–82 at 65–6, with permission from the publisher.

[163] Sorensen, *Possession and Exorcism*, 184–5; A. Nicolotti, *Esorcismo cristiano e possessione diabolica tra II e III secolo* (Turnhout: Brepols, 2011), 69–70, 76.

name of Jesus. Justin, for instance, speaks several times of demons being cast out 'by the name of Jesus Christ, crucified under Pontius Pilate'.[164] On one occasion his description of Jesus' life is more detailed, drawing on what appears to have been an early summary of faith regarding Jesus: 'For every demon is overcome and subdued when exorcised in the name of this very Son of God and "first-born of all creation" (cf. Col. 1: 15), who was born of a virgin and became a human being susceptible to suffering, who was crucified under Pontius Pilate by your people and died, who rose from the dead and ascended into heaven.'[165] This sort of summary may be what Origen refers to when he states that Christians drive out demons 'by the name of Jesus, together with a recital of narratives about him'.[166] In the same passage Origen notes that Christians also add 'other reliable words, in accordance with the divine scripture'.[167] Tertullian offers a few more details, explaining that the demons flee at the name of Jesus and the reminder of the punishments they will receive from him—which Tertullian refers to as adjurations[168]—accompanied by laying on of hands and blowing of air.[169]

The practice described by these writers in general terms manifests itself in amulets in a number of ways. First, in incantations to dispel fevers or other ills worked by evil spirits, the name or power invoked is often that of Jesus.[170] Sometimes the invocation is simple and direct, as in *SM* I 22: 'Power of Jesus Christ, heal Eremega, whom Anilla bore, of all illness and pain of the head and temples, and of fever, and of fever with shivering', or *SM* I 34, which, as we saw in Chapter 4,[171] juxtaposes an invocation of Jesus with the name 'Erichthonius' written in a diminishing grape-cluster and an invocation of the white wolf: 'Jesus Christ heals the shivering and the fever and every illness of the body of Joseph,

---

[164] Justin, *Dial.* 30.3, in *Justin Martyr, Dialogue avec Tryphon*, ed. P. Bobichon, 2 vols (Fribourg: Academic Press and Éditions Saint-Paul, 2003), 1.256; Justin, *2 Apol.* 5(6).6 (SC 507.334).

[165] Justin, *Dial.* 85.2, in Bobichon, *Justin Martyr*, 1.416: κατὰ γὰρ τοῦ ὀνόματος αὐτοῦ τούτου τοῦ υἱοῦ τοῦ θεοῦ καὶ πρωτοτόκου πάσης κτίσεως, καὶ διὰ παρθένου γεννηθέντος καὶ παθητοῦ γενομένου ἀνθρώπου, καὶ σταυρωθέντος ἐπὶ Ποντίου Πιλάτου ὑπὸ τοῦ λαοῦ ὑμῶν καὶ ἀποθανόντος, καὶ ἀναστάντος ἐκ νεκρῶν καὶ ἀναβάντος εἰς τὸν οὐρανόν, πᾶν δαιμόνιον ἐξορκιζόμενον νικᾶται καὶ ὑποτάσσεται. On *regulae fidei* such as this one in the second century, see P. Smulders, 'Some Riddles in the Apostles' Creed: II. Creeds and Rules of Faith', *Bijdragen*, 32 (1971), 350–66, doi: 10.1080/00062278.1971.10596938.

[166] Origen, *Cels.* 1.6 (SC 132.90): Οὐ γὰρ κατακλήσεσιν ἰσχύειν δοκοῦσιν ⌊ἀλλὰ τῷ ὀνόματι Ἰησοῦ⌋ μετὰ τῆς ἀπαγγελίας τῶν περὶ αὐτὸν ἱστοριῶν; *Cels.* 3.24 (SC 136: 56).

[167] Origen, *Cels.* 1.6 (SC 132.90): σαφὲς ὅτι ⌊Χριστιανοὶ οὐδεμιᾷ μελέτῃ ἐπῳδῶν χρώμενοι τυγχάνουσιν ἀλλὰ τῷ ὀνόματι τοῦ Ἰησοῦ μετ' ἄλλων λόγων πεπιστευμένων κατὰ τὴν θείαν γραφήν⌋.

[168] Tertullian, *Apol.* 32.2–3 (CCSL 1.143).

[169] Tertullian, *Apol.* 23.15–16 (CCSL 1.132–3); with Nicolotti, *Esorcismo*, 492–509.

[170] T. S. de Bruyn, 'Christian Apocryphal and Canonical Narratives in Greek Amulets and Formularies in Late Antiquity', in P. Piovanelli and T. Burke (eds), *Rediscovering the Apocryphal Continent: New Perspectives on Early Christian and Late Antique Apocryphal Texts and Traditions* (Tübingen: Mohr Siebeck, 2015), 153–74 at 166–8.

[171] See Section 4.2.1.

who wears the amulet—the quotidian and tertian.' In other incantations the petition or adjuration is prefaced by a *historiola* recounting the healings that Jesus performed. The allusion may be brief, as in *SM* I 30 (*P.Coll.Youtie* II 91): 'You who healed every illness [and every infirmity,] Jesus Christ, heal the man or [woman] who wears [this amulet] . . . and soul and body and spirit . . . from every evil.' Or it may be more expansive, as in *PGM* P18, which we discussed and quoted in Chapter 4.[172] Such *historiolae* may in fact echo liturgical prayers for healing. The Coptic rite for the anointing of the sick also recalls healings and miracles performed by Jesus, using a form similar to that in amulets: 'You who healed so-and-so' or 'As you healed so-and-so'.[173] Though we must be cautious in citing parallels from later liturgical books, the similarity reveals a point of intersection between incantations in amulets and prayers of the church.

Second, two amulets preface their petition or injunction with an acclamatory form of the second article of the Christian creed: *SM* I 23 (*P.Haun.* III 51), assigned to the fifth century, and *SM* I 35 (*P.Batav.* 20), assigned to the sixth century. From an exorcism to be said over the oil for the sick in the fourth-century Montserrat Euchologion (mentioned in Section 6.1.2 in connection with the *Sanctus*),[174] we know that christological summaries like those described by Justin in the second century continued to be used in prayers so that, in the words of the exorcism, 'everyone who is anointed with [this oil] may be healed completely from every evil activity of Satan, every visitation of wickedness, and every tyranny of the Devil'.[175] The two amulets add to this evidence. The fact that they are separated by a century—assuming that the palaeographical dating is correct—suggests that the recitation of christological acclamations in rituals to dispel or expel evil spirits was an established practice. This is confirmed by exorcistic and healing incantations in medieval and early modern Byzantine manuscripts, where, too, the injunction is preceded by a christological acclamation.[176]

[172] See Section 4.2.2.

[173] H. Denzinger (ed.), *Ritus orientalium Coptorum Syrorum et Armenorum in administrandis sacramentis*, 2 vols (Würzburg, 1863–4; repr. Graz: Akademische Druck- u. Verlagsanstalt, 1961), 2.489–90, 492–3, 497; ET: *Coptic Offices*, tr. R. M. Woolley (London: Society for Promoting Christian Knowledge, 1930), 95–6, 99–100, 106. For a description of the modern rite, see G. Viaud, *La Liturgie des Coptes d'Égypte* (Paris: Librairie d'Amérique et d'Orient, 1978), 44–5.

[174] Roca-Puig, *Anàfora de Barcelona*, 103–11, with plates at 133–5 (P.Monts.Roca inv. 156a.6–156b.3); R. Merkelbach (ed.), *Abrasax: Ausgewählte Papyri religiösen und magischen Inhalts*, vol. 4: *Exorzismen und jüdisch/christlich beeinflusste Texte* (Cologne: Westdeutscher, 1996), 64–70.

[175] See now Merkelbach, *Abrasax*, 4.66, for the transcription of P.Monts.Roca inv. 156a.20–3: ὅπως πάντα τὸν ἀλιφόμενον [read: ἀλειφόμενον] ἐξ αὐτοῦ [i.e., τοῦ ἐλαίου] ἰάσῃ [subsequently expanded to: ἰάσηται] | ἀπὸ πάσης ἐνεργείας τοῦ Σατανᾶ καὶ παντὸς συν- | εντήματος [read: συναντήματος] πονηρία<ς> καὶ πάσης καταδυναστείας | τοῦ διαβόλου.

[176] A. Vassiliev (ed.), *Anecdota Graeco-Byzantina: Pars Prior* (Moscow: Universitatis Caesareae, 1893), 339; Pradel, *Griechische und süditalienische Gebete*, §§13.23–14.6 with 48–9; Delatte, *Anecdota Atheniensia*, 1.146, 616; A. Tselikas, 'Spells and Exorcisms in Three Post-Byzantine Manuscripts', in J. C. B. Petropoulos (ed.), *Greek Magic: Ancient, Medieval and Modern* (Abingdon and New York: Routledge, 2008), 72–81 at 75, 77–8.

The wording of the christological acclamations in the amulets varies some-what and does not correspond to known creeds, indicating that the practice of recalling the action of Christ was a 'lived' one, executed with some freedom. In *SM* I 23 the acclamation reads: '⁜ Christ was born, amen. Christ was crucified, amen. Christ was buried, amen. Christ arose, amen. He has woken to judge the living and the dead. You too, fever with shivering, flee from Kale, who wears this phylactery.'[177] In *SM* I 35 it reads: '⁜ Christ was proclaimed in advance. ⁜ Christ appeared. ⁜ Christ suffered. ⁜ Christ died. ⁜ Christ was raised. ⁜ Christ was taken up. ⁜ Christ reigns. Christ saves Vibius, whom Gennaia bore, from all fever and from all shivering, daily, quotidian, now now, quickly quickly'.[178] In both amulets each clause of the acclamation is given its own line—a visual reflection of its oral proclamation. In *SM* I 23 the ensuing injunction takes the form of a customary 'flee-formula', whereas in *SM* I 35 the acclamation is followed by an indicative declaring that Christ saves Vibius, the certainty of Christ's protection taken as given.[179] As in the Montserrat exorcism, the distinction between warding off or expelling evil spirits and healing is not a sharp one;[180] since sickness is perceived to be the work of evil spirits, the christological acclamation avails against both. We have evidence of this from quite a different context, in a sermon Ambrose preached to catechumens about the creed. Ambrose concludes his sermon by encouraging the catechu-mens to learn the creed from memory so that, among other things, they may be able to recite it when they are assailed by the Devil or beset by illness.[181]

In both amulets the acclamation is part of an otherwise customary incan-tation. In *SM* I 35 the incantation concludes with the traditional accelerating formula: 'now now quickly quickly'. In *SM* I 23 the customary character of the amulet is even more marked. The amulet has not one, but two incantations, a relatively common feature of amulets against fever and other illnesses in Late Antiquity.[182] The second part of the amulet has a drawing of a stele with the letters *sigma* and *eta* (ϲϲϲ | ϲϲ | ηη | η) written inside, flanked by two eight-pointed *charaktêres* (see Fig. 6.1). (As it happens, the title of the exorcism in

---

[177] *SM* I 23.1–9: ⁜ Χριστὸς ἐγεννήθη, ἀμήν. | Χριστὸς ἐσταυρόθη, ἀμήν. | Χριστὸς ἐτάφη, ἀμήν. | Χριστὸς ἀνέστη, ἀμή<ν>. | γεγέρθη κρῖνε ζο̃ντας | καὶ νεκρούς. φύγε καὶ σοί, | ῥιγοπυρέτιν, ἀπὸ Καλῆς | τῆς φορούσης τὸ φυλ<α>κτή- | ριον τοῦτο.

[178] *SM* I 35.1–14: ⁜Χ(ριστὸ)ς προεκ[ηρύχθη] | ⁜ Χ(ριστὸ)ς ἐφάνη | ⁜ Χ(ριστὸ)ς ἔπαθεν | ⁜ Χ(ριστὸ)ς ἀπέθανεν | ⁜ Χ(ριστὸ)ς ἀνηγέρθη | ⁜ Χ(ριστὸ)ς ἀνελήμφθη | ⁜ Χ(ριστὸ)ς βασιλεύε | Χ(ριστὸ)ς σῴζει Οὐίβιον, | ὃν ἔτεκεν Γενναία, | ἀπὸ παντὸς πυρετοῦ | καὶ παντὸς ῥίγους | [[.]] ἀμφημερινοῦ, | καθημερινοῦ, | ἤδη ἤδη, ταχὺ ταχύ.

[179] *SM* I 35.8 comm.   [180] See n. 175.

[181] Ambrose, *Expl. symb.* 9 (SC 25 *bis*.56–8). I am grateful to Gillian Clark for bringing this to my attention. In both East and West, catechumens preparing for baptism memorized the creed and recited it in a rite prior to their baptism; see P. L. Gavrilyuk, *Histoire du catéchuménat dans l'Église ancienne*, tr. F. Lhoest, N. Mojaïsky, and A.-M. Gueit (Paris: Les Éditions du Cerf, 2007), 208–9, 231, 298–9, 304.

[182] See Chapter 4 n. 58.

Fig. 6.1. *SM* I 23 (*P.Haun.* III 51; inv. 312). Courtesy of the Papyri Haunienses Collection.

the Montserrat Euchologion is also flanked by an eight-pointed *charaktêr*.[183]) The invocation accompanying these visual elements reads: 'Holy stele and mighty *charaktêres*, chase away the fever with shivering from Kale, who wears this amulet, now now now, quickly quickly quickly.'[184] This part of the amulet trades on the power attributed to stelae engraved with deities and inscribed with hieroglyphs in temple courts and other public places in Graeco-Roman

---

[183] See the plate at Roca-Puig, *Anàfora de Barcelona*, 133.

[184] *SM* I 23.10–17: ἁγία | στήλη |καὶ εἰσ- | χυροὶ χαρακτῆραις, ἀπο- | διόξαται τὸ ῥιγοπύρετον | ἀπὸ Καλῆς τῆς φορούσης | τὸ φυλακτήριον τοῦτο, | ἤδε ἤδε ἤδε, ταχὺ ταχὺ ταχύ.

Egypt.[185] Manuals of procedures not only name such stelae as the source of their incantations,[186] they also refer to the incantation itself as a 'stele'.[187]

The scribe of *SM* I 35, who wrote in a practiced but untidy cursive hand,[188] was evidently accustomed to writing incantations incorporating an acclamatory creed. The manner in which he combines a staurogram with Χριστός written as a *nomen sacrum* (·₽χͩ) at the beginning of each acclamation betrays an ease with scribal conventions: a single stroke rises from the bottom left of the *rho* to form the cross bar of the staurogram and the diagonal of *chi*. The scribe of *SM* I 23, on the other hand, wrote in a rather deliberate upright majuscule hand,[189] inadvertently dropping a few letters in the first acclamation.[190] He also writes 'Christ' out in full, but this may not be significant, since in documents and letters scribes did not always use *nomina sacra*.

In sum, the different and yet similar manner in which these two amulets incorporate a christological acclamation suggests that the practice of reciting such acclamations was sufficiently well known to be adopted by practitioners who were nevertheless free to adapt the resources available to them. It is yet another instance of an individualized appropriation of a tradition.

Although Christian apologists insist on the simplicity of Christian exorcisms, the reality was at times rather different, as we learn from a pseudonymous tract on the way of life of itinerant Christian ascetics,[191] written in the third or early fourth century and circulating in Egypt within the next century.[192] One of the practices the writer disapproves of is the use of lengthy incantations when praying over demoniacs. When visiting them, one is to pray to God with faith, 'not by combining many words or declaiming adjurations for human display so as to appear eloquent or endowed with a good memory'.[193]

---

[185] Frankfurter, *Religion in Roman Egypt*, 47–9.　　　[186] *PGM* VIII.41–3.

[187] *PGM* IV.1115, 1167, 2567–9, 3245–7; V.95, 422–3; XIII.54, 61, 127, 131–2, 425, 566–7, 684–5, 688.

[188] *P.Batav.* 10, plate XIV.　　　[189] *P.Haun.* III 51 intro., p. 31, and plate III; fig. 6.1 above.

[190] Indicated at n. 177 between angled brackets.

[191] Pseudo-Clement, *Ep. ad virgines*, in *Patres apostolici*, ed. F. Diekamp and F. X. Funk, 2 vols, 3rd edn (Tübingen: Laupp, 1913), 2.1–28. For the versions of this work, see M. Geerard (ed.), *Clavis patrum graecorum*, 6 vols in 5 (Turnhout: Brepols, 1974–2003), 1.6–7 (no. 1004). On the date and provenance, see Nicolotti, *Esorcismo*, 621, and the literature cited there.

[192] The writer censures cohabitation or mingling of male and female ascetics, an innovation that church authorities in the fourth century sought to end, substituting more socially acceptable institutions, such as separate monasteries for women and men. See pseudo-Clement, *Ep. ad virgines* 1.10.1–4, in Diekamp and Funk, *Patres apostolici*, 2.17–18; and S. Elm, *Virgins of God: The Making of Asceticism in Late Antiquity* (Oxford: Oxford University Press, 1996), 47–51, 162–4, 341, 374–5.

[193] Pseudo-Clement, *Ep. ad virgines* 1.12.2, in Diekamp and Funk, *Patres apostolici*, 2.22–3: ... μὴ ἐκ συνθέσεως πολλῶν λόγων ἢ μελέτας ἐξορκισμῶν πρὸς ἐπίδειξιν ἀνθρωπαρεσκείας πρὸς τὸ φανῆναι εὐλάλους ἢ μνήμονας ἡμᾶς. For the Coptic version, see *Les pères apostoliques en copte*, ed. and tr. L.-Th. Lefort, 2 vols, CSCO 135–6 (Louvain: L. Dubecq, 1952), 135.41–2 (text), 136.35 (translation). The Greek, Syriac, and Coptic versions can be conveniently compared at Nicolotti, *Esorcismo*, 622–4.

Presumably, this instruction was necessary because Christian incantations, like non-Christian ones, could be elaborate. The incantation with which we opened this chapter, *PGM* P10, could be an example of what the writer had in mind. It consists of six elaborate adjurations; a simple command was evidently insufficient. We see this as well in a Coptic amulet that may date from the early Islamic period. It combines LXX Ps. 90: 1–2 and the *incipits* of the four gospels with twelve short adjurations to protect a certain Philoxenos from 'all [harm] and all evil and all sorcery and all injury induced by the stars and all the demons and all the deeds of the hostile adversary'.[194] The tendency to pile up adjurations would prove to be tenacious. The later Byzantine liturgical exorcisms that parallel the language of *PGM* P10 at a number of points[195]—particularly, as we saw, in using the verb ἀναχωρεῖν to command the evil spirits to depart[196]—contain a seemingly endless series of adjurations, to be uttered until the demon leaves.[197]

Lengthy exorcistic adjurations were already in circulation in non-Christian circles by the fourth century, and probably earlier. We have already encountered two extended exorcistic procedures in our discussion of the Graeco-Egyptian manuals in Chapter 3. The most explicit in label, incantation, and instructions is *PGM* IV.1227–64,[198] which, as we have seen, includes a Christian formula. It is said to be 'an excellent ritual for driving out demons';[199] the incantation takes the classic form of adjuring the demon (ἐξορκίζω σε, δαῖμον) to come out and stay away from the client;[200] and the procedure includes preparing a protective amulet for the client to wear after the demon has been expelled. Similarly, the procedure replete with adjurations drawing on Jewish lore, *PGM* IV.3007–86,[201] carries the label 'For those possessed by a demon',[202] and instructs the exorcist to utter the command 'Come out of so-and-so' while preparing a compound.[203] (The label 'For those possessed by

---

[194] J. Drescher, 'A Coptic Amulet', in T. Whittemore (ed.), *Coptic Studies in Honor of Walter Ewing Crum* (Boston: The Byzantine Institute, 1950), 265–70, with discussion of the date at 266; ET: *ACM*, no. 62.

[195] *PGM* P10 apparatus.   [196] See n. 5.

[197] E.g., Vassiliev, *Anecdota Graeco-Byzantina*, 332–3; Delatte, *Anecdota Atheniensia*, 1.228–62; L. Delatte, *Un office byzantin d'exorcisme (Ms. de la Lavra du Mont Athos, θ 20)* (Gembloux: J. Duculot, 1954), *passim*, with remarks at 102, 141–6. See R. P. H. Greenfield, *Traditions of Belief in Late Byzantine Demonology* (Amsterdam: Adolf M. Hakkert, 1988), 141–7.

[198] See Section 3.1.2.

[199] *PGM* IV.1227: πρᾶξις γενναία ἐκβάλλουσα δαίμονας.

[200] *PGM* IV.1243–4: ἔξελθε . . . καὶ ἀπόστηθι ἀπὸ τοῦ δεῖνα. On this formula see Kotansky, 'Greek Exorcistic Amulets', 261; Leicht, 'Mashbia' Ani 'Alekha'.

[201] See Section 3.1.1.

[202] *PGM* IV.3007: πρὸς δαιμονιαζομένους. The writers of the gospels use ὁ δαιμονιζόμενος to refer to those who are possessed by a demon; see W. Bauer (ed.), *A Greek-English Lexicon of the New Testament and Other Early Christian Literature*, 3rd edn, ed. and rev. F. W. Danker (Chicago: University of Chicago Press, 2000), *s.v.* δαιμονίζομαι.

[203] *PGM* IV.3013: ἔξελθε ἀπὸ τοῦ δεῖνος.

a demon' is also applied to another amulet in the same manuscript, *PGM* IV.86–7,[204] as well as to an amulet in a later fragmentary collection of medico-magical prescriptions, *SM* II 94.17–21 [*P.Ant.* II 66].)

We do not know whether lengthy, iterative liturgical exorcisms were used in the church in Egypt in Late Antiquity. No liturgical exorcisms from that period are extant. However, given the precedent for such repeated adjurations in exorcisms in Graeco-Egyptian manuals and in occasional amulets with Christian elements, as well as the evident predilection for elaborate incantations in some Coptic rituals, we may expect that at least some Christian clerics and monks replicated this particular cultural model.

6.4 THE VENERATION OF SAINTS

The period when the great majority of Greek amulets with Christian elements were composed in late antique Egypt was also the period when veneration of saints became widely institutionalized in the Egyptian church. The papyrological, epigraphic, and material sources of evidence of such veneration, though not without their own difficulties, are relatively rich when compared with the literary sources. Arietta Papaconstantinou's thorough and judicious weighing of the evidence from the fifth to the ninth century yielded an inventory of 167 entries.[205] These entries do not, however, correspond to individual saints, since in many instances it is impossible to tell when a single name refers to more than one individual. A small number—between sixteen and twenty-three—are biblical saints, most them evangelists, apostles, or witnesses to Christ mentioned in the New Testament, such as Longinus the centurion, whom we shall meet again below. A slightly larger number— between twenty-nine and thirty-three—are saints from other regions of the eastern empire, most notably from Asia Minor, where the Forty Martyrs of Sebaste originated, and Syria-Palestine, the provenance of the twin brothers and physicians Cosmas and Damian, as well as the anti-Chalcedonian champion Severus of Antioch. The great majority of saints documented in Egypt, however, are of Egyptian origin—between 111 and 116 of the 167. Most of these—about one hundred—appear to have been local saints, attested and honoured in only one place. A handful were venerated in more than one region, some in Lower and Middle Egypt, others in Middle and Upper Egypt.

---

[204] See *PGM* IV.86 comm.; *GMPT*, 38 n. 26.

[205] For what follows, see A. Papaconstantinou, *Le culte des saints en Égypte des Byzantins aux Abbassides: l'apport des inscriptions et des papyrus grecs et coptes* (Paris: CNRS Éditions, 2001), 229–33.

Only a small number of saints—far smaller than the known pool—are invoked in amulets. Several of these saints had multiple sanctuaries and a dedicated feast day in Egypt—evidence of an organized, institutional cult:[206] George (invoked along with Mary in one amulet),[207] Mary (whom we shall discuss separately in Section 6.4.1), and Victor (invoked among the Oxy-rhynchite saints in *PGM* P5b).[208] The archangels Michael and Gabriel (invoked in an amulet and a prayer for justice) were also venerated in Egypt,[209] though they are as likely to be named at the head of a series of archangels,[210] as was customary in incantations,[211] as singly.[212] Locally venerated Egyptian saints are almost entirely absent, the only exception being several Oxyrhynchite saints invoked in *PGM* P5b (*P.Oxy.* VIII 1151). Thus, although the sample is small, it would appear that Greek amulets with Christian elements are not profoundly shaped by veneration of local saints in the Egyptian chôra.

One can discern at least three different reasons for invoking a saint. Some saints appear to have been invoked because of their specific protective or healing powers. As we saw in Chapter 4, St Phocas' power to heal people from snake bites is almost certainly the reason he is invoked in *PGM* P2 (*P.Oxy.* VII 1060), an amulet against scorpion stings.[213] So too, the centurion and martyr Longinus was reputed to heal eye injuries and diseases on account of his having restored the sight of a blind woman.[214] It has been suggested that this is why he is invoked in *P.Bon.* I 9, the concluding fragment of what was probably an amulet,[215] quoted in Section 6.1.3.[216] Other saints are invoked in a manner that suggests that the person calling upon them saw them as a personal

---

[206] Papaconstantinou, *Le culte des saints*, 255–63.

[207] Brashear, *Magica Varia*, 64, lines 8–10 (*SB* XVIII 13602). On the cult of George, see Papaconstantinou, *Le culte des saints*, 129–32.

[208] *PGM* P5b.48–9 (*P.Oxy.* VIII 1151). On the cult of Victor, see Papaconstantinou, *Le culte des saints*, 62–8.

[209] P.Vindob. inv. G 60398 (see Chapter 2 n. 23); *SM* II 61.1 (see Chapter 4 n. 269). On the cult of Gabriel and Michael, see Papaconstantinou, *Le culte des saints*, 68–9, 154–9. For wider evidence, see C. D. G. Müller, *Die Engellehre der koptischen Kirche: Untersuchungen zur Geschichte der christlichen Frömmigkeit in Ägypten* (Wiesbaden: Otto Harrassowitz, 1959).

[210] E.g., *P.Prag.* II 119.3; *SM* I 32.11–12.

[211] J. Michl, 'Engel IV', *RAC* 5.109–200 at 183–6; *AKZ* 3.70–83. On Michael in particular, see T. J. Kraus, 'Angels in the Magical Papyri: The Classic Example of Michael, the Archangel', in F. V. Reiterer, T. Nicklas, and K. Schöpflin (eds), *Angels: The Concept of Celestial Beings—Origins, Development and Reception* (Berlin: De Gruyter, 2007), 611–27.

[212] E.g., *PGM* P6a.3 (*P.Oxy.* VIII 1152); *PGM* P21.14–16, 33–5; *SM* I 29.3–4 (*P.Princ.* II 107).

[213] See Chapter 4 n. 34.

[214] O. De Lacy, *The Saints of Egypt in the Coptic Calendar* (London and New York: Church Historical Society, 1937; repr. Amsterdam: Philo Press, 1974), 179–80. The miracle is recounted in an apocryphal sermon attributed to Hesychius of Jerusalem, *Hom.* 19.12–15, in *Les homélies festales d'Hésychius de Jérusalem*, ed. M. Aubineau, 2 vols (Brussels: Société des Bollandistes, 1978), 2.836–42. The sermon, which Aubineau assigns to the sixth or seventh century (2.796–800), is repeated at greater length in a later apocryphal sermon that is derivative of *Hom.* 19, Hesychius of Jerusalem, *Hom.* 20.

[215] *P.Bon.* I 9 intro.   [216] See n. 101.

protector or intermediary. This would appear to be why *PGM* P5c (*P.Cairo. Cat.* 10696)—an amulet that recites LXX Ps. 21: 20–3, appeals to four named martyrs to protect a certain woman from illnesses of body and soul, and recites the *incipits* of Luke, Matthew, and John—concludes with the petition: 'Saint Phocas, Saint Mercurius, protect your (female) servant.'[217] This is also probably why, in another amulet, *PGM* P9 (*BGU* III 954), Silvanus, son of Sarapion, asks God and Saint Serenus to drive away from him 'the demon of envy and the one of evildoing and the one of enmity' and to take away from him 'every illness and every infirmity' so that he may be healthy and may be able to pray 'the gospel prayer'.[218] After reciting text of the Lord's Prayer and the *incipits* of the Gospels of John and Matthew, the amulet concludes with the petition: 'Saint Serenus, supplicate on my behalf, that I may be perfectly healthy.'[219] (The amulet was found in Herakleopolis [Ihnasya el-Medina],[220] in the same administrative district as the Oxyrhynchite amulet that invokes this Egyptian saint, *PGM* P5b.[221]) Finally, the saints invoked could be those honoured in a given locale. This is the case with *PGM* P5b, which appeals to Christ to heal and protect a certain Joannia 'through the prayers and intercessions of our lady the *Theotokos* and the glorious archangels and Saint John, the glorious apostle and evangelist and theologian, and Saint Serenus and Saint Philoxenus and Saint Victor and Saint Justus and all the saints.'[222] As we saw in Chapter 4,[223] all the saints named here as intermediaries were honoured with sanctuaries in Oxyrhynchus, and several of them—John the Evangelist, Justus, and Philoxenus—were, to the best of our knowledge, venerated only there.

6.4.1 Mary

The saint named most frequently in amulets is Mary.[224] Even though we are dealing with chance finds and not a representative sample of materials, Mary's relative prominence in amulets is in all likelihood a reflection of the prominence of her cult throughout Egypt.[225] Evidence for devotion to Mary in the

---

[217] *PGM* P5c.6.   [218] *PGM* P9.3–15; ET: *ACM*, no. 18.   [219] *PGM* P9.29–30.

[220] U. Wilcken, 'Heidnisches und Christliches aus Ägypten', *APF*, 1 (1901), 396–436 at 431, doi: 10.1515/apf.1901.1.3-4.396; *BGU* III 954 intro.

[221] On the cult of Serenus, see Papaconstantinou, *Le culte des saints*, 187–8, with a map at 469.

[222] *P.Oxy.* VIII 1151.38–51, with D. Hagedorn, 'Bemerkungen zu Urkunden', *ZPE*, 145 (2003), 224–7 at 226, <http://www.jstor.org/stable/20191724>.

[223] See Chapter 4 n. 116.

[224] On the cult of Mary in Egypt, see A. Papaconstantinou, 'Les sanctuaires de la Vierge dans l'Égypte byzantine et omeyyade: l'apport des textes documentaires', *JJP*, 30 (2000), 81–94; S. Higgins, 'Embodying the Virgin: The Physical Materialization of the Cult of Mary in Late Antique Egypt (Fifth–Ninth Centuries CE)', PhD thesis, University of Ottawa, Ottawa, 2015.

[225] Papaconstantinou, 'Les sanctuaires de la Vierge', 93–4. The number of confirmed Marian churches is now thirty-three; see Higgins, 'Embodying the Virgin', 55.

fifth, sixth, seventh, and eighth centuries can be found in documentary references to churches dedicated to her, archaeological evidence of churches and monasteries dedicated to her, and wall paintings of her.[226] The evidence from amulets coincides roughly with this material record.[227]

In several amulets the petitioner appeals to Christ through the intercessions of Mary, as in *PGM* P5b, already discussed above. *PGM* P18, an amulet from the fifth or sixth century to which we referred earlier in this chapter,[228] concludes by asking Christ to heal the woman wearing the amulet 'through the prayers and intercession [*sic*] of the ever-virgin mother, the *Theotokos*, and all...'[229] *P.Oxy.* LXXV 5024,[230] a strip of parchment written in a regular, informal sloping majuscule hand assigned to the late sixth or early seventh century,[231] preserves a prayer for salvation with a petition for the flooding of the Nile similar to that found in the anaphoral intercessions of St Mark/ St Cyril.[232] It concludes with a somewhat less formulaic appeal: 'through the intercession of the woman who bore you, we beseech you, Lord, good and abounding in mercy, hear us and have mercy on us'.[233] There are traces of folds, suggesting that the parchment may have been carried as a memory-aid or an amulet.[234] Finally, a parchment assigned to the seventh century appeals to Christ to relieve a woman of her afflictions 'through the intercessions of your holy martyr George' and 'through the intercessions of our Lady, the all-glorious *Theotokos* and ever-virgin Mary'.[235] The more developed formula is consistent with the dating: the epithet 'all-glorious' is relatively rare in Marian formulae in Late Antiquity.[236] It is worth noting that two of the more common

---

[226] Higgins, 'Embodying the Virgin'.

[227] I discuss the following evidence in greater detail in T. S. de Bruyn, 'Appeals to the Intercessions of Mary in Greek Liturgical and Paraliturgical Texts from Egypt', in L. M. Peltomaa, A. Külzer, and P. Allen (eds), *Presbeia Theotokou: The Intercessory Role of Mary across Times and Places in Byzantium (4th–9th Century)* (Vienna: Verlag der Österreichischen Akademie der Wissenschaften, 2015), 115–29.

[228] See n. 172.

[229] *PGM* P18.12–17, with M. Naldini, 'Due papiri cristiani della collezione fiorentina', *SIFC*, 33 (1961), 212–18 at 217.

[230] *P.Oxy.* LXXV 5024. Although the parchment is published in the Oxyrhynchus series, it and *P.Oxy.* LXXV 5023 may not have been found there; see *P.Oxy.* LXXV, p. 8.

[231] *P.Oxy.* LXXV 5024 intro. Image at *P.Oxy.* LXXV, plate VIII, and <http://www.papyrology. ox.ac.uk/> (Oxyrhynchus Online).

[232] *P.Oxy.* LXXV 5024.14–17 comm.; Cuming, *The Liturgy of St Mark*, 14, 26, 111–13. For a detailed survey of feasts or prayers for the flooding of the Nile in eastern liturgies, see K. Treu, 'Liturgische Traditionen in Ägypten (zu *P.Oxy.* 2782)', in P. Nagel (ed.), *Studia Coptica* (Berlin: Akademie-Verlag, 1974), 43–66, noting earlier studies at 47 n. 12.

[233] *P.Oxy.* LXXV 5024.18–23.   [234] *P.Oxy.* LXXV, p. 8.

[235] Brashear, *Magica Varia*, 64, lines 8–10, 12–14 (*SB* XVIII 13602).

[236] The epithet is applied to Mary by writers from the seventh century; see G. H. E. Lampe (ed.), *A Greek Patristic Lexicon* (Oxford: At the Clarendon Press, 1961), *s.v.* πανένδοξος. (A search of *Thesaurus Linguae Graecae* yielded no earlier instances.) It appears in one of the Fraction Prayers in the principal medieval manuscript of the Greek Liturgy of St Gregory; see Renaudot, *Liturgiarum orientalium collectio*, 1.106, with Gerhards, *Die griechische Gregoriosanaphora*, 14–19.

epithets—'Lady' and '*Theotokos*'—gave the scribe some trouble.[237] The scribe was familiar with the formula, but not its spelling, which suggests that his knowledge of the formula was primarily oral.

In a few other amulets the petitioner appeals directly to Mary. *SM* I 26 = *BKT* IX 206, assigned to the fifth century, reads as follows: '·✝· Having received grace from your only-begotten Son, stop the discharge, the pains of the eyes of Phoibammon, son of Athanasius. "He who dwells in the help of the Highest will reside in the shelter of the God of heaven" (LXX Ps. 90: 1).' The request is expressed in metre.[238] It follows a structure found in other iambic incantations to stop some discharge or pain: the imperative στῆσον ('stop'), followed by the discharge or pain, and then the affected part of the body.[239] Among the finds of Egypt, a precedent exists in a late third- or early fourth-century incantation against pain in the feet, written on a silver *lamella*.[240] Thus, this way of formulating a command against a discharge was not unknown. Consistent with the studied quality of the metric composition is the relative absence of phonetic spellings and what may be an uncommon use of a single dot above *upsilon* to indicate a rough breathing.[241] As it happens, the other amulet that contains a direct appeal to Mary, *PGM* P15b, also reveals a particular cultural debt. Assigned to the fifth or sixth century, it reads:

·✝· O angels, archangels, who guard the floodgates of heaven, who bring forth light upon the whole earth: because I am having a clash with a headless dog, seize him when he comes and release me through the power of the Father and the Son and the Holy Spirit, amen. A Ô Sabaôth. O *Theotokos*, incorruptible, undefiled, unstained mother of Christ, remember that you have said these things. Again heal her who wears this, amen. ✝·[242]

The first part of the amulet is a formula. It appears in another amulet with small variations, where it is followed by an appeal to 'the blood of my Christ,

---

[237] Brashear, *Magica Varia*, 64, lines 12–16: διὰ τῶν πρεσ- | βιῶν [read: πρεσβειῶν] τῆς' δετετουσης μ ⟦·····⟧ | τῆς δεσπήνης [read: δεσποίνης]· ὑμῶν [read: ἡμῶν] τῆς παν- | νενδόξου [read: πανενδόξου] θεωτωγουκου (read: θεοτόκου) καὶ ἀει- | παρθένου Μαρίας. Regarding δετετουσης μ ⟦·····⟧, Brashear, 68, comments: 'It appears that the writer was attempting to correct something erroneously written into δεσποίνης, gave up, crossed out the rest of the line and recommenced in the following line.'

[238] D. R. Jordan, 'Choliambs for Mary in a Papyrus Phylactery', *HTR*, 84 (1991), 343–6, doi: 10.1017/S0017816000024056, first recognized the metric quality of the lines. C. A. Faraone, 'Stopping Evil, Pain, Anger, and Blood: The Ancient Greek Tradition of Protective Iambic Incantations, *GRBS*, 49 (2009), 227–55 at 243 n. 46, <http://grbs.library.duke.edu/article/view/1121>, suggests that the metre may be, in part, iambic.

[239] Faraone, 'Stopping Evil', 243–6.

[240] *P.Köln* VIII 339; Faraone, 'Stopping Evil', 244–5.

[241] *SM* I 26.5: ϋιου; 7: ὑψι[στο]υ; see *SM* I 26.5 and 7 comm. The short left diagonal in the *upsilon* in υἱοῦ at line 2 is a blob that may be the unintended result of a stroke and a dot. Image at <http://smb.museum/berlpap/index.php/04918> (Berliner Papyrusdatenbank).

[242] ET: *ACM*, no. 24, slightly modified.

which was poured out in the place of a skull'.[243] The second part of the amulet betrays the influence of liturgical speech. The alpha-privative epithets ascribed to Mary recall the language of hymns and sermons,[244] as does the appellation 'mother of Christ'.[245] Yet the appeal was formulated in response to a specific encounter: the phrase 'remember that you have said these things' suggests that Mary had been consulted at a shrine or had appeared in a dream.

For the most part, the appeals to Mary or to her intercessions in the amulets we have just reviewed echo the language of the liturgy of the church. In none of the amulets do we find an incantation in which Mary herself, in the first person, summons healing power from God.[246] The absence is noteworthy because such incantations appear in a number of Coptic texts that have been classified as forms of the prayer of Mary 'in Bartos'.[247] An illustrative instance of this type of incantation is found in a group of incantations prepared for a certain 'Severus, son of Joanna' around the year 600.[248] This group is thus roughly contemporaneous with the Greek amulets we have been considering. The incantations combine Jewish, gnostic, apocryphal, canonical, and liturgical elements in vivid invocations, narratives, and adjurations. In the second incantation prepared for Severus, the speaker, Mary, first invokes power from God so that 'all things be subject to me [i.e., Mary], those of heaven and those of earth, and those that are beneath the earth'. Then the speaker continues in the first person: 'I am Mary, I am Miriam, I am the mother of life of the whole world, I am Mary. Let the stone [break], let the darkness break before me. [Let] the earth break. Let the iron dissolve. Let the demons retreat before me. Let the [...] appear to me. Let the archangels and angels come and speak with me until the Holy Spirit clears my path'.[249]

---

[243] *PGM* P15a (*P.Ross.Georg.* I 24); ET: *ACM*, no. 23.

[244] On the application of alpha-privative epithets to Mary, see N. Constas, *Proclus of Constantinople and the Cult of the Virgin in Late Antiquity: Homilies 1–5, Texts and Translations* (Leiden: E. J. Brill, 2003), 61 n. 55. For instances among hymns found in Egypt, see, e.g., *O.Camb.* 117.4–5, *O.Camb.* 118.4; *P.David* 5, no. e.27 (*O.Crum* Add. 39); I owe these references to Ágnes Mihálykó. For instances in the wider corpus of Greek hymns and sermons, see de Bruyn, 'Appeals to the Intercessions', 125 n. 124.

[245] Of thirty-eight instances of μήτηρ Χριστοῦ in *Thesaurus Linguae Graecae*, twenty are in hymns: one in Romanus Melodus, *Cant.*18, str. 18.1 (SC 110.302), and the remainder in *Analecta Hymnica Graeca*.

[246] What follows draws on T. S. de Bruyn, 'Greek Amulets from Egypt Invoking Mary as Expressions of "Lived Religion"', *JCSCS*, 3–4 (2012), 55–69 at 60–1, with permission from the publisher, Lockwood Press.

[247] See M. Meyer, *The Magical Book of Mary and the Angels (P. Heid. Inv. Kopt. 685): Text, Translation, and Commentary* (Heidelberg: Universitätsverlag C. Winter, 1996), 58, for extant versions of the prayer, with bibliography of editions, re-publications, and translations.

[248] London, British Library, Or. Ms. 6794; 6795; 6796 (2), (3), (1); 6796 (4), 6796, in *AKZ* 1.29–49; ET: *ACM*, nos. 129–32. Severus is named as the client in the first three incantations. The date is that assigned to the group by W. E. Crum at *AKZ* 1.xi.

[249] *AKZ* 1.35–40 at 36.20–30; ET: *ACM*, no. 131.

The only known Greek version of this prayer has recently been discovered in a crypt prepared for the twelfth-century archbishop of ancient Toungoul (modern Old Dongola) in Nubia.[250] The walls of the crypt are written with a series of texts that form an apotropaic programme. Prominent among them are Marian texts, including, on the north wall, a Greek text of the prayer of Mary 'in Bartos'. The scribe, who was more proficient in Coptic than in Greek, may have been copying from an exemplar. Though the evidence is medieval, it suggests that the prayer was circulating in Greek at an earlier time. So it is all the more interesting that the prayer does not surface in Greek amulets. Incidentally, the tradition to which the incantation alludes—the story of Mary offering her prayer in order to deliver the apostle Matthias from prison[251]—still informs devotional practices among Coptic Christians in Egypt today.[252]

6.4.2 The Forty Martyrs of Sebaste

By all indications the cult of the Forty Martyrs of Sebaste arrived relatively late in Egypt.[253] Whereas the Forty Martyrs were venerated in sanctuaries in Cappadocia, Pontus, and Armenia in the fourth century and in Constantinople, Syria, and Palestine in the fifth century,[254] the first mention of a sanctuary dedicated to the Forty Martyrs in Egypt, at Hermonthis, dates from the seventh century, as does a litany referring to them.[255] We know from various sources that the names of the martyrs had entered the repertoire of protective or powerful texts in Egypt around that time:[256] an amulet consisting of Mark 1: 2 and nine names of the forty;[257] an incantation to which four of the forty names are appended;[258] the Leiden codex mentioned in Chapter 3, containing many common Christian exorcistic and protective texts

---

[250] A. Łajtar and J. van der Vliet, 'Wall Inscriptions in a Burial Vault under the Northwest Annex of the Monastery on Kom H (Dongola 2009)', *PAM*, 21 (2009), 330–7, <http://www.pcma.uw.edu.pl/fileadmin/pam/PAM_2009_XXI/PAM21_Lajtar_Vliet.pdf>. On Toungoul, see <http://www.trismegistos.org/place/5080> (Trismegistos Geo). The town was located on the eastern bank of the Nile between the third and fourth cataract, about 80 kilometres south of New Dongola.

[251] Meyer, *The Magical Book of Mary*, 58; M. Meyer, 'The Prayer of Mary Who Dissolves Chains in Coptic Magic and Religion', in P. Mirecki and M. Meyer (eds), *Magic and Ritual in the Ancient World* (Leiden: Brill, 2002), 407–15.

[252] Meyer, 'The Prayer of Mary', 412–14.

[253] P. Maraval, 'Les premiers développements du culte des XL Martyrs de Sébastée dans l'Orient byzantin et en occident', *VetChr*, 36 (1999), 193–211 at 206–7.

[254] Maraval, 'Les premiers développements', 195–206.

[255] Papaconstantinou, *Le culte des saints*, 197.

[256] For an excellent overview of the evidence, see *P.Leid.Inst.*, pp. 32–6.

[257] *P.Ryl.Copt.* 101; see J. E. Sanzo, *Scriptural Incipits on Amulets from Late Antique Egypt: Text, Typology, and Theory* (Tübingen: Mohr Siebeck, 2014), 99.

[258] *BKU* I 8; see n. 102.

(including the correspondence between Abgar and Jesus, the names of the Forty Martyrs, the names of the Seven Sleepers of Ephesus, the titles and *incipits* of the gospels, and the *incipit* of LXX Ps. 90);[259] and inscriptions in a tomb reused as a Coptic church near ancient Pachora (modern Faras) in Nubia,[260] which, like the Leiden codex, include Jesus' letter to Abgar, the names of the Forty Martyrs (accompanied by the 'Sator' palindrome),[261] and the names of the Seven Sleepers.[262]

Greek and Coptic amulets with names of the Forty Martyrs are distinctive in that, apart from a few exceptions, they simply list names of the martyrs without any accompanying incantation or appeal. It is hard to imagine that the names would have been recognized as a source of protection or help apart from other dimensions of the cult, such as the regular reading of their martyrdom, services on feast days, accounts of healings or miracles, and the like. Therefore, despite the absence of incantations or appeals, amulets listing names of the Forty Martyrs offer additional evidence of the underlying importance of the broader cult of saints in making saints sources of power and assistance.

Almost all the Greek and Coptic amulets listing the names of the Forty Martyrs have been assigned to the seventh century or later;[263] one is assigned, tentatively, to the sixth century;[264] the remainder cannot be assigned with any certainty.[265] By the seventh century the names were circulating in lists with an established order, since most (but not all) of the extant amulets fall into groups

---

[259] Leiden, ms. AMS 9, published in W. Pleyte and P. A. A. Boeser, *Manuscrits coptes du Musée d'Antiquités des Pays-Bas à Leide* (Leiden: Brill, 1897), 441–77, with the list of the Forty Martyrs at 475–6. See Section 3.4.

[260] On Pachora, see <http://www.trismegistos.org/place/3170> (Trismegistos Geo). The town is located on the eastern bank of the Nile between Abu Simbul and the second cataract.

[261] On the 'Sator' palindrome, see, for an exhaustive review of the evidence, H. Hofmann, 'Satorquadrat', *PWSup*, 15.477–565, with examples from late antique Egypt at 483–7; and, on its meaning, M. Marcovich, 'Sator arepo = ΓΕΩΡΓΟC ἈΡΠΟΝ (ΚΝΟΥΦΙ) ἈΡΠΩC, arpo(cra), harpo(crates)', *ZPE*, 50 (1983), 155–71, <http://www.jstor.org/stable/20183770>.

[262] A. H. Sayce, 'Gleanings from the Land of Egypt', *RTPE*, 20 (1898), 169–76 at 174–6; R. Pietschmann, 'Les inscriptions coptes de Faras', *RTPE*, 21 (1899), 133–6; D. Hagedorn, 'PUG I 41 und die Namen der vierzig Märtyrer von Sebaste', *ZPE*, 55 (1984), 146–53 at 148 n. 14, <http://www.jstor.org/stable/20184025>.

[263] *BKU* I 8, in Beltz, 'Die koptischen Zauberpapyri', 68–70 (eighth century); *BKU* I 20, in Beltz, 'Die koptischen Zauberpapyri', 78 (ninth century); *P.Genova* I 41 (seventh–eighth century); *P.Leid.Inst.* 12 (*P.Select.* 25[iii]) (seventh–eighth century), probably but not certainly an amulet, as discussed at *P.Leid.Inst.*, p. 35; C. Gallazzi, 'O. Mil. Vogl. Inv. Provv. CE 2: amuleto coi nomi dei Martiri di Sebastia', *ZPE*, 75 (1988), 147–9, <http://www.uni-koeln.de/phil-fak/ifa/zpe/downloads/1988/075pdf/075.html> (seventh–eighth century).

[264] *P.Eleph.Wagner* 322, re-edited in A. Delattre, 'Noms rares et noms fantômes dans trois ostraca grec d'Éléphantine', *CdE*, 85 (2010), 363–73 at 363–6, doi: 10.1484/J.CDE.1.102045 (sixth century?).

[265] *BKU* I 19, in Beltz, 'Die koptischen Zauberpapyri', 67–8 (no date given); *O.CrumST* 443 (no date given); D. Hagedorn and K. A. Worp, 'Ostraka der Sammlung Kaufmann in Beuron', *ZPE*, 146 (2004), 159–64 at 164, <http://www.jstor.org/stable/20191759> (Byzantine era).

according to the ordering of the names.[266] This indicates that veneration for the Forty Martyrs was already being advanced in a systematic way in Egypt. At the same time, the format of the lists could vary (written down in columns or across in rows),[267] as could the spelling of the names.[268] Such variability is to be expected, given independent channels of transmission and shifts due to the language and orthography of the transmitter. It shows that appeals to saints like the Forty Martyrs were subject to a measure of variation as a consequence of being spread across different locales.

6.4.3 Summary

Amulets appealing to saints constitute part of the evidence for the cult of saints in late antique Egypt. There are numerous indications that appeals to saints in amulets are an extension of the role and function of saints in the liturgy of the church and the lives of Christians. The fact that most of the saints invoked in amulets were widely venerated with sanctuaries and feast days is one indication. In one amulet, as we have seen, we can identify the saints named with sanctuaries and feast days in the town where the amulet was found. The formulaic phrasing of appeals to the intercessions of saints would also appear to derive from formal or liturgical prayers. Sometimes the appeal is more direct and informal, but nevertheless suggests a prior interaction with the saint in the context of a wider cult. As Arietta Papaconstantinou has observed,[269] when the house phylactery from Oxyrhynchus declares that 'Saint Phocas is here', it could be referring to the presence enacted by the incantation itself or it could be referring to a eulogion of the saint already present in the house (an inscription, an image, or some other token).[270] Such a eulogion could have been procured through a visit to the saint's sanctuary in Oxyrhynchus. Likewise, the amulet that alludes to a promise received from Mary suggests that the petitioner had some prior communication with the saint. One possible context for such communication could, again, have been a church dedicated to Mary. The amulets, exercises, graffiti, and manuscripts listing all or some of the names of the Forty Martyrs of Sebaste, too, can be explained only as a product of growing veneration for that group of martyrs in the Egyptian church after the sixth century, which in time found expression in an important feast day in the Coptic calendar, dedicated sanctuaries and monasteries, a wall painting, and distinctively Coptic hagiographical texts.[271]

---

[266] *P.Leid.Inst.*, p. 36.   [267] *P.Leid.Inst.*, p. 36.

[268] Hagedorn, 'PUG I 41', 147–51.   [269] Papaconstantinou, *Le culte des saints*, 345.

[270] On eulogia, see A. Stuiber, 'Eulogia', *RAC*, 6.900–28 at 925–7.

[271] J. Simon, 'Le culte des XL Martyrs dans l'Égypte chrétienne', *Orientalia*, 3 (1934), 174–6, <http://www.jstor.org/stable/43581001>.

6.5 'ALTERNATIVE' DOXOLOGICAL TRADITIONS

The expressions used to refer to God in the liturgy of the church were traditional in the sense that they repeated formulae received from previous generations of worshipers. But these received ways of offering praise and prayers to God were at the same time susceptible to innovation, as when, for example, the earliest followers of Jesus began to address prayers to God 'through Jesus Christ'—an innovation that would become a tradition. Sometimes these innovations were programmatic. An obvious example is the adoption of coordinate trinitarian formulae toward the end of the fourth century in reaction to subordinationist trinitarian theologies.[272] Sometimes the impetus is more diffuse and harder to pinpoint, as in the emergence of formulae highlighting the intercessory role of Mary *Theotokos*, Mary venerated as the 'God-bearer'.[273] Even when the impetus is evident, the process is hardly tidy, as one can see from the various trinitarian formulations used by Christian writers in the fourth and fifth centuries.[274] While some theologians adopted a purely coordinate trinitarian formula, praising God 'with' the Son and 'with' the Holy Spirit, others made use of a hybrid formula as well, offering praise to God 'through and with' the Son and 'with' the Holy Spirit.[275] The latter, preferred by Cyril of Alexandria, appears in early witnesses to the anaphora of St Mark/St Cyril,[276] and is widely used in Greek and Coptic prayers from the sixth to the eighth century.[277]

The doxological formulae that make their way into incantations with Christian elements echo, for the most part, the theological and liturgical usage of the institutional church after the fourth century. For instance—to focus for the moment on trinitarian language in incantations—praise is offered 'to the Father and the Son and the Holy Spirit',[278] prayer is given 'in the name of the Father and the Son and the Holy Spirit',[279] and deliverance is sought 'through the power of the Father and the Son and the Holy Spirit'.[280] The coordinate trinitarian formula was heard and spoken so often in Christian rituals—in salutations,

---

[272] Jungmann, *The Place of Christ*, 184–6, 192–13.

[273] L. M. Peltomaa and A. Külzer, '*Presbeia Theotokou*: An Introduction', in Peltomaa, Külzer, and Allen, *Presbeia Theotokou*, 11–21.

[274] For an analysis of the various formulae and their frequencies in the sources, see J. M. Hanssens, *La liturgie d'Hippolyte: documents et études* (Rome: Università gregoriana, 1970), 167–8, 178–83.

[275] Hanssens, *La liturgie d'Hippolyte*, 190–1.

[276] Hammerstaedt, *Griechische Anaphorenfragmente*, 24, 29–31 (P.Strasb. G inv. 254r.10–11 text and commentary); Cuming, *The Liturgy of St. Mark*, 79.

[277] Mihálykó, 'Writing the Christian Liturgy in Egypt', 205 (comment on *O.Frangé* 730.12–15).

[278] *PGM* P5d.1–2 (*P.Lond.Lit.* 231); *PGM* P19.5–6 (*PSI* VI 719).

[279] *BKT* VI 7.1.1; *SM* I 31.4 (*P.Turner* 49) = *BKT* IX 134; *SM* I 36.1.

[280] *PGM* P15a.18–22 (*P.Ross.Georg.* I 24); *PGM* P15b.5–6.

invocations, doxologies, and benedictions—that it is hardly surprising that it appears with some regularity in incantations. But for that very reason it is intriguing when the phrasing of the formula is irregular, as in the case of *PGM* P16 (*P.Ross.Georg.* I 23), where, as we discussed in Chapter 4, the scribe writes: 'For there is only one Lord, [only one] God, in the Son [and] in the Father and the Holy Spirit, for ever and ever, amen.'[281] Variants like this, as well as the more frequent and less substantive vagaries of phrasing or spelling, remind us that in the decentralized sphere of amulet production tradition is malleable, whether by intention, informality, ignorance, or carelessness.

In much of this chapter we have focused on the relationship between incantations with Christian elements and the rituals of the institutionally established church in Egypt. This is not accidental. When incantations with Christian elements echo liturgical language or evoke ritual practices, an association can usually be made (and documented) with the rituals of the institutional church, which themselves varied over time and from place to place. But a number of amulets reveal that the traditions on which some scribes drew or within which some scribes worked fell outside of what had come to be accepted as, more or less, 'orthodox' Christianity.

Sometimes all we have to go on is a liturgical phrase or allusion. This is the case with the *historiola* in *P.Oxy.* XI 1384, the sheet of recipes we discussed in Chapter 3, that refers to '[those] who believe in the [name of the] Father and the Holy [Spirit and the] Son'. A similar, but even more enigmatic, reference is found in three amulets from Oxyrhynchus written by a single scribe for three different women. One amulet has long been known, *PGM* P5a (*P.Oxy.* VI 924);[282] the two others have just been published, *P.Oxy.* LXXXII 5306 and 5307.[283] All three are written in a compressed semi-cursive hand with frequent adjoining letters,[284] assigned to the fourth century.[285] These amulets give us another rare glimpse of how a scribe might adapt resources with which he was familiar to the occasion at hand when writing amulets for different individuals.[286] *P.Oxy.* LXXXII 5306, composed for a certain Eulogia, is considerably longer than the other two and incorporates, in a somewhat discombobulated way, material which will not be discussed here.[287] *P.Oxy.* VI 924 and *P.Oxy.*

---

[281] *PGM* P16.19–23 (*P.Ross.Georg.* I 23).

[282] See now the re-edition by F. Maltomini, 'PGM P 5a rivisitato', *Galenos*, 9 (2015), 229–34, which supersedes the transcription in M. de Haro Sanchez, 'Le vocabulaire de la pathologie et de la thérapeutique dans les papyrus iatromagiques grecs: fièvres, traumatismes et "épilepsie"', *BASP*, 47 (2010), 131–53 at 135, <http://hdl.handle.net/2027/spo.0599796.0047.001>.

[283] *P.Oxy.* LXXXII, published in 2016, includes three formularies and nine amulets, several of which have Christian elements. Regrettably, I was unable to take these items into account more extensively, as they were published after the manuscript of this book was completed.

[284] Images at de Haro Sanchez, 'Le vocabulaire', 136; *P.Oxy.* LXXXII, plate III.

[285] *P.Oxy.* VI 924 intro., followed by *P.Oxy.* LXXXII, p. 76.

[286] Cf. the discussion in Section 4.3.2 of the Coptic curses written for Mary and Jacob.

[287] See F. Maltomini's detailed comments at *P.Oxy.* LXXXII, pp. 79–89.

LXXXII 5307, composed for Aria and Bassa respectively, are similar to one another in length and formulation; without naming the power addressed, the incantations enjoin that the women be protected from several types of fever. All three incantations conclude with a formulaic rationale for what is enjoined (which in all three instances has a redundant *eta*, possibly the result of an earlier conflation of two expressions),[288] followed by an acclamation written out in a visual scheme and framed by a line border. The language of the formulaic rationale, which is almost identical in *P.Oxy.* VI 924 and *P.Oxy.* LXXXII 5307 ('in accordance with your will first and in accordance with her faith, because she is a servant of the living God, in order that your name may be glorified forever'),[289] corresponds in many ways to the phraseology of Christian scriptures and prayers.[290] Either the scribe of these amulets or his sources were formed in a Christian milieu. Particularly distinctive are two echoes from the Book of Daniel: the expression 'servant of the living God', found in Theodotion's translation of Dan. 6: 21 (but not in the LXX),[291] and the clause 'that your name may be glorified forever', recalling Dan. 3: 26 (reprised in Ode 7: 26).

What interests us here is the final acclamation written out in a visual scheme. Since it is present in all three amulets with only minor variations,[292] its design can now be established despite lacunae on account of wear in each individual instance. In the centre of the scheme is a large cross with 'Father, Son, Mother' (πατήρ υἱός μήτηρ) straddling the two upper quadrants and *alpha* and *omega*, 'Holy Spirit' (with 'Spirit' written as the *nomen sacrum* π̅ν̅α̅ and 'Holy' written, irregularly, as ἅγιος rather than ἅγιον), and 'Abrasax' straddling the two lower quadrants. Above and alongside the top half of the scheme is the acclamation 'Power of Jesus Christ', employing *nomina sacra* for 'Jesus' and Christ in the genitive (ι̅υ̅, χ̅υ̅) written in large letters alongside the cross formation, 'Jesus' on the left and 'Christ' on the right. (This reading, initially proposed by Karl Preisendanz when reconstructing the lacunose line in *P.Oxy.* VI 924,[293] is now confirmed by the other two amulets.[294]) Circling

---

[288] *P.Oxy.* LXXXII 5306.11–13 comm.

[289] *P.Oxy.* VI 924.7–13; *P.Oxy.* LXXXII 5307.12–17.

[290] *P.Oxy.* LXXXII 5306.39–42 comm.; *P.Oxy.* LXXXII 5307.12–13 comm.

[291] A. Rahlfs (ed.), *Septuaginta: id est, Vetus Testamentum Graece iuxta lxx interpretes, editio minor*, 2 vols in 1 (Stuttgart: Württembergische Bibelanstalt, 1935), 2.908. While incantations with and without Christian elements may refer to a person as a 'servant' (or 'slave') of God, the expression 'servant of the living God' is not attested elsewhere; see, e.g., *PGM* XII.71; *PGM* XIII.637; *PGM* P5b.10, 29 (*P.Oxy.* VIII 1151); *PGM* P5c.4, 10 (*P.Cair.Cat.* 10696); *PGM* P6d.4; *PGM* P9.8, 29 (*BGU* III 954).

[292] *P.Oxy.* VI 924.14–18; *P.Oxy.* LXXXII 5306.43–7; *P.Oxy.* LXXXII 5307.18–23.

[293] *PGM* P5a.15.

[294] Maltomini, 'PGM P 5a rivisitato', 233; *P.Oxy.* LXXXII 5306.43–4 comm. I arrived at the same reading when examining *P.Oxy.* VI 924 for a paper delivered at the Seventeenth International Conference on Patristic Studies in 2015, T. S. de Bruyn, 'Historians, Bishops, Amulets, Scribes, and Rites: Interpreting Christian Practice', *StudPatr*, forthcoming.

the left, top, and right sides of the cross are a series of dots that vary in number on account of lacunae; six can be observed in *P.Oxy.* VI 924, which is intact in this regard. Flanking the scheme are the seven vowels written vertically in two columns, $a \; \epsilon \; \eta \; \iota$ along the left and $o \; \upsilon \; \omega$ along the right (the position varies slightly in *P.Oxy.* LXXII 5306).

What are we to make of this visual display, particularly the sequence 'Father, Son, Mother'? It has been suggested that 'Mother' refers to the Holy Spirit.[295] Indeed, as Roberta Mazza observes in her discussion of the sequence Father–Holy Spirit–Son in *P.Oxy.* XI 1384,[296] the Holy Spirit or Mother appears as a figure between the Father and the Son in several ancient Christian traditions.[297] But then why is the Holy Spirit named in the next line? I have suggested that the scheme in the amulet may derive from a Sethian tradition.[298] In Sethian writings, a triad of beings comprises the first unfolding of the transcendent invisible Spirit.[299] The members of the triad are given various names,[300] but in one christianizing strand of the tradition, they are identified as Father, Mother, and Son.[301] Normally Mother is in the second position,[302] but there are exceptions. In *Melchizedek* (NH IX,1) 5.23–6.10, 'a basically Christian work which has been Sethianized',[303] the first three acclamations in a 'thrice holy' litany are addressed to the Father of All, an incomplete name that appears to refer to the Son, and the Mother of the aeons, Barbelo.[304] In some versions of the Sethian system, the Holy Spirit is presented as a figure immediately below the primary triad,[305] as in our amulets, while Abrasax appears among the last set of beings to unfold from the triad.[306] As regards the seven vowels, in one Sethian work, *The Gospel of the Egyptians*, they issue from

---

[295] *ACM*, p. 39; for supporting evidence, see R. Mazza, '*P.Oxy.* XI, 1384: medicina, rituali di guarigione e cristianesimi nell'Egitto tardoantico', *ASE*, 24/2 (2007), 437–62 at 449–50.

[296] Mazza, '*P.Oxy.* XI, 1384', 449–50.   [297] See Chapter 3 nn. 68–72.

[298] De Bruyn, 'Historians'.

[299] A. Böhlig, 'Triade und Trinität in den Schriften von Nag Hammadi', in B. Layton (ed.), *The Rediscovery of Gnosticism*, vol. 2: *Sethian Gnosticism* (Leiden: Brill, 1981), 617–34; J. D. Turner, *Sethian Gnosticism and the Platonic Tradition* (Leuven: Peters, 2001), 60–4.

[300] Turner, *Sethian Gnosticism*, 255–301.   [301] Turner, *Sethian Gnosticism*, 284–90.

[302] E.g., *Ap. John* (NH II,1 9.10–11; BG 2 19; NH III,1 13.15–6), in *The Apocryphon of John: Synopsis of Nag Hammadi Codices II,1; III,1; and IV,1 with BG 8502,2*, ed. M. Waldstein and F. Wisse, NHMS 33 (Leiden: Brill, 1995), 54–5; *Gos. Eg.* (NH III,2 41.9; NH IV,2 50.25–6), in *Nag Hammadi Codices III,2 and IV,2: The Gospel of the Egyptians (The Holy Book of the Great Invisible Spirit)*, ed. A. Böhlig and F. Wisse, NHMS 4 (Leiden: Brill 1975), 54–5.

[303] Turner, *Sethian Gnosticism*, 101.

[304] *Melch.* (NH IX,1) 5.23–7, in *Melchisédek (NH IX,1): oblation, baptême et vision dans la gnose séthienne*, ed. W.-P. Funk, comm. C. Gianotto, BCNH, section 'Textes' 28 (Laval: Presses de l'Université Laval; Louvain and Paris: Peeters, 2001), 72; commentary at 132. See Turner, *Sethian Gnosticism*, 176–7.

[305] Turner, *Sethian Gnosticism*, 288.

[306] *Gos. Eg.* (NH III,2 52.26–53.1; NH IV,2 64.21–3), in Böhlig and Wisse, *Nag Hammadi Codices III,2 and IV,2*, 104–5; exposition at 26–8.

the Son in the course of the primary unfolding the transcendent invisible Spirit as an expression of his plenitude and his mysterious name.[307]

However persuasive such observations may be, in the end we must admit that we cannot determine exactly what tradition(s) the scribe of these amulets (or his sources) may have been drawing upon, in part because of the simplicity of the scheme, which provides too little specificity to allow us to match it with more elaborate and developed liturgical or theological texts. In fact, the scribe may not have been all that cognizant of the tradition(s) that generated the sequence of names and letters that appear in the scheme—tradition(s) which, evidently, were different from those which prevailed in the institutional church after the fourth century. The syntactical redundancy in the formulaic rationale and the irregular spelling of 'holy' in the visual scheme certainly suggest that the scribe was depending on a model which he did not fully comprehend. Nevertheless, the scheme must have held some significance for him, however inarticulate, since he employs it as a talismanic signature in all three of the amulets. Indeed, this the most remarkable feature of these amulets: the repeated use of a symbolic scheme whose execution reveals that it was customary and habitual for the scribe, and whose formulation varies from what would become the authorized tradition of the institutional church.

Our second example, *PGM* P21,[308] gives us a bit more to work with. It is a formulaic incantation intended to bring the client favour and success (a *charitêsion*).[309] Originally assigned to the fourth century, then to the fifth or sixth century, it would appear to have been written in the fourth or fifth century.[310] The invocation is replete with Christian phraseology.[311] It follows the pattern of early Christian prayers in calling upon 'God almighty … through our Lord Jesus Christ, the beloved child'.[312] The attributes ascribed to God—'who is above every ruler and authority and lordship and every name that is named'[313]—echo Eph. 1: 21. The epithet applied to Christ—'the beloved child'[314]—recalls

---

[307] *Gos. Eg.* (NH III,2 42.21–43.4, 43.23–44.9; NH IV,2 52.15–24, 53.26–54.13), in Böhlig and Wisse, *Nag Hammadi Codices III,2 and IV,2*, 62–3, 66–9; commentary at 172–3.

[308] The first edition remains valuable: T. Hopfner, 'Ein neuer griechischer Zauberpapyrus (Pap. Wessely Pragens. Graec. No. 1)', *ArOr*, 7 (1935), 355–66. For a revised reading of line 45, see T. S. de Bruyn, 'A Late Witness to Valentinian Devotion in Egypt?' *ZAC*, 18 (2013), 120–33 at 124 n. 17, doi: 10.1515/zac-2014-0008. I thank Professor Rosario Pintaudi for providing me with a digital image of the papyrus. ET: *ACM*, no. 36 (based on the text in *PGM*).

[309] On *charitêsia*, see J. F. Quack, 'From Ritual to Magic: Ancient Egyptian Precursors of the Charitesion and their Social Setting', in G. Bohak, Y. Harari, and S. Shaked (eds), *Continuity and Innovation in the Magical Tradition* (Leiden: Brill, 2011), 43–84; T. S. de Bruyn, 'An Anatomy of Tradition: The Case of the *Charitêsion*', *ARG*, 16 (2015), 31–50, doi: 10.1515/arege-2014-0005.

[310] On the successive datings, see de Bruyn, 'A Late Witness', 126–7.

[311] *PGM* P21.1–8.

[312] *PGM* P21.7–8. On prayer addressed to God through Christ, see J. A. Jungmann, *The Place of Christ in Liturgical Prayer*, tr. A. Peeler, 2nd edn (Staten Island: Alba House, 1965), 144–71.

[313] *PGM* P21.2–5.   [314] *PGM* P21.8.

the phraseology of ante-Nicene Christian prayers,[315] still employed in Christian discourse in the fourth century but no longer used after the fifth century.[316]

The prayer, so begun, continues with a customary request,[317] found in other Greek and Coptic incantations,[318] to be surrounded on all sides by divine or angelic powers:

> Send forth to me, Master, your holy archangels, who stand opposite your holy altar, appointed to your holy services, Gabriêl,[319] Michaêl, Raphaêl, Sarouêl, Ragouêl, Nouriêl, Anaêl. Let them accompany me today, during all the hours of day and night, granting me victories, favour, success with N, good luck with all people, small and great, with whom I may have dealings today, during all the hours of day and night. For I have before me Jesus Christ, who travels with me and accompanies me; behind me Iaô Sabaôth Adônai; on my right and left the God of Abraham, Isaac, Jacob; before my face and my heart (?) Gabriêl, Michaêl, Raphaêl, Sarouêl, Ragouêl, Nouriêl, Anaêl. Protect me from every demon, male or female, and from every stratagem and from every name, for I am sheltered under the wings of the cherubim.[320]

The *charitêsion* concludes with an unusual doxology, which brings it into our purview here: 'Jesus Christ, you king of all the aeons, almighty, inexpressible creator, nourisher, master, almighty; you child, benevolent son, my unutterable and inexpressible name, truly true form, unseen forever and ever, amen.'[321] I have argued elsewhere that this doxology recalls language used in Valentinian writings to describe the relationship of the Son to the Father and, in turn, of the Christian to the Father.[322] The transcendent Father is known only in the Son. The Son is the 'Name' and the 'Form' of the Father. The saving self-revelation of the Father in the Son is analogous to giving a name or giving form. In the rite of baptism, accordingly, the initiated are said to receive the 'Name'. In Valentinian treatises all of this is articulated in complex language that strains to convey the transcendence of the Father and

---

[315] A. von Harnack, 'Die Bezeichnung Jesu als "Knecht Gottes" und ihre Geschichte in der alten Kirche', *SPAW*, 28 (1926), 212–38; repr. in A. von Harnack, *Kleine Schriften zur alten Kirche: Berliner Akademieschriften 1908–1930* (Leipzig: Zentralantiquariat der Deutschen Demokratischen Republik, 1980), 730–56; W. Zimmerli and J. Jeremias, 'παῖς θεοῦ', *TDNT*, 5.654–717 at 702–3.

[316] D. Ison, 'ΠΑΙΣ ΘΕΟΥ in the Age of Constantine', *JTS*, n.s. 38 (1987), 412–19, <http://www.jstor.org/stable/23962954>; C. Horn and J. W. Martens, *'Let the Little Children Come to Me': Childhood and Children in Early Christianity* (Washington, D.C.: The Catholic University of America Press, 2009), 61–5.

[317] Hopfner, 'Ein neuer griechischer Zauberpapyrus', 363–4.

[318] *P.Kramer* 2; *AKM*, 3.76–8.

[319] It is unusual, but not without parallel, that Gabriel is named first in the list of seven archangels; see *SM* II 61.1 (n. 209 above).

[320] Translation mine.

[321] *PGM* P21.41–9, revised in de Bruyn, 'A Late Witness', 118–19.

[322] De Bruyn, 'A Late Witness', 121–3.

the generation of the Son in the Father. The superlatives in the doxology in the *charitêsion* likewise strive to express the inexpressible.

A scribal peculiarity of the *charitêsion* offers further evidence of a Valentinian connection. The scribe uses a four-letter abbreviation for Χριστός (rather than the more common two- or three-letter form) with *eta* instead of *iota*.[323] *Nomina sacra* with *eta* are rare.[324] But the full form χρηϲτοϲ is frequently used in Valentinian works in the Nag Hammadi codices,[325] and the abbreviation ⲡⲉⲭⲣ̄ⲏ̄ⲥ occurs once in the Valentinian *Tripartite Tractate*,[326] along with the more common ⲡⲉⲭⲣ̄ⲥ̄ and ⲡⲉⲭ̄ⲥ̄. Such forms could have been known to the scribe, since he wrote in Coptic as well as Greek, as the Coptic postscript to the *charitêsion* shows.[327]

We cannot know to what extent the writer of this amulet was improvising on an established manner of speaking about Christ, but we should assume that composers of incantations could modulate doxological materials with a certain amount of freedom and creativity. We have a remarkable instance of this in *PGM* P13 (*P.Cair.Cat.* 10263). This long invocation and request for protection, originally published by Adolf Jacoby in 1900,[328] has now been thoroughly re-examined by Ágnes Mihálykó,[329] who assigns it to the first half of the fifth century.[330] The invocation is indebted to credal summaries of Christ's career for the structure and substance of its narrative of the incarnation, childhood, crucifixion, resurrection, post-resurrection appearance, and ascension of Jesus (lines 1–5). The writer expands on that narrative in ways that are unexpected, though not necessarily without parallel in wider Christian tradition. He refers, for instance, to Jesus as 'the fullness of the aion' who 'broke the claw of Charon' and 'came through Gabriel in the womb of Mary'.[331]

---

[323] Line 8: ⲓ̄ⲏ̄ⲩ̄ χρ[η]ῡ (the right vertical of *eta* is visible); lines 26–7: ⲓ̄ⲏ̄ⲩ̄ χρης (as an accusative); line 41: ⲓ̄ⲏ̄ⲥ̄ χρης.

[324] De Bruyn, 'A Late Witness', 124.

[325] *Treatise on the Resurrection* (NHC I,5) 43.37, 48.19, 50.1, in *Nag Hammadi Codex I (The Jung Codex)*, ed. H. W. Attridge et al., 2 vols, NHMS 22–3 (Leiden: E. J. Brill, 1985), 1.148, 154, 156; *Tripartite Tractate* (NHC I,5) 122.19, in *Le Traité Tripartite (NH I, 5)*, ed. E. Thomassen, BCNH, section 'Textes' 19 (Québec: Les Presses de l'Université Laval, 1989), 222; *Valentinian Exposition* (NHC XI,2) 26.23, 28.23, 33.17, 39.30, 40.13, 40.19, 40.33, 41.17, 42.32–3, 43.37–8, in *Concordance des textes de Nag Hammadi: les codices X et XIA*, ed. W.-P. Funk, BCNH, section 'Concordances' 6 (Québec: Presses de l'Université Laval and Louvain: Peeters, 2000), 321, 323, 325, 326, 327.

[326] *Tripartite Tractate* (NHC I,5) 136.1, in Thomassen, *Le Traité Tripartite (NH I, 5)*, 254.

[327] *PGM* P21.50–3; see de Bruyn, 'A Late Witness', 125–6.

[328] A. Jacoby, *Ein neues Evangelienfragment* (Strassburg: Karl J. Trübner 1900), 31–47; ET: *ACM*, no. 10 (now superseded by that of Mihálykó, n. 329).

[329] A. T. Mihálykó, 'Christ and Charon: PGM P13 Reconsidered', *SO*, 89 (2016), 183–209, doi: 10.1080/00397679.2015.1108051. Image at <http://ipap.csad.ox.ac.uk/Varia.html> (Photographic Archive of Papyri in the Cairo Museum).

[330] Mihálykó, 'Christ and Charon', 184.

[331] On this phraseology, see Mihálykó, 'Christ and Charon', 189–93 (lines 1–3 comm.) As Mihálykó explains, 'the claw of Charon' probably derives from the biblical expression 'the sting

The account of Christ's career culminates in a form of the *Sanctus* that echoes the pre-*Sanctus* and *Sanctus* of the Eucharist, but also deviates from it (lines 5–8)—another instance of a debt that is modulated with considerable freedom. The invocation continues—the division of the text into an invocation and an epiclesis (as I once supposed) can no longer be sustained in view of the corrected reading of ἐλεεθ ἐλε ̓ε ̓θ instead of ἐλθ[έ] τὸ ἔλεο[s] at line 8[332]— with what is by now a well and widely established tradition of Christ's descent into Hades.[333] The author recounts how souls are released from Hades, how its gates opened up and its bars are shattered, how Death is made impotent and the Devil is bound and cast down (lines 9–14). After this long invocation, the incantation concludes with a request for protection from 'the principalities and powers and cosmic rulers of darkness, or an unclean spirit, or fall of a demon at noontide, or chill, or fever, or ague, or harm from people or powers of the adversary' (lines 15–17).[334] Throughout the entire text the author freely adapts biblical phraseology to a Hellenistic idiom in an effort at rhetorical sophistication.[335] The result is a unique yet layered product that attests to both the scope of traditions available to the author and the author's individuality in appropriating those traditions.

In each of the above examples (as well as elsewhere in this chapter) we are obliged to infer a hypothetical liturgical or doxological context from the text of the amulet, since we have only the artefacts as our point of departure, without any information about their archaeological or social context. In the case of amulets from Kellis (modern Ismant el-Kharab) in the Dakhleh Oasis, how-ever, we have the rare good fortune to treat artefacts that were unearthed in a controlled archaeological excavation and published in the context of other materials. This context is particularly relevant for our consideration of 'alter-native' liturgical and doxological traditions, since a significant concentration of Manichaean materials was found in a group of houses in a residential quarter in the town (Group 1, comprising Houses 1, 2, and 3 and the adjacent North Building).[336] Among these materials are fragments of a Coptic codex containing canonical works by Mani, Manichaean psalms and liturgical texts, Coptic-Syriac glossaries of Manichaean technical terms, fragments from the Letter to the Romans and the Letter to the Hebrews, and personal letters written in Greek and Coptic that contain distinctive Manichaean terminology

---

of death' (Hos. 13: 14; 1 Cor. 15: 55) by way of its Coptic translation, given that the Coptic word for 'sting' (ϩⲓⲃ) can also take the meaning 'claw'.

[332] Mihálykó, 'Christ and Charon', 186–7, 195 (line 8 comm.)

[333] See R. Gounelle, *La descente du Christ aux enfers: institutionnalisation d'une croyance* (Paris: Institut d'Études Augustiniennes, 2000).

[334] ET: Mihálykó, 'Christ and Charon', 188.   [335] Mihálykó, 'Christ and Charon', 201–4.

[336] For a description of the site and the stratigraphy, see *P.Kellis* V, pp. 99–102; additional bibliography at *P.Kellis* VII, p. 6 n. 2.

and were presumably written by Manichaean believers.[337] The majority of these materials were found in House 3, though there are links among documents or fragments found in all the houses in Group 1.[338] Datable documents and coins found on the site span most of the period from the closing years of the third century to the second last decade of the fourth.[339] Most of the Coptic documents appear to have been written between 355 and 380.[340] They include letters written over several generations by and to members of the family of Macarius, a Manichaean family group living in House 3.[341] The site appears to have been abandoned in the early 390s.

Two sorts of evidence from this site are of particular interest to us—texts that were undoubtedly formularies or amulets and texts that, it has been suggested, were used as amulets. We begin with the former. Fragments of a Greek formulary preserving portions of three prescriptions were found in House 3 (*P.Kellis* I 85a and 85b), as well as several Greek amulets against fever (*P.Kellis* I 86 and 87, and a mostly illegible amulet noted at *P.Kellis* I 86.16 comm.). *P.Kellis* I 87 was found in the same room as the fragments of the formulary (in adjoining sedimentary layers), and was very likely copied from it, as it repeats much of what is found in *P.Kellis* I 85b.[342] The texts are customary incantations that incorporate many elements typical of such formulations, such as *charaktêres*, *voces mysticae*, the seven vowels written in diminishing and increasing word-shapes, the injunction to 'deliver' (ἀπάλλαξον) the person in question, and the accelerating formula (only in the mostly illegible amulet). None of the texts contains elements that are distinctively Christian (whether non-Manichaean or Manichaean),[343] although the incantation in *P.Kellis* I 86 is flanked by the names 'Raphaêl, Michaêl' in the left margin and the names 'Ouriêl, Gabriêl' in the right margin. In short, there is nothing distinctively Manichaean in these materials.

---

[337] For an overview, see I. Gardner, 'The Manichaean Community at Kellis: A Progress Report', in P. Mirecki and J. D. BeDuhn (eds), *Emerging from Darkness: Studies in the Recovery of Manichean Sources* (Leiden: Brill, 1997), 161–75 at 162–7. The Manichaean and associated texts have been published in *P.Kellis* II and VI, the Greek documents have been published in *P.Kellis* I, and the Coptic documents have been published in *P.Kellis* V and VII. Many of the Coptic personal letters contain Manichaean terminology or were written by Manichaeans; see *P.Kellis* V, pp. 72–82; *P.Kellis* VII, pp. 29–30. One Greek letter, *P.Kellis* I 63, has been identified as Manichaean.

[338] *P.Kellis* VII, p. 7. [339] *P.Kellis* V, pp. 109–15 and table 6.

[340] *P.Kellis* V, pp. 8–11; *P.Kellis* VII, p. 6. [341] *P.Kellis* V, pp. 56, 107.

[342] See *P.Kellis* I, p. 214; *P.Kellis* I 85b.16–19 comm.; and *P.Kellis* I 87.1 comm.

[343] As Gardner, 'The Manichaean Community at Kellis', 171–3, argues, Manichaeans at Kellis (and elsewhere) regarded themselves as 'true' Christians and the 'true' church. On the slow trend in scholarship to recognize in Manichaeism a form of Christianity, see T. Pettipiece, 'Manichaeism at the Crossroads of Jewish, Christian, and Muslim Traditions', in B. Bitton-Ashkelony, T. S. de Bruyn, and C. Harrison (eds), *Patristic Studies in the Twenty-first Century: Proceedings of an International Conference to Mark the 50th Anniversary of the International Association of Patristic Studies* (Turnhout: Brepols, 2015), 299–313 at 301–3.

The same can be said of an incantation copied in a letter sent by a Mani-chaean scribe, Valens (in Greek, Ouales), to his colleague, Pshai, *P.Kellis* V 35.[344] The incantation, a 'separation curse' meant to create discord between two people, happened to be in Valens' possession. He sent it instead of another incantation that he intended to send but could not find.[345] (The small fragment of papyrus on which the latter was written had gone missing—a telltale detail as to how incantations were kept by individuals.) There is nothing distinctively Manichaean in the incantation that Valens copied (unless one thinks that the Chaldeans mentioned in the *historiola* discussed below are an oblique reference to Zoroastrian opponents to Mani in the Persian Empire).[346] The invocation calls upon 'the one who has been from the beginning; the one sitting above the Cheroubin and Sarouphin; the one who stands (in judgement) over disputes and quarrels; the one who has stopped the winds with his great power!'[347] It is likely that 'the one who has stopped the winds with his great power' is an allusion to the story of Jesus stilling the storm (Mark 4: 35–41 = Matt. 8: 23–7 = Luke 8: 22–5).[348] But this story, like the other elements of the invocation,[349] would be part of a wider tradition that both non-Manichaean and Manichaean Christians might draw upon. The incantation is followed by an enigmatic *historiola* that appears to refer to the retreat of the Chaldeans from the city of Jerusalem at the approach of an army from Egypt, events recounted in Jer. 37: 1–11. The *historiola* suggests that the retreat was precipitated by division within the Chaldean ranks; hence its relevance for this particular curse.[350] The rest of the incantation consists of pronouncements and procedures typical of separ-ation curses.[351]

The absence of obvious Manichaean references in all these incantations reminds us that purveyors and users of incantations in Late Antiquity did not always think it important or necessary that an incantation draw upon a specific doxological or liturgical tradition, even if they themselves did in fact identify with a particular tradition. Invocations and adjurations that drew on more general and widely used vocabulary might well be acceptable to them. The fact that an incantation was preserved in a recipe or sent by a friend may

---

[344] For extensive commentary on this letter, see P. Mirecki, I. Gardner, and A. Alcock, 'Magical Spell, Manichaean Letter', in Mirecki and BeDuhn, *Emerging from Darkness*, 1–32.

[345] *P.Kellis* V 35.28–31; ET: *P.Kellis* V, pp. 226–7.

[346] See Mirecki, Gardner, and Alcock, 'Magical Spell, Manichaean Letter', 23.

[347] *P.Kellis* V 35.1–5.

[348] See Mirecki, Gardner, and Alcock, 'Magical Spell, Manichaean Letter', 19–21. In Matthew's gospel, Jesus is said to have 'rebuked the winds' (Matt. 8: 26: ἐπετίμησεν τοῖς ἀνέμοις), which may account for the plural here. Compare Brashear, *Magica Varia*, 64, lines 1–2 (*SB* XVIII 13602).

[349] See Mirecki, Gardner, and Alcock, 'Magical Spell, Manichaean Letter', 18–19.

[350] See Mirecki, Gardner, and Alcock, 'Magical Spell, Manichaean Letter', 22–3.

[351] See Mirecki, Gardner, and Alcock, 'Magical Spell, Manichaean Letter', 23–8.

have been more salient in convincing people of its utility or effectiveness than the precise phrasing of the incantation.

At the same time, incantations discussed earlier in this section show that people did draw on specific doxological traditions when formulating an amulet. Unfortunately, among the materials found at Kellis we do not have an unambiguous instance of an amulet devised in specifically Manichaean terms. It was initially suggested that a board written with a prayer for healing, *P.Kellis* I 88, was an amulet.[352] But on the basis of an almost identical prayer in the Montserrat Euchologion,[353] the Kellis text was subsequently identified as a prayer for the laying on of hands on the sick.[354] The absence in the Kellis text of the appeal and doxology addressed to Jesus Christ in the Montserrat text may have been the result of a Manichaean redaction.[355] But the board itself probably belonged to a liturgical codex, as the two pairs of holes and the two v-shaped collational marks on right side suggest.[356] The oblique strokes that mark phrases throughout the text likely served as reading aids when the prayer was spoken over a sick person.

It has likewise been suggested that several Manichaean prayers or hymns of praise, *P.Kellis* II 91, 92, and 94, could have been used as amulets.[357] *P.Kellis* II 91 and 92 are each written in the form of a small bifolium like those used to create miniature codices.[358] They would therefore have been portable. It is conceivable that the text on *P.Kellis* II 91 would have had a protective value, since it includes the request, 'Make us worthy to be your faithful',[359] and concludes with the petition, 'Deliver us'.[360] But it not at all certain that the text on *P.Kellis* II 91 constitutes a single prayer. The bifolium is likely all that is left of a codex with one or more intervening pages, since there is a break in continuity from page 2 to page 3 of the present bifolium and there are slots in its centre fold that could have been used to stitch several bifolio into a

---

[352] *P.Kellis* I, pp. 221–2.

[353] Roca-Puig, *Anàfora de Barcelona*, 99–101, with plates at 131–3 (P.Monts.Roca inv. 155b.19–156a.5).

[354] C. E. Römer, R. W. Daniel, and K. A. Worp, 'Das Gebet zur Handauflegung bei Kranken in P. Barc. 155, 19–156 , 5 und P. Kellis I 88', *ZPE*, 119 (1997), 128–31, <http://www.uni-koeln. de/phil-fak/ifa/zpe/downloads/1997/119pdf/119.html>.

[355] Römer, Daniel, and Worp, 'Das Gebet zur Handauflegung', 129.

[356] *P.Kellis* I 88 intro. and plate.

[357] *P.Kellis* II, pp. 132, 134, 137, 143; Gardner, 'The Manichaean Community at Kellis', 165.

[358] *P.Kellis* II 91 intro. and plate 21 (5.7 cm w × 4.2 cm h; each page 2.85 cm w); *P.Kellis* I 92 intro. and plate 22 (7.4 cm w × 4.6 cm h; each page 3.7 cm w).

[359] *P.Kellis* II 91.20–2.

[360] *P.Kellis* II 91.36. What was meant to follow this petition—possibly a doxology to be recalled from memory—is unclear. See G. Jenkins, 'A Single Codex Sheet from Kellis: A Manichaean Miniature Greek Codex (Papyrus 2)', in J. N. Bremmer (ed.), *The Apocryphal Acts of John* (Kampen: Kok Pharos, 1995), 217–30 at 223; C. E. Römer, 'Christliche Texte II (1996–1997)', *APF*, 44 (1998), 129–39 at 137, doi: 10.1515/apf.1998.44.1.129.

codex.[361] While miniature codices could serve as amulets (as we have already seen), they appear to have been created and valued by Manichaeans for other reasons, as the remarkable Manichaean miniature codex in the Cologne collection indicates.[362] It is even more doubtful that *P.Kellis* II 92 was written to be used as an amulet,[363] since its text, to the extent that it has been deciphered, consists entirely of a hymn of praise to the Father, the supreme deity in Mani's cosmogony. So too, although *P.Kellis* II 94,[364] a short hymn of praise to the Father 'of Greatness' (a typical Manichaean epithet[365]) written on two sides of a small wooden tablet (5 cm w × 8.2 cm h), could have been worn or carried as an amulet, the tablet shows no signs of wear or abrasion to suggest that it was.[366]

6.5.1 Summary

The amulets we have discussed in this section, few though they are, reveal that creators of amulets could draw on diverse Christian traditions, beyond those that were eventually approved as 'orthodox' by the institutional church and incorporated into its rituals. Since we have less of a context to go by with regard to such 'alternative' traditions, our efforts to associate a particular formulation in an amulet with a specific tradition must be tentative. Moreover, formulations in amulets (as in other unofficial forms of communication, such as private letters) are typically simpler than in the more technical genres that are our main sources of information about these 'alternative' traditions (cosmogonies, liturgies, polemics, and so on).[367] Therefore, more than one genealogy may be possible. In addition, the means whereby a particular formulation was suggested to the creator or copier of the incantation remains hidden. We do not know whether it was generated by communal worship, private devotion, individual creativity, or some other impetus.

Nevertheless, these few amulets show that liturgical or doxological material from traditions other than those accepted by the institutional church

---

[361] *P.Kellis* II 91.18–19: κυβερνήτην | θωσυνην. Given the care taken by the scribe in writing the text, an omission of five letters and an error in writing the final *nu* in line 19, as suggested by the editor in *P.Kellis* II, is unlikely. Jenkins, 'A Single Codex Sheet', 219–25, and Römer, 'Christliche Texte II', 136, argue for an original document comprising more than one bifolium.

[362] See the personal communication of C. E. Römer at Mirecki, Gardner, and Alcock, 'Magical Spell, Manichaean Letter', 10 n. 41. For the Cologne codex, see L. Koenen and C. E. Römer (eds), *Der Kölner Mani-Kodex: Abbildungen und diplomatischer Text* (Bonn: R. Habelt, 1985).

[363] Thus Römer, 'Christliche Texte II', 136.

[364] See now the re-edition in N. Gonis and C. E. Römer, 'Ein Lobgesang an den Vater der Grösse in P. Kellis II 94', *ZPE*, 120 (1998), 299–300, <http://www.uni-koeln.de/phil-fak/ifa/zpe/downloads/1998/120pdf/120.html>.

[365] Gonis and Römer, 'Ein Lobgesang', 300 (lines 9–10 comm.).

[366] Image at *P.Kellis* II, plate 24.   [367] See *P.Kellis* V, p. 79.

continued to circulate. I suspect that an exhaustive study of Coptic incantations would yield a richer array of material. What this tells us about the
religious or institutional affiliation of the scribes of this material is, however,
difficult to say. The scribe of *PGM* P21, for instance, may not have associated
the doxology with which he concludes his *charitêsion* with a particular form of
Christianity, 'orthodox' or 'alternative'. Moreover, we see from the correspondence between Valens and Pshai that incantations that scribes had in their
possession and copied for others might not bear any relation to their own
personal religious affiliation. (This could equally be true for the scribe of the
manual with the extensive 'Sethian' invocation discussed in Chapter 3.) Still, it
is significant that diverse doxological formulations are preserved in incantations. They attest to continuing and evolving diversity within late antique
Christianity.

6.6 CONCLUSION

The starting point for this study was a set of Greek incantations and amulets
from late antique Egypt that contain Christian elements. In Chapters 4 and 5
we investigated various types of amulets, observing how Christian material
was either incorporated into customary incantations or displaced such incantations altogether. While those chapters focused on the nature of the Christian
material and the manner in which it was appropriated, this chapter addressed
a prior question, namely, what led creators of incantations and amulets to
draw on, out of all the resources available to them, certain types of Christian
material? The answer, I have argued, lies, at least in part, in the role of ritual in
authorizing and maintaining specific ways of appealing to or associating with
divine power. Whether as creators or copiers, immediately or indirectly,
consciously or not, scribes of incantations and amulets were shaped by rituals
of the Christian church and ritualizing behaviour of Christians.

Sometimes we can document a close connection between the formulation of
an incantation or amulet and the rituals or ritualizing behaviour of a particular
community or tradition, most notably that of the institutionally established
church in Egypt. Thus, we can reasonably posit that acclamations such as the
Sanctus or the trinitarian response to the invitation to communion came to be
used in incantations because of the power and authority they derived from
regular chanting in the liturgy of the Eucharist. The reason that verses of LXX
Ps. 62 (and possibly LXX Ps. 3) appear relatively frequently in amulets, one
may infer, is in part because the psalm was recited daily in the morning
service. So too, the phrasing of appeals to the intercessions of saints reveals
a debt not only to the form of liturgical prayer but also to the cult of particular
saints in Egypt. Likewise, the numerous papyri and parchments written with

verses from a psalm, whether they are amulets or not, undoubtedly derives from the monastic and clerical practice of reciting, praying with, and meditating upon the Psalms.

At other times we are forced to connect the dots between disparate sources of evidence. Even so, the evidence, such as we have it, points to a ritual context. Thus, from the testimony of Christian writers and the formulation of several incantations, I have argued that christological acclamations were used in exorcisms and healings. It is unlikely that writers of amulets generated this form of acclamation; it is more likely that they replicated it from rituals performed by Christian clerics and monks. So too, the presence in an incantation of what appears to be Valentinian doxological language must have derived at one point, if not in its current iteration, from the use of such language in communal or private prayer.

This is not to say that scribes of incantations and amulets were conscious of the ways in which rituals and ritualizing behaviour shaped the resources on which they drew. The debt that a particular element may have owed to rituals or ritualizing behaviour could over time or in specific instances be attenuated to the point of seeming insignificance. We cannot really know, for instance, what it meant for a scribe to begin an incantation with the sign of the cross, even though we know that the sign was used frequently in Christian rituals; or what it meant for a scribe to incorporate a threefold 'holy' without the remainder of the *Sanctus*, even if the acclamation that perpetuated the chanting of the threefold 'holy' in Late Antiquity was the *Sanctus* in the liturgy of the Eucharist. But this is the nature of 'lived religion'. Resources generated collectively are appropriated individually. Individuals may alter the traditions they receive and attach their own meanings to them. In that regard, evidence of tradition, on the one hand, and of diversity in the way a tradition is received, on the other, is more important than our ability to explain precisely how a particular amulet may have come about or what it may have meant.

Conclusion

The impetus for this study was a desire to get beyond the generalities of normative Christian pronouncements about incantations and amulets by delving into the specificity and individuality of artefacts that people in fact produced and used in late antique Egypt. One of the objectives was to see, in an array of particular instances, how the formulation of amulets perpetuated pre-existing conventions and how it diverged from them as the institutional Christian church gained in stature and influence in Egypt. Another objective was to observe at close hand how individual amulets were written, in order to locate them, if only provisionally, in a culture and society undergoing 'christianization'. A third objective was to investigate how rituals of the Christian church and ritualizing behaviour of Christians generated and shaped the resources on which writers of incantations and amulets drew.

Drawing conclusions from a study of many different artefacts entails a certain loss of specificity, as the individual character of each artefact recedes from view. Nevertheless, some observations deserve to be drawn out, with due recognition of their inferential character, since patterns in the formulation and writing of amulets take us some distance in devising plausible scenarios for their production in an increasingly Christian Egypt.

Many of the amulets we have examined were more or less formulaic. This is hardly surprising. The formulaic character of an incantation is what rendered it recognizable as an effective remedy. Knowing and recognizing trusted formulations (whether entire incantations or portions of incantations) would have been inherent to writing an amulet.

The formulaic character of an amulet is especially obvious when an incantation appears in more than one amulet, as in amulets using the 'Hôr Hôr' sequence against scorpions or amulets consisting of the Lord's Prayer or LXX Ps. 90. In the amulets against scorpions, the speed with which several writers executed the incantation reveals how well known it had become. Likewise, the frequent occurrence of amulets reciting the Lord's Prayer or LXX Ps. 90 (or both) shows how conventional those texts had become as means of protection, and the variety of hands in which they were written reveals how familiar these texts were to people of differing degrees of training or literacy. The value of the

Lord's Prayer as a protective incantation would have been reinforced by its regular recitation in any number of settings—whether in private prayer, in communal services of morning and evening prayer, or in the liturgy of the Eucharist. In fact, the wording of the prayer in several amulets, inserting the vocative 'Lord' between 'and lead us not into temptation' and 'but deliver us from evil', shows that it was recalled from liturgical recitation.

The formulaic character of incantations is equally evident in incantations that employ customary phraseology at key points, but otherwise vary in their formulation. The repertoire of customary formulae includes, for instance, commands to heal, deliver, or flee in amulets against sickness; commands to strike down in curses or prayers for justice; phraseology used to identify the person or the types of fevers or evils targeted by the incantation; or the accelerating formula 'now now quickly quickly'. Since the wording of the incantation had to be filled out around these formulaic elements, the scope for individuality in these incantations is obviously greater than in relatively set incantations like the 'Hôr Hôr' sequence or the Lord's Prayer. We rarely have the luxury of comparing two or more amulets written by the same scribe to see how scribes developed their incantations; the two Coptic curses discussed in Chapter 4 and the three amulets from Oxyrhynchus discussed in Chapter 6 are exceptions. But even without such chance finds, we can see that composers of incantations worked with common elements, modulating them to create a more or less integrated incantation. On the customary side of this repertoire, one finds a selection of the elements we surveyed in Chapter 2—sequences of vowels, the esoteric words 'Ablanathanalba' and 'Akrammachamari', the most familiar *charaktêres*. On the Christian side of this repertoire, one finds credal summaries, liturgical invocations, echoes of the *Sanctus*, gospel *incipits*, repetitive *historiolae*, and concluding formulae or doxologies found in liturgical prayers.

The amulets produced out of this repertoire of conventions can be located on a spectrum, ranging from those composed almost entirely of customary elements with only the slightest of Christian elements (e.g., *PGM* P11, though incomplete; *SM* I 20) to those that are composed only of a scriptural passage (e.g., amulets written with verses from LXX Ps. 3 and/or Ps. 62). Within this spectrum one finds amulets that combine fully developed Graeco-Egyptian and Christian idioms (e.g., *SM* I 34); amulets that are customary in structure but Christian in idiom (e.g., *SM* I 25 [*P.Prag.* I 6] and *BKT* X 27); amulets that, like the previous ones, incorporate customary phrases, but whose Christian elements are more expansive (e.g., *PGM* P5b [*P.Oxy.* VIII 1151] or *SM* I 31 [*P.Turner* 49] = *BKT* IX 134); amulets that consist only or mainly of a particular type of Christian element, such as amulets comprising the *incipits* of the gospels or appealing to a specific passage from the gospels; amulets that recite the Lord's Prayer and/or LXX Ps. 90; and amulets that recite some other passage of scripture whose value or purpose is more personal and less definite.

The prominence, and indeed wording, of certain types of Christian material within amulets, I have argued, are owing to its repeated use in Christian rituals, such as the liturgy of the Eucharist or the services of morning and evening prayer. The most obvious examples are the *Sanctus* and the trinitarian response to the call to communion in the Eucharist, the Lord's Prayer in various settings, and LXX Ps. 62 in the service of morning prayer. This material was rendered both familiar and powerful by repeated participatory chanting. Indeed, the frequent collective recitation of this material meant that it made its way into amulets across the spectrum described above, produced by scribes of varying capabilities. So, for example, the *Sanctus* or the trinitarian response is invoked in customary incantations by scribes who are seemingly not familiar with the liturgical form, as well as in incantations composed in a wholly Christian idiom by scribes who replicate the liturgical form. Likewise, the Lord's Prayer is written down by practiced writers with more or less regular hands, less practiced writers, and 'slow writers'. The channels by which these various writers might have come to learn of or incorporate this material into their amulets were no doubt diverse, since some would have known this material from participation in church services, others by copying from amulets or recipes available to them, and others from schooling or other indirect channels. It is telling, however, that often the spelling of such familiar material—particularly the Lord's Prayer or a psalm like LXX Ps. 90—is phonetic. The material was recalled from memory.

Much of the material in amulets that is liturgical in character can be correlated fairly closely to liturgies and other cultic activities of the established institutional church in late antique Egypt. The acclamations follow the phraseology of early witnesses to the Liturgy of St Mark/St Cyril, and the closing appeals or doxologies follow the phraseology of what were evidently liturgical prayers. In one rare instance, *PGM* P5b, we can correlate the saints named in the closing appeal of the incantation with dedicated shrines and churches in Oxyrhynchus—tangible evidence of the connection between the language of incantation and the local cult of saints. Usually the correlation is more diffuse but still specific to Egypt.

Such apparent debts are not limited to the doxological or liturgical traditions of what came to be the established institutional church in Egypt. Though many amulets are informed by its traditions, some amulets echo or elaborate on other Christian traditions, such as those putatively termed 'Valentinian' or 'Sethian' on the basis of schools of thought and bodies of literature associated with those figures. Since words and phrases drawn from doxological traditions are typically expressed more simply in popular forms of communication (such as letters) than in technical literary genres, it is difficult to situate this 'alternative' doxological language precisely. Nevertheless, it is clear that the writers of some amulets (or their exemplars) were drawing on 'alternative' doxological traditions.

There was evidently room for individuality in the creation of amulets. Very few amulets are identical. Yet, as others have noted in their investigations of expressions of individuality in antiquity,[1] the individuality of writers of amulets was conditioned or circumscribed. The types of amulets they produced and how they produced them was influenced by their training as a scribe, their occupation and position in society, their relative proximity to institutional forms of worship, the knowledge or techniques they acquired in the writing of incantations, the models or examples they happened to possess, and the like. It is these qualities that lead us to posit different cultural horizons for writers of different types of amulets or to posit different levels of training and skill for diverse writers of a given type of amulet. The capacity for individual expression makes it difficult to know where the influence of the ambient culture ends and the creativity of the scribe begins. This dilemma is especially noticeable in some of the more intriguing artefacts considered in this study. For instance, how *does* one account for the insertion of a well-developed christological injunction-cum-doxology in a conventional incantation against scorpions (*PGM* P3 [*P.Oslo* I 5])? For the amulet against fever that appeals to Christ and the white wolf (*SM* I 34)? For the *charitêsion* that concludes with what appears to be a Valentinian doxology (*PGM* P21)? For the long invocation that recounts, in an idiosyncratic and at times Hellenistic idiom, the descent and ascent of Christ (*PGM* P13 [*P.Cair.Cat.* 10263])? But the dilemma is also present, albeit in a more prosaic way, in the selection, omission, and transcription of verses in a scriptural amulet. While some of the variation observed in such amulets may be due to carelessness or unimportance (it did not matter how much of an *incipit* was recited), at times it appears that the writer may have selected a passage for a particular, if opaque, reason (as in, e.g., *P.Oxy.* LXXVI 5073 or *SPP* XX 294). Indeed, the exercise of individuality extends to writers who wrote down a few verses from a psalm not often or ever found in amulets. We cannot know why they selected those verses, but for some reason they did.

One aspect of individuality that we have singled out throughout this study is the character of the hand. This expression of individuality was also circumscribed or conditioned. Most of the writers of amulets, it is safe to assume, wrote in a hand to which they were accustomed. This would be true of practiced as well as unpracticed writers. It is difficult to imagine a practiced writer choosing to write in an unpracticed hand—why would one? It was certainly impossible for an unpracticed or 'slow' writer to write in a practiced hand. A practiced writer could well have been able to write in more than one style, as one finds in 'mixed' archives that include literary as well as documentary texts written by 'multifunctional' scribes capable of writing in both a book

---

[1] See the Introduction n. 36.

hand and a documentary hand.[2] In fact, we see this in one amulet, *PGM* P2 (*P.Oxy.* VII 1060), written in both an informal sloping majuscule hand and a documentary cursive hand. But this is a rare instance. Most amulets are written in a single type of hand. Of course, in the case of a practiced hand, we cannot know whether the writer could have written the amulet in another style but chose not to do so. All we have is the hand before us in the amulet.

If one considers the hands of amulets across the spectrum described above,[3] one can observe suggestive, but not definitive, patterns. Irregular writing in compressed lines occurs more often in incantations that mix customary and Christian elements (e.g., *SM* I 32; *SM* I 34) than in incantations written in a wholly Christian idiom. The latter tend to be written in more evenly spaced and regular hands (e.g., *PGM* P18; *SM* I 26; *SM* I 31), which in some instances broach on book hands (e.g., *PGM* P5b). But there are exceptions, as in the elegantly written amulet against scorpions that concludes with a Christian doxology (*PGM* P3).

In amulets consisting mainly of scriptural material, one sees a wide range of hands, extending from writers capable of writing in a formal style to 'slow writers' who wrote individual letters deliberately and awkwardly. Many are written by practiced writers in regular or irregular informal hands. One sees both roughly bilinear, evenly spaced writing and compressed, sloping writing. While the content of these amulets is wholly Christian, their scribes do not necessarily use *nomina sacra* or, when they use them, apply the technique consistently. A feature in these amulets that appears to derive from practices associated with the writing and reading of scriptural and liturgical books is the organization or recollection of psalms in verse-units (*stichoi*) and the use of reading aids to demarcate sections of text (e.g., *ekthesis*) or phrases in a passage (e.g., oblique strokes).

By combining observations about how the amulets examined in this study were formulated with observations about how they were written (in the manner of overlaying images), one can begin to situate their writers in the context of a late antique Egyptian town or village. This has to be a tentative exercise, since there are limits to what one can safely infer from an artefact about the context of its production. We saw this, for example, in the case of the incantation copied by the Manichaean scribe Valens, which is not distinctively Manichaean. If one had only the incantation, one would not suspect that it was kept by a Manichaean scribe. Instances like this one take us into the complex territory of religious affiliation, identity, and salience. What individuals recognized and valued about their association with a particular cult or tradition, be that pagan or Jewish or Christian, no doubt varied among participants in

---

[2] K. Haines-Eitzen, *Guardians of Letters: Literacy, Power, and the Transmitters of Early Christian Literature* (Oxford: Oxford University Press, 2000), 32–4.

[3] See p. 236.

that cult and certainly varied between people more closely involved in official functions and those not so involved. Into this diversity one must factor uncertainty about what exactly in an incantation was salient for its producer or user. Valens evidently deemed it worthwhile to send an incantation that was not specifically Manichaean to his colleague. It may have been enough that it had been written down, passed on, and fallen into his possession. The perfunctory way in which some incantations were written down, with and without Christian elements, suggests that they were regarded simply as common remedies, used by people irrespective of how they might have affiliated themselves socially or culturally by other practices or beliefs. We must be careful about investing either customary or Christian elements with a salience that they might not have had for a scribe, as one sees from two amulets that appeal to *charaktêres* to heal someone who is ill—the appeal preceded in one amulet by the trinitarian acclamation 'One Father, one Son, one holy Spirit' and 'Ablanathanabla' written as a diminishing grape-cluster (*SM* I 21); in the other, by an acclamatory form of the second article of the Christian creed (*SM* I 23 [*P.Haun.* III 51]).

That said, the formulation of various amulets suggests that their original composers, and possibly also their copiers, were conditioned by different cultural competencies or affinities. One differentiation, suggested by the character of incantations composed in a Christian idiom, is between compositions that lie closer, culturally, to the institutional centre of the Egyptian church and those that are more distant from that centre. This differentiation is based primarily on how closely Christian acclamations, doxologies, petitions, or scriptural citations in the incantation correspond to what we know of the liturgy and scriptures of the Egyptian church. This differentiation assumes that most, if not all, people officially or routinely involved in worship services would have replicated those elements fairly closely, particularly since most of the elements would have been recalled from frequent oral recitation. This body of people includes, of course, clergy, both priests and deacons, since they were expected to learn parts of the liturgy and portions of scripture from memory.[4] It would also include monks and nuns, who would have recited much of this material repeatedly in their own prayers or meditation as well as in communal worship services.[5] And it could encompass some laity—those literate enough to be able to reiterate liturgical and scriptural material in writing.

Similarly, among amulets reciting one or more passages of scripture, differences in how such amulets were formulated and written suggest that their writers worked with slightly different understandings of what they were doing and why they were doing it. The impetus for amulets reciting *incipits* from the gospels and LXX Ps. 90 (sometimes along with other short passages) or

---

[4] See n. 13.   [5] For evidence of such knowledge among nuns, see Chapter 4 n. 132.

amulets explicitly invoking a short passage from a gospel for a particular purpose (which I have termed 'gospel' amulets) is different than the impetus for amulets reciting verses from one or two psalms. Whereas the scribes of the former type of amulets operate out of a knowledge that certain forms of scriptural citation are effective and powerful devices, the scribes of the later type of amulets appear to have been motivated by associations that the passage had acquired through regular recitation, whether that occurred in communal services or individual meditation. The difference can be seen in how the passages are cited. Whereas the verse-units in amulets written with portions of one or more psalms are usually complete (except for inadvertent omissions), *incipits* or short passages cited together with a heading, invocation, or injunction can stop in mid-phrase. While some scribes may have been equally conversant with both modes of scriptural recitation, others were probably not: people who wrote down verses of one or two psalms for themselves or someone else to wear may have been unaware of the technique of composing amulets with *incipits*.

Finally, we must ask, who *could* have written these various kinds of amulets? Who would have had the requisite ability to read and write Greek (since this study deals primarily with amulets written in Greek)?

In Late Antiquity, as in earlier periods, only a small proportion of the population in Egypt was able to read and write.[6] However, even though most of the population communicated orally, the ability to read and write was necessary for the functioning of Egyptian society.[7] It was required for the operation of the imperial and municipal government, for communicating with officials, for legal agreements between private parties, for commercial transactions and records, and for the liturgy and administration of the church. Greek was the official language used in all of these domains well into Late Antiquity; Coptic, used for literary texts and private correspondence from the fourth century onward, only begins to be used for legal documents toward the end of the sixth century.[8] The need for written communication ensured that

---

[6] For overviews, see E. Wipszycka, 'Le degré d'alphabétisation en Égypte byzantine', *REAug*, 30 (1984), 279–96, <http://hdl.handle.net/2042/1194>, repr. in E. Wipszycka, *Études sur le christianisme dans l'Égypte de l'antiquité tardive* (Rome: Institutum Patristicum Augustinianum, 1996), 107–26; R. S. Bagnall, *Egypt in Late Antiquity* (Princeton: Princeton University Press, 1993), 240–51. On continuing levels of literacy in Late Antiquity, as opposed to the decline postulated by W. V. Harris, *Ancient Literacy* (Cambridge, M.A., and London: Harvard University Press, 1989), see Wipszycka, *Études*, 127–35.

[7] A. E. Hanson, 'Ancient Illiteracy', in J. H. Humphrey (ed.), *Literacy in the Roman World* (Ann Arbor: Journal of Roman Archaeology, 1991), 159–98; Wipszycka, *Études*, 108; R. S. Bagnall, *Everyday Writing in the Graeco-Roman East* (Berkeley: University of California Press, 2012), 1–3.

[8] J.-L. Fournet, 'The Multilingual Environment of Late Antique Egypt: Greek, Latin, Coptic, and Persian Documentation', in R. S. Bagnall (ed.), *The Oxford Handbook of Papyrology* (Oxford: Oxford University Press, 2009), 418–51 at 434–41; Bagnall, *Everyday Writing*, 75–94.

children of the propertied elite in villages and of the commercial, professional, and propertied classes in towns were taught to read and write Greek. Still, this education was available for the most part only to boys. Moreover, the ability to write could be rudimentary and did not necessarily entail an ability to read. Finally, not all children from a given family would achieve the same level of literacy; the documentary archives of families reveal that some members were literate, but others not.[9]

Given the social parameters of literacy in late antique Egypt, men able to read and write Greek could be found in the families of the civic elite (along with some women); working as scribes, notaries, and clerks in government offices; working (enslaved or free) for guilds, on private estates, or in wealthy families as scribes or secretaries; available for hire as public scribes to write petitions, letters, and the like; employed as teachers; and appointed to the higher offices of the church (bishops, priests, and deacons).[10] In addition, the formation and routines of monks and nuns entailed an ability to read, if not write.[11] The proficiency one could expect of people in these positions varied. Professional scribes employed in public or private administration would have been highly proficient, capable of writing fast documentary hands and, in the most prestigious offices of the state, chancery hands. Such scribes might well be 'multifunctional', able to write in book hands as well as documentary hands. While the hands of some private secretaries could match those of professional scribes, one also finds less regular, more uneven hands among letters penned by such writers.[12] Among the clergy and monks

---

[9] H. C. Youtie, '*ΑΓΡΑΜΜΑΤΟΣ*: An Aspect of Greek Society in Egypt', *HSCP*, 75 (1971), 161–76 at 170–1, <http://www.jstor.org/stable/311224>, repr. in H. C. Youtie, *Scriptiunculae*, 2 vols (Amsterdam: Adolf M. Hakkert, 1973), 2.611–27; Wipszycka, *Études*, 108.

[10] On the literacy of the higher clergy, see E. Wipszycka, *Les ressources et les activités économiques des églises en Égypte du IVᵉ au VIIIᵉ siècle* (Brussels: Fondation égyptologique Reine Élisabeth, 1972), 165–70; A. Martin, 'L'Église et la khôra égyptienne au IVᵉ siècle', *REAug*, 25 (1979), 3–26 at 11–17, <http://hdl.handle.net/2042/1068>; Wipszycka, *Études*, 117–21; E. Wipszycka, *The Alexandrian Church: People and Institutions* (Warsaw: Journal of Juristic Papyrology, 2015), 119–21.

[11] See C. Rapp, 'Christians and their Manuscripts in the Greek East in the Fourth Century', in G. Cavallo, G. de Gregori, and M. Maniaci (eds), *Scritture, libri e testi nelle aree provinciali di Bisanzio*, 2 vols (Spoleto: Centro italiano di studi sull'alto Medioevo, 1991), 1.127–48 at 133–6; Wipszycka, *Études*, 121–5, 133; E. Wipszycka, *Moines et communautés monastiques en Égypte (IVᵉ–VIIIᵉ siècles)* (Warsaw: Journal of Juristic Papyrology, 2009), 361–5; M. J. Albarrán Martínez, 'Women Reading Books in Egyptian Monastic Circles', in J. P. Monferrer-Sala, H. Teule, and S. Torallas Tovar (eds), *Eastern Christians and their Written Heritage: Manuscripts, Scribes and Context* (Leuven: Peeters, 2012), 199–212; J. Timbie, 'The Education of Shenoute and Other Cenobitic Leaders: Inside and Outside the Monastery', in P. Gemeinhardt, L. Van Hoof, and P. Van Nuffelen (eds), *Education and Religion in Late Antiquity: Reflections, Social Contexts, and Genres* (London and New York: Routledge, 2016), 34–46. On learning how to read and write in monastic contexts, see L. I. Larsen, 'Early Monasticism and the Rhetorical Tradition: Sayings and Stories as School Texts', in Gemeinhardt, Van Hoof, and Van Nuffelen, *Education and Religion in Late Antiquity*, 13–33.

[12] R. S. Bagnall and R. Cribiore, *Women's Letters from Ancient Egypt, 300 BC–AD 800* (Ann Arbor: The University of Michigan Press, 2006), 42–4.

of the church, one would expect to find a range of ability: a small number of highly trained writers able to copy books in a formal, even calligraphic, hand; practiced writers able to write in a fluent regular hand; writers whose hand is more uneven and less controlled; and writers who can only write laboriously and clumsily. Such irregular or laborious hands might also be found among informal networks—family and friends for whom writing was not a daily activity.

Most of the amulets we have studied were produced by writers across the middle of this range: practiced writers with regular hands, practiced writers with irregular hands, and unpracticed or clumsy writers. A few come from writers outside this range: at one end, those written in a rapid documentary cursive or a formal book hand (excluding leaves from biblical codices whose use as an amulet appears to have been secondary to their original purpose); on the other end, those written by a 'slow writer' or, in one case (*PGM* P17 [*P.Iand.* I 6] = *P.Giss.Lit.* 5.4), someone who could not read Greek. Thus, we must look for the writers of our amulets among the sorts of people who would have populated this large middle ground, with glances to either side of the range of scribal competence.

Christian clergy and monks were undoubtedly a source of certain types of amulets. Their familiarity the liturgy of the church, with the phraseology of liturgical prayer, and with portions of the scriptures (particularly the gospels and the Psalms, parts of which they were expected to memorize) would have given them, more than most other writers, the cultural expertise to formulate incantations in a wholly Christian idiom or to recall and transcribe verses from scripture.[13] Their position and role in the church and society would also have made them credible sources of such remedies. What is harder to determine is the extent to which Christian clergy and monks would have been familiar with customary techniques of incantation, as well as the extent to which their knowledge of Christian phraseology and scripture would have diverged from the 'standard' forms attested in liturgical and biblical manuscripts. On the one hand, the presence of customary formulae (such as the flee-formula or the accelerating formula) in incantations composed in a Christian idiom indicates that these were quite acceptable to scribes writing in a Christian milieu. Moreover, the manual of recipes found in the floor of a monk's cave near the monastery Deir el-Bakhit indicates that some monks were acquainted with customary resources. Thus, the presence of customary

---

[13] On the liturgical and biblical knowledge expected of priests and deacons, see G. Schmelz, *Kirchliche Amtsträger im spätantiken Ägypten nach den Aussagen der griechischen und koptischen Papyri und Ostraka* (Munich: K. G. Saur, 2002), 55; Wipszycka, *The Alexandrian Church*, 325–7. On the correlation between close citation of the New Testament and a monastic context in fourth-century letters, see M. Choat, 'Echo and Quotation of the New Testament in Papyrus Letters to the End of the Fourth Century', in T. J. Kraus and T. Nicklas (eds), *New Testament Manuscripts: Their Texts and their World* (Leiden: Brill, 2006), 267–92 at 280–1.

elements—vowels, *charaktêres*, phraseology—does not preclude clerical or monastic authorship, as we see, for instance, with *PGM* P3 or *SPP* XX 244. On the other hand, we should expect that most clerics (as well as most monks and nuns) would have reproduced frequently recited liturgical material, such as the *Sanctus* and the Lord's Prayer, in a form that was relatively close to that used in the liturgy of the church. Therefore, it is unlikely, in my view, that members of the higher clergy composed amulets that diverged considerably from the 'standard' form, such as *SM* I 29 (*P.Princ.* II 107) or *SM* I 32. If this supposition proves to be incorrect, we would be obliged to revise the current scholarly view of the competencies normally required of and found among such clerics.

Some of the Christian material used in amulets would have been familiar to lay Christians as well, particularly those who participated regularly in Christian services. Moreover, they may have learned certain texts, such as the Lord's Prayer or individual psalms, in school.[14] However, writing exercises differed in what they required of students. In one exercise tablet, *SB* XXVI 16597,[15] the opening words of LXX Ps. 90 appear twice in the hand of a teacher and then several times in the hand of a student still learning to write letters. Although the tablet shows that the psalm was used in exercises, it also reveals that rudimentary exercises such as the one found there would not have enabled a student to recall and copy more than a line or two of the psalm, if that. The ability to recall and copy several verses of the psalm, or the entire psalm, would have required more education, access to a text of the psalm, or continuous recitation.

Whether the writer of an amulet was a cleric, a monk or nun, or a layperson, the social and economic value attached to the ability to read and write brings another consideration into view. Experienced writers would have had numerous outlets for their skill, even if they were not professional scribes and were not able to maintain an entirely regular hand. We should not imagine that such writers made a living only by producing amulets or similar remedies. It is clear from the examples of Dioscorus of Aphrodite and Valens in Kellis that copying an incantation was incidental to the principal activity of writers working as scribes or in other professional positions. This is likely true of

---

[14] For (possible) instances of the in exercises, see T. J. Kraus, 'Manuscripts with the *Lord's Prayer*—They Are More Than Simply Witnesses to That Text Itself', in Kraus and Nicklas, *New Testament Manuscripts*, 227–66 (nos. 1, 14–16); J. Chapa, 'Su demoni e angeli: il Salmo 90 nel suo contesto', in G. Bastianini and A. Casanova (eds), *I papiri letterari cristiani: atti del convegno internazionale di studi in memoria di Mario Naldini, Firenze, 10–11 Giugno 2010* (Florence: Istituto Papirologico 'G. Vitelli', 2011), 59–90 at 68. On *P.Ant.* II 54 (no. 1 in Kraus's catalogue), see Section 5.5.

[15] J.-L. Fournet, 'Nouveaux textes scolaires grecs et coptes', *BIFAO*, 101 (2001), 159–81 at 160–2, with fig. 1, <http://www.ifao.egnet.net/bifao/101/>; D. R. Jordan, 'Another Example of LXX Ps. 90.1', *Eulimene*, 3 (2002), 201.

less-skilled writers as well. Thus, the writers of the amulets we have studied probably did other types of work, whether as clerics, monastics, teachers, public scribes, or in some other capacity.

We may wish to distinguish between writers who copied or recalled incantations and writers who generated new incantations, particularly extended incantations. The latter presumably required more experience and facility in the techniques of incantation than the former. But the distinction between copying and generating is not a sharp one, since scribes drew on pre-existing models and techniques when generating incantations and introduced personal idiosyncrasies when copying them. It can be difficult to determine that an amulet was generated rather than copied. The absence of telltale clues, such as verbatim coping of the generic phrase 'so-and-so born of so-and-so', is not sufficient.

In the end, the distinction may not be so crucial. The text of an amulet reveals something of the cultural location of the scribe, regardless of whether the scribe generated it or copied it. For instance, the cultural competencies and affinities of a scribe who produces a customary incantation with Christian acclamations that do not correspond to their liturgical form and whose use of Christian scribal conventions is uneven are different than those of a scribe who produces an incantation in a wholly Christian idiom using Christian scribal conventions. Similarly, a scribe who produces an amulet consisting of verses from a psalm has a different understanding of what constitutes an amulet than a scribe who produces an amulet consisting of an incantation. Sometimes the difference between these putative cultural locations is not great: it could be that a single scribe may have produced various types of amulets. But at other times the difference is considerable.

Such a model also fits with what we know about the 'conditioned individuality' of 'lived religion'. What individuals do in the course of their religious observances will inevitably be conditioned by socially inculcated outlooks, expectations, customs, habits, and speech. But it will not be wholly determined by such cultural proclivities. The amulets examined in this study permit us to see not only diversity in the cultural proclivities of purveyors of remedies in late antique Egypt, but also individuality among purveyors who share a particular cultural proclivity. The artefacts produced by these purveyors do not correspond, therefore, to what was described or recommended in normative Christian discourse. That discourse, generated in an effort to keep Christians from doing what pagans or Jews did, allowed for only a few polarized alternatives: 'demonic' amulets comprising incantations and 'magical' signs, and 'acceptable' amulets consisting of the gospel, the cross, or water and oil that had been blessed. Scribes working in a Christian context were not unaffected by such norms. It is telling that many incantations with Christian elements do not invoke Graeco-Egyptian deities and heroes (though some still do); the range of what is deemed permissible or efficacious has shifted from what had been the norm in the Graeco-Egyptian manuals. But the media through which such scribes encountered Christian norms—in the liturgy of the church and the devotional habits of Christians (themselves or others)—and the interactive way in which they worked with these norms left room for individual agency. The same might be said of the ways in which scribes worked with customary resources, such as manuals of procedures and recipes, copies of applied incantations, or training and experience in techniques of incantation. In short, the writers of incantations and amulets were both receivers and creators of tradition. The work of making amulets Christian was very much their individual doing. They would not have expected that we would be poring over the results of their work a millennium and a half later. But it is a fitting tribute to the religious life of 'everyday' people that we are.

Bibliography

Ancient Sources

Selected Corpora of Manuals and Incantations

Audollent, A., *Defixionum tabellae* (Paris: A. Fontemoing, 1904).

Betz, H. D. (ed.), *The Greek Magical Papyri in Translation, Including the Demotic Spells*, 2nd edn (Chicago and London: University of Chicago Press, 1992).

Borghouts, J. F. (tr.), *Ancient Egyptian Magical Texts* (Leiden: Brill, 1978).

Gager, J. G. (ed.), *Curse Tablets and Binding Spells from the Ancient World* (New York: Oxford University Press, 1992).

Daniel, R. W., and F. Maltomini (eds), *Supplementum Magicum*, 2 vols (Opladen: Westdeutscher Verlag, 1991–1992).

Kotansky, R. (ed.), *Greek Magical Amulets: The Inscribed Gold, Silver, Copper, and Bronze Lamellae, Part I: Published Texts of Known Provenance* (Opladen: Westdeutscher Verlag, 1994).

Kropp, A., *Ausgewählte koptische Zaubertexte*, 3 vols (Brussels: Édition de la Fondation égyptologique Reine Élisabeth, 1930–1).

Meyer, M., and R. Smith (eds), *Ancient Christian Magic: Coptic Texts of Ritual Power* (San Francisco: HarperCollins, 1994).

Preisendanz, K., and A. Henrichs (eds), *Papyri Graecae Magicae: Die griechischen Zauberpapyri*, 2 vols, 2nd edn (Stuttgart: Teubner, 1973–4; repr. Munich and Leipzig: K. G. Saur, 2001).

Literary and Legal Sources

The following list includes only editions; bibliographical details of translations are given in the notes at the point of reference. For bibliographical details of the series PG, PL, and PLS, see the List of Abbreviations.

Acta apostolorum apocrypha post Constantinum Tischendorf, ed. R. A. Lipsius and M. Bonnet, 2 vols in 3 (1891–1903; repr. Hildesheim: G. Olms, 1990).

Acta Iohannis (A. Io.) [*The Acts of John*]—*Acta Iohannis*, ed. E. Junod and J.-D. Kaestli, 2 vols in 1 (Turnhout: Brepols, 1983).

Acta Pauli et Theclae (A. Paul. et Thecl.) [*The Acts of Paul and Thecla*]—*Acta apostolorum apocrypha post Constantinum Tischendorf*, ed. R. A. Lipsius and M. Bonnet, 2 vols in 3 (Leipzig, 1891–1903; repr. Hildesheim: G. Olms, 1990), 1.235–72.

Akten der ephesinischen Synode vom Jahre 449, ed. J. Flemming (Berlin: Weidmann, 1917).

Alexander Salaminus
De inventione crucis (Cruc.) [*On the Discovery of the Cross*]—PG 87.4016–76.

Ambrose of Milan

De sacramentis (Sacr.) [*On the Sacraments*]—Ambroise de Milan, Des sacrements, Des mystères, Explication du symbole, ed. B. Botte, SC 25 *bis* (Paris: Les Éditions du Cerf, 1961), 60–155.

Explanatio symboli ad initiandos (Expl. symb.) [*Explanation of the Creed*]—Ambroise de Milan, Des sacrements, Des mystères, Explication du symbole, ed. B. Botte, SC 25 *bis* (Paris: Les Éditions du Cerf, 1961), 46–59.

Ammianus Marcellinus

Res gestae (Res gest.) [*Roman History*]—Ammianus Marcellinus, *History*, tr. J. C. Rolfe, 3 vols, LCL (Cambridge, M.A.: Harvard University Press, 1939–1950).

Analecta hymnica graeca e codicibus eruta Italiae inferioris, vol. 11: *Canones iulii*, ed. A. A. Longo (Rome: Istituto di Studi Bizantini e Neoellenici, Università di Roma, 1978).

Apocryphon of John (Ap. John)—*The Apocryphon of John: Synopsis of Nag Hammadi Codices II,1; III,1; and IV,1 with BG 8502,2*, ed. and tr. M. Waldstein and F. Wisse, NHMS 33 (Leiden: Brill, 1995).

Apostolic Church Order—A. Stewart-Sykes, *The Apostolic Church Order: The Greek Text with Introduction, Translation and Annotation* (Strathfield: St Pauls Publications, 2006).

Aristides

Apologia (Apol.) [*Apology*]—Aristide, Apologie, ed. B. Pouderon, M.-J. Pierre, B. Outtier, and M. Guiorgadzé, SC 470 (Paris: Les Éditions du Cerf, 2003).

Arnobius of Sicca

Disputationes adversus nationes (Adv. nat.) [*The Case against the Pagans*]—Arnobius adversus nationes libri VII, ed. A. Reifferscheid, CSEL 4 (Vienna: Apud C. Geroldi filium, 1875).

Athanasius of Alexandria

De amuletis [*On Amulets*]—PG 26.1320.

Epistula festalis xxxix (fragmentum) *(Ep. fest. 39)* [*Festal Letter Thirty-Nine*]— P.-P. Joannou, *Discipline générale antique (IVᵉ–IXᵉ s.)*, vol. 2: *Les canons des Pères Grecs* (Vatican: Tipografia Italo-Orientale 'S. Nilo', 1963), 71–6.

Vita Antonii (V. Anton) [*Life of Antony*]—Athanase d'Alexandrie, Vie d'Antoine, ed. G. J. M. Bartelink, SC 400 (Paris: Les Éditions du Cerf, 1994).

Augustine

De Doctrina Christiana (Doct. chr.) [*On Christian Teaching*]—Augustine: De Doctrina Christiana, ed. R. P. H. Green (Oxford: Clarendon Press, 1995).

Enarrationes in Psalmos (Psal.) [*Explanations of the Psalms*]—Sancti Aurelii Augustini Enarrationes in Psalmos I–CL, ed. E. Dekkers and J. Fraipont, 3 vols, CCSL 38–40 (Turnhout: Brepols, 1956).

In evangelium Iohannis tractatus (Tract. Io.) [*Tractates on the Gospel of John*]—Sancti Aurelii Augustini In Iohannis evangelium tractatus CXXIV, ed. R. Willems, CCSL 36 (Turnhout: Brepols, 1954).

Sermones (Serm.) [*Sermons*]—PL 38–9; PLS 2.417–743, 1348–56; Augustin d'Hippone: vingt-six sermons au peuple d'Afrique, ed. F. Dolbeau (Paris: Institut d'Études Augustiniennes, 1996).

Basil of Caesarea

Epistulae (Ep.) [*Letters*]—*Saint Basile, Lettres*, ed. Yves Courtonne, 3 vols (Paris: Belles Lettres, 1957–66).

Homiliae in Psalmos (Hom. in Ps.) [*Homilies on the Psalms*]—PG 29.209–494.

Regulae fusius tractatae (Reg. fus.) [*Long Rules*]—PG 31.889–1052.

Caesarius of Arles

Sermones (Serm.) [*Sermons*]—*Sancti Caesarii Arelatensis Sermones*, ed. G. Morin, 2 vols, CCSL 103–4 (Turnhout: Brepols, 1953).

Canones Hippolytus (Can. Hipp.) [*The Canons of Hippolytus*]—*Les Canons d'Hipplyte*, ed. R.-G. Coquin, PO 31/2 (Paris: Firmin-Didot, 1966).

Canons of Athanasius of Alexandria—W. E. Crum and W. Riedel, *The Canons of Athanasius of Alexandria* (London: Williams and Norgate, 1904).

Codex Iustinianus (C.Iust.) [*Code of Justinian*]—*Corpus juris civilis*, vol. 2: *Codex Iustinianus*, ed. P. Krueger (Berlin: Weidmann, 1892).

Codex Theodosianus (C.Th.) [*Theodosian Code*]—*Theodosiani libri XVI cum Constitutionibus Sirmondianis et Leges novellae ad Theodosianum pertinentes*, ed. T. Mommsen and P. M. Meyer, 2 vols in 3 (Berlin, 1905; repr. Berlin: Weidmann, 1962).

Constitutiones apostolorum (Const. apost.) [*Apostolic Constitutions*]—*Les Constitutions apostoliques*, ed. M. Metzger, SC 320, 329, 336 (Paris: Les Éditions du Cerf, 1985–7).

Cyril of Alexandria

Commentarius in Johannem (Jo.) [*Commentary on John*]—*Sancti patris nostri Cyrilli archiepiscopi Alexandrini in d. Joannis evangelium*, ed. E. P. Pusey, 3 vols (Oxford, 1872; repr. Brussels: Culture et Civilisation, 1965).

De adoratione et cultu in spiritu et veritate (Ador.) [*The Adoration and Worship of God in Spirit and in Truth*]—PG 68.132–1125.

De recta fide ad Arcadiam et Marinam (Arcad.) [*On the True Faith, to Arcadia and Marina*]—*Concilium Universale Ephesenum*, ed. E. Schwartz, ACO 1.1.1.5 (Berlin: Walter de Gruyter, 1927), 62–118.

De recta fide ad Theodosium (Thds.) [*On the True Faith, to Theodosius*]—*Concilium Universale Ephesenum*, ed. E. Schwartz, ACO 1.1.1.5 (Berlin: Walter de Gruyter, 1927), 26–61.

Commentarii in Lucam in catenis (Lc.) [*Commentaries on Luke*]—PG 72.475–950.

Cyril or John of Jerusalem

Catecheses mystagogicae (Catech. myst.) [*Mystogogical Catecheses*]—*Cyrille de Jérusalem, Catéchèses mystagogiques*, ed. A. Piédagnel, SC 126 *bis* (Paris: Les Éditions du Cerf, 2004).

Didache XII apostolorum (Did.) [*The Teaching of the Twelve Apostles*]—*La Doctrine des Douze Apôtres (Didachè)*, ed. W. Rordorf and A. Tuilier, SC 248 *bis* (Paris: Les Éditions du Cerf, 1998).

Didymus of Alexandria
Commentarius in Ecclesiasten (Eccl.) [Commentary on Ecclesiastes]—Didymos der Blinde: Kommentar zum Ecclesiastes (Tura-Papyrus), ed. G. Binder et al., 7 vols in 6, PTA 9, 13, 16, 22–6 (Bonn: Rudolf Habelt, 1969–89).
Commentarius in Psalmos (Ps.) [Commentary on the Psalms]—Didymos der Blinde: Psalmenkommentar (Tura-Papyrus), ed. L. Doutreleau, A. Gesiché, and M. Gronewald, 5 vols, PTA 4, 6–8, 12 (Bonn: Rudolf Habelt, 1968–1970).

Dioscorides
De materia medica, ed. M. Wellmann, 3 vols (Berlin: Weidmann, 1958).

Doctrina apostolorum (Doct. apost.) [The Teaching of the Apostles]—La Doctrine des Douze Apôtres (Didachè), ed. W. Rordorf and A. Tuilier, SC 248 *bis* (Paris: Les Éditions du Cerf, 1998), 207–10.
Epitome of the Canons of the Holy Apostles (Epitome)—Eine Elfapostelmoral oder die X-Rezension der 'beiden Wege', ed. T. Schermann (Munich: Lentner'sche Buchhandlung, 1903), 16–18; repr. in A. Stewart-Sykes, *The Apostolic Church Order: The Greek Text with Introduction, Translation and Annotation* (Strathfield: St Pauls Publications, 2006), 117–18.

Eusebius of Caesarea
Commentarius in Psalmos (Ps.) [Commentary on the Psalms]—PG 23.65–1396; PG 24.9–78.
Demonstratio evangelica (D.e.) [The Proof of the Gospel]—Eusebius Werke: Die Demonstratio evangelica, ed. I. A. Heikel, 2 vols, GCS 23 (Leipzig: J. C. Hinrichs, 1913).
Historia ecclesiastica (H.e.) [Ecclesiastical History]—Eusebius Werke: Die Kirchengeschichte, ed. E. Schwartz and T. Mommsen, 2nd edn, ed. F. Winkelmann, 3 vols, GCS N.F. 6 (Berlin: Akademie Verlag, 1999).

Fulgentius Ferrandus of Carthage
Breviatio canonum (Breu. can.) [Digest of Canons]—Concilia Africae a. 345–a. 525, ed. C. Munier, CCSL 149 (Turnhout: Brepols, 1974), 287–306.

Gospel of the Egyptians (Gos. Eg.)—Nag Hammadi Codices III,2 and IV,2: The Gospel of the Egyptians (The Holy Book of the Great Invisible Spirit), ed. A. Böhlig and F. Wisse, NHMS 4 (Leiden: Brill 1975).

Gregory of Nyssa
Epistula canonica (Ep. can.) [Canonical Letter]—PG 45.221–36; P.-P. Joannou, *Discipline générale antique (IVe–IXe s.)*, vol. 2: *Les canons des pères grecs* (Vatican: Tipografia Italo-Orientale 'S. Nilo', 1963), 203–26.

Hermas
Similitudines pastoris (Sim.) [Similitudes]—Die apostolischen Väter I: Der Hirt des Hermas, ed. M. Whittaker, GCS 48 (Berlin: Akademie Verlag, 1956), 46–113.

Hesychius of Jerusalem
Homiliae (Hom.) [Homilies]—Les homélies festales d'Hésychius de Jérusalem, ed. M. Aubineau, 2 vols (Brussels: Société des Bollandistes, 1978).

Hilary of Poitiers
Collectanea antiariana Parisina—S. Hilarii Pictaviensis Opera, Pars IV, ed. A. Feder, CSEL 65 (Vienna: F. Tempsky, 1916), 43–177.

Hippolytus of Rome
Refutatio omnium haeresium (Haer.) [*Refutation of All Heresies*]—*Hippolytus, Refutation omnium haeresium*, ed. M. Marcovich, PTS 25 (Berlin: Walter de Gruyter, 1986).

Historia monachorum in Aegypto (Hist. mon.) [*History of the Monks of Egypt*]—*Historia monachorum in Aegypto*, ed. A.-J. Festugière (Brussels: Société des Bollandistes, 1961).

Irenaeus of Lyon
Aduersus haereses (Haer.) [*Against Heresies*]—*Irénée de Lyons, Contre les hérésies*, ed. A. Rousseau and L. Doutreleau, SC 100, 152–3, 210–11, 263–4, 293–4 (Paris: Les Éditions du Cerf, 1965–82).

Jerome
Commentariorum in Mattheaeum libri IV (Matt.) [*Commentary on Matthew*]—*Jérôme, Commentaire sur S. Matthieu*, ed. E. Bonnard, SC 242, 259 (Paris: Les Éditions du Cerf, 1977–9).
Vita S. Hilarionis eremitae (V. Hil.) [*Life of Hilarion*]—*Jérôme, Trois vies de moines (Paul, Malchus, Hilarion)*, ed. E. M. Morales, SC 508 (Paris: Les Éditions du Cerf, 2007), 212–99.

John Cassian
De institutis coenobiorum (Inst. coen.) [*The Institutes*]—*Jean Cassien, Institutions cénobitiques*, ed. J.-C. Guy, SC 109 (Paris: Les Éditions du Cerf, 1965).

John Chrysostom
Ad populum Antiochenum de statuis (Stat.) [*Homilies on the Statues*]—PG 49.15–222.
Expositiones in Psalmos (Exp. in Ps.) [*Explanations of the Psalms*]—PG 55.
Homiliae in epistolam ad Colossenses (Hom. in Col.) [*Homilies on Colossians*]—PG 62.299–392.
Homiliae in epistolam primam ad Corinthios (Hom. in 1 Cor.) [*Homilies on 1 Corinthians*]—PG 61.9–382.
Homiliae in epistolam primam ad Timotheum (Hom. in 1 Tim.) [*Homilies on 1 Timothy*]—PG 62.503–600.
Homiliae in Matthaeum (Hom. in Matt.) [*Homilies on Matthew*]—PG 57–8.

John of Gaza
Epistulae (Ep.) [*Letters*]—*Barsanuphe et Jean de Gaza, Correspondance*, ed. F. Neyt and P. de Angelis-Noah, SC 426–7, 450–1, 468 (Paris: Les Éditions du Cerf, 1997–2002).

John of Thessalonica
Orationes in dormitionem B M V (Dorm. B M V) [*Orations on the Dormition of the Blessed Virgin Mary*]—*Homélies mariales byzantines II*, ed. M. Jugie, PO 19/3 (Paris: Firmin-Didot, 1926), 375–438.

Julius Africanus
Cesti—Iulius Africanus. Cesti: The Extant Fragments, ed. M. Wallraff et al., GCS N. F. 18 (Berlin: Walter de Gruyter, 2012).

Justin Martyr
Apologia I, II (1 Apol.; 2 Apol.) [*First Apology; Second Apology*]—*Justin, Apologie pour les chrétiens*, ed. C. Munier, SC 507 (Paris: Les Éditions du Cerf, 2006).
Dialogus cum Tryphone Judaeo (Dial.) [*Dialogue with Trypho the Jew*]—*Justin Martyr, Dialogue avec Tryphon*, ed. P. Bobichon, 2 vols (Fribourg: Academic Press and Éditions Saint-Paul, 2003).

Le synaxaire éthiopien: mois de terr, ed. G. Colin, PO 45/1 (Turnhout: Brepols, 1990), 214–31.
Life of Aaron—Miscellaneous Coptic Texts in the Dialect of Upper Egypt, ed. E. A. Wallis Budge (London: British Museum, 1915).
Melchizedek (Melch.)—Melchisédek (NH IX,1): oblation, baptême et vision dans la gnose séthienne, ed. W.-P. Funk, BCNH, section 'Textes' 28 (Laval: Presses de l'Université Laval; Louvain and Paris: Peeters, 2001).
Metaphrasis martyrii sanctae Tatianae—F. Halkin (ed.), *Légendes grecques de 'Martyres romaines'* (Brussels: Société des Bollandistes, 1973), 56–81.

Origen
Contra Celsum (Cels.)—Origène, Contre Celse, ed. M. Borret, SC 132, 136, 147, 150, 227 (Paris: Les Éditions du Cerf, 1967–76).
Dialogus cum Heraclide (Dial.) [*Dialogue with Heraclides*]—*Entretien d'Origène avec Héraclide*, ed. J. Scherer, SC 67 (Paris: Les Éditions du Cerf, 1960).

Palladius
Historia Lausiaca (H. Laus.) [*The Lausiac History*]—*The Lausiac History of Palladius*, ed. C. Butler, Texts and Studies 6/2 (Cambridge: Cambridge University Press, 1904).

Pseudo-Athanasius
De virginitate (Virg.) [*On Virginity*]—*De virginitate: Eine echte Schrift des Athanasius*, ed. F. von der Goltz, TU 29/2A (Leipzig: J. C. Hinrichs, 1905).

Pseudo-Clement
Epistulae ii ad virgines (Ep. ad virgines) [*Two Letters to Virgins*]—*Patres apostolici*, ed. F. Diekamp and F. X. Funk, 2 vols, 3rd edn (Tübingen: Laupp, 1913), 2.1–49; *Les pères apostoliques en copte*, ed. and tr. L.-Th. Lefort, 2 vols, CSCO 135–6 (Louvain: L. Dubecq, 1952), 1.35–43, 2.29–37.

S. Eligii episcopi Noviomensis vita (Vit. Elig.) [*Life of Eligius*]—PL 87.478–594.

Severus of Antioch
Homiliae (Hom.)—Les Homiliae cathedrales de Sévère d'Antioche: homélies LXXVIII à LXXXIII, ed. M. Brière, PO 20/2 (Paris: Firmin-Didot, 1927).

Shenoute
Acephalous work A14—*Shenute: Contra Origenistas*, ed. T. Orlandi (Rome: C.I.M., 1985), 16–21 [§§200–62].

Sophronius of Jerusalem
Miracula Cyri et Joannis (Mir. Cyr. et Jo.) [Miracles of Cyrus and John]—N. F. Marcos, Los Thaumata *de Sofronio: contribucion al estudio de la* incubatio *Cristiana* (Madrid: Instituto 'Antonio de Nebrija', 1975), 243–400.

Tatian
Oratio ad Graecos (Orat.) [Oration to the Greeks]—Tatiani Oratio ad Graecos, ed. M. Marcovich, PTS 43 (Berlin: Walter de Gruyter, 1995).

Tertullian
Apologeticus (Apol.) [Apology]—Tertulliani Opera, ed. E. Dekkers et al., 2 vols, CCSL 1–2 (Turnhout: Brepols, 1954), 1.85–171.

Theodore of Mopsuestia
Catechetical Homilies—Les homélies catéchétiques de Théodore de Mopsueste, tr. R. Tonneau and R. Devreesse (Vatican: Biblioteca apostolica vaticana, 1949).

Theodoret of Cyr
Expositio rectae fidei (Exp. rect. fid.) [Explanation of the True Faith]—Corpus apologetarum Christianorum saeculi secundi, ed. J. C. T. Otto, 9 vols in 7, 3rd edn of vols 1–5 (Jena: In libraria Maukii, 1851–81), 4.2–66.

The Teaching of Addai—The Doctrine of Addai the Apostle, ed. and tr. G. Phillips (London: Trübner, 1876); repr. in *The Teaching of Addai*, tr. G. Howard (Chico: Scholars, 1981).
The Tripartite Tractate (Tri. Trac.)—Le Traité Tripartite (NH I, 5), ed. E. Thomassen, BCNH, section 'Textes' 19 (Québec: Les Presses de l'Université Laval, 1989).
Traditio apostolica ,(Trad. ap.)—Hippolyte de Rom, La Tradition apostolique, ed. B. Botte, SC 11 *bis* (Paris: Les Éditions du Cerf, 1968); *Der koptische Text der Kirchenordnung Hippolyts*, ed. W. Till and J. Leipoldt, TU 58 (Berlin: Akademie Verlag, 1954).
Treatise on the Resurrection (Treat. Res.)—Nag Hammadi Codex I (The Jung Codex), ed. H. W. Attridge et al., 2 vols, NHMS 22–3 (Leiden: E. J. Brill, 1985).
Valentinian Exposition (Val. Exp.)—Concordance des textes de Nag Hammadi: les codices X et XIA, ed. W.-P. Funk, BCNH, section 'Concordances' 6 (Québec: Presses de l'Université Laval and Louvain: Peeters, 2000).

Secondary Literature

The following bibliography includes only items cited more than once in the notes.

Albarrán Martínez, M. J., 'Women Reading Books in Egyptian Monastic Circles', in J. P. Monferrer-Sala, H. Teule, and S. Torallas Tovar (eds), *Eastern Christians and their Written Heritage: Manuscripts, Scribes and Context* (Leuven: Peeters, 2012), 199–212.
Amundsen, L., 'Christian Papyri from the Oslo Collection', *Symbolae Osloenses*, 24 (1945), 121–47, doi: 10.1080/00397674508590389.

Bagnall, R. S., 'Religious Conversion and Onomastic Change in Early Byzantine Egypt', *Bulletin of the American Society of Papyrologists*, 19 (1982), 105–24, <http://hdl. handle.net/2027/spo.0599796.0019.003:02>.

Bagnall, R. S., 'Conversion and Onomastics: A Reply', *Zeitschrift für Papyrologie und Epigraphik* 69 (1987), 243–50, <http://www.jstor.org/stable/20186672>.

Bagnall, R. S., *Egypt in Late Antiquity* (Princeton: Princeton University Press, 1993).

Bagnall, R. S., *Reading Papyri, Writing Ancient History* (London: Routledge, 1995).

Bagnall, R. S., *Early Christian Books in Egypt* (Princeton: Princeton University Press, 2009).

Bagnall, R. S. (ed.), *The Oxford Handbook of Papyrology* (Oxford: Oxford University Press, 2009).

Bagnall, R. S., *Everyday Writing in the Graeco-Roman East* (Berkeley: University of California Press, 2012).

Bagnall, R. S., and R. Cribiore, *Women's Letters from Ancient Egypt, 300 BC–AD 800* (Ann Arbor: The University of Michigan Press, 2006).

Bélanger Sarrazin, R., 'Le syncrétisme en Égypte dans l'Antiquité tardive: l'apport des papyrus iatromagiques grecs', MA thesis, Université d'Ottawa, Ottawa, 2015.

Beltz, W., 'Die koptischen Zauberpapyri der Papyrus-Sammlung der Staatlichen Museen zu Berlin', *Archiv für Papyrusforschung*, 29 (1983), 59–86, doi: 10.1515/ apf.1983.1983.29.59.

Biondi, A., 'Le citazioni bibliche nei papiri magici cristiani greci', *Studia Papryologica*, 20 (1981), 93–127.

Blumell, L. H., *Lettered Christians: Christians, Letters, and Late Antique Oxyrhynchus* (Leiden: Brill, 2012).

Bohak, G., *Ancient Jewish Magic: A History* (Cambridge: Cambridge University Press, 2008).

Bohak, G., Y. Harari, and S. Shaked (eds), *Continuity and Innovation in the Magical Tradition* (Leiden: Brill, 2011).

Bonner, C., *Studies in Magical Amulets, Chiefly Graeco-Egyptian* (Ann Arbor: University of Michigan, 1950).

Boustan, R., and J. E. Sanzo, 'Christian Magicians, Jewish Magical Idioms, and the Shared Magical Culture of Late Antiquity', *Harvard Theological Review*, 110 (forthcoming).

Bowman, A. K., et al. (eds) *Oxyrhynchus: A City and its Texts* (London: Egypt Exploration Society, 2007).

Bradshaw, P. F., *The Search for the Origins of Christian Worship: Sources and Methods for the Study of Early Liturgy*, 2nd edn (Oxford: Oxford University Press, 2002).

Bradshaw, P. F., and M. E. Johnson, *The Eucharistic Liturgies: Their Evolution and Interpretation* (Collegeville: Liturgical Press, 2012).

Bradshaw, P. F., M. E. Johnson, and L. E. Phillips, *The Apostolic Tradition: A Commentary* (Minneapolis: Fortress, 2002).

Brakmann, H., 'Le déroulement de la messe copte: structure et histoire', in A. M. Triacca and A. Pistoia (eds), *L'Eucharistie: célébrations, rites, piétés* (Rome: C.L.V.-Edizioni liturgiche, 1995), 107–32.

Brashear, W. M., *Magica Varia* (Brussels: Fondation Égyptologique Reine Élisabeth 1991).

Brashear, W. M., 'The Greek Magical Papyri: An Introduction and Survey; Annotated Bibliography (1928–1994)', in W. Haase (ed.), *Aufstieg und Niedergang der römischen Welt*, Part II, vol. 18/5: *Heidentum: Die religiösen Verhältnisse in den Provinzen* (Berlin: Walter de Gruyter, 1995), 3380–684.

Brashear, W. M., and R. Kotansky, 'A New Magical Formulary', in P. Mirecki and M. Meyer (eds), *Magic and Ritual in the Ancient World* (Leiden: Brill, 2002), 3–24.

Bremmer, J. N., and J. R. Veenstra (eds), *The Metamorphosis of Magic from Late Antiquity to the Early Modern Period* (Leuven: Peeters, 2002).

Brightman, F. E. (ed.), *Liturgies Eastern and Western*, vol. 1: *Eastern Liturgies* (Oxford: Clarendon Press, 1896).

Budde, A., *Die ägyptische Basilios-Anaphora: Text—Kommentar—Geschichte* (Münster: Aschendorff, 2004).

Bülow-Jacobsen, A., 'Writing Materials in the Ancient World', in R. S. Bagnall (ed.), *The Oxford Handbook of Papyrology* (Oxford: Oxford University Press, 2009), 3–29.

Burton-Christie, D., *The Word in the Desert: Scripture and the Quest for Holiness in Early Christian Monasticism* (New York: Oxford University Press, 1993).

Carlig, N., and M. de Haro Sanchez, 'Amulettes ou exercises scolaires: sur les difficultés de la catégorisation des papyrus chrétiens', in M. de Haro Sanchez (ed.), *Écrire la magie dans l'antiquité: actes du colloque international (Liège, 13–15 octobre 2011)* (Liège: Presses Universitaires de Liège, 2015), 69–83.

Cavallo, G., *La scrittura greca e latina dei papiri: una introduzione* (Pisa: Fabrizio Serra, 2008).

Cavallo, G., and H. Maehler, *Greek Bookhands of the Early Byzantine Period: A.D. 300–800* (London: Institute of Classical Studies, 1987).

Chapa, J., 'Su demoni e angeli: il Salmo 90 nel suo contesto', in G. Bastianini and A. Casanova (eds), *I papiri letterari cristiani: atti del convegno internazionale di studi in memoria di Mario Naldini, Firenze, 10–11 Giugno 2010* (Florence: Istituto Papirologico 'G. Vitelli', 2011), 59–90.

Charlesworth, S. D., 'Consensus Standardization in the Systematic Approach to *nomina sacra* in Second- and Third-Century Gospel Manuscripts', *Aegyptus*, 86 (2006), 37–68, <http://www.jstor.org/stable/41217448>.

Choat, M., *Belief and Cult in Fourth-Century Papyri* (Turnhout: Brepols, 2006).

Ciraolo, L. J., 'Supernatural Assistants in the Greek Magical Papyri', in M. Meyer and P. Mirecki (eds), *Ancient Magic and Ritual Power* (Leiden: Brill, 1995), 279–95.

Cline, R., *Ancient Angels: Conceptualizing Angeloi in the Roman Empire* (Leiden: Brill, 2011).

Collart, P., 'Un papyrus Reinach inédit: Psaume 140 sur une amulette', *Aegyptus*, 13 (1933), 208–12, <http://www.jstor.org/stable/41214260>.

Collart, P., 'Psaumes et amulettes', *Aegyptus*, 14 (1934), 463–7, <http://www.jstor.org/stable/41214438>.

Cramer, M., *Das altägyptische Lebenszeichen [ankh] im christlichen (koptischen) Ägypten: Eine kultur- und religionsgeschichtliche Studie*, 3rd edn (Wiesbaden: Harrassowitz, 1955).

Cribiore, R., *Writing, Teachers, and Students in Graeco-Roman Egypt* (Atlanta: Scholars Press, 1996).

Cribiore, R., *Gymnastics of the Mind: Greek Education in Hellenistic and Roman Egypt* (Princeton: Princeton University Press, 2001).

Crum, W. E., 'La magie copte: nouveaux textes', in *Recueil d'études égyptologiques dédiées à la mémoire de Jean-François Champollion* (Paris: E. Champion, 1922), 539–40.

Crum, W. E., *A Coptic Dictionary* (Oxford: Clarendon Press, 1939).

Crum, W. E., and H. G. Evelyn White (eds), *The Monastery of Epiphanius at Thebes, Part II* (New York: The Metropolitan Museum of Art, 1926).

Cuming, G. J., *The Liturgy of St Mark* (Rome: Pontificium Institutum Studiorum Orientalium, 1990).

Daniel, R. W., 'A Christian Amulet on Papyrus', *Vigiliae Christianae*, 37 (1983), 400–4, doi: 10.2307/1583548.

Daniel, R. W., 'Some *ΦΥΛΑΚΤΗΡΙΑ*', *Zeitschrift für Papyrologie und Epigraphik*, 25 (1977), 145–54, <http://www.jstor.org/stable/20181354>.

Daniel, R. W., and F. Maltomini, 'From the African Psalter and Liturgy', *Zeitschrift für Papyrologie und Epigraphik*, 74 (1988), 253–65, <http://www.uni-koeln.de/phil-fak/ifa/zpe/downloads/1988/074pdf/074.html>.

Dasen, V., and J.-M. Spieser (eds), *Les savoirs magiques et leur transmission de l'Antiquité à la Renaissance* (Florence: SISMEL—Edizioni del Galluzzo, 2014).

Davis, C., 'The *Didache* and Early Monasticism in the East and West', in C. N. Jefford (ed.), *The Didache in Context: Essays on its Text, History, and Transmission* (Leiden: Brill, 1995), 352–67.

de Bruyn, T. S., 'Appeals to Jesus as the One "Who Heals Every Illness and Every Infirmity" (Matt 4: 23, 9: 35) in Amulets in Late Antiquity', in L. DiTommaso and L. Turcescu (eds), *The Reception and Interpretation of the Bible in Late Antiquity* (Leiden: Brill, 2008), 65–81.

de Bruyn, T. S., 'Papyri, Parchments, Ostraca, and Tablets Written with Biblical Texts in Greek and Used as Amulets: A Preliminary List', in T. J. Kraus and T. Nicklas (eds), *Early Christian Manuscripts: Examples of Applied Method and Approach* (Leiden: Brill, 2010), 145–89.

de Bruyn, T. S., 'A Late Witness to Valentinian Devotion in Egypt?' *Zeitschrift für antikes Christentum*, 18 (2013), 120–33, doi: 10.1515/zac-2014-0008.

de Bruyn, T. S., 'An Anatomy of Tradition: The Case of the *Charitêsion*', *Archiv für Religionsgeschichte*, 16 (2015), 31–50, doi: 10.1515/arege-2014-0005.

de Bruyn, T. S., 'Appeals to the Intercessions of Mary in Greek Liturgical and Para-liturgical Texts from Egypt', in L. M. Peltomaa, A. Külzer, and P. Allen (eds), *Presbeia Theotokou: The Intercessory Role of Mary across Times and Places in Byzantium (4th–9th Century)* (Vienna: Verlag der Österreichischen Akademie der Wissenschaften, 2015), 115–29.

de Bruyn, T. S., 'Christian Apocryphal and Canonical Narratives in Greek Papyrus Amulets in Late Antiquity', in P. Piovanelli and T. Burke (eds), *Rediscovering the Apocryphal Continent: New Perspectives on Early Christian and Late Antique Apocryphal Texts and Traditions* (Tübingen: Mohr Siebeck, 2015), 153–74.

de Bruyn, T. S., 'Historians, Bishops, Amulets, Scribes, and Rites: Interpreting Christian Practice', *Studia Patristica* (forthcoming).

de Bruyn, T. S., and J. H. F. Dijkstra, 'Greek Amulets and Formularies from Egypt Containing Christian Elements: A Checklist of Papyri, Parchments, Ostraka, and Tablets', *Bulletin of the American Society of Papyrologists*, 48 (2011), 163–216, <http://hdl.handle.net/2027/spo.0599796.0048.001>.

de Haro Sanchez, M., 'Le vocabulaire de la pathologie et de la thérapeutique dans les papyrus iatromagiques grecs: fièvres, traumatismes et "épilepsie"', *Bulletin of the American Society of Papyrologists*, 47 (2010), 131–53, <http://hdl.handle.net/2027/spo.0599796.0047.001>.

Deissmann, A., *Light from the Ancient East: The New Testament Illustrated by Recently Discovered Texts of the Graeco-Roman World*, tr. L. R. M. Strachan from the 4th German edn (New York, 1927; repr. Peabody: Hendrickson, 1995).

Delatte, A., *Anecdota Atheniensia. Tome I. Textes grecs inédits relatifs à l'histoire des religions* (Liège and Paris: H. Vaillant-Carmanne and Édouard Champion, 1927).

Delattre, A., and K. A. Worp, 'Trois tablettes de bois du Musée de Leyde', *Chronique d'Égypt*, 87 (2012), 361–82, doi: 10.1484/J.CDE.1.103137.

Depauw, M., and W. Clarysse, 'How Christian was Fourth Century Egypt? Onomastic Perspectives on Conversion', *Vigiliae Christianae*, 67 (2013), 407–35, doi: 10.1163/15700720-12341144.

Dickie, M. W., 'The Fathers of the Church and the Evil Eye', in H. Maguire (ed.), *Byzantine Magic* (Washington, D.C.: Dumbarton Oaks Research Library and Collection, 1995), 9–34.

Dickie, M. W., *Magic and Magicians in the Greco-Roman World* (London: Routledge, 2001).

Dieleman, J., *Priests, Tongues, and Rites: The London-Leiden Magical Manuscripts and Translation in Egyptian Ritual (100–300 CE)* (Leiden: Brill, 2005).

Dijkstra, J. H. F., *Philae and the End of Ancient Egyptian Religion: A Regional Study of Religious Transformation (298–642 CE)* (Leuven: Peeters, 2008).

Dijkstra, J. H. F., 'The Interplay between Image and Text on Greek Amulets Containing Christian Elements from Late Antique Egypt', in D. Boschung and J. M. Bremmer (eds), *The Materiality of Magic* (Munich: Wilhelm Fink, 2015), 271–92.

Dijkstra, J. H. F., and M. van Dijk (eds), *The Encroaching Desert: Egyptian Hagiography and the Medieval West* (Leiden: Brill, 2006).

Dinkler-Von Schubert, E., '*ΣΤΑΥΡΟΣ*: Vom "Wort vom Kreuz" (1 Kor. 1,18) zum Kreuz-Symbol', in C. Moss and K. Kiefer (eds), *Byzantine East, Latin West: Art-Historical Studies in Honor of Kurt Weitzmann* (Princeton: Department of Art and Archaeology, Princeton University, 1995), 29–39.

Dornseiff, F., *Das Alphabet in Mystik und Magie*, 2nd edn (Leipzig: Teubner, 1925).

Dosoo, K., 'A History of the Theban Magical Library', *Bulletin of the American Society of Papyrologists*, 53 (2016), 251–74.

Draper, J. A. (ed.), *The Didache in Modern Research* (Leiden: Brill, 1996).

Drioton, E., 'Un apocryphe anti-arien: la version copte de la correspondence d'Abgar, roi d'Édesse, avec Notre-Seigneur', *Revue de l'orient chrétien*, 20 (1915–17), 306–26 and 337–73.

Dzwiza, K., *Schriftverwendung in antiker Ritualpraxis anhand der griechischen, demotischen und koptischen Praxisanleitungen des 1.–7. Jahrhunderts*, 4 vols in 2 (Erfurt and Heidelberg, 2013), <http://www.db-thueringen.de/servlets/DocumentServlet?id=23500>.

Eitrem, S., *Some Notes on the Demonology in the New Testament*, 2nd edn (Oslo: Universitetsforlaget, 1966).

Entwistle, C., and N. Adams (eds), *'Gems of Heaven': Recent Research on Engraved Gemstones in Late Antiquity c. AD 200-600* (London: The British Museum, 2011).

Faraone, C. A., 'The Agonistic Context of Early Greek Binding Spells', in C. A. Faraone and D. Obbink (eds), *Magika Hiera: Ancient Greek Magic and Religion* (New York: Oxford University Press, 1991), 3–32.

Faraone, C. A., 'New Light on Ancient Greek Exorcisms of the Wandering Womb', *Zeitschrift für Papyrologie und Epigraphik*, 144 (2003), 189–200, <http://www.jstor.org/stable/20191675>.

Faraone, C. A., and D. Obbink (eds), *Magika Hiera: Ancient Greek Magic and Religion* (New York: Oxford University Press, 1991).

Förster, H., 'Alltag und Kirche', in J. Henner, H. Förster, and U. Horak (eds), *Christliches mit Feder und Faden: Christliches in Texten, Textilien und Alltagsgegenständen aus Ägypten* (Vienna: Österreichische Verlagsgesellschaft, 1999), 40–51.

Fournet, J.-L., 'The Multilingual Environment of Late Antique Egypt: Greek, Latin, Coptic, and Persian Documentation', in R. S. Bagnall (ed.), *The Oxford Handbook of Papyrology* (Oxford: Oxford University Press, 2009), 418–51.

Fowler, R. L., 'The Concept of Magic', in *Thesaurus Cultus et Rituum Antiquorum (ThesCRA)*, 9 vols (Los Angeles: J. Paul Getty Museum, 2004–2012), 3.283–6.

Frankfurter, D., 'The Magic of Writing and the Writing of Magic: The Power of the Word in Egyptian and Greek Traditions', *Helios*, 21 (1994), 179–221.

Frankfurter, D., *Religion in Roman Egypt: Assimilation and Resistance* (Princeton: Princeton University Press, 1998).

Froschauer, H., 'Ⱥ = Ligatur von Alpha und Omega?', *Analecta Papyrologica*, 14–15 (2002–2003), 91–9.

Frøyshov, S. S. R., 'The Cathedral-Monastic Distinction Revisited. Part I: Was Egyptian Desert Liturgy a Pure Monastic Office?', *Studia Liturgica*, 37 (2007), 198–216.

Gardner, I., 'The Manichaean Community at Kellis: A Progress Report', in P. Mirecki and J. D. BeDuhn (eds), *Emerging from Darkness: Studies in the Recovery of Manichean Sources* (Leiden: Brill, 1997), 161–75.

Gemeinhardt, P., L. Van Hoof, and P. Van Nuffelen (eds), *Education and Religion in Late Antiquity: Reflections, Social Contexts, and Genres* (London and New York: Routledge, 2016).

Gerhards, A., *Die griechische Gregoriosanaphora: Ein Beitrag zur Geschichte des eucharistischen Hochgebets* (Münster: Aschendorff, 1984).

Gignac, F. T., *A Grammar of the Greek Papyri of the Roman and Byzantine Periods*, 2 vols (Milan: Istituto Editoriale Cisalpino-La Goliardica, 1976–1981).

Giversen, S., 'Ad Abgarum: The Sahidic Version of the Letter to Abgar on a Wooden Tablet', *Acta Orientalia*, 24 (1958), 71–82.

Gonis, N., 'An "Our Father" with Problems', *Zeitschrift für Papyrologie und Epigraphik*, 181 (2012), 46–7, <http://www.jstor.org/stable/41616956>.

Gonis, N., and C. E. Römer, 'Ein Lobgesang an den Vater der Grösse in P. Kellis II 94', *Zeitschrift für Papyrologie und Epigraphik*, 120 (1998), 299–300, <http://www.uni-koeln.de/phil-fak/ifa/zpe/downloads/1998/120pdf/120.html>.

Gordon, R., 'Imaging Greek and Roman Magic', in B. Ankarloo and S. Clark (eds), *Witchcraft and Magic in Europe: Ancient Greece and Rome* (Philadelphia: University of Pennsylvania Press, 1999).

Gordon, R., 'Shaping the Text: Innovation and Authority in Graeco-Egyptian Malign Magic', in H. F. J. Horstmanshoff et al. (eds), *Kykeon: Studies in Honour of H. S. Versnel* (Leiden: Brill, 2002), 69–111.

Gordon, R., '*Signa nova et inaudita*: The Theory and Practice of Invented Signs (*charaktêres*) in Graeco-Egyptian Magical Texts', *MHNH: Revista internacional de investigación sobre magia y astrología antiguas*, 11 (2011), 15–44.

Gordon, R., '*Charaktêres* between Antiquity and Renaissance: Transmission and Re-Invention', in V. Dasen and J.-M. Spieser (eds), *Les savoirs magiques et leur transmission de l'Antiquité à la Renaissance* (Florence: SISMEL—Edizioni del Galluzzo, 2014), 253–300.

Graf, F., 'Augustine and Magic', in J. N. Bremmer and J. R. Veenstra (eds), *The Metamorphosis of Magic from Late Antiquity to the Early Modern Period* (Leuven: Peeters, 2002), 87–103.

Guignard, C., 'Technical and/or Magical Character', in M. Wallraff et al. (eds), *Iulius Africanus. Cesti: The Extant Fragments*, GCS N.F. 18 (Berlin: Walter de Gruyter, 2012), xxvii–xxxii.

Hagedorn, D., 'PUG I 41 und die Namen der vierzig Märtyrer von Sebaste', *Zeitschrift für Papyrologie und Epigraphik*, 55 (1984), 146–53, <http://www.jstor.org/stable/20184025>.

Hagedorn, D., 'Bemerkungen zu Urkunden', *Zeitschrift für Papyrologie und Epigraphik*, 145 (2003), 224–7, <http://www.jstor.org/stable/20191724>.

Hammerstaedt, J., *Griechische Anaphorenfragmente aus Ägypten und Nubien* (Opladen: Westdeutscher Verlag, 1999).

Hanssens, J. M., *La liturgie d'Hippolyte: documents et études* (Rome: Università gregoriana, 1970).

Harari, Y., 'What is a Magical Text? Methodological Reflections Aimed at Redefining Early Jewish Magic', in S. Shaked (ed.), *Officina Magica: Essays on the Practice of Magic in Antiquity* (Leiden: Brill, 2005), 91–124.

Harmless, W., *Desert Christians: An Introduction to the Literature of Early Monasticism* (New York: Oxford University Press, 2004).

Harrauer, H., 'Bücher in Papyri', in H. W. Lang (ed.), *Flores litterarum Ioanni Marte sexagenario oblati: Wissenschaft in der Bibliothek* (Vienna: Böhlau Verlag, 1995), 59–77.

Harrauer, H., 'Strafaufschub', *Zeitschrift für Papyrologie und Epigraphik*, 30 (1978), 209–10, <http://www.jstor.org/stable/20181621>.

Harrauer, H., 'Von Silber beschützt', in H. Lang and H. Harrauer (eds), *Mirabilia artium librorum recreant te tuosque ebriant: dona natalicia Ioanni Marte oblata* (Vienna, Phoibos, 2001), 90–3.

Harrauer, H., *Handbuch der griechischen Paläographie*, 2 vols (Stuttgart: Anton Hiersemann, 2010).

Harrauer, H., and C. Gastgeber, 'Bibeltexte im Alltag: Schutzamulette', in H. Froschauer, C. Gastgeber, and H. Harrauer (eds), *Ein Buch verändert die Welt: Älteste Zeugnisse der Heiligen Schrift aus der Zeit des frühen Christentums in Ägypten* (Vienna: Phoibos, 2003), 35–43.

Heid, S., 'Kreuz', in T. Klauser et al. (eds), *Reallexikon für Antike und Christentum*, 26 vols (Stuttgart: A. Hiersemann, 1950–2015), 21.1099–148.

Henner, J., *Fragmenta Liturgica Copta* (Tübingen: Mohr Siebeck, 2000).

Hopfner, T., 'Ein neuer griechischer Zauberpapyrus (Pap. Wessely Pragens. Graec. No. 1)', *Archiv Orientální*, 7 (1935), 355–66.

Horak, U. (ed.), *Illuminierte Papyri, Pergamente und Papiere I* (Vienna: A. Holzhausens, 1992).

Hübner, W., 'Planets. II. Astrology and Mythology', in H. Cancik and H. Schneider (eds), *Brill's New Pauly: Encyclopaedia of the Ancient World: Antiquity*, 16 vols (Leiden: Brill, 2002–10), 11.328–34.

Hunger, H., 'Zwei unbekannte neutestamentliche Papyrusfragmente der Österreichischen Nationalbibliothek', *Biblos*, 8 (1959), 7–12.

Hunger, H., 'Ergänzungen zu zwei neutestamentlichen Papyrusfragmenten der Österreichischen Nationalbibliothek', *Biblos*, 19 (1970), 71–5.

Hurtado, L. W., *The Earliest Christian Artifacts: Manuscripts and Christian Origins* (Grand Rapids: Eerdmans, 2006).

Jenkins, G., 'A Single Codex Sheet from Kellis: A Manichaean Miniature Greek Codex (Papyrus 2)', in J. N. Bremmer (ed.), *The Apocryphal Acts of John* (Kampen: Kok Pharos, 1995), 217–30.

Joannou, P.-P., *Discipline générale antique (IVᵉ–IXᵉ s.)*, vol. 1/2: *Les canons des synodes particuliers* (Vatican: Tipografia Italo-Orientale 'S. Nilo', 1962).

Joannou, P.-P., *Discipline générale antique (IVᵉ–IXᵉ s.)*, vol. 2: *Les canons des pères grecs* (Vatican: Tipografia Italo-Orientale 'S. Nilo', 1963).

Johnson, M. E., *The Prayers of Sarapion of Thmuis: A Literary, Liturgical, and Theological Analysis* (Rome: Pontificio Istituto Orientale, 1995).

Jones, B. C., *New Testament Texts on Greek Amulets from Late Antiquity* (London: Bloomsbury T & T Clark, 2016).

Jordan, D. R., 'A Survey of Greek Defixiones Not Included in the Special Corpora', *Greek, Roman and Byzantine Studies*, 26 (1985), 151–97, <http://grbs.library.duke.edu/issue/view/1131>.

Jordan, D. R., 'New Greek Curse Tablets (1985–2000)', *Greek, Roman and Byzantine Studies*, 41 (2000), 5–46, <http://grbs.library.duke.edu/issue/view/321>.

Jördens, A. (ed.), *Ägyptische Magie und ihre Umwelt* (Wiesbaden: Harrassowitz, 2015).

Jungmann, J. A., *The Place of Christ in Liturgical Prayer*, 2nd edn, tr. A. Peeler (Staten Island: Alba House, 1965).

Kasser, R., 'Paleography', in A. S. Atiya (ed.), *The Coptic Encyclopedia*, 8 vols (New York: Macmillan, 1991), 8.175–84.

Kelhoffer, J. A., '"Hippolytus" and Magic: An Examination of *Elenchos* IV 28–42 and Related Passages in Light of the Papyri Graecae Magicae', *Zeitschrift für antikes Christentum*, 11 (2008), 517–48, doi: 10.1515/ZAC.2007.028.

Klijn, A. F. J., *Jewish-Christian Gospel Traditions* (Leiden: Brill, 1992).

Klingshirn, W. E., *Caesarius of Arles: The Making of a Christian Community in Late Antique Gaul* (Cambridge: Cambridge University Press, 1994).

Knox, W. L., 'Jewish Liturgical Exorcism', *Harvard Theological Review*, 31 (1938), 191–203, <http://www.jstor.org/stable/1508308>.

Kotsifou, C., 'Books and Book Production in the Monastic Communities of Byzantine Egypt', in W. E. Klingshirn and L. Safran (eds), *The Early Christian Book* (Washington, D.C.: Catholic University of America Press, 2007), 48–66.

Kraus, T. J., 'Septuaginta-Psalm 90 in apotropäischer Verwendung: Vorüberlegungen für eine kritische Edition und (bisheriges) Datenmaterial', *Biblische Notizen*, n.f. 125 (2005), 39–73.

Kraus, T. J., 'Manuscripts with the *Lord's Prayer*—They Are More Than Simply Witnesses to That Text Itself', in T. J. Kraus and T. Nicklas (eds), *New Testament Manuscripts: Their Texts and their World* (Leiden: Brill, 2006), 227–66.

Kraus, T. J., 'Βους, Βαινχωωχ und Septuaginta-Psalm 90? Überlegungen zu den sogenannten "Bous"-Amuletten und dem beliebtesten Bibeltext für apotropäische Zwecke', *Zeitschrift für antikes Christentum*, 11 (2008), 479–91, doi: 10.1515/ZAC.2007.025.

Kraus, T. J., 'P.Berol. 11710', in T. Nicklas, M. J. Kruger, and T. J. Kraus (eds), *Gospel Fragments* (Oxford: Oxford University Press, 2009), 227–39.

Kraus, T. J., and T. Nicklas (eds), *New Testament Manuscripts: Their Texts and their World* (Leiden: Brill, 2006).

Krebs, F., 'Altchristliche Texte im Berliner Museum', *Nachrichten der Königlichen Gesellschaft der Wissenschaften zu Göttingen*, 4 (1892), 114–20.

La'da, C. A., and A. Papathomas, 'A Greek Papyrus Amulet from the Duke Collection with Biblical Excerpts', *Bulletin of the American Society of Papyrologists*, 41 (2004), 93–113, <http://hdl.handle.net/2027/spo.0599796.0041.001:06>.

Lampe, G. H. E. (ed.), *A Greek Patristic Lexicon* (Oxford: Clarendon Press, 1961).

Leclercq, H., 'Croix, crucifix', *Dictionnaire d'archéologie chrétienne et de liturgie*, 15 vols (Paris: Letouzey et Ané, 1907–53), 3/2.3045–131.

Leicht, R., 'Mashbia' Ani 'Alekha: Types and Patterns of Ancient Jewish and Christian Exorcism Formulae', *Jewish Studies Quarterly*, 13 (2006), 319–34, <http://www.jstor.org/stable/40753414>.

Liddell, H. G., R. Scott, and H. S. Jones (eds), *A Greek-English Lexicon*, 9th edn with a revised supplement (Oxford: Clarendon Press, 1996).

LiDonnici, L., '"According to the Jews": Identified (and Identifying) "Jewish" Elements in the *Greek Magical Papyri*', in L. LiDonnici and A. Lieber (eds), *Heavenly Tablets: Interpretation, Identity and Tradition in Ancient Judaism* (Leiden: Brill, 2007), 87–108.

Limongi, D., 'La diffusione dei Vangeli in Egitto (secc. I–VIII): osservazioni sul *Vangelo secondo Marco*', *Analecta Papyrologica*, 7 (1995), 49–62.

Llewelyn, S. R., 'The Christian Symbol *ΧΜΓ*, an Acrostic or an Isopsephism?' in S. R. Llewelyn (ed.) *New Documents Illustrating Early Christianity*, vol. 8: *A Review of the Greek Inscriptions and Papyri Published 1984–85* (Sydney and Grand Rapids: Ancient History Documentary Research Centre, Macquarie University, and Eerdmans, 1998), 156–68.

Lotz, A., *Der Magiekonflikt in der Spätantike* (Bonn: Rudolf Habelt, 2005).

Luijendijk, A., 'A Gospel Amulet for Joannia (P.Oxy. VIII 1151)', in K. B. Stratton and D. S. Kalleres (eds), *Daughters of Hecate: Women and Magic in the Ancient World* (New York: Oxford University Press, 2014), 418–43.

Maltomini, F., 'I papiri greci', *Studi classici e orientali*, 29 (1979), 55–124.

Maltomini, F., 'Cristo all'Eufrate. P.Heid.G.1101: amuleto cristiano', *Zeitschrift für Papyrologie und Epigraphik*, 48 (1982), 149–70, <http://www.jstor.org/stable/20183648>.

Maltomini, F., 'Osservazioni al testo di alcuni papiri magici greci. (III.)', *Studi classici e orientali*, 32 (1982), 235–41, <http://www.jstor.org/stable/24181825>.

Maltomini, F., 'PGM P 5a rivisitato', *Galenos*, 9 (2015), 229–34.

Maraval, P., 'Les premiers développements du culte des XL Martyrs de Sébastée dans l'Orient byzantin et en occident', *Vetera Christianorum*, 36 (1999), 193–211.

Markschies, C., 'Wer schrieb die sogenannte *Traditio Apostolica*? Neue Beobachtungen und Hypothesen zu einer kaum lösbaren Frage aus der altkirchlichen Literaturgeschichte', in *Tauffragen und Bekenntnis: Studien zur sogenannten 'Traditio Apostolica', zu den 'Interrogationes de fide' und zum 'Römischen Glaubensbekenntnis'* (Berlin: Walter de Gruyter, 1999), 1–74.

Marrassini, P., 'I frammenti aramaici', *Studi classici e orientali*, 29 (1979), 125–30.

Martín-Hernández, R., 'Reading Magical Drawings in the Greek Magical Papyri', in P. Schubert (ed.), *Actes du 26ᵉ Congrès internationale de papyrologie, Genève, 16–21 août 2010* (Geneva: Librarie Droz, 2012), 491–8.

Martín-Hernández, R., and S. Tovar Torallas, 'The Use of the *Ostracon* in Magical Practice in Late Antique Egypt: Magical Handbooks vs. Material Evidence', *Studi e materiali di storia delle religioni*, 80/2 (2014), 780–800.

Mastrocinque, A., 'Le pouvoir de l'écriture dans la magie', *Cahiers 'Mondes anciens'*, 1 (2010) [online], doi: 10.4000/mondesanciens.168.

Mazza, R., 'P.Oxy. XI, 1384: medicina, rituali di guarigione e cristianesimi nell'Egitto tardoantico', *Annali di storia dell'esegesi*, 24/2 (2007), 437–62.

Merkelbach, R. (ed.), *Abrasax: Ausgewählte Papyri religiösen und magischen Inhalts*, vol. 4: *Exorzismen und jüdisch/christlich beeinflusste Texte* (Cologne: Westdeutscher Verlag, 1996).

Metzger, M., 'Introduction', in M. Metzger (ed.), *Les Constitutions Apostoliques. Tome I: Livres I et II*, SC 320 (Paris: Les Éditions du Cerf, 1985), 11–94.

Meyer, M., *The Magical Book of Mary and the Angels (P. Heid. Inv. Kopt. 685): Text, Translation, and Commentary* (Heidelberg: Universitätsverlag C. Winter, 1996).

Meyer, M., 'The Prayer of Mary Who Dissolves Chains in Coptic Magic and Religion', in P. Mirecki and M. Meyer (eds), *Magic and Ritual in the Ancient World* (Leiden: Brill, 2002), 407–15.

Meyer, M., and P. Mirecki (eds), *Ancient Magic and Ritual Power* (Leiden: Brill, 1995).

Michel, S., *Magischen Gemmen im Britischen Museum*, 2 vols (London: British Museum Press, 2001).

Mihálykó, A. T., 'Christ and Charon: PGM P13 Reconsidered', *Symbolae Osloenses*, 89 (2016), 183–209, doi: 10.1080/00397679.2015.1108051.

Mihálykó, A. T., 'Writing the Christian Liturgy in Egypt (3rd to 9th cent.)', PhD thesis, University of Oslo, Oslo, 2016.

Mirecki, P., 'The Coptic Wizard's Hoard', *Harvard Theological Review*, 87 (1994), 435–60, <http://www.jstor.org/stable/1509968>.

Mirecki, P., I. Gardner, and A. Alcock, 'Magical Spell, Manichaean Letter', in P. Mirecki and J. D. BeDuhn (eds), *Emerging from Darkness: Studies in the Recovery of Manichean Sources* (Leiden: Brill, 1997), 1–32.

Mirecki, P., and M. Meyer (eds), *Magic and Ritual in the Ancient World* (Leiden: Brill, 2002).

Nagy, A. M., 'Engineering Ancient Amulets: Magical Gems of the Roman Imperial Period', in D. Boschung and J. M. Bremmer (eds), *The Materiality of Magic* (Munich: Wilhelm Fink, 2015), 205–40.

Naldini, M., 'Due papiri cristiani della collezione fiorentina', *Studi italiani di filologia classica*, 33 (1961), 212–18.

Nicolotti, A., *Esorcismo cristiano e possessione diabolica tra II e III secolo* (Turnhout: Brepols, 2011).

Nongbri, B., 'The Lord's Prayer and *XMΓ*: Two Christian Papyrus Amulets', *Harvard Theological Review*, 104 (2011), 59–64, doi: 10.2307/41234070.

Ogden, D., 'Binding Spells: Curse Tablets and Voodoo Dolls in the Greek and Roman Worlds', in B. Ankarloo and S. Clark (eds), *Witchcraft and Magic in Europe: Ancient Greece and Rome* (Philadelphia: University of Pennsylvania Press, 1999), 1–90.

Orsini, P., and W. Clarysse, 'Early New Testament Manuscripts and their Dates: A Critique of Theological Palaeography', *Ephemerides Theologicae Lovanienses*, 88 (2012), 443–74, doi: 10.2143/ETL.88.4.2957937.

Otranto, R., *Antiche liste di libri su papiro* (Rome: Edizioni di storia e letteratura, 2000).

Otto, B.-C., *Magie: Rezeptions- und diskursgeschichtliche Analysen von der Antike bis zur Neuzeit* (Berlin: De Gruyter, 2011).

Paap, A. H. R. E., *Nomina Sacra in the Greek Papyri of the First Five Centuries A.D.: The Sources and Some Deductions* (Leiden: Brill, 1959).

Papaconstantinou, A., 'La liturgie stationnale à Oxyrhynchos dans la première moitié du 6ᵉ siècle: réédition et commentaire du POxy XI 1357', *Revue des Études Byzantines*, 54 (1996), 139–59, 146, doi: 10.3406/rebyz.1996.1921.

Papaconstantinou, A., 'Les sanctuaires de la Vierge dans l'Égypte byzantine et omeyyade: l'apport des textes documentaires', *Journal of Juristic Papyrology*, 30 (2000), 81–94.

Papaconstantinou, A., *Le culte des saints en Égypte des Byzantins aux Abbassides: l'apport des inscriptions et des papyrus grecs et coptes* (Paris: CNRS Éditions, 2001).

Papathomas, A., 'Ein griechisches Papyrusamulett mit Teilen aus zwei Septuaginta Psalmen', *Tyche*, 27 (2012), 113–18, doi: <http://dx.doi.org/10.15661/tyche.2012.027.05>.

Peltomaa, L. M., A. Külzer, and P. Allen (eds), *Presbeia Theotokou: The Intercessory Role of Mary across Times and Places in Byzantium (4th–9th Century)* (Vienna: Verlag der Österreichischen Akademie der Wissenschaften, 2015).

Pernigotti, S., 'Una rilettura del P.Mil. Vogl. Copto 16', *Aegyptus*, 73 (1993), 93–125, <http://www.jstor.org/stable/41217102>.

Pintaudi, R., 'Per la datazione di PSI VI 719', *Analecta Papyrologica*, 2 (1990), 27–8.

Pleyte, W., and P. A. A. Boeser, *Manuscrits coptes du Musée d'Antiquités des Pays-Bas à Leide* (Leiden: Brill, 1897).

Pradel, F., *Griechische und süditalienische Gebete, Beschwörungen und Rezepte des Mittelalters* (Giessen: Alfred Töpelmann, 1907).

Quack, J. F., 'From Ritual to Magic: Ancient Egyptian Precursors of the Charitesion and their Social Setting', in G. Bohak, Y. Harari, and S. Shaked (eds), *Continuity and Innovation in the Magical Tradition* (Leiden: Brill, 2011), 43–84.

Quecke, H., *Untersuchungen zum koptischen Stundengebet* (Louvain: Université catholique de Louvain, Institut Orientaliste, 1970).

Rahlfs, A. (ed.), *Psalmi cum Odis*, 3rd edn (Göttingen: Vandenhoek and Ruprecht, 1979).

Rapp, C., 'Christians and their Manuscripts in the Greek East in the Fourth Century', in G. Cavallo, G. de Gregori, and M. Maniaci (eds), *Scritture, libri e testi nelle aree provinciali di Bisanzio*, 2 vols (Spoleto: Centro italiano di studi sull'alto Medioevo, 1991), 1.127–48.

Rebillard, E., *Christians and their Many Identities in Late Antiquity, North Africa, 200–450 CE* (Ithaca: Cornell University Press, 2012).

Rémondon, R., 'Un papyrus magique copte', *Bulletin de l'Institut français d'archéologie orientale*, 52 (1953), 157–61, <http://www.ifao.egnet.net/bifao/52/>.

Renaudot, E. (ed.), *Liturgiarum orientalium collectio*, 2 vols, 2nd edn (Paris, 1716; repr. Frankfurt am Main and London: Joseph Baer and John Leslie Bibliopolam, 1847).

Ritner, R. K., 'Egyptian Magical Practice under the Roman Empire: The Demotic Spells and their Religious Context', in W. Haase (ed.), *Aufstieg und Niedergang der römischen Welt*, Part II, vol. 18/5: *Heidentum: Die religiösen Verhältnisse in den Provinzen* (Berlin: Walter de Gruyter, 1995), 3333–79.

Roca-Puig, R., *Anàfora de Barcelona i altres pregàries (Missa del segle IV)*, 2nd edn (Barcelona: Grafos, 1996).

Römer, C. E., 'Christliche Texte II (1996–1997)', *Archiv für Papyrusforschung*, 44 (1998), 129–39, doi: 10.1515/apf.1998.44.1.129.

Römer, C. E., R. W. Daniel, and K. A. Worp, 'Das Gebet zur Handauflegung bei Kranken in P. Barc. 155, 19–156 , 5 und P. Kellis I 88', *Zeitschrift für Papyrologie und Epigraphik*, 119 (1997), 128–31, <http://www.uni-koeln.de/phil-fak/ifa/zpe/down loads/1997/119pdf/119.html>.

Rordorf, W., 'An Aspect of the Judeo-Christian Ethic: The Two Ways', in J. A. Draper (ed.), *The Didache in Modern Research* (Leiden: Brill, 1996), 148–64.

Rüpke, J. (ed.), *The Individual in the Religions of the Ancient Mediterranean* (Oxford: Oxford University Press, 2013).

Sanzo, J. E., 'Brit. Lib. Or. 4919(2): An Unpublished Coptic Amulet in the British Library', *Zeitschrift für Papyrologie und Epigraphik*, 183 (2012), 98–9, <http://www.jstor.org/stable/23849875>.

Sanzo, J. E., *Scriptural Incipits on Amulets from Late Antique Egypt: Text, Typology, and Theory* (Tübingen: Mohr Siebeck, 2014).

Sanzo, J. E., 'Wrapped Up in the Bible: The Multifaceted Ritual on a Late Antique Amulet (P. Oxy. VIII 1077)', *Journal of Early Christian Studies*, 24 (2016), 569–97.

Sanzo, J. E., and L. Zelyck, 'The Text and Function of P. Berol. 11710 Revisited', *Journal of Theological Studies* (forthcoming).

Schäfer, P., and H. G. Kippenberg (eds), *Envisioning Magic: A Princeton Seminar and Symposium* (Leiden: Brill, 1997).

Schäfer, P., and S. Shaked (eds), *Magische Texte aus der Kairoer Geniza*, 3 vols (Tübingen: J. C. B. Mohr, 1994–9).

Scheidel, W., *Death on the Nile: Disease and the Demography of Roman Egypt* (Leiden: Brill, 2001).

Scibilia, A., 'Supernatural Assistance in the Greek Magical Papyri: The Figure of the *Parhedros*', in J. N. Bremmer and J. R. Veenstra (eds), *The Metamorphosis of Magic from Late Antiquity to the Early Modern Period* (Leuven: Peeters, 2002), 71–86.

Shandruk, W. M., 'Christian Use of Magic in Late Antique Egypt', *Journal of Early Christian Studies*, 20 (2012), 31–57, doi: 10.1353/earl.2012.0003.

Shandruk, W. M., 'The Interchange of ι and η in Spelling χριστ- in Documentary Papyri', *Bulletin of the American Society of Papyrologists*, 47 (2010), 205–19, <http://hdl.handle.net/2027/spo.0599796.0047.001:16>.

Smith, M., 'Jewish Elements in the Magical Papyri', in S. J. D. Cohen (ed.), *Studies in the Cult of Yahweh: New Testament, Early Christianity, and Magic* (Leiden: Brill, 1996), 241–56.

Sorensen, E., *Possession and Exorcism in the New Testament and Early Christianity* (Tübingen: Mohr Siebeck, 2002).

Spier, J., *Late Antique and Early Christian Gems* (Wiesbaden: Reichert, 2007).

Spier, J., 'Late Antique Gems: Some Unpublished Examples', in C. Entwistle and N. Adams (eds), *'Gems of Heaven': Recent Research on Engraved Gemstones in Late Antiquity c. AD 200–600* (London: The British Museum, 2011), 193–213.

Spier, J., 'An Antique Magical Book Used for Making Sixth-Century Byzantine Amulets?', in V. Dasen and J.-M. Spieser (eds), *Les savoirs magiques et leur transmission de l'Antiquité à la Renaissance* (Florence: SISMEL—Edizioni del Galluzzo, 2014), 43–66.

Spinks, B. D., *The Sanctus in the Eucharistic Prayer* (Cambridge: Cambridge University Press, 1991).

Stander, H. F., 'Amulets and the Church Fathers', *Ekklesiastikos Pharos*, 75 (1993), 55–66.

Stegemann, V., *Die koptischen Zaubertexte der Sammlung Papyrus Erzherzog Rainer in Wien* (Heidelberg: Carl Winters Universitätsbuchhandlung, 1934).

Stewart(-Sykes), A. (ed.), *On the Two Ways: Life or Death, Light or Darkness: Foundational Texts in the Tradition* (Yonkers: St Vladimir's Seminary Press, 2011).

Stratton, K. B., *Naming the Witch: Magic, Ideology, and Stereotype in the Ancient World* (New York: Columbia University Press, 2007).

Sullivan, K. P., and T. G. Wilfong, 'The Reply of Jesus to King Abgar: A Coptic New Testament Apocryphon Reconsidered (P. Mich. Inv. 6213)', *Bulletin of the American Society of Papyrologists*, 42 (2005), 107–23, <http://hdl.handle.net/2027/spo.0599796.0042.001:09>.

Szirmai, J. A., *The Archaeology of Medieval Bookbinding* (Aldershot: Ashgate, 1999).

Taft, R. F., *The Liturgy of the Hours in East and West: The Origins of the Divine Office and its Meaning for Today*, 2nd edn (Collegeville: Liturgical Press, 1993).

Taft, R. F., *A History of the Liturgy of St. John Chrysostom*, vol. 5: *The Precommunion Rites* (Rome: Pontificio Istituto Orientale, 2000).

Taft, R. F., 'Christian Liturgical Psalmody: Origins, Development, Decomposition, Collapse', in H. W. Attridge and M. E. Fassler (eds), *Psalms in Community: Jewish and Christian Textual, Liturgical, and Artistic Traditions* (Atlanta: Society of Biblical Literature, 2003), 7–32.

Thee, F. C. R., *Julius Africanus and the Early Christian View of Magic* (Tubingen: J. C. B. Mohr, 1984).

Tod, M. N., 'The Scorpion in Graeco-Roman Egypt', *Journal of Egyptian Archaeology*, 25 (1939), 55–61, <http://www.jstor.org/stable/3854932>.

Traube, L., *Nomina Sacra: Versuch einer Geschichte der christliche Kürzung* (Munich: Beck, 1907).

Treu, K., 'Neue neutestamentliche Fragmente der Berliner Papyrussammlung', *Archiv für Papyrusforschung*, 18 (1966), 23–38, doi: 10.1515/apf.1966.1966.18.23.

Trzcionka, S., *Magic and the Supernatural in Fourth-Century Syria* (London and New York: Routledge, 2007).

Turner, E. G., *The Typology of the Early Codex* (Philadelphia: University of Pennsylvania, 1977).

Turner, E. G., *Greek Manuscripts of the Ancient World*, 2nd edn, ed. P. J. Parsons (London: Institute of Classical Studies, 1987).

Turner, J. D., *Sethian Gnosticism and the Platonic Tradition* (Leuven: Peters, 2001).

van de Sandt, H., and D. Flusser, *The Didache: Its Jewish Sources and its Place in Early Judaism and Christianity* (Assen: Van Gorcum, 2002), 140–90.

van der Horst, P. W., 'The Great Magical Papyrus of Paris (PGM IV) and the Bible', in P. W. van der Horst (ed.), *Jews and Christians in their Graeco-Roman Context: Selected Essays on Early Judaism, Samaritanism, Hellenism, and Christianity* (Tübingen: Mohr Siebeck, 2006), 269–79.

van der Vliet, J., 'Les anges du soleil: à propos d'un texte magique copte récemment découvert à Deir en-Naqlun (N. 45/95)', in N. Bosson (ed.), *Études coptes VII: neuvième journée d'études, Montpellier 3–4 juin 1999* (Leuven: Peeters, 2000), 319–37.

Vassiliev, A. (ed.), *Anecdota Graeco-Byzantina: Pars Prior* (Moscow: Universitatis Caesareae, 1893).

Versnel, H. S., 'Beyond Cursing: The Appeal to Justice in Judicial Prayers', in C. A. Faraone and D. Obbink (eds), *Magika Hiera: Ancient Greek Magic and Religion* (New York: Oxford University Press, 1991), 60–106.

Versnel, H. S., 'Some Reflections on the Relationship Magic–Religion', *Numen*, 38 (1991), 177–97, doi: 10.1163/156852791X00114.

Versnel, H. S., 'Prayers for Justice, East and West: Recent Finds and Publications since 1990', in R. Gordon and F. M. Simón (eds), *Magical Practice in the Latin West* (Boston: Brill, 2010), 275–354.

von Dobschütz, E., 'Der Briefwechsel zwischen Abgar und Jesus', *Zeitschrift für wissenschaftliche Theologie*, 43 (1900), 422–86.

Wallraff, M., 'Magie und Religion in den Kestoi des Julius Africanus', in M. Wallraff and L. Mecella (eds), *Die Kestoi des Julius Africanus und ihre Überlieferung* (Berlin: Walter de Gruyter, 2009), 39–52.

Wallraff, M., and L. Mecella (eds), *Die Kestoi des Julius Africanus und ihre Überlieferung* (Berlin: Walter de Gruyter, 2009).

Wessely, C., 'Neue griechische Zauberpapyri', *Denkschriften der kaiserlichen Akademie der Wissenschaften in Wien, Philosophisch-historische Classe*, 42 (1893), 1–96.

Wessely, C. (ed.), 'Les plus anciens monuments du christianisme écrits sur papyrus II', *Patrologia orientalis*, 18/3 (Paris: Firmin-Didot, 1924), 341–509.

Winkler, G., *Das Sanctus: Über den Ursprung und die Anfänge des Sanctus und sein Fortwirken* (Rome: Pontificio Istituto Orientale, 2002).

Winkler, G., *Die Basilius-Anaphora: Edition der beiden armenischen Redaktionen und der relevanten Fragmente, Übersetzung und Zusammenschau aller Versionen im Licht der orientalischen Überlieferungen* (Rome: Pontificio Istituto Orientale, 2005).

Winlock, H. E., and W. E. Crum (eds), *The Monastery of Epiphanius at Thebes, Part I* (New York: Metropolitan Museum of Art, 1926).

Wipszycka, E., *The Alexandrian Church: People and Institutions* (Warsaw: Journal of Juristic Papyrology, 2015).

Worrell, W. H., 'A Coptic Wizard's Hoard', *The American Journal of Semitic Languages and Literatures*, 46 (1930), 239–62, <http://www.jstor.org/stable/529100>.

Worrell, W. H., 'Coptic Magical and Medical Texts', *Orientalia*, 4 (1935), 1–37, <http://www.jstor.org/stable/43581034>.

Wortmann, D., 'Der weisse Wolf: Ein christliches Fieberamulett der Kölner Papyrussammlung', *Philologus*, 107 (1963), 157–61.

Wortmann, D., 'Neue magische Texte', *Bonner Jahrbücher*, 168 (1968), 56–111.

Youtie, H. C., *Scriptiunculae*, 2 vols (Amsterdam: Adolf M. Hakkert, 1973).

Index of Sources

Literary and Legal Sources

For the full form of titles abbreviated below, *see* the Bibliography, 'Ancient Sources'.

General Index